Why do states in arid regions fail to cooperate in sharing water resources when cooperation would appear to be in their mutual interest? And under what circumstances could they be encouraged to negotiate even when protracted conflict characterizes interstate relations? Through in-depth analysis of the history and current status of the dispute over the waters of the Jordan River basin among Israel, Jordan, Lebanon, and Syria, and its relationship to the Arab–Israeli conflict, Dr. Miriam Lowi explores the answers to these critical questions. By comparing the Jordan waters conflict with disputes in the Euphrates, Indus, and Nile River basins, she evaluates the material and ideal concerns of states with regard to sharing scarce resources with adversarial neighbors, and highlights the significance of water to both conceptions of national security and to the local environment.

Water and power: the politics of a scarce resource in the Jordan River basin is a provocative study of an issue which is rapidly emerging on the international agenda because of the intimate links between environmental factors and their effects on the welfare of populations. This book will be of value to all those with an interest in the recent history and politics of the Middle East, the politics of scarcity, and resource conflicts.

Cambridge Middle East Library: 31

WATER AND POWER

Cambridge Middle East Library: 31

Editorial Board

The *Cambridge Middle East Library* aims to bring together outstanding scholarly work on the history, politics, sociology and economics of the Middle East and North Africa in the nineteenth and twentieth centuries. While primarily focussing on monographs based on original research, the series will also incorporate broader surveys and in-depth treatments.

A list of books in this series will be found at the end of this volume.

WATER AND POWER

The politics of a scarce resource in the Jordan River basin

MIRIAM R. LOWI

CAMBRIDGE
UNIVERSITY PRESS

Published by the Press Syndicate of the University of Cambridge
The Pitt Building, Trumpington Street, Cambridge CB2 1RP
40 West 20th Street, New York, NY 10011–4211, USA
10 Stamford Road, Oakleigh Melbourne 3166, Australia

First published 1993
First paperback edition 1995

Printed in Great Britain at the University Press, Cambridge

A catalogue record for this book is available from the British Library

Library of Congress cataloguing in publication data
Lowi, Miriam R.
Water and power: the politics of a scarce resource in the Jordan
River basin / Miriam R. Lowi.
p.   cm. – (Cambridge Middle East Library: 31)
Includes bibliographical references.
ISBN 0 521 43164 6 (hardback)
1. Water resources development – Jordan River region – International
cooperation. 2. Riparian rights – Jordan River region. 3. Water-
supply – Political aspects – Middle East. 4. Jewish–Arab relations.
I. Title. II. Series.
HD1698.M53L69   1993
333.91′0095694 – dc20   92–38277   CIP

ISBN 0 521 43164 6 hardback
ISBN 0 521 55836 0 paperback

UP

For
Abdellah,
Jazia and Ismael

Contents

Contents

Illustrations

Maps

Figure

Tables

Preface

When Israeli forces invaded Lebanon in June 1982, some observers claimed that one of Israel's objectives was to seize control of the Litani River. At the time, I found the allegation intriguing. Why would a state launch such a costly military operation for the sake of a river that, even by regional standards, was not particularly abundant? What Israeli national security concerns could possibly be epitomized by a Lebanese river? When I began graduate school at Princeton University in the fall of that year, I told my teacher, Charles Issawi, that I was interested in exploring the role – if indeed there was one – that rivers, and water in general, have played in the ongoing and unresolved Arab–Israeli confrontation. He chuckled and said: "That should keep you busy for a while." Little did I know that ten years later I would still be studying the complex relationship between riparian dispute and inter-state conflict.

No doubt my initial curiosity with the "lure of the Litani" was quickly dwarfed by the larger, and far more engaging political issues raised by the experience in the Jordan River basin. For one, it became clear to me that there was, indeed, an intimate link between water resources and national security. In arid and semi-arid regions, such as the Middle East, water scarcity is not only a fact of life, but also, and more importantly, a material constraint to survival. Without unimpeded access to water resources, states cannot pursue the multiplicity of tasks they are expected to fulfill: provision of drinking water, development of the economy, settlement of population, provision of health care, to name but a few. The survival of the state as both a physical and political entity is dependent upon the provision of these goods. On one level, this book is addressed to the "security community" and the current debate over definitions of security that explicitly incorporate environmental concerns.

Second, my reading of the history of the conflict in the Jordan basin led me to believe that past efforts at resolving the water dispute had been misguided. In the mid-fifties and somewhat less so in the late seventies, the United States government hoped that solving the water dispute would reduce tensions in the region and facilitate the resolution of the Arab–Israeli conflict. By establishing a web of interdependencies in economic and welfare matters, adversaries would come to recognize their need for each other. Thus, technical cooperation would spill over into political peace. Experience would show, however, that the water dispute could not be solved, precisely because of the larger political conflict and the visceral concerns that lay at its core. Cooperation in economic and welfare matters required the prior, or perhaps, simultaneous, resolution of the "high politics" conflict. On another level, therefore, this book is addressed to the policy community. Implicitly, it cautions against trying to resolve protracted conflict by "nibbling at the edges."

Related to the policy focus is the central issue that pervades the book: the potential for cooperation in international river basins. On yet another level, the book makes a contribution to the ongoing debate between political realists and liberal institutionalists about how to explain cooperation, and its absence, among nations. It comes out in favor of the classical realist tradition and its emphasis on the distribution of power, modified by a greater understanding of culture, history, and ideology and the ways in which they may influence political behavior. In the introductory and concluding chapters especially, the international relations community is the principal audience.

In light of the current talks within the framework of a Middle East peace process, the timely nature of the subject matter of the book is obvious. To wit, a water resources working group has been meeting as part of the multilateral track of the talks. It may well be that one of the implicit objectives of the peace process is to establish "epistemic communities" in the principal issue-areas. Furthermore, with the collapse of the Soviet Union, Middle Eastern states have less room to maneuver than previously was the case. The Arabs, despairing of attaining their perceived rights in a unipolar world, may be more inclined to curry the favors of the United States, and more likely to cut a deal with Israel. Israel, in turn, may well find that the current political situation is more precarious than ever before. It too may be willing to make some compromises for the sake of bringing the protracted conflict to a close. Needless to say, this book is also addressed to the vast community of Middle East specialists and observers of Middle Eastern affairs.

In the course of working on this book many people assisted me in a variety of ways. I am happy to have the opportunity to record my gratitude to them. My greatest debt is to John Waterbury of Princeton University, whose generosity and commitment to his students are both remarkable and inspiring. Over the years, he has been my teacher, advisor, and friend.

Michael Brecher of McGill University and Janice Stein of the University of Toronto, international relations theorists with a Middle East focus, deserve special mention as well. Both read the manuscript in its entirety and offered valuable suggestions. Stephen Lintner, a senior environmental specialist with the World Bank, went through the manuscript with a fine-tooth comb. He shared with me his vast expertise on the conflict in the Jordan basin and reacted at length to my interpretations of it.

At different stages, several other people read all or parts of the manuscript and made helpful comments. I wish to thank Sion Assidon, Jameson Doig, Michael Doyle, Richard Falk, Thomas Homer-Dixon, Charles Issawi, Robert Keohane, Charles Kupchan, Marc Levy, Richard Matthew, Tim Mitchell, Thomas Naff, Susan Ossman, Robert Vitalis, Steve Walt, and Arthur Westing. Needless to say, as important as their contributions have been in shaping the final version of the project, I alone bear responsibility for its contents.

The sudden death of John Vincent was a terrible blow to the international relations community and to all those who knew him. He was a superb teacher and a fine human being. He believed profoundly in the importance of dialogue and exchange among peoples and perspectives. It is with gratitude for his guidance, support, and friendship that I invoke his memory.

In the field, numerous people helped me considerably. In Syria, Egypt, Jordan, and Israel, interlocutors answered my many questions, sometimes at personal risk. Because of the sensitivity of the subject matter of this book, I promised to protect the identities of those whom I interviewed. They know who they are. I hereby express my appreciation to them. I do wish to single out for special mention a number of key figures who did not request anonymity: Sadiq al-Azm and Aziz Shukri in Syria, Mahmoud Riad in Egypt, Hamed al-Farhan and Munther Haddadin in Jordan, Mordechai Gazit, Elisha Kally and Aharon Wiener in Israel.

It is important to note that because water is a national security issue in the countries of the central Middle East, certain data are not accessible to the public, let alone to foreign researchers. As a result, in writing this book, I have had to resort to making conjectural assertions on occasion. Moreover, while I was able to review several key feasibility studies, I have refrained from citing them directly, out of respect for the concerns and interests of those who allowed me to consult them. I do not believe, however, that these "holes" detract from the larger picture I have drawn.

The conditions of my work in the Middle East were enhanced by affiliations with a number of institutions. I would like to thank the American Center for Oriental Research in Amman, the Institut Français des Etudes Arabes in Damascus, and the Dayan Center for Middle Eastern Studies at

Tel-Aviv University. The staffs of the national archives in Jerusalem and in Washington, D.C., and the Freedom of Information Act services of the United States government extended assistance to me, as well.

Various stages of the research and writing were funded by the Social Science Research Council (New York), the Fonds pour la formation des chercheurs et l'aide à la recherche (FCAR, Québec), the Center of International Studies (Princeton University), the Sternberg Family Fund, and the Institute for the Study of World Politics (Washington). I am grateful to these institutions for their support and generosity.

A number of other people remain to be thanked. Mildred Kalmus has been a great source of assistance and encouragement over the years. Gwendolyn Prothro helped with bibliographic searches, photocopying, and mailing materials when I was overseas. Bernard Lewis gave me the idea for the jacket design, and Oleg Grabar provided me with the photograph of the Madaba mosaic map from his personal library. Marigold Acland, the editor of the Middle East Library series at Cambridge University Press, and her staff, very ably handled the production and publication of the manuscript.

Finally, my husband, Abdellah Hammoudi, has contributed to this book in many ways. Most important of all, he has been my dear friend and comrade.

Preface to the paperback edition

Since *Water and power* went to press in the fall of 1992, the Middle Eastern region has witnessed a number of historic developments, some of which impact directly upon the politics of water. I am pleased, therefore, that this new edition allows me the opportunity to continue the story of the Jordan waters conflict up to the present.

Most significant of the recent developments is that the peace process that was set in motion at the Madrid conference in the fall of 1991, in the wake of the Gulf war, has taken on a life of its own. This, I may add, had not been anticipated; prior to Iraq's invasion of Kuwait, no one in the public domain could have predicted with any degree of certainty that a resolution of the four-decade-long Arab–Israeli conflict was about to be put back onto the negotiating table and, more importantly, would remain there for as long as it has.

These were particularly fortuitous developments for *Water and power*, as well. Despite the fact that the subject matter of the book had represented the focus of my research interests since the early 1980s – before the water dimension of the Arab–Israeli relationship became highly publicized – the book suddenly found itself at the center of the arena of Middle Eastern affairs and squarely within the agenda of the peace process. This, I believe, has enhanced the value of the book and suggested the need for its wider accessibility. In addition to whatever scholarly merits it may have, it can provide readers with a context within which to understand and follow these historic developments.

Following the Madrid conference, participants in the multilateral track of the peace talks met for the first time in Moscow in January of 1992. At that meeting, working groups were established in five substantive areas of mutual concern to the Arab "frontline" states and Israel: arms control, economic development, the environment, refugees, and water resources. These groups were to meet separately from the bilateral negotiating teams. The objective was twofold: first, that the multilaterals would provide support for and complement the bilaterals, with each track drawing inspiration from progress in the other, and second, that technical arrangements would be elaborated and agreed upon in the multilateral meetings by the time the bilateral negotiations came to a successful completion. It was hoped that some technical arrangements could be implemented even before peace.

By the spring of 1995, the water resources working group had met seven times: in Moscow in January 1992, Vienna in May 1992, Washington in September 1992, Geneva in April 1993, Beijing in October 1993, Muscat in April 1994, and Athens in November 1994. However, until September 1993 and the signing of the *Declaration of principles* by Palestine Liberation Organization Chairman Yasir Arafat and Israeli Prime Minister Yitzhak Rabin, discussions within the water resources working group remained at a very preliminary level. There was general consensus on the obvious: that there was not enough water in the region, that demand was growing, that water quality was deteriorating. Lengthy discussions took place on the problem of data collection, and the parties agreed that in a more favorable political climate, it would be important to share data.

In these first four meetings, substantive progress was impeded by the "high politics" conflict – the Arab–Israeli confrontation that has dominated Middle Eastern affairs, defined relations, and been at the center of wars and diplomacy since 1948. Both sides, but especially the Arabs, were reluctant to come to consensus, even on very small matters, in the absence of considerable progress toward a political settlement of the core issue of conflict: Palestinian statehood and the future status of the territories occupied by Israel in the 1967 war.

After the signing of the *Declaration of principles* on September 13, 1993, the atmosphere in the water resources working group improved considerably. At the meetings in Beijing and Muscat, for example, participants were beginning to think in the long term. There was a sense that for the first time, parties were entertaining the possibility – even the likelihood – that the Arabs and Israelis would be interacting on a regular basis and for the indefinite future in matters of mutual concern. The idea of common water projects of broad scope no longer seemed farfetched.

At the most recent meeting, in Athens in November 1994, the mood was especially upbeat because of the peace treaty that had been signed between Israel and Jordan just three weeks before. Despite some imprecise language and vagueness on certain details, the treaty opens up possibilities for a future of cooperation between these two former adversaries.

Progress in the water resources working group reflects progress in the bilateral (political) negotiations and "on the ground," on the core issue of conflict. When treaties are signed or when the Palestinian Authority and the Government of Israel are making significant headway in implementing the *Declaration of principles*, participants in the water resources working group are inclined to resolve matters cooperatively. This being said, they continue to be reluctant to address the issue of regional water management and cooperation – what is considered to be optimal when exploiting the waters of an international river basin. This condition, I would argue, results from the absence of genuine political commitment thus far. A history of animosity and protracted conflict, uncertainty about the future and the intentions of "the other," a melange of preferences and concerns, and most recently, general frustration with the stalled implementation of the *Declaration of principles*, lie at the core of this lack of commitment. It seems fair to conclude that considerably more progress toward the implementation of a broad political settlement – one that expands the areas of Palestinian authority beyond the Gaza Strip and Jericho – would be required before the parties entertain the specifics of basin-wide cooperation. This conclusion echoes one of the central arguments I make in *Water and power*.

My analysis of the Jordan waters conflict indicates that over the course of its history, the parties to the conflict were reluctant to come to technical agreements on sharing and managing water resources in the absence of a resolution of their political differences. Comparative evidence from the riparian disputes in the Euphrates and Indus basins corroborates this finding, as well. States engaged in "high politics" conflicts do not allow extensive collaboration in the sphere of "low politics," centered around economic and welfare issues. Indeed, technical cooperation is impeded by the "high politics" conflict, because all technical matters are subsumed under the political condition and are perceived as dimensions of it. Hence, a political settlement must precede technical cooperation, and not vice versa.

Indeed, I believe that a number of arguments I made have been substantiated by recent developments in the region and within the peace process. Let me highlight these by focusing first on the Israel–Jordan *Treaty of peace* and second, on the implementation of certain aspects of the *Declaration of principles*.

On October 26, 1994, Israel and Jordan signed the *Treaty of peace*, bringing to a close the state of war between the two countries. *Annex II* of the treaty, which is reprinted at the back of this book as Appendix 5, concerns water-related matters. What is noteworthy about the water agreement is how close to or removed from the preferences of the parties it actually is. For one, there is no discussion of a large storage dam on the Yarmouk River – akin to the Maqarin dam project or later, the Unity (al-Wahdah) dam – to impound the winter flow for Jordan's usage during the long, dry summer months. Since the early 1950s, Jordan had been insisting on the need for such a facility. Over the years, its efforts in this regard were stymied by a variety of sources, both political and financial. This time, no doubt, the fact that Syria is not a party to the treaty while it is the upstream state on the Yarmouk and hence would have to be included in any discussion of a dam project, goes a long way to explaining the lacuna.

There is, however, mention of two other storage facilities on the Yarmouk. The first is a very small dam – a regulating weir, in fact – to control the flow into the King Abdullah Canal (the former East Ghor Canal). The Jordanians maintain that this will allow them access to an additional 10–20 million cubic meters (mcm) of Yarmouk water. But downstream of the diversion into the Canal, Israel has the right to offtake the excess floodwaters. A second storage dam would be built on the Jordan River somewhere south of the confluence with the Yarmouk. It is expected to provide Jordan with an average of 20 mcm per annum, as well.

By the terms of the treaty, Israel is obligated to provide Jordan with 10 mcm of desalinated water per year. For several decades, Israel had been diverting water from saline springs around Lake Tiberias into the Lower Jordan River. The treaty stipulates that within a period of four years from the signing, a desalination plant will have to be built and become operational in Israel. After giving Jordan its due, Israel will keep some portion of the remaining desalinated water. However, until completion of the plant, Israel will have to give Jordan 10 mcm of water directly from the lake.

According to the treaty, Israel has the right to pump 12 mcm per annum directly from the Yarmouk River during the summer months, and 13 mcm during the winter. Jordan is entitled to the remainder of the flow. This combined allocation is, curiously enough, what was earmarked from the Yarmouk for Israel in the Johnston Plan of the 1950s, discussed in chapter 4 of this book. (It also is somewhat less than the quantity that Israel has been taking directly from the river in recent years, although exact figures are unavailable.) Moreover, Jordan allows Israel to pump an additional 20 mcm of water from the Yarmouk in the winter, but during the summer months, Israel must transfer 20 mcm to Jordan. These quantities cancel each other out; their significance is simply one of timing. Jordan has no means of storing winter flow, although its demand during the dry season is great. Israel, in contrast, does have storage capacity, so that it can manage with a smaller allocation in the dry season. On balance, Israel has access to more or less the same amount of water from the Yarmouk as it had prior to the signing of the treaty, while Jordan has an additional 40–50 mcm. Furthermore, the two parties are enjoined to cooperate in finding for Jordan an additional 50 mcm of water of potable quality. Absolutely no mention is made of the Palestinians' claim to water from the Jordan–Yarmouk system.

Needless to say, the water-related portion of the treaty is, at least on paper, very important. If implemented, Jordan will be somewhat better off, while Israel will not be worse off. Besides, the document opens the door to an era of cooperation in water matters. This, in itself, makes *Annex II* a historic document. Nonetheless, as those in the policy domain know all too painfully well, signing a treaty and all that that entails may be considered relatively easy when compared with the next step in the process – the implementation of the treaty. If the process of implementation bogs down, the local population may become frustrated and the treaty itself is threatened. This is precisely what we have been witnessing in the Israeli–Palestinian arena in the winter of 1994–95. But before turning to the *Declaration on interim self-government arrangements*, let me speculate on why the Israel–Jordan treaty was signed in the first place, and its implications for the central thesis of this book, that adversarial states will not come to technical agreements over sharing water resources in the absence of a resolution of their political conflict.

The peace treaty between Israel and Jordan was signed in October 1994 in the absence of a *bona fide* Israeli–Palestinian settlement on the core issue of statehood. No doubt, a combination of factors urged Jordan in this direction. For one, King Hussein must have felt that the economic crisis that had beset Jordan since the Gulf war was not on the wane, and that there would be no respite until there was peace with Israel. On a number of occasions over the decades, as I document in *Water and power*, Jordan had been interested in arrangements with Israel that would have provided relief from economic constraints. Insofar as the water dispute was concerned, Jordan had hoped for the implementation of some variation of the "Johnston Plan" in the 1950s. And it certainly wanted a riparian agreement with Israel and Syria in the late 1970s and early 1980s so that it could build a dam on the Yarmouk River. Jordan's public posture had always been one of non-collaboration with Israel. However, it is fair to assume that because of the long border it shares with Israel, as well as a number of mutual concerns – not least among them, access to a common body of water – Jordan would have sought cooperative arrangements with Israel long ago, had the political situation permitted.

When the Palestinian leadership and the Israeli government entered into the process that culminated in the signing of the *Declaration of principles*, both the Jordanian and the Syrian governments were annoyed; they perceived the Palestinians' having gone ahead without them as a betrayal of Arab solidarity. However, once the Palestinians signed the *Declaration*, the Jordanians probably felt that the stage was set for them to make their own move. It was not that Jordan viewed the *Declaration of principles* as a "high politics" settlement – it would be very difficult to sustain such a claim. Rather, the Jordanian government most likely viewed the document as a step in the direction of a "high politics" settlement: a prelude to other international agreements. This provided Jordan with the opportunity to proceed openly in the pursuit of its own national interests. Indeed, for about one year prior to the signing of the treaty, Jordan and Israel had been meeting regularly with the United States in a *Trilateral economic committee* to discuss technical issues of mutual concern. Nonetheless, for a variety of reasons which are elucidated in chapters 4, 5 and 7, Jordan would not have taken the initiative to sign an agreement with Israel before the Palestinian leadership.

As for the Israeli–Palestinian relationship, joint committees have been set up, in keeping with the stipulations of the *Declaration of principles*, in a variety of technical areas, including water resources. Unfortunately, several of these bilateral committees have made little headway to date, and the water resources committee has barely gotten off the ground, precisely because of the impasse at the political level. Progress toward the transfer of rule in the West Bank to the Palestinian Authority has reached a bottleneck, and the Palestinian people, with their future uncertain and their expectations faltering, have become increasingly disillusioned. Besides, with the question of Palestinian statehood in limbo, water resources have low priority as a subject for immediate discussion. Again, this is what I argue in *Water and power*: that states engaged in a protracted conflict will not make progress in resolving seemingly technical matters of mutual concern when their political differences remain unresolved.

It is important to bear in mind just how little water there is in Israel, Jordan, and the West Bank. This factor, coupled with the rising demands of states and peoples in arid and semi-arid regions, with high population growth rates and considerable agricultural sectors, illuminates the extent to which margins are narrow in the development and utilization of water resources. Even if we assume that a mutually satisfactory political settlement is implemented and unitary basin-wide development is adopted, it is highly likely that the waters of the Jordan–Yarmouk system will prove to be insufficient for meeting the needs of the peoples of the basin. (Needless to say, Jordan and Israel were well aware of this when they signed the peace treaty. They may have felt that it made little sense to fuss about a few tens of mcms of water when, in fact, potential water deficits in the coming decades may be in the order of several hundreds of mcms.) This being the case, a variety of solutions to scarcity must be considered.

Technological solutions at the national level in the form of water augmentation and management systems are one obvious avenue to explore. To date, the Israelis and the Jordanians have independently pursued a number of such techniques: cloud-seeding, desalination, wastewater reuse, dam-building, etcetera. Obviously, if these techniques were to be implemented cooperatively, they could have a greater mutual benefit by virtue of states sharing technology, expertise, and data. Intra-regional solutions are another avenue to explore. There are a number of possible scenarios. For one, water could be "imported" from outside the immediate area. The past decade has witnessed a flurry of research activity in the domain of water transfers, with the result that there are currently a variety of imaginative schemes to transport water from relatively wet zones. Another intra-regional solution that could be envisioned is the trade of oil for water in the Middle East. Iraq and Turkey would be logical partners in such an enterprise at some future date. Yet another possibility is that Gulf states would help finance desalination schemes in exchange for some other valued good. There is certainly no shortage of potential solutions. However, all of them – indeed, all except for unilateral solutions – require a favorable political climate.

No doubt, the resolution of protracted conflict would open up vast possibilities for functional cooperation. But this must not be viewed as the entire solution to resource scarcity. In addition to resolving their political disputes, the states of the central Middle East must take bold steps to curtail excessive and wasteful consumption of water, especially by their agricultural sectors. This means that they must reconsider the size and importance of agriculture in their economies, revise the choice of crops grown, and adopt the most effective water-conservation technologies.

Revamping agriculture does not require the end of regional political conflict. However, if conflict is not brought to an end, states in arid regions will be forced to rely on sub-optimal solutions of a purely domestic and piecemeal nature. Given the stresses on water supplies in Israel, Jordan, the West Bank, and the Gaza Strip – among them, the absence of additional unexploited sources, population growth trends, and recurrent drought conditions – basin-wide and intra-regional arrangements for sharing and utilizing water are crucial for the long-term stability of the region. The implementation of the *Declaration of principles* in its entirety and progress towards final status negotiations are the essential first steps in that direction.

Princeton, March 1995

Abbreviations

AMER   Associates for Middle East Research, Data Base
          (Philadelphia, Pa.: University of Pennsylvania)

BBC   *BBC: Summary of World Broadcasts*, part 4: the
          Middle East

FBIS   United States, *Foreign Broadcast Information
          Service*, Daily Report: Middle East, Africa, and
          Western Europe, 1967

FOI   Freedom of Information Act, Government of the
          United States

FRUS   *Foreign Relations of the United States, 1952–1954*
          vol. 9

INA   National Archives of the State of Israel

USG/CFA   Testimony before the House Committee on
          Foreign Affairs: Subcommittee on Europe and
          the Middle East, *The Middle East in the 1990s:
          Middle East Water Issues* (Washington, D.C.,
          26 June 1990)

USG/DS   Declassified document on West Bank water
          provided to the author by the Government of the
          United States, Department of State (n.d.)

USNA   United States National Archives

1 Introduction: conflict and cooperation in international river basins

Well before the emergence of the nation-state, the arbitrary political division of a unitary river basin – the area of land drained by a river and its tributaries – led to problems regarding the interests of the states and/or communities located within the basin and the manner in which conflicting interests should be resolved.[1] Geography suggests that, by virtue of its physical unity, a river basin should be developed as a single, indivisible whole, irrespective of political divisions. This is so, because moving water, flowing toward an outlet (or outlets), binds land areas together, and interference with the water and its movement at any point has repercussions elsewhere in the basin.[2] Indeed, the river basin can be considered a common property resource by virtue of the fact that its exploitation by one beneficiary may diminish the benefits enjoyed by all others.[3] From the point of view of economic efficiency, as well, the basin should be treated as a unit; in that way, "a careful inventory of soils, feasibility of irrigation and drainage, values of alternative crops, domestic and industrial water needs, could be factored into a basin-wide model that might... yield an 'optimal' pattern of water utilization."[4] To wit, the situation in international river basins exemplifies the pervasive collective action problem: the pursuit of interests defined in purely individualistic terms would lead to socially undesirable outcomes. Hence, the ideal solution to the satisfaction of competing needs and conflicting interests is unitary basin-wide development of water resources under some system of supranational authority or management.[5]

While the ties of geography prescribe the unitary development of the river basin, the contingent ties of history may stymie the process. Only reluctantly will states relinquish control over land or resources that lie, even partially, within their borders.[6] Furthermore, the concern to maximize individual benefits provides a powerful incentive to exploit resources unilaterally. States are constrained in their behavior by structural factors as well. For one, and as political realists argue, power and capabilities define relations in the international system.[7] However, systems of government, ideologies and emotions, and historical experience – in other words, the unique character of states – also influence the conduct of international affairs and the character of conflicts, wars, and cooperation. Yielding sovereignty is always a dubious proposition. Even under favorable circumstances, states may shy away from cooperating, when they can afford to. Hence, the challenge in international river basins remains the achievement of cooperative solutions to the provision of a common property resource, and avoidance of the tragedy of the commons.[8]

This book is an inquiry into the conduct and resolution of riparian disputes in protracted conflict settings, in arid or semi-arid regions.[9] By riparian dispute, we refer to a dispute among two or more sovereign states over access to or control over the water resources of an international river basin that traverses their territories. Protracted conflicts can be defined as:

hostile interactions which extend over long periods of time with sporadic outbreaks of open warfare fluctuating in frequency and intensity. These are conflict situations in which the stakes are very high – the conflicts involve whole societies and act as agents for defining the scope of national identity and social solidarity.[10]

Our focus is on riparian disputes that co-exist with a larger political conflict among the states in question. In addressing this problem – the failure to achieve cooperative solutions to riparian disputes in protracted conflict settings – we aim to answer two broad questions: what guides the behavior of states in international river basins and what determines the potential for cooperation among adversaries in the utilization of scarce water resources?

The empirical material on which this inquiry is based is drawn from the dispute over the waters of the Jordan River basin, an area which spans the territories of Israel, Jordan, Lebanon and Syria. This region has been the locus of an intense political conflict since mid-century and the establishment of a Jewish state in Palestine. The riparian dispute has been and continues to be an integral part of the protracted Arab–Israeli confrontation.[11]

For comparative evidence, we analyze three other cases of riparian dispute that share certain basic similarities with the principal case. They are: (1) the conflict in the Euphrates basin, among Turkey, Syria, and Iraq, (2) in the Indus basin, between India and Pakistan, and (3) in the Nile basin, between Egypt and the Sudan primarily, but involving seven other riparians, as well. Of the four cases, all are located, at least partially, in arid or semi-arid zones. In all, the water is used in productive activities – agriculture, industry, and households. For some or all of the riparian states in each basin, unimpeded access to the water resources is linked to national security concerns. In all but the Nile case, a protracted political conflict characterizes relations among some, if not all, of the riparian states. And in all four cases, efforts have been made to reach a cooperative, basin-wide arrangement for the utilization of the waters of the river system. In none of the cases, however, has the result been the "optimal" pattern of river basin development – via unitary, basin-wide planning and management.[12]

The problem of cooperation

Why do states fail to achieve, or even strive for, the ideal solution to resource development? Alternatively, under what conditions would they relinquish sovereign control over resources that lie within their territory and submit to supra-national authority? How could they be induced to do so, given that this would serve the "common good" in the basin? More generally, how can we explain why it is that in international affairs, states tend to have sub-optimal preferences: they elect non-cooperation when, under certain circumstances and in a specific domain, cooperation would appear to be in their mutual interest? At issue is the long-standing debate in International relations theory between two schools of thought: political realism and liberal institutionalism.[13]

In both the realist and liberal world views, states are purposive, rational actors: they possess "consistent, ordered preferences, and ... calculate costs and benefits of alternative courses of action in order to maximize their utility in view of those preferences."[14] In interactions with other states, therefore, a core interest is to achieve the greatest possible individual gain. Moreover, both views agree that in international affairs, states "first define their preferences and then engage in a process of inter-state strategic inter-action ... to reach a common outcome." Seen within this simplified model, one of the principal differences between realism and liberalism lies in emphasis: liberals focus on states' preferences, realists on inter-state strategic interaction.[15] Similarly, for realists, the behavior of states is a reflection of their power and capabilities, while for liberals, it is a reflection of their preferences and purposes.

Realists argue that the political–structural condition of anarchy, the absence of a common government, in the international system has an impact on the willingness of states to engage in cooperation.[16] Implicit in anarchy is that there is no capacity to enforce sanctions as a means to protect states from each other or to prevent states from doing damage to others. Given this condition, states are motivated by fear and distrust, and their principal concern is with their security and survival.[17] Since ensuring their security is their chief objective, states are preoccupied with their power and capabilities. Indeed, capabilities, in the form of economic, military, and political resources, are "the ultimate basis for state security and independence in the self-help context of international anarchy."[18] That is to say, states have to rely on the means they can generate and the arrangements they can make for themselves. Before all else, they must make provisions for their security in the power struggle among states.[19] The preoccupation with autonomy, power, and security predisposes states toward conflict and competition.

Neo-realists add that since states fear for their security, they are preoccupied not only with power, but also with the fear that if they were to cooperate their partners could eventually turn out to be better off than them by virtue of having achieved relatively greater gains. Given the right set of circumstances, the advantaged partner would then be in a position to use its superior power resources to inflict harm.[20] Because of this possibility, a state would be wise not to cooperate, even if cooperation offered the promise of absolute gains; no state wants to realize fewer absolute gains than any other. That is to say, the concern that a division of gains from joint endeavors may favor others more than oneself acts as a barrier to cooperation; as relative gains concerns increase, cooperation becomes more difficult.[21] It follows that the achievement of an equitable distribution of gains, one "that roughly maintains pre-cooperation balances of capabilities,"[22] would promote cooperation.

States, therefore, worry about and seek to prevent increases in the relative power of others. That being the case, they assess cooperative arrangements in terms of their likely impact upon the distribution of power.[23] In sum, neo-realism identifies the relative gains problem (and the related concern for relative status) as a central impediment to cooperation in a world of anarchy.[24]

Until recently, liberal institutionalists had little to say about why states reject cooperation. Functionalists, neo-functionalists and interdependence theorists refuted the realist contention that states are disinclined to cooperate.[25] For them, cooperation is the norm. States are becoming increasingly interdependent in economic and welfare matters. As a result, they argue, states rightly consider each other as partners in growth and development. The liberals' analyses are prescriptive: they suggest how cooperation can be achieved, not why it is rejected.

In contrast to their predecessors, the neo-liberal institutionalists identify what they view as the principal barrier to cooperation: the compliance problem in international arrangements.[26] Synthesizing elements of realism and liberalism, they argue that states reject cooperation because, in an anarchic world, where there is no agency to "enact and enforce rules of behavior,"[27] the intentions of others are opaque and their reliability, uncertain. Hence, cheating is both feasible and profitable. However, states, in their international relations, are anxious to achieve the greatest possible individual gain.[28] Thus, while it is easy for states to misjudge the intentions of others, they cannot take a chance on being wrong. Anarchy "impedes cooperation through its generation of uncertainty about the compliance of partners."[29] Furthermore, in the absence of an institutional framework, the costs of verifying compliance and sanctioning cheaters would be very high.

In sum, liberal institutionalists identify asymmetrical information and uncertainty as the main impediments to cooperation; related to them is the problem of transaction costs.

On the question of how states could be encouraged to elect cooperation, the realists do not have much to say. For them, cooperation in a world of anarchy is an anomaly. When cooperative arrangements do emerge, they are surface reflections of underlying power relationships. In the realist view, the behavior of states is proportional to their capabilities or power resources, and outcomes in the international arena reflect the distribution of power.[30] It follows that the potential for cooperation is determined by the distribution of power, as well. Indeed, a variant of the theory of hegemonic stability lies at the core of realist thought. The theory states that order in world politics is dependent upon the leadership of a single dominant power, and that the maintenance of order requires the persistence of hegemony.[31] Likewise, cooperation and the formation of international regimes depend upon hegemony and its persistence. In sum, therefore, states cooperate when cooperation serves the interests of a dominant power, that takes the lead in creating cooperative arrangements and enforces compliance to their rules.[32]

Liberals, in contrast, have been prolific with regard to the question of how to achieve cooperation. Given that at least within the stronger structuralist models of liberal institutionalist thought[33] cooperation is an implicit expectation, even though it is often rejected because of the compliance problem, efforts must be made to alter the "payoff structure" and thereby facilitate cooperation. What unifies the various strands of liberal institutionalism is the focus on meta-national institutions – specialized agencies, interest groups, transgovernmental policy networks, multinational corporations, epistemic communities – as the principal agents of cooperation.

Following on the heels of World War II, functionalists maintained that peace would be attained only if the intrusion of power politics was checked, national sovereignty sacrificed, and efforts made toward material unity in an increasingly interdependent world.[34] This, they argued, could be accomplished by functional cooperation across national boundaries and the creation of supra-national task-related organizations. "Every activity organized in that way would be a layer of peaceful life," insofar as "economic unification would build up the foundation for political agreement..."[35] No doubt, politics would have to be by-passed, ideological issues neutralized.[36]

Broadly based cooperation would evolve by virtue of the "spill-over effect." A process of integration would proceed from areas thought to be less contentious and would be pushed on by the "felt needs" of citizens. Functions would be taken up by international institutions, operating across national frontiers according to the requirements of the particular function. The development among states of an ever-widening range of interdependencies in economic, technical, and welfare areas would not only enmesh governments, but would also encourage actors to set aside their political and/or ideological differences. Moreover, a learning process involving attitude change would accompany the process of continuous interaction. Functional integration would eventually spill over into regional peace.

The neo-functionalists were less sanguine about the integrative potential and the spillover process. Although they did not outline a formula for the achievement of cooperation, they modified that of their predecessor. For one, they went beyond the compliance problem and took note of the importance of preference issues as well. They were more realistic about the possibility of totally separating welfare from politics, and recognized the crucial role played by values and ideology in the decision-making of actors. The inception and success of institutional arrangements, they argued, were dependent upon some degree of ideological or philosophical commitment, or, "elite value complementarity."[37] In addition, they acknowledged that spillover was not automatic; states decide, on the basis of their interests, whether or not to "adapt integrative lessons learned in one context to a new situation..."[38] And as with subsequent strains of liberal institutionalism, the neo-functionalists argued that not only was the perception of likely individual gain an important incentive to cooperate, but so was the perception that cooperation would be virtually cost-free.[39] Hence, the greater the political content of an issue-area, for example, the less amenable states would be to accept cooperative arrangements in that domain.

Neo-liberals do not assume that international agreements are easy to make or to keep. However, like the functionalists, they are more optimistic about the potential for cooperation in economic and welfare matters than in military and security affairs. Nonetheless, they caution that their perspective is relevant to international politics only if three conditions exist.[40] First and foremost, states must have mutual interests; they must stand to gain from their cooperation. Second, variations in the degree of institutionalization account for variations in state behavior. And third, states do not expect others to threaten them with force. In situations where mutual interest is minimal or absent,

neoliberal theory's predictions considerably overlap with those of neorealism. Under these conditions, states will be reluctant to cooperate with each other and will choose less durable rather than more durable arrangements. Linkages, furthermore, may well impede cooperation.[41]

Neo-liberals maintain that although the realists are correct insofar as the condition of anarchy impedes cooperation, states in non-zero-sum situations can collaborate with the assistance of institutions.[42] This is because "international regimes," patterned norm- and rule-governed behavior among states in a particular issue area, reduce the uncertainties states may have about the intentions of others.[43] They do this by codifying expectations, providing information, establishing and imposing rules, and sanctioning misconduct.[44] And unlike individual states, they can do this at relatively low cost. Similarly, an "epistemic community" – a professional, knowledge-based group that "believes in the same cause-and-effect relationships, truth tests to assess them, and shares common values...a common interpretive framework..."[45] – can, under certain circumstances, foster cooperation. It does this by providing information, and reducing uncertainty and transaction costs.[46]

In addition, regimes (and epistemic communities) reduce the attractiveness of cheating by imposing a strategy of reciprocity on parties. A direct connection is thus established between a state's present behavior and anticipated future benefits: "a promise to respond to present cooperation with future cooperation and a threat to respond to present defection with future defection can improve the prospects for cooperation."[47] However, for reciprocity to be a viable strategy, states must expect to continue to interact over the indefinite future.[48] Echoing the functionalists and their focus on the spillover effect that proceeds from ongoing technical operation and the resultant enmeshing of states, some neo-liberals maintain that international regimes, by their very nature, increase the iterative character of the context of interaction and thereby promote cooperation.[49]

If, indeed, the "emergence of cooperation among egoists" is dependent upon the existence of international institutions, insofar as the latter mitigate the problems of uncertainty, asymmetrical information and high transaction costs, how then can we facilitate the creation of such institutions? How are cooperative arrangements arrived at in the first place? On these questions, the neo-liberals are vague.[50] On the one hand, they say that a hegemonic state or group of states supply institutions when it "see(s) a potential profit in organizing collaboration."[51] On the other hand, they maintain that in an increasingly interdependent world, shared economic interests create a demand for international institutions. The demand for cooperation creates its supply.[52] That, in combination with the success of existing institutions, provides the impetus for the spread of institutional arrangements.[53] Furthermore, once an international regime is in place, they argue, cooperation can be assured by making the costs of exit from the arrangement extremely high. Not only would it be very expensive for a state to renege on the deal, but also, by doing so, its reputation would be at stake.[54] Thus, high exit costs reassure all players that no one would dare defect.

In part, this book explores the application of realism and liberalism to explaining the conduct of riparian dispute and the potential for cooperation in international river basins in arid regions and characterized by an overarching political conflict. Essentially, our approach and conclusions run counter to rational and extended game-theoretic models of political behavior. Instead, they build upon the reservations about functionalism expressed by the neo-functionalists, support the hegemonic stability theory, and posit what could be termed a hegemonic theory of cooperation. Indeed, the classical realist tradition, informed by history, culture and ideology, lies at the core of this study.

Cooperation in international river basins: an evaluation of realism and liberalism

Conflicts over the waters of international river basins provide rich empirical material for exploring the efficacy of realism and liberalism in explaining: (1) why states reject cooperation when it would appear to be in their mutual interest to accept it and, (2) under what circumstances states would elect cooperation, and how they could be encouraged to do so. For one, some of the basic tenets of liberal institutionalism are integral to conceptions of river basin development. As we recall, unitary development of a basin under the control and management of a supra-national authority, equivalent to an international regime, has been advocated as optimal in terms of both the physical landscape and human welfare.

Moreover, on two occasions in the history of the Jordan waters conflict, the United States' Government actively supported the idea of a regional scheme for water utilization and, in the first case, the creation of a regime for the basin, as well.[55] As suggested by functionalist theory, the third party viewed regional development as a stepping-stone to regional peace, given that projects would require ongoing multilateral cooperation in the use of water resources. It believed that solving water problems would provide the climate necessary for resolving larger inter-state conflicts. Collaboration among adversaries in the functional matter of sharing water would bind the countries close together and eventually spill over into political association. Thus, the waters of the river basin would be utilized in the optimal fashion, and political rivalry – the Arab–Israeli conflict – would come to an end. Nonetheless, on both occasions, efforts to implement the schemes fell short of their objective.

Functional cooperation was advocated in the Indus River basin, as well. For eight years, the World Bank left no stone unturned in its efforts to secure agreement to a basin-wide accord. Eventually, an agreement was reached in 1960, but one that explicitly rejected cooperation and interdependence. In essence, the river system was partitioned, as the subcontinent had been in 1947. Hence, the outcome of the mediation effort in the basin was, in (narrowly defined) game-theoretic terms, sub-optimal. In both the Jordan and Indus basins, the nature and scope of the larger political conflict was the proximate reason for the failure to reach truly cooperative solutions.

In response to functionalists and their prescription that the "distorting elements" of politics and ideology be circumvented in efforts to achieve cooperation, we suggest that when a dispute over water resources is embedded in a larger political conflict, the former can neither be conceived of as a discrete conflict over a resource, nor be resolved as such. The riparian dispute in a protracted conflict setting is not simply about water; it takes on many of the attributes of the inter-state conflict. Indeed, the parties involved view the riparian dispute and the political conflict as one and the same. More accurately, the former is perceived as a manifestation, or microcosm, of the latter. Both conflicts trigger a similar discourse; both arouse a similar attitude toward the adversary.

Hence, given the experiences in the river basins analyzed in this book, we argue that states which are antagonists in the "high politics" of war and diplomacy tend not to agree willingly to extensive collaboration in the sphere of "low politics," centered around economic and welfare issues. They would have to be induced to do so. This is the case because, in addition to the material interest to secure access to water resources, historically situated states, as the realists point out, face structural constraints. They also face ideational constraints.[56] But this neo-realists, functionalists, and most neo-liberals, in general, fail to take sufficient note of. Concerns with regard to: (1) relative power resources – the means available to achieve objectives and, (2) basic organizing principles – values and beliefs, factor into states' decision-making and regional behavior at least as much as do their material interests.[57] Functional cooperation in international river basins characterized by protracted conflict is impeded by the persistence of political rivalry. Hence, cooperation in water utilization requires, at the outset, the positive resolution of political conflict and not vice versa, as the functionalists suggest.[58]

Despite the failure to create a basin-wide regime, there was, from 1956 to June 1967, implicit cooperation between Israel and Jordan over utilization of the waters of the Upper Jordan River.[59] Moreover, since 1967, the two states have been able to establish a few delimited cooperative arrangements in highly specific technical matters of mutual concern. In 1960, an agreement on a "non-cooperative" water scheme in the Indus basin was signed between India, Pakistan, and the World Bank. And in the Nile basin, there have been two explicit, negotiated water regimes between two of the nine riparians, albeit in the absence of protracted conflict. How, then, can we explain that on occasion, states in international river basins have been able either to establish a regime or to agree to informal arrangements for water utilization? Stated differently, under what circumstances will states accept cooperation, under what circumstances will they reject it?

In response to this set of questions, we argue that while the persistence of protracted conflict impedes the optimal resolution of riparian dispute, two factors will induce states to minimize the salience of the inter-state conflict for this issue-area. Instead, they will seek cooperation in river basins. First, states which need the resources in question and are (heavily) dependent upon the basin waters will be motivated to cooperate with some or all of the riparians. This is especially the case when access to the water is linked to security concerns, by virtue of being a necessary element of national survival. Second, and employing a variant of the theory of hegemonic stability in which the relevant "structure" is the distribution of power in the river basin, if the dominant power in the basin will benefit from regional cooperation in water utilization, it will take the lead in creating and maintaining a regime, and will enforce compliance with its rules. (It was the combination of these two factors that resulted in a cooperative agreement between Egypt and the Sudan on the Nile waters.) However, the dominant power will have no interest in basin-wide cooperation if its superior power resources coincide with a superior riparian position. (This is the case of Turkey and the dispute in the Euphrates basin.) Indeed, geographic position, as with other "natural"–environmental variables, influences the capabilities of states.[60] Therefore, it must be included among a state's power resources, either enhancing them, when geographic position is advantageous, or detracting from them, when unfavorable. The state which is the furthest upstream and hence, in the most favorable geographic position, will have no obvious incentive to cooperate. Being at the source of the river, it can utilize as much of the water as it chooses unilaterally, irrespective of downstream needs. It will not cooperate unless it is coerced to do so. (This is similar to the case of India and the Indus waters conflict.) In contrast, downstream states (Egypt, Jordan, Pakistan), irrespective of their relative power resources, will seek a cooperative solution because, given their inferior riparian position, they are needier than and, at least in theory, at the mercy of those upstream. Hence, insofar as international river basins in arid regions are concerned, we find cooperative arrangements *only* where threats to national security, in the form of resource need, exist, and where such arrangements have been advocated or imposed by a hegemonic power.

To take one example from the history of the Jordan waters conflict as an illustration of the pre-eminence of these two factors, let us consider briefly the failure, in 1955, of the first attempt to establish a regime in the basin. For Israel and Jordan, an agreement on the distribution of the Jordan waters was crucial, since both states were heavily dependent on the river system; it provided one-third of Israel's total water supply and more than two-thirds of Jordan's. Because of their acute need and the fact that neither of them was the upstream riparian, nor the dominant power in the basin, both were anxious for the implementation of a regional plan, despite the political conflict. However, for Lebanon and Syria, the Jordan River represented only a tiny fraction of the water resources to which they had access. Besides, as the upstream states, they were in the most favorable position in the basin. And Syria was the most powerful of the Arab riparians. Hence, because need was not acute and power resources were in their favor, the upstream states had no interest in cooperation. Given the circumstances, the political conflict took precedence in their calculations. In examinations of transboundary resource disputes in dry climate conditions, the centrality of resource need and relative power in both the interest in basin-wide cooperation and the creation of a regime is brought to the fore repeatedly.

Research design and methodology

Three principal methods are employed in our study of the conduct of riparian dispute and the potential for cooperation in international river basins. First, we reconstruct the history of the Jordan waters conflict from its inception in the 1950s until 1992. And for comparative purposes we outline the experiences in three other river basins. Second, we posit a framework for analyzing riparian disputes in protracted conflict settings. This framework has emerged by identifying and isolating those variables that have been of primary concern to states in riparian disputes and in the specific case of the Jordan waters conflict, and have influenced considerably decisions with regard to cooperation in the basin.[61] They are:

(1) resource need/dependence: the degree to which a state is dependent upon the water supply of the basin for its socio-economic development, both absolutely and relative to the other riparian states;
(2) relative power resources: the composite of capabilities – economic, military, and political resources – in terms of both their quantity and composition, available to one state relative to that of the other state(s) with which it interacts. In the realist tradition, relations among states are relations of power, and the behavior of states is a function of the distribution of power;[62]
(3) character of riparian relations or the impact of the larger political conflict; subsumed are three inter-related variables:
  (a) the protracted nature of conflict
  (b) core values and organizing principles: parties' concerns for identity, recognition, legitimacy, and survival
  (c) perceptions of the adversary;[63]
(4) efforts at conflict resolution and third party involvement.[64]

Each of the four cases is analyzed in terms of these variables to determine both the roles they have played in the course and evolution of the riparian dispute, and their importance in promoting or impeding cooperation in international river basins.[65] It is against the background of this complex of forces that state behavior must be understood. In essence, we want to learn how and to what degree these variables have determined outcomes in the four river basins.

Third, we use the principal case study, as well as the three secondary cases, to answer five research questions about the conduct of riparian dispute in protracted conflict settings and the potential for cooperation. Of these, two illuminate salient contextual features of riparian disputes: the influence of inter-state relations and perceptions in conflict settings:

(1) In the specific case of the Jordan basin how has the larger political conflict shaped the various efforts to find a negotiated solution to the water dispute?

(2) What determines whether a state perceives a dimension of its international relations as conflictual? How can we explain that, when a particular issue concerns two (or more) states, one may consider it a source of conflict, while the other(s) may not?

Three questions focus on the potential for cooperation in international river basins and are inspired by, and in fact are responses to, the various incarnations of liberal institutionalist thought.

(3) When a riparian dispute co-exists with a larger political conflict, is it reasonable to aim to resolve the former as a first step to resolving the latter? In other words, is the functionalist argument feasible: can we expect to achieve overall political cooperation among hostile states via an ongoing process of task-based arrangements for the satisfaction of shared interests? Similarly, is the neo-liberal argument, about the efficacy of international institutions in promoting cooperation by binding states in "a long-term, multilevel game," convincing?[66] More generally, if regime formation is indeed the answer to conflict, how, and under what conditions, can it be achieved?

(4) Related to the question above and to the functionalist and neo-liberal perspectives, is it possible to de-link issues when a riparian dispute co-exists with a protracted political conflict, so that the former could be resolved without reference to the latter?

(5) How can we explain that states engaged in a protracted conflict have been able, on occasion, to make cooperative arrangements, not unlike implicit regimes, with regard to water resources? What characterizes these occasions? Would liberals be correct to assume that such arrangements have more general implications for inter-state relations and the potential for peace?

Taken together, the answers to these questions link up with the second analytical method to provide the central argument of the study and to illustrate that the tenets of classical realism, modified by a more pointed focus on historically formed cultural and ideological dimensions, offer the most convincing explanation for the conduct of riparian dispute and the potential for cooperation in international river basins.

Structure of the book

This book is divided into three sections. The first considers the general problem of riparian dispute in protracted conflict settings by highlighting the landscape of conflict in the principal case study, as well as in the three secondary cases. The second and third sections analyze various episodes in the Jordan waters conflict, and draw comparisons with the other cases to provide the evidence with which to substantiate the arguments outlined above.

Chapter 2 sets the scene for the bulk of the study by providing the background necessary for understanding the riparian dispute in the Jordan River basin and its relationship to the Arab–Israeli confrontation. The focus is on those aspects of the regional environment, broadly defined, that bring to the fore the significance of the Jordan system and have had considerable conflict potential.

Chapter 3 outlines the three cases of riparian dispute that are introduced for comparative evidence. The conflicts in the Euphrates, Indus, and Nile basins are analyzed in terms of the four variables that are posited above as a framework for studying riparian dispute. We elucidate the ways in which the different values attached to the variables have governed each dispute and the extent to which they have determined outcomes. Comparisons are drawn among the four cases, including the conflict in the Jordan basin, and the variations in outcome are assessed in terms of the four variables.

The core empirical material, on the conflict over the waters of the Jordan River system, is treated in the remaining chapters. The historical analysis of the conflict begins in Chapter 4, with a discussion of the Johnston mission to the Middle East (1953–56), the first attempt to implement a functional arrangement and establish a "regime" for the utilization of the waters of the Jordan system among the basin states. We analyze the outcome of the Johnston effort in terms of the variables that guide state behavior. We note that the mission failed to achieve its objectives, because Syria, the most powerful Arab riparian (and one of the upstream states), had little to gain from a basin-wide accord. The Arab League, reflecting the interests of its member states, could not accept cooperation.

Chapter 5 continues the historical analysis of the Jordan waters conflict from the breakdown of the American-sponsored mediation effort until the outbreak of the June war (1967), concentrating primarily on the Jordan waters crisis of 1964. As in the preceding chapter, this event is analyzed in terms of the variables that constitute our framework. However, the focus is on inter-state relations or, more specifically, the importance of cognitive dynamics in guiding foreign policy behavior. Here we employ another methodology – that of systematic textual analysis of speeches, editorials, and radio broadcasts from that period. The aim is to demonstrate just how intractable the conflict has been, by providing a detailed case study of perceptions and sketching the psychological environment in the region.

Chapter 6 begins the discussion of the Jordan waters conflict since June 1967, when Lebanon and Syria were effectively removed from the dispute over the main trunk of the river, by virtue of the fact that their parts of the basin had come under Israeli occupation. Now, only Israel and Jordan would compete for the waters of the Jordan River proper, with the former the upstream state. Syria and the West Bank would be included in matters concerning the Yarmouk waters, on the one hand, and groundwater sources, on the other. Nonetheless, the principal actors during this period are Israel and Jordan, and it is they that receive the bulk of our attention in the remaining chapters.

Chapter 6 delineates the profound resource constraints faced by Israel and Jordan, and outlines the various efforts the two states have made in recent years to develop domestic water supplies. The chapter is geared to those readers who have considerable interest in hydrodynamics and resource development. Those who are more concerned with the larger theoretical arguments of the book may proceed to the next chapter.

Chapter 7 shifts the focus back to cognitive dynamics. We discuss the relationship that has developed between Israel and Jordan, and link Jordan's attitude toward its avowed enemy to its domestic needs and national interests, as well as to its perception of the distribution of power in the basin. Then we consider the discrepancy in the respective perceptions of Israelis and Jordanians with regard to the persistence of water conflict in the basin. We argue that just as the combination of resource need and relative power determines the possibility for cooperation in international river basins, so does it explain the variation in perceptions of the conflict potential of any particular issue.

Chapter 8 substantiates this argument by exploring four areas of actual or potential conflict in the basin since 1967. The chapter concludes with the stunning case of Israel's dependence on the subterranean water sources of the West Bank for more than one-quarter of its consumption demand.

Chapter 9 weaves together the different threads of the book. The five research questions are addressed, drawing evidence from the empirical material of the principal case study and the secondary cases. The four variables are evaluated in terms of the role each plays and the importance of that role in promoting or impeding cooperation in water utilization. Finally, the argument about the potential for cooperation in international river basins is refined, drawing upon the classical realist tradition.

PART I

Riparian dilemmas

2 The environment of conflict in the Jordan basin

In two seminal articles from the 1950s, Harold and Margaret Sprout discuss the importance played by the environment, or *milieu*, in international politics.[1] They argue that to make sense of the political behavior of states and of individuals requires understanding the environment, or context, in which actors operate and the variety of constraints and possibilities it poses.[2] In response to geopolitical theories of international behavior which assumed the pre-eminence of geographic variables – in vogue from World War I until mid-century[3] – the Sprouts posit an integrated, holistic view of the environment, taking account of both physical and non-physical features. The environment is a multi-dimensional system in which no one variable occupies a pre-eminent position. And because human activity is affected by environmental factors, broadly defined, politics can only be understood by exploring the multiplicity of "man–milieu relationships."

However, the Sprouts caution that it is not enough to study objective environmental conditions to make sense of political behavior. Perceptions of the environment – what the Sprouts refer to as the "psychomilieu" – are themselves important objects of study and analysis. Indeed, it is on the basis of perceptions that decisions are made and policy carried out. Nonetheless, the outcome of decisions is conditioned by the actual environment, or, "operational milieu."

We begin our study of riparian dispute by describing the environment in the Jordan River basin. Our aim is to underscore those aspects of the physical, human, political, and psychological environments that elucidate the significance of the Jordan system to the riparian states. In one way or another, the aspects described in the following sections have functioned as constraints upon state behavior *vis-à-vis* the river system and/or the other riparians. This discussion provides the necessary background for understanding the dispute over the Jordan waters, its relationship to the larger political conflict in the region, and the potential for cooperation.

The physical environment

The locus of our study, the Jordan River basin, is an elongated valley in the central Middle East. Draining an area of some 18,300 square kilometres, it extends from Mount Hermon in the north to the Dead Sea in the south and lies within the pre-June 1967 territories of Israel, Jordan, Lebanon, and Syria (see map 2.1). Physiographically, the basin is characterized by mountainous ranges in the north and on both flanks of the river, and alluvial plains in the central part.[4] Its waters, which originate in rainfall, in rivers and streams in the riparian states, drain land east and west of the Jordan Rift Valley. The Rift, a geological formation consisting of a fault, or deep scar in the earth's rock crust, forms the bed of the Jordan River by cutting through hilly terrain.

While the basin covers parts of four states, about 80 percent of it is located in present-day Israel, Jordan and the West Bank. Moreover, of the four riparians, Israel and Jordan are the most dependent on its waters. On average, the river system supplies Israel with almost one-third of its total water consumption, and the Kingdom of Jordan with slightly less than one-half.

Israel

On the southeastern coast of the Mediterranean, Israel borders Lebanon to the north, Syria to the northeast, Jordan to the east, and Egypt to the south. Covering an area of 20,699 square kilometres, it is one of the smallest states in the Middle East and the second smallest in the Jordan basin. Despite its size, its territory embraces coastal plains, hill regions, valley lands, and desert, each with a distinct topography and development potential.

The Negev desert and Arava Valley in the south cover an area of approximately 12,000 square kilometres, equivalent to more than 60 percent of the State of Israel within its pre-1967 borders.[5] In this region, rainfall varies from a maximum of 50 millimetres per year in the most arid parts to 200 millimetres in the northern Negev.[6] In addition to its relative sparseness, rainfall is capricious, and intense rainstorms are not uncommon. The desert climate allows no perennial streams.[7] Nonetheless, over the years there have been pronounced efforts at settlement and agricultural development in the Negev and Arava Valley.

Parallel to the Mediterranean shore and toward the center of the country, the coastal plain is a relatively fertile zone, with precipitation ranging from 250 millimetres in the southern extremity to 800 millimetres in its northernmost parts.[8] It is rich in water resources, either stored in different groundwater horizons or appearing in springs along the coastline. Rain

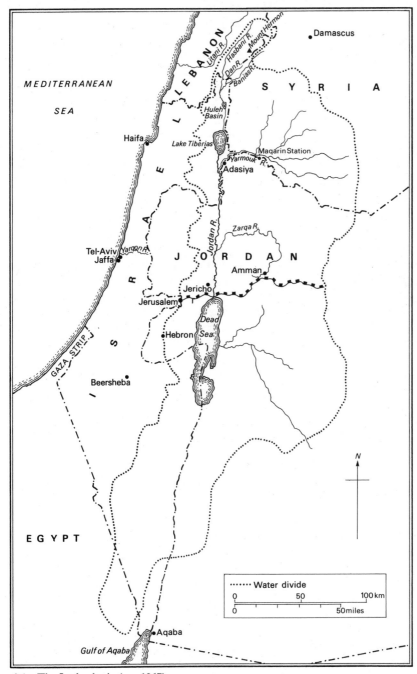

2.1   The Jordan basin (pre-1967)

falling on the hill regions east of the coastal plain seeps into the ground and flows westward toward the sea.[9]

The hill regions lie in the north, the center, and the east. Before June 1967, both the Golan Heights in the northeast and what Israel refers to as "Judea and Samaria" in the east lay within the territories of Syria and the Kingdom of Jordan, respectively. The Golan Heights were annexed by Israel in 1982, while part of the Judean foothills and most of the Judean hills and desert constitute the West Bank of the Jordan River, under Israeli occupation since 1967. Although there is significant variation from one hill region to the other, they tend to be relatively rich in rainfall, ranging from 400 to 500 millimetres in the foothills to 800 millimetres per annum in the Judean hills.[10]

Finally, the Jordan Rift, including the Dead Sea and Arava Valley, runs the length of the country from north to south. This geological formation is divided into four sections: (1) The Upper Jordan and Huleh Valley in the north is an area of relatively abundant precipitation – 900 to 1,500 millimetres per annum. It is the meeting point of the three headwaters of the Jordan system: the Banias, Dan, and Hasbani Rivers.[11] (2) The central Jordan Valley includes Lake Tiberias, which provides natural storage for the State of Israel, and the surrounding valleys. (3) The Lower Jordan extends southward from Lake Tiberias as far as the Dead Sea. A number of tributaries meet the river from the west. (However, much larger ones, the Yarmouk and the Zarqa, for example, originate east of the Jordan, either in Syria or in the Kingdom of Jordan.) To the south, soil salinity increases gradually, so that the higher terraces near the Dead Sea can hardly support any vegetation.[12] (4) The Dead Sea, which measures 80 kilometres from north to south, covers the deepest continental depression in the world, approximately 400 metres below sea level. Its waters register the highest salt content in the world.[13]

Kingdom of Jordan

Jordan is bordered on the west by Israel, the north by Syria, the east by Iraq, and the east and south by Saudi Arabia. Nearly landlocked, it has a 26-kilometre coastline on the Red Sea at the Gulf of Aqaba. The kingdom covers a territory of about 90,649 square kilometres on the East Bank of the Jordan River. The West Bank, which is bounded on the north, west, and south by Israel and separated from the East Bank by the Jordan River and Dead Sea, covers approximately 5,584 square kilometres (5,946 square kilometres with East Jerusalem).[14] Considered as a whole, only 11 percent of the land of Jordan is arable and 1 percent is forested. The remaining 88 percent is mostly desert.[15]

The country's terrain is marked by stark contrasts. The Jordan Rift, which extends for much of the length of the State of Israel, extends the entire length of Jordan from north to south and separates the East Bank from the West Bank. Stretching from the Red Sea northward, two-thirds of the arid Arava Valley lie within Jordan. By the terms of the 1949 United Nations Armistice Agreement, the western half of the Dead Sea, from its southern-most tip until its mid-way point, is in Israel, while the rest, equivalent to roughly three-quarters, is entirely within Jordan or the Israeli-occupied territories. To the north lies the Jordan Valley, the most fertile region of the country when provided with irrigation water. East of the valley, precipitous hills run almost the entire length of the country, quickly petering out to form the central highland region. The terrain of this plateau varies from extensive, slightly sloped plains to abrupt hills, too steep to cultivate.[16] Beyond this region lies the vast Syrian (or North Arabian) Desert which, as noted above, covers most of the East Bank.

Like its terrain, the country's rainfall is highly variable. It ranges from more than 640 millimetres annually to virtually nil. Nowhere does it reach 1,500 millimetres as it can on Israel's northern border. To reiterate, precipitation in the Israeli-occupied West Bank tends to be relatively abundant in the central hill region and slightly less so in the foothills to the west. Rainfall diminishes rapidly as one moves eastward toward the Jordan River and the Dead Sea. In the Jordan Valley, precipitation ranges between 50 millimetres in the south to 200 millimetres in the north. This regime renders agriculture possible only with irrigation.[17] Continuing eastward, the northern portion of the Jordanian highlands is a well-watered zone. Not only can it receive as much as 640 millimetres of rainfall, but also, it is from here that the Yarmouk, the country's most important river, and the smaller Zarqa River flow toward the Jordan. On the flatter, open slopes of the northern highlands, settled agriculture is possible. The southern portion, however, averages only 300–60 millimetres of rainfall per annum, which is just adequate for the cultivation of some grains.[18] To the east and south of the plateau, precipitation decreases rapidly to a maximum of 100 millimetres. For the most part, this vast and arid zone can support only pastoral nomads.[19]

The river system

The Jordan River's spring-fed sources rise on the western and southern slopes of Mount Hermon about 2,000 metres above sea level.[20] (See map 2.2.) They flow in three separate tributaries, the Dan (Hebrew: Nahal Liddani), Hasbani (Nahal Senir), and Banias (Nahal Hermon) Rivers, before converging in Israeli territory about twenty-five kilometres north of Lake Tiberias to form the Upper Jordan. From the confluence of the headwaters, the Jordan River flows through northern Israel into Lake Huleh and then

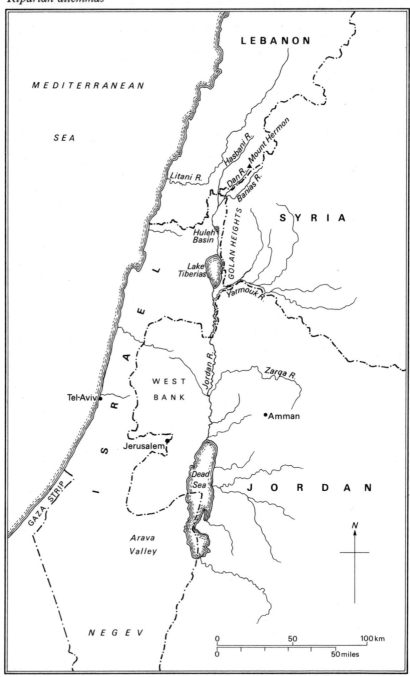

2.2   Jordan River system

continues in a narrow channel before entering Lake Tiberias. From 1949 to June 1967, the lake, which is the only natural reservoir in the basin, lay within Israeli territory, except for about one-half of its eastern bank which was a de-militarized zone. At the southern tip of the lake, the Jordan re-emerges, and after a course of 6·5 kilometres through Israeli territory, is joined from the east by the Yarmouk, the river's principal tributary. The main trunk of the Yarmouk forms the present boundary between Syria and Jordan for about 40 kilometres before it becomes the border between Jordan and Israel in its lower reaches. From its point of confluence with the Yarmouk, the Jordan River twists through the Lower Jordan Valley for approximately 110 kilometres, forming the boundary between Israel and Jordan for the first 40 kilometres, before flowing entirely within Jordanian territory (between the East and West Bank) for the remaining distance. (It is in this region that the river flows in a deep gorge called the *Zor*, on either side of which there is a series of terraces rising steeply to the top of the hills and referred to as the *Ghor*.)[21] During the course of its meandering, the Jordan receives many tributaries running parallel to each other from the east and the west, the majority of which are *wadis*, or seasonal streams that carry water only on a limited number of days each winter. Finally, the river discharges into the Dead Sea, 395 metres below sea level.[22]

The headwaters of the Upper Jordan River rise in the territories of pre-June 1967 Israel, Lebanon, and Syria.[23] The Dan, the largest of the three, lies wholly within Israel. It has a relatively steady flow, averaging 245 mcm (million cubic metres) per year, equivalent to 50 percent of the discharge of the Upper Jordan.[24] The Hasbani River is formed by springs at the foot of Mount Hermon in Lebanon, some fifty kilometres from the border with Israel. Before entering Israel, the river traverses a corner of Syrian territory for about two kilometres. The Hasbani's discharge is subject to very great seasonal and annual fluctuations. On average, it contributes 138 mcm per annum to the main stream.[25] The third and smallest of the headwater tributaries is the Banias. It flows for less than two kilometres in Syria before crossing into Israel. Its volume of discharge, which averages 121 mcm, also varies considerably.[26] Combined, the contribution of these three tributaries to the surface watershed of the Upper Jordan River is approximately 500 mcm per annum.

Over the course of the Upper Jordan, from the confluence of the tributaries to the northern tip of Lake Tiberias, an additional 150 mcm of water is added to the river system. Thus, an average of 650 mcm is discharged into the lake.[27] In the 1950s, about 500 mcm per annum left the lake's southern outlet.[28] Today, no more than 40 mcm is released.[29] Ten kilometres further south, the Jordan receives water from the Yarmouk River. This tributary originates in the Hauran plain in Syria and drains a basin measuring 7,252

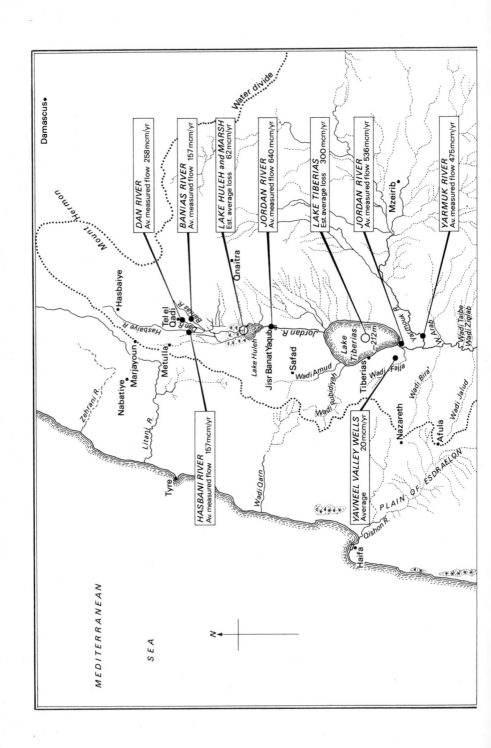

DAN RIVER
Av. measured flow 258mcm/yr

BANIAS RIVER
Av. measured flow 157 mcm/yr

LAKE HULEH and MARSH
Est. average loss 62mcm/yr

JORDAN RIVER
Av. measured flow 640 mcm/yr

LAKE TIBERIAS
Est. average loss 300 mcm/yr

JORDAN RIVER
Av. measured flow 536mcm/yr

YARMUK RIVER
Av. measured flow 475mcm/yr

HASBANI RIVER
Av. measured flow 157mcm/yr

YAVNEEL VALLEY WELLS
Average 20mcm/yr

Damascus

Water divide

Mount Hermon

Hasbaiye

Qnaitra

Mzeirib

Tel el Qadi

Marjayoun

Nabatiye

Metulla

Hasbaiye R.

Banias R.

Zehrani R.

Litani R.

Lake Huleh

Jisr Banat Yaqub

Jordan R.

Safad

Wadi Amud

Lake Tiberias

-212m

Wadi Rubidiya

Tiberias

Wadi Fajja

Yarmouk R.

W. Arab

Wadi Taibe

Wadi Ziqlab

Wadi Qarn

Nazareth

Wadi Bira'

Afula

Wadi Jalud

PLAIN OF ESDRAELON

Qishon R.

Haifa

Tyre

MEDITERRANEAN

SEA

N

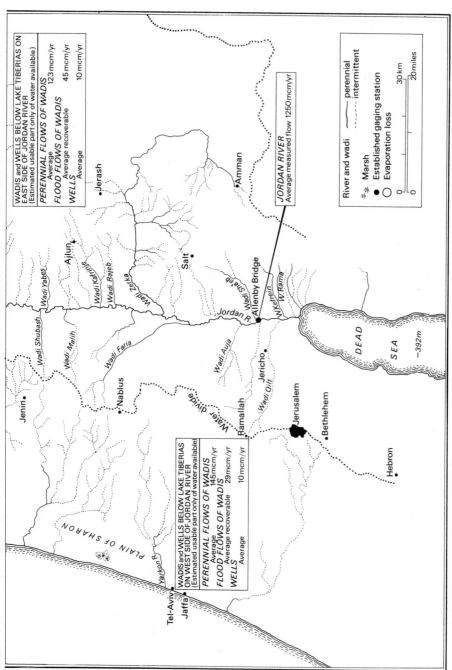

2.3 Water available in Jordan River Valley region, 1953

Table 2.1 *Major tributaries of the Jordan River*

Tributary	Source of headwaters	Discharge (mcm per year)
Hasbani	Lebanon	138
Banias	Syria	121
Dan	Israel	245
Yarmouk	Syria	400

Source : Alasdair Drysdale and Gerald H. Blake, *The Middle East and North Africa : A political geography* (New York: Oxford University Press, 1985), p. 99; Naff and Matson, *Water in the Middle East.*

square kilometres, of which 80 percent lies within Syria and the remainder in the Kingdom of Jordan.[30] (See table 2.1.) Under normal climatic conditions and prior to withdrawals upstream, the Yarmouk's contribution to the Lower Jordan amounted to some 400 mcm. (Today, however, it is virtually nil.) Thus, the natural average annual runoff of the Lower Jordan at its point of confluence with the Yarmouk River is about 900 mcm. Together, the wadis on the eastern and western sides of the river, north of the Dead Sea, contribute approximately 300 mcm of water per annum.[31]

Prior to the inception of major development schemes using Jordan waters, the river system delivered an annual average of more than 1,200 mcm of water to the Dead Sea.[32] This figure, however, was subject to extreme seasonal fluctuations. The Jordan carries much water in the winter and spring, but from April or May until November, it is only a small and slow brook. In February, for example, the river may carry as much as 40 percent of its total annual flow, but in each of the summer and autumn months, when water is most needed, it carries only 3–4 percent of its annual discharge.[33] (See map 2.3.)

Water balances

It is important to bear in mind just how little water there is in the Jordan system. This factor, coupled with the rising demands of states in arid or semi-arid regions, with high population growth rates and considerable agricultural sectors, illuminates the extent to which margins are narrow in the development and utilization of water resources. By world standards, the Jordan is a small stream. Its total discharge, of between 1,200 and 1,800 mcm (1·2 and 1·8 bcm) depending on the author, is equivalent to about 2 percent of the annual flow of the Nile, 6 percent of the Euphrates, less than 2 percent of the Indus, and less than 1 percent of the Congo (see table 2.2). Despite its

Table 2.2 *Some rivers of the Middle East : lengths and discharge*

	Length (km)	Total Discharge (bcm per year)
Euphrates	2,333	31·8
Tigris	1,840	49·2
Jordan	*c*. 800	1·2
Yarmouk	*c*. 60	0·4
Nile	6,825	83·6

Source : compiled by author.

size and the relative meagreness of its flow, the river is crucial for Israel and Jordan in their efforts to meet consumption demand.

Israel's overall water inventory is extremely limited, unevenly and unfavorably distributed, and subject to rather high, climatically determined fluctuations.[34] As noted above, the country has a Mediterranean climate, varying from semi-arid in the north to arid in the south. More than one-half the area of the country receives an annual average of less than 200 millimetres of rainfall.

Israel's water resources are unfavorably located in relation to main areas of demand. While they are most plentiful in the north and northeast, the densest concentrations of population, industry, and irrigable land are in the central part of the country and the coastal plain. And because of considerable development efforts there, the arid south has also become an area of high demand.[35]

Throughout the country, the temporal distribution of water resources is problematic. Streamflow and storm-water runoff are at their peak during the winter months, whereas consumption peaks at the height of the irrigation season in July and August. Moreover, drought years and even successions of drought years are not at all uncommon.[36]

In order to mitigate the difficulties that may be incurred as a result of spatial and temporal distributions, the storage of water resources is necessary. Thus, the discrepancy between supply and demand within the year, as well as the effects of long-time fluctuations in water availability can be overcome. Unfortunately, the country's only natural reservoir, Lake Tiberias, has a storage capacity of no more than 520 mcm, which is not sufficient to assure uncurtailed supply to various parts of the country during periods of adverse climatic conditions.[37]

Finally, compared to some of the other countries of the region, the extent of stream flow available to Israel is small. The annual volume of the Upper Jordan River, the largest exploitable body of surface water available,

Table 2.3 *Israel: renewable fresh water resources, 1984/85*

Source	Quantity (mcm per year)
River flow	
Upper Jordan	580
Yarmouk[a]	100–125
Groundwater	1,200
Floodwater[b]	15
Recycled wastewater	30–110
Losses	−60
Total	1,865–1,970

[a] Including floodflow.
[b] Excluding Yarmouk floodflow.
Source: compiled from Schwarz, "Israeli Water Sector"; interviews (1985–86, 1991).

Table 2.4 *Israel: water consumption data*

Year	Total (mcm per year)	Consumption sector (Percentage of total)		
		Agriculture	Domestic	Industrial
1960	1,138	81·2	14·7	4·1
1965	1,330	80·9	15·0	4·1
1970	1,570	79·7	15·3	5·0
1975	1,600	75·7	18·4	5·9
1979	1,700	73·5	19·5	7·0
1988[a]	1,950	68·0	24·0	9·0

[a] Approximate figures
Source: Vardi, "National Water Resources," p. 42; 1988 figures derived from, AMER; Schwarz, "Israeli Water Sector."

constitutes less than one-third of the country's total demand. In contrast, about three-fifths of total renewable water potential – that is, 1·2 bcm out of 1·9 bcm in the mid-1980s – originate from groundwater.[38] The coastal plain basin and the more abundant western basin provide the bulk of Israel's groundwater supply.[39] (See table 2.3.)

Because of the rapid increase in population and the marked expansion of the irrigated area since 1949, demands on the limited resources of the country have been great (see table 2.4). By 1989, population had quadrupled in size, while irrigated area witnessed a sevenfold increase. Total water consumption increased more than eight times (see table 2.5). As of the mid-1970s, in fact,

Table 2.5 *Indicators of Israeli development*

	Population	Irrigation area	Water consumption (mcm per year)		
	(thousands)	(thousand ha)	Agriculture	M and I[a]	Total
1949	1,059	30·0	180	50	230
1955	1,750	89·0	760	190	950
1960	2,117	130·5	1,060	251	1,338
1965	2,563	150·8	1,153	265	1,418
1970	2,958	172·4	1,233	311	1,544
1975	3,410	182·5	1,297	379	1,676
1977	3,575	186·5	1,258	402	1,660
1988	4,200	217·0	*c.* 1,300	*c.* 600	*c.* 1,900

[a] Municipal and Industrial.
Source: Itzhak Galnoor, "Water Policymaking in Israel," p. 289; AMER; Schwarz, "Israeli Water Sector."

demand for fresh water has exceeded supply.[40] And the prospects for the development of yet unexploited conventional fresh water resources remain limited.[41]

In the absence of additional sources of surface water, groundwater tends to be over-exploited, thereby diminishing its quality and threatening its future availability. Since the sustainable annual water yield is a fixed quantity, excess withdrawals from it by over-pumping or depletion of underground reserves constitute an overdraft that could cause irreversible damage. Over-pumping lowers the groundwater horizons so that infiltration of sea water is imminent. When the reserve of underground flow sinks below a certain level, the interface, or dividing line, between fresh and sea water is drawn upward and causes salination.[42] Israel has been over-pumping groundwater since 1970; some hydrologists maintain that since 1980, as much as 200 mcm have been over-pumped on an annual basis.[43]

In absolute terms, the water resources available to the Kingdom of Jordan are substantially inferior to those of the State of Israel. As we recall, 88 percent of the total area of the country is desert and steppe, and only a narrow strip of territory in the northwest, equivalent to one-tenth the total area, receives a minimum of 200 mm of rainfall. However, owing to unfavorable topographic features, no more than one-half of that area, equivalent to 5 percent of the country, can be cultivated.[44] Moreover, rainfall patterns are subject to considerable irregularity, and this can be very costly for agricultural production.[45]

In addition to the unfavorable rainfall regime, there are no perennial

Table 2.6 *Kingdom of Jordan: water availability, 1989/90 (mcm per year)*

Surface water	
Yarmouk River (at Adasiye)	120
Zarqa River	92
East Ghor wadis	120
Groundwater	388
Wastewater reuse	30
Total	750

Source: Abu-Taleb *et al.*, "Water Resources Planning and Development in Jordan: Problems, Future Scenarios, and Recommendations," in Guy Le Moigne, Shawki Barghouti, Gershon Feder, Lisa Garbus, and Mie Xie (eds.) *Country Experiences with Water Resources Management: Economic, Institutional, Technological and Environmental Issues*, World Bank Technical Paper no. 175 (Washington, D.C.: The World Bank, 1992); Jordan Valley Commission, *Rehabilitation and Development Plan of the Jordan Valley (East Bank), 1973–1975*, (Amman, October 1972) p. 12.

surface water sources available to the kingdom other than the Lower Jordan, the Zarqa and Yarmouk Rivers. However, because of the high degree of salinity of the waters leaving Lake Tiberias, the Lower Jordan cannot be used for most agricultural purposes. In fact, over the years it has become little more than a drainage ditch.[46] Besides, during the 1980s, an average of less than 50 mcm of water was released into the Lower Jordan on an annual basis, as opposed to some 500 mcm in the 1950s.[47] The Yarmouk River, with an average annual natural discharge of about 450 mcm, is the country's single most abundant source.[48] Unfortunately, Jordan is unable to make use of more than a small portion of its flow. Much of its yield is in the form of winter floodwaters that would have to be stored in order to be exploitable, but unlike Israel, Jordan has no natural reservoir within its territory.[49] In addition, the Yarmouk's annual discharge has fallen to less than 380 mcm, as a result of the drought conditions in the basin in the 1980s. Coupled with that, both Israel and Syria have been increasing their withdrawals from the river for their own development projects. Jordan has access to no more than about 120 mcm per annum.[50] As for non-perennial surface flow, it is important to note that in June 1967 the West Ghor wadis were lost to Israeli occupation, thereby depleting the kingdom's overall water balance by about 140 mcm.

In contrast to Israel, where groundwater represents as much as three-fifths of the country's total resource potential, in Jordan, groundwater is less abundant. In recent years, between one-third and one-half of total resource potential has been drawn from subterranean sources.[51] (See table 2.6.)

If Jordan had storage on the Yarmouk River, it would have access to an additional 75 mcm of water, at least. That, in combination with the implementation of other supply augmentation projects, would increase water availability to the estimated ceiling of 862–900 mcm under normal climatic conditions. It was only during the drought years of the 1980s that resources were fully exploited and insufficient for meeting demand.[52]

The human environment: population and settlement

In discussing the human geography of the State of Israel, there are a number of important features of its population and settlement experience that must be taken note of if we are to highlight those aspects of the environment that were likely to promote conflict in the Jordan basin. First, Israel is different from its Arab neighbors and unique in the Middle East in terms of population structure, ethnic composition, degree of urbanization, and rapid growth rate largely through immigration. Second, as with other countries of the Middle East, the population is unevenly distributed between the semi-arid and well-watered zones. Nonetheless, there have been considerable efforts at agricultural settlement and the development of some industry in desert areas, especially in the northern Negev. Third, population distribution and settlement patterns reflect deliberate planning policies related to ideological concerns and perceived needs of national security; principles of social and economic theory based on environmental factors have not been their primary influence, as would be the case in most other countries of the region.[53]

Approximately 85 percent of the population of the State of Israel within its pre-June 1967 borders is Jewish.[54] Despite virtual homogeneity on the basis of creed, its population is heterogenous in terms of ethnic, racial, linguistic, and cultural origin.[55] For the most part, the Jewish population of Israel is composed of immigrants and their offspring who, since the beginning of the Zionist Movement in 1882, have left their countries of origin in Asia, Africa, Europe, and the Americas, to settle in Palestine, and later, Israel. Consistently, Jewish leaders, whether in the Diaspora or in Palestine/Israel, have encouraged immigration for political and idealistic reasons. Moreover, in Israel's Declaration of Independence, it is proclaimed that the state would be open to "the ingathering of the exiles," and the Law of Return of July 1950 provides that every Jew is entitled to "return" to *Eretz Yisrael*, the Land of Israel.

While Jewish immigration has continued almost uninterruptedly since 1920, its pace has been dependent upon changing political conditions in the countries of origin, as well as in Palestine/Israel (see table 2.7). Thus, in the first three and one-half years following independence, immigration was massive; a total of 687,000 people entered the country, thereby more than doubling its Jewish population.[56]

33

Table 2.7 *Immigration of Jews into Israel, 1948–86 (in thousands)*

Year	Immigrants	Total population	Total Jewish population
1948	101·8	914·7	758·7
1949	239·4	1,173·9	1,013·9
1950	169·7	1,370·1	1,203·0
1951	174·0	1,577·8	1,404·4
1952	23·4	1,629·5	1,450·2
1953	10·4	1,669·4	1,483·6
1954	17·5	1,717·8	1,526·0
1955	36·3	1,789·1	1,590·5
1956	55·0	1,872·4	1,667·5
1957	71·1	1,976·0	1,762·7
1958	26·1	2,031·7	1,810·1
1959	23·0	2,088·7	1,858·8
1960	23·6	2,150·4	1,911·2
1961	46·7	2,233·6	1,985·5
1962	59·6	2,331·8	2,068·9
1963	62·2	2,430·1	2,155·5
1964	52·5	2,525·6	2,239·2
1965	28·8	2,598·4	2,299·1
1966	13·6	2,657·4	2,344·9
1967[a]	12·3	2,776·3	2,383·6
1968[b]	20·5	2,841·1	2,434·8
1969	37·8	2,922·0	2,500·0
1970	36·7	3,022·1	2,582·0
1973	54·8	3,338·2	2,845·0
1974	31·9	3,421·6	2,906·9
1975	20·0	3,493·2	2,959·4
1978	26·4	3,737·6	3,141·2
1979	37·2	3,836·2	3,218·4
1980	20·4	3,921·7	3,282·7
1981	12·6	3,977·9	3,320·3
1984	19·9	4,199·7	3,471·7
1985	10·6	4,266·2	3,517·2
1986	9·5	4,331·3	3,561·4

[a] Following 1967 only those years in which there was a considerable increase or decrease in immigration appear in the table.
[b] All years from 1968 onwards include the population of East Jerusalem.
Source: Blake, "Israel," p. 185; Orni and Efrat, *Geography of Israel*, p. 260; State of Israel, *Statistical Abstract*, 1987.

The growth of Israel's Jewish population is largely a reflection of the rate of immigration. Between 1948 and 1951, the annual rate of population increase was 23·7 percent.[57] It slowed down to 3 percent or less from 1952 to 1957 and picked up to around 5 percent in 1957.[58] Since 1977, it has hovered around 2 percent per annum, as compared with a growth rate of about 3·5 percent in Jordan.[59] By the end of 1969, the population of the state had increased threefold, from some 720,000 Jews (and 156,000 Arabs and Druze) in November 1948 to 2,500,000 (and 422,000 Arabs and Druze).[60] It numbered about 4·4 million in 1990.[61]

While there has been steady immigration of Jews to Israel since 1948, there has also been a steady decline in the Jewish population as a percentage of the total.[62] In 1954, Jews represented 89 percent of the population of the country; in 1967, 86 percent; in 1982, 83 percent. Moreover, if the territories captured in the 1967 war are included in the calculation, then the proportion of Jews is significantly lower. In 1982, the figure was no more than 64 percent of the total.[63] This progressive decline has been the result of a number of factors. First, Jewish emigration from Israel has been estimated at between 10 and 15 percent of immigration over time. Second, since the 1967 war, the state has maintained control over captured territories that had a non-Jewish population. And third, the non-Jewish communities of Israel and its occupied territories – Arabs, Christians, Druze – have consistently had higher birth rates than the Jewish population.[64] Thus, Jews have constituted a smaller and smaller majority of the population of *Eretz Yisrael* over time. This has been a source of concern to the Israeli political establishment, since it flies in the face of the *raison d'être* of the state and calls into question basic notions of identity and identification with the state. Although this is discussed at length in the following section, it is important to take note of the view that if Israel is to be the homeland of the Jews, the society must be homogenous and Jewish.

From the outset of Jewish immigration, settlement in Palestine concentrated in the coastal zone and in the three largest towns. With the inception of statehood in 1948, the particular distribution of Jewish population was of especial concern to the Zionist leadership and its perceptions of the security of the newly founded Israel. The hinterland was sparsely inhabited. The majority of Jewish settlements were within a thirty-kilometre radius of Tel-Aviv or Haifa, and only a few were as far away as fifty kilometres. Small and medium-sized settlements were scarce. The south, comprising close to 70 percent of the country, was virtually empty. Much of the relatively well-watered north was underpopulated and had a substantial Arab majority. And for the most part, the boundaries of the country were not guarded by frontier settlement.[65]

As a result, a self-conscious settlement strategy was instituted in order to bring about an optimum spatial pattern and distribution of population that in terms of national security and development were considered more rational. It was a deliberate policy to disperse Jewish settlement throughout the country in urban and rural settings, and especially where it was deemed too thin. Hence, immigrants were induced to settle in peripheral areas – the hill regions in the north, the arid Negev in the south, and the Huleh and Jordan Valleys in the east, bordering Syria and Jordan respectively.[66] In the words of David Ben-Gurion, Israel's first prime minister, "we must go to the borders or the borders will come to us."[67]

As with Israel, there are certain features of the population structure and settlement pattern of the Kingdom of Jordan that are particular to the state and place certain constraints on its regional behavior. First, Jordan is alone among the Middle Eastern countries and probably unique in the world in that refugees and displaced persons form a majority of its population. Second, the demographic character of Jordan has been profoundly affected by the alternation of expansion and retraction of the geographic extent of the state, that has accompanied wars and the occupation of territory. Third, because of the aridity and unfavorable topographic features of much of the East Bank, the population is concentrated in a very small portion of the country, in the high rainfall belt in the northwestern corner and in the Jordan Valley, where there is a recently developed irrigation system.

At the time of independence in 1946, the east bank of the Jordan River constituted what became the Kingdom of Jordan. According to one estimate, the "East Bankers," descendants of nomadic tribes that roamed between the Arabian Peninsula and the Fertile Crescent, then numbered 433,659. Of these, more than three-quarters lived in rural and semi-rural settings and most of the remainder were non-settled bedouin.[68] In the aftermath of the first Arab–Israel war in 1948–49, this picture changed radically. Abdullah, then king of Jordan, annexed the area of Palestine that his forces had occupied during the fighting: the region that later became known as the "West Bank," because of its location relative to the Jordan River. As a result of this maneuver, West Bank inhabitants – Palestine Arabs, who numbered some 400,000 – became subjects of the Hashemite monarchy. Their incorporation effectively doubled the population of Jordan. In addition, approximately 450,000 Palestine Arabs fled or were expelled from the newly founded State of Israel and poured into neighboring Jordan. Of these refugees, about one-quarter settled on the East Bank; the balance, on the West Bank. Thus, almost overnight, the population of the kingdom trebled, from a mere 400,000 plus to close to 1,300,000. And refugees formed a clear majority, constituting two-thirds of the population.[69]

The next major population shift occurred in 1967, in the aftermath of another Arab–Israel war. Since the West Bank fell to Israeli military occupation, the Kingdom of Jordan lost direct control over part of its territory and approximately one-third of its subjects. Nonetheless, about 265,000 West Bank Palestinians and some 45,000 Gaza Strip Palestinians fled to the East Bank.[70] According to Israel's Central Bureau of Statistics, the flow of West Bank Arabs to the East Bank has continued since 1968, at a rate varying from two to three thousand per year, totalling more than twenty thousand by 1981.[71] By 1990, the population of the East Bank had reached roughly 3,200,000 of whom at least 60 percent were Palestinian.[72]

It is important to note – and this will be explored at greater length in the section below – that important cultural, educational, social and political differences have existed between the East Bank Jordanians and the Palestinian population residing in Jordan, especially in the early years.[73] In 1948, East Jordan was rural and had a significant nomadic population, while Palestine was primarily urban, with an almost exclusively sedentary population. On the whole, the Palestinians were better educated than the East Bankers, and engaged in a variety of professional and commercial occupations. Moreover, the Palestinians in Jordan constituted a foreign population that had not settled there by choice. Their national identity and hence, their loyalties, differed from that of the indigenous population.

As to settlement patterns, they conform, for the most part, to the climatic and topographic features of the country. Where precipitation is relatively abundant, as in the narrow strip of highlands east of the Jordan Valley, population density is at its maximum. Since the mid-1960s and the implementation of an irrigation scheme using Yarmouk waters, the Jordan Valley north of the Dead Sea has become the second most densely populated region of the country, and this despite having a meagre rainfall regime. As would be expected, density diminishes markedly as one moves east and south into the desert regions of the country. Bedouins, constituting 5–7 percent of the population in 1980, live in the eastern two-thirds of the country, either scattered in small villages around water sources or, for those who are nomadic, in tents.[74] Thus, unlike Israel, where the population has been spread deliberately throughout the country, the vast majority of the East Bank population is squeezed into a very small area, in close proximity to the Jordan River. In fact, the capital city of Amman, including its metropolitan area, had nearly 50 percent of the total population of the kingdom in the early 1980s – a remarkable proportion given the country's size.[75]

National sentiment – implications of the nature of population

In the cases of both Israel and Jordan, the very particular sorts of population that make up their constituents have had a profound influence on them as states. The nature of the population impacts upon what political geographers refer to as the "idea of the state," that which binds people to the political entity and defines its purpose and functions.[76] At the heart of the idea of the state lies the notion that there exists some degree of identification with, allegiance or sense of belonging to the state on the part of its citizens. This relationship of society to the state can be the result of deeply rooted national sentiment or the prevalence of an all-encompassing political, economic, or religious "organizing ideology." If there are strong ties of nationhood and/or widespread support for a dominant ideology, one can assume that the state is fairly secure internally in terms of this component.[77] Furthermore, the strength or weakness of the idea of the state, or the degree to which it is rooted in society, has a bearing on the relative strength of the state and hence, on its international relations.

Israel is a unique state in the international system insofar as it was established as the national home for those of one particular religion the world over – the Jews. The background to the *raison d'être* of the state lies in the ideology of late nineteenth-century European Zionists, who argued that Jews would continue to be persecuted until they constituted a majority in a territory over which they held sovereign control. Hence, the answer to what was referred to as the "Jewish Question," the problems arising from the existence of a largely unassimilated ethnic–religious minority throughout the world, was the founding of a Jewish national home and the "ingathering of the exiles."[78] This solution was given irreversible momentum with the rise of Nazism in central Europe in the 1930s, and the subsequent extermination of six million Jews.

Thus, when the State of Israel was declared on 14 May 1948, the idea of the state was firmly established in the minds of world Jewry, as well as in the "minds" of those nations which had supported its creation. It was a sovereign, independent Jewish state, open to Jews throughout the Diaspora, who were called upon to "return" to *Eretz Yisrael* after two thousand years of wandering and persecution. By 1951, Jews constituted 89 percent of the total population of the new state, as opposed to some 30 percent at the outbreak of the first Arab–Israel war.[79]

In keeping with the *raison d'être* of the state (and perception of its external environment), Israel's primary and most sternly guarded values have remained its security and its Jewishness. Moreover, since the inception of statehood, the society has been prepared to fight and die for the idea of the state and its organizing ideology, Israeli Jewish patriotism. In fact, it has done so on several occasions: 1948–49, 1956, 1967, and 1973.

The twin sentiments, that the state is the national homeland of the Jewish people, and that it constitutes Israeli Jewish society, are deeply rooted in Israeli Jews (as well as in a majority of world Jewry, who provide the state with substantial material and psychological support). The strength of nationality and of patriotism has been a tremendous asset to the state, enhancing significantly its power resources.

In contrast, the idea of the state in the Kingdom of Jordan is not firmly established. That which inspires allegiance – a feeling of belonging to and identification with the state – is sorely lacking.[80] The kingdom was carved out of Greater Syria and created by the British in 1921 to reward the Hashemites. Nor did this family, of Arabian origin, have any traditional ties to the indigenous population of what became Transjordan. Allegiance to central power and the simultaneous breaking-down of tribal loyalties of the predominantly Bedouin communities of the new state were acquired painstakingly, mainly through the provision of arms and political favors. Furthermore, until independence in 1946, the state remained a patrimonial autocracy, absolutely dependent upon British funds, soldiers, and advisors.[81]

The tenuous nationality question in the kingdom was strained yet further following the Arab–Israel wars of 1948 and 1967, when on both occasions, several hundred thousand Palestine Arabs poured into the country. A situation of severe tension quickly developed. On the one hand, the absorptive capacity of the fledgling, resource-poor state was strained to the breaking point. On the other hand, and as mentioned above, the Palestinian exile community, comprising approximately 60 percent of the population of Jordan, had different cultural ties and political aspirations from the indigenous "East Bankers." Besides, their national sentiment was directed *not* to the Jordanian state, but to Palestine. With more than half the population feeling that it belonged elsewhere and that its residence in Jordan was temporary, the degree of identification of society with the state could only be uncertain. Nor was there any strongly held ideology – like liberal democracy or Islam, capitalism, communism or Arab Socialism – that predominated in the life and governance of the peoples of Jordan (except for the prevalence of Palestinian nationalism among the refugees and their offspring).

Given that ties of nationhood have been ambivalent and the state lacks nation-building power, harmony between the state and its subjects has had to be cultivated and nurtured constantly. Moreover, because the idea of the state in Jordan is weakly developed, the kingdom is vulnerable to challenges and interference from within and without. The fragile foundations of the state and resultant threats to it translate into profound constraints upon the regime's maneuverability both domestically and internationally.

Political environment: land and water in the Jordan basin until mid-century

The roots of conflict over the waters of the Jordan River lie in the convergence of two phenomena, one material, the other historical and ideological. First, and as noted above, scarcity characterizes the natural resource endowment of Palestine. However, a viable economy is dependent upon a minimum degree of land and food security, plus the development of sources of energy. Second, the Zionist movement sought to establish a Jewish national home in Palestine. Not only is land the basic requirement of settlement, but also, the actual land of Israel (Biblical Zion or *Eretz Yisrael*) – the need to "return" to it, to work and "redeem" it – was an essential ingredient of Zionist thought in the early part of the twentieth century.[82] The fact of scarcity impinged upon the contending aspirations of Arabs and Jews in Palestine.

No doubt therefore, the territorial aspirations of the Zionist movement, especially in the initial stages of its endeavors, were guided by economic criteria. With time, however, historic and strategic criteria gained in importance, as well. From the outset, unrestricted access to water resources was perceived as a non-negotiable prerequisite for the survival of a Jewish national home in Palestine. At the Paris Peace Conference on 3 February 1919, the World Zionist Organization expressed its concern thus: "The economic life of Palestine, like that of every other semi-arid country depends on the available water supply. It is, therefore, of vital importance not only to secure all water resources already feeding the country, but also to be able to conserve and control them at their sources."[83] Hence, the frontier claim it submitted to the Conference demanded "a line starting on the Mediterranean just south of the port of Sidon and then running north-east up the slopes of the Lebanon, to include the greater part of the Litani and the whole of the Jordan catchment area up to its northernmost source... From there, the frontier was to run along the crest of the Hermon, then turning due east to run along the northern watershed of the Yarmouk tributaries..."[84] The Organization justified its claim: "The boundaries above outlined are what we consider essential for the necessary economic foundation of the country. Palestine must have its natural outlets to the seas and the control of its rivers and their headwaters."[85]

Despite Zionist efforts and largely at the insistence of the French, the frontiers of Mandatory Palestine were delineated in such a way that the country was deprived of the areas containing the Litani River, the Banias and Hasbani tributaries, the spring of Mount Hermon, and the greater part of the Yarmouk Valley. They remained within the territories of French-mandated Lebanon and Syria.[86] Furthermore, by the terms of Winston Churchill's "White Paper" (1922), Transjordan was detached from the territory of the

British Mandate for Palestine. In its final form, the Mandate system extended the right to the United Kingdom to set up a separate state east of the Jordan River. Hence, not only were the land and water resources in government hands limited, but also, the actual size of the resource that was part of the conflict between Jews and Arabs was significantly diminished. Nonetheless, by the terms of the Anglo-French border agreements of 1920 and 1922, all of Lake Tiberias was included in Palestine, as were a narrow strip of territory along the eastern shores of the Lake and, "a fertile, triangular area bounded by the Jordan, the Yarmuk, and the Lake" – often referred to as the Adasiye or Yarmouk Triangle.[87] These areas would later prove to be important economic and strategic gains, even though at the time, they fell short of the territorial aspirations of the Zionist Organization.

Hence, given the convergence of the two phenomena outlined above – the aridity and resource scarcity of Palestine on the one hand, and the aspirations of the Zionist movement to establish a Jewish national home in the ancient land of Israel on the other – the Mandate Powers, by delineating the boundaries thus, set the stage for a future contest over land and water resources; a contest that was bound to intensify with the advance of settlement, state-building, socio-economic development, and inter-communal hostility in the region.

With the immigration of Jews to Palestine, beginning in 1882, the Zionist movement quickly realized that its "target land" for settlement was not a rich and wide-open frontier in the Turnerian sense.[88] The country was found to be resource-poor, with low economic potential. Moreover, the land was settled. All land, even if not inhabited, was owned by some person or agency – the Ottoman Sultan, or later, the British Crown – and the local population, which was far more numerous than had been estimated, had well-developed economic and legal ties to the land.[89] Both communities, Arab and Jewish, came to perceive that for their purposes, land and water resources were limited; resources could not be divided in a way that would be mutually satisfactory.

Throughout the period of the British Mandate (1922–48), the concerns of the World Zionist Organization with regard to the economic viability and the security of a Jewish state in Palestine were paramount. Efforts were made to exercise control over as much territory as possible. To this end, a fairly sophisticated institutional structure, consisting of such organizations as the Jewish National Fund, the Jewish Colonization Association, and the Palestine Land Development Company, was developed to enhance Jewish land purchase and settlement.

Not only was the *Yishuv*, the Jewish community in Palestine as a social and political entity, successful at buying up land, but also, it had acquired the most extensive and most significant water concession in the country. In 1926, the Mandatory Power granted a concession to the Zionist, Palestine Electric Corporation, giving it exclusive rights for seventy years to harness the Jordan and Yarmouk waters, whether from the Palestinian or the Transjordanian side, for the generation of hydro-electric power.[90] By the terms of the concession, ratified by Transjordan in 1928, basin states had to apply to the corporation for access to river water. Transjordan was granted the right to take Yarmouk water that was in excess of the needs of the corporation. Thus, with a monopoly of control over much of the river system, the "Rutenburg Concession," so-called after Pinhas Rutenburg, the president of the Corporation, was greatly involved in the industrial development of the Jewish economy prior to the establishment of the State of Israel. It exercised control over much of the economic development of Transjordan, as well, by virtue of its control of the water supply and its absolute right to priority of usage of the Jordan and Yarmouk rivers.[91]

Also during the period of the British Mandate and in keeping with the Balfour Declaration (1917), Palestine was opened up, yet further, to Jewish immigration. Under the initial assumption that there were vast empty tracts of land, aching for settlement and the settler's plough, European Jews arrived in increasing numbers. The Arab inhabitants of Palestine, who had expected to have an independent state once the Mandate was terminated, were perturbed by the influx; and they viewed with suspicion and growing animosity the Jewish National Fund's extensive land purchases, the appropriation of some of the best agricultural land, and the establishment throughout much of the country of agricultural and quasi-military settlements.[92] By the early 1930s, the Jews had gained control of the Jezreel Valley, the Huleh Valley, and much of the coastal plain. The Arabs perceived these developments as undermining the existence of the entire Arab community in Palestine.

While Arab concern regarding Jewish immigration and land purchases dated back to the 1890s, tensions and resistance escalated markedly as of the 1920s, when average annual land purchases by the *Yishuv* had increased considerably and the problem of the alienation of Arab *fellaheen* from their land had become acute.[93] Territorial accumulation went along with a complementary process of power accumulation. Violent clashes accompanied the conquest of the land by the Jews.

In response, the British government imposed quotas on Jewish immigration, as of 1922, in an effort to appease the Arabs. This initiative followed the Arab riots of the previous year, and was formalized in Churchill's "White Paper."[94] The government also sent missions to Palestine to investigate the disturbances. The Jews complained about the government's numerical restrictions on immigration and the Arabs complained about the growing Jewish presence in Palestine.[95] The *Yishuv*'s attitude was that, "in order to accumulate maximum territory, ever-increasing rates of immigration…were necessary, while extensive land purchases were perceived as essential for the absorption of both the ongoing immigration and the immigration the Zionist movement hoped for in the future."[96] The Arabs, however, were hostile to Jewish immigration. They perceived the situation as zero-sum: the country could maintain only a fixed or limited population, hence, "the arrival of any Jew was at the expense of an Arab."[97] One feared for the future of a Jewish national home; the other feared expropriation by colonizers. Both perceived threats to their existence and identity. Britain's concern was with the absorptive capacity of the country: was there room enough and the appropriate resources in Palestine for the two communities?

After the Arab revolt of 1936, the British Colonial Office sent a Royal Commission to Palestine to find ways to alleviate the tensions.[98] In its report, the Peel Commission proposed the partition of Palestine into three parts: a Jewish state, an Arab state, and a British enclave. The Jewish state would include the coastal region, the Jezreel Valley, and the Galilee; the Arab state would be annexed to Transjordan and would include the hills of Judea and Samaria, as well as the Negev; the British enclave would consist of Jerusalem and Bethlehem. The Arabs living in Jewish areas would have to move to the designated Arab part of Palestine and Transjordan.[99] In addition, the Commission recommended that in light of an eventual partition and the population transfers, a hydrographic survey be made of Palestine and Transjordan in order to ascertain the region's potential for agricultural development and land settlement (see map 2.4).

By the end of 1938, the British Government withdrew its support for the partition proposal; the report of another (Woodhead) Commission suggested that land and water resources were insufficient to support two workable, homogeneous areas. Nonetheless, a hydrographic survey of Transjordan had already been solicited for the Peel Commission from an irrigation engineer and Director of Development in the Transjordan Administration.

In his, *Report on the water resources of Transjordan and their development*, Michael Ionides described the results of his survey and outlined a few preliminary projects for exploiting the agricultural and settlement potential of the country.[100] After investigating the country's resource endowment, he found that the only possibility for providing substantial new areas of land was by irrigating the Jordan Valley between Lake Tiberias and the Dead Sea.[101] However, he maintained that, "there is no escape from the conclusion that the only source of water on a scale large enough to affect the capacity of the country to any appreciable extent is from the two main rivers of the country, the Jordan and the Yarmouk." Therefore, "the sole means of gaining a substantial increase in agricultural development, in the quantitative

43

2.4   The Peel Partition Plan for Palestine, 1937

sense of providing room for increased population, lies in the canalization of
the Jordan and the Yarmouk."[102]

Ionides outlined his scheme to irrigate the most fertile land in Transjordan,
"the long narrow Terrace of the Ghor, the old bed of the sea in the Valley
from Lake Tiberias in the north to the Dead Sea in the south," a stretch of
about 100 kilometres.[103] He proposed laying a canal from north to south
alongside the Ghor, diverting the Jordan and Yarmouk waters to irrigate the
Terrace down to the Dead Sea. A feeder canal from the southern tip of Lake
Tiberias would link up with the larger Ghor canal just below the Yarmouk
diversion. He suggested, as well, that the floodwaters of the Yarmouk could
be diverted to Lake Tiberias and stored there for summer use, rather than
continue to go to waste. Although his project was confined to the east bank

44

of the river, Ionides also made a few suggestions with regard to the possibility of carrying water to the west bank and conveying it along a west Ghor canal. The Ionides project never materialized, since the partition proposal of 1937, for which it had been commissioned, was rejected. Nonetheless, it served as the basis for all subsequent Jordan system irrigation projects proposed by the Arabs.

On the other side of the Jordan River, the Jewish Agency for Palestine had been studying land development possibilities to settle increasing numbers of immigrants.[104] The aim was to settle land far and wide, in order to establish a strong and defensible presence throughout the territory that the *Yishuv* sought to protect as the future Jewish state.[105] To assist it in its task, the Agency enlisted the services of the American soil conservationist, Walter Clay Lowdermilk, to investigate the absorptive capacity of Palestine. In his book, *Palestine Land of Promise*, published in 1944, Lowdermilk elaborated an imaginative plan for water development, with highly optimistic claims as to the country's economic and land settlement potential.[106] The scheme, which was to remain the basic Israeli plan for water utilization, recommended the creation of a Jordan Valley Authority to oversee the irrigation of the valley lands on both sides of the river, the diversion of Upper Jordan waters to the coastal plain and Negev desert, and the channelling of Mediterranean water through a system of canals and tunnels to the Dead Sea for the production of hydro-electricity. The plan presupposed the existence of vast empty lands awaiting settlement, with the resources to accommodate no less than four million new immigrants in addition to the approximately two million Arabs and Jews already living there.[107] Furthermore, the realization of his plan involved the diversion of water from outside the territory of Mandatory Palestine; the headwaters of the Jordan and Yarmouk Rivers, in mandated Lebanon and Syria, would have to be used to help support Jewish immigrants. Implicitly, Lowdermilk recognized the inadequacy of Palestine's absorptive capacity.

Lowdermilk's proposals were made operational in an engineering study prepared by James Hays, an American engineer and consultant for the Jewish Agency. In *TVA on the Jordan*, Hays elaborated eight stages for the realization of his predecessor's scheme, including the drainage of the Huleh marshes, the division of the Yarmouk waters between Palestine and Transjordan on a fifty–fifty basis, and the utilization of Upper Jordan waters for the irrigation of land outside the Jordan catchment – in the coastal plain, the lower Galilee, and the Negev. He was only slightly less optimistic than Lowdermilk with regard to the country's absorptive capacity.[108]

The Lowdermilk–Hays proposals were not well received by the Arabs. The plan gave further weight to the erroneous belief that in Palestine and Transjordan, there was plenty of land and plenty of water for all the Arabs

2.5   The UN Partition Plan for Palestine, 1947

and all the Jews. The Arabs feared that unprecedented Jewish immigration would follow in its wake. Besides, the plan was clearly designed to benefit the areas of Jewish settlement in Palestine – the coastal, fertile plains and the south. Finally, the Arabs rejected the basic concept of the scheme: to take as much of the Jordan waters as possible out of the river valley and away from its inhabitants, to irrigate lands outside the basin before the needs of the basin had been met.[109] In contrast, the Jews were relieved by the conclusions of the study. Events in central Europe in the late thirties and early forties had made the need for a viable Jewish national home far more urgent than ever before. The World Zionist Organization was anxious to settle hundreds of thousands of Jews in Palestine. According to the Lowdermilk–Hays scheme, this seemed feasible.

On 29 November 1947, the United Nations General Assembly voted in favor of a resolution to partition Palestine into a Jewish state, an Arab state, and an internationalized Jerusalem under UN trusteeship (see map 2.5). On 14 May 1948, one day before Britain withdrew its forces from Palestine, Israel declared itself a sovereign, independent Jewish state. The following day, armies from the neighboring Arab countries attacked, marking the beginning of the first Arab–Israel war.[110]

By the time the fighting ended, Israel had gained political control over an area 20 percent larger than what had been allocated to it under the 1947 Partition Plan. The Arab population in Israel's total area was reduced by about 80 percent of that which had been in the same area prior to the war. And "abandoned" Arab lands within Israel's boundaries were transferred to Israeli sovereign control and, later, to Jewish ownership.[111] Moreover, according to the Armistice Agreements (1949) between Israel and its four contiguous Arab neighbors, the demarcation lines between the states were established in such a way that Israel had within its boundaries several important bodies of water: much of the upper catchment of the Jordan, one of the three headwater tributaries – the Dan, Lake Huleh, Lake Tiberias including its southern outlet, and part of the western shoreline of the Dead Sea (see map 2.6). Israel had secured physical access to some of the areas it needed in order to execute the basic concept of the Lowdermilk–Hays plan – the irrigation of the coastal plain and the south.

Israel's gains weighed especially heavily on the Kingdom of Jordan which, in the aftermath of the fighting, had to contend with an influx of about 450,000 Palestine Arab refugees who had fled or were expelled from Israel, and needed food and shelter. This was in addition to the approximately 400,000 Palestinians living on the West Bank, who had become dependents of the Jordanian state. From a pre-war figure of some 430,000, the population of the kingdom trebled in less than two years.[112] The young state was desperately in need of exploiting its development potential. However, the Jordan Valley was the sole region of the country with land and water resources to provide for the increased numbers. In an impassioned article, Michael Ionides made a plea for the implementation of his scheme to develop the valley's resources – the only hope for refugee survival in Jordan.[113]

The development tasks of Israel were no less formidable. Once Jewish sovereignty had been achieved, all barriers to immigration were removed. From a population of about 700,000 Jews when the new state was declared, the figure doubled within the first four years of the State's existence. The percentage of Jews in the total population of Palestine/Israel jumped from 30 percent in 1948 to 89 percent in 1951. By 1952, about 684,000 new immigrants had arrived from Europe and the Arab countries of the Middle East and North Africa.[114] Israel had to settle increasing numbers of people, from a variety of linguistic, cultural, and ethnic backgrounds, and develop

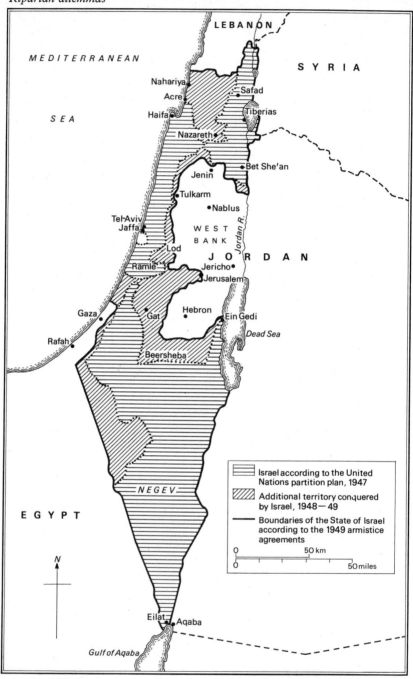

2.6 Post-1949 Israel

the economy in a harsh environment, under conditions of severe constraint. The Jordan system figured significantly in the State's development plans.

From the time the Armistice Agreements were signed, there was a clear division of interests between the Jews and the Arabs in the waters of the Jordan River. The former were principally concerned with development in the coastal plain; the latter, with development in the Jordan Valley. Israel and Jordan began to plan separately. It was inevitable that the two would eventually come to loggerheads over the exploitation of this scarce, but essential resource.

In 1949, Jordan hired a British firm of consulting engineers, Sir Murdoch MacDonald and Partners, to formulate an irrigation scheme, using the Ionides project as the basis. Two years later, the firm published its *Report on the Proposed Extension of Irrigation in the Jordan Valley*.[115] Its recommendations closely followed those of Ionides, with an extension of the canalization of the river system to include the west Ghor, most of which was now within Jordanian territory. It outlined a scheme for irrigating both sides of the valley between Lake Tiberias and the Dead Sea, based on the assumption that a joint Israel–Jordan scheme would eventually be possible. Lake Tiberias would be used as the reservoir for the winter flow of the Jordan and Yarmouk Rivers for both the Arabs and the Jews, since no satisfactory dam site on the Yarmouk was then known. The project was based on the principle that "the waters in a catchment area should not be diverted outside that area unless the requirements of all those who use or genuinely intend to use the waters within the area have been satisfied." The plan thus crystallized what soon became a fundamental issue of conflict between the Arabs and Israel, reflecting their divergent interests in resource development: should the waters of the Jordan system be used outside the Jordan basin, or must they be reserved for intra-basin usage alone?

In the meantime, Israel was proceeding with its Lowdermilk–Hays inspired national water plan. The Seven Year Plan, drawn up by a special water department within the Ministry of Agriculture, aimed at integrating "all the water resources of the country into a comprehensive country-wide network which would collect water wherever it is available and distribute it to the areas where it is needed."[116] A central irrigation system would carry water from the north, where it is plentiful and where land reserves are limited, to the south, where the reverse is the case. The system would draw on the sources of the Jordan north of Lake Huleh and carry its water through a central conduit to a main reservoir in the Galilee. From there, a canal would continue southward to a central point in the northern Negev, whence the water would be distributed by pipelines to various parts of the territory. As in Lowdermilk's proposals, the plan would also provide for hydropower generation, derived from a Mediterranean–Dead Sea canal.[117] The Plan, made public in October 1953, contemplated more than doubling the water supply by 1961 so as to triple the area of irrigated land. The objective was to increase local agricultural production, which then supplied only one-half of Israel's total food requirements, to the point where, by 1960, it could furnish three-quarters of total requirements for an estimated population of two million.[118]

From the outset, the control over land and water resources in Palestine was intimately related to both Zionist aspirations and the eventual establishment of the State of Israel. With regard to Arab–Jewish relations, land emerged as the major source of conflict soon after the beginnings of mass immigration to Palestine. Conflict over land intensified as Jewish land purchases increased and Arab-owned lands were expropriated.

Zionist immigration and settlement created a condition of interminable conflict between Jewish settlers and the indigenous Arab population, which revolved around the striving of both sides for sole control of the land of Palestine. The main focus of Arab anxiety was the Jews' accumulation of territory. Not only did the accumulation of power accompany the accumulation of territory, but also, from the beginning, the Arab community viewed the situation in Palestine as zero-sum.[119] There was an acute conflict of interest over resources which were perceived to be permanently limited. Hence, one side's gain was necessarily the other side's loss. Land thus became a central issue in the struggle for Palestine. Land was the basic requirement of settlement, but without water (and manpower), land could not be made productive.

As for the *Yishuv* prior to 1948, it rejected – at least in its official discourse – the notion that resources were permanently limited.[120] In part to pay lip service to the Balfour Declaration (1917), which had laid down protective clauses for "existing populations," the Zionists tried to present all conflicts as variable-sum. Once the Balfour Declaration had become obsolete after 15 May 1948, Israel no longer had to maintain that posture. In fact, the *Yishuv*'s land purchase and settlement activities demonstrated concurrence with the sentiment that resources were permanently limited. This perception became explicit immediately following the first Arab–Israeli war.[121] The building of a sovereign Jewish society on the same territory as an Arab social and political entity, and the continued existence of the latter, were viewed by both Arab and Jew as antithetical; one side could achieve its goals only at the expense of the other.

In the aftermath of the 1948–49 war, the resource bases of Israel and Jordan underwent tremendous strain. Both countries were hard-pressed to develop their land and water resources for the settlement and subsistence of outsiders: Jewish immigrants on the one hand, and Palestine Arab refugees on the other. Both states were dealing with far greater numbers than ever before, and both needed access to bountiful water supplies. Yet water in the immediate region was known to be scarce. There certainly was not enough to realize simultaneously both Israel's Seven Year Plan and Jordan's Murdoch MacDonald scheme. Furthermore, there was only one source of water of note in the region, the Jordan River system, and it was shared by Israel and the Kingdom of Jordan, the two countries in desperate need to develop their respective water supplies.

The dispute over water resources in the Jordan basin is intrinsically bound up with the larger Arab–Jewish conflict over Palestine. The seeds of conflict lie in Jewish immigration to Palestine as of the late 1880s and the concerted efforts to establish a permanent and growing Jewish community alongside an indigenous Arab community. The conflict intensified and became institutionalized after 1948 and the establishment of the State of Israel. Water came to be viewed as an extension of the land.

The psychological environment: perceptions of the importance of water

The importance of water to Zionists/Israelis

To the Zionist movement, which had been dominated by socialist trends from its inception through the 1930s, water was important insofar as it was part of the "ideology of agriculture" in Zionist thought.[122] Of primary concern to the Zionists in their endeavors at promoting the establishment of a sovereign Jewish state was to restore to Jews that which they lacked in the Diaspora and to create what they considered to be the "ideal" man. The creation of these "new" people was essential because:

> The Land of Israel will not be Jewish, even if Jews settle in it and buy land, unless they work the land with their own hands. For the land is not really that of its owners, but of its workers.[123]

Encouraging agricultural activity in Palestine was central to the achievement of their goals. By working the land, Jews would be returning to the Land of Israel (*Eretz Yisrael*) in the most literal sense. They would become productive, in the Marxian sense of the term, rather than continue to engage in trade and commerce as had been their tendency in the Diaspora. Besides, to Socialist Zionism, the "ideal man" is he who tills the land. And in keeping with socialist doctrine, he who tills the land has rights to it. It followed logically that if Jews worked the land, the Land of Israel, that land would belong to them. Hence, in this early period, the emphasis on agriculture had both social and ideological components. Moreover, it served a dual function. On the one hand, it sanctified the Jewish farmer. On the other hand, it sanctified the possession of land.[124]

In time, however, agriculture became related to defense and defense imperatives insofar as it was viewed as the means by which the Jews could be dispersed and an uninterrupted physical presence established throughout the country. Not only was it essential to be on the land in order to lay claim to it, but also, to quote one Israeli interviewed: "Jews must work the land – all the land. If not, it will be occupied by Arabs; first by their grazing animals and then, by them, themselves. This would be the end of the Jewish state."[125] Agricultural development has remained a national goal, embodying a socially accepted value and dictated by ideology.

Water, because it is an essential ingredient of agriculture, was and continues to be considered important by Zionists and the State of Israel. Moreover, it has always been linked in some fashion to their ideological, economic, political, and security-related concerns.[126] Water would help to make possible the absorption of increasing numbers of immigrants in *Eretz Yisrael*. It would also make it possible for Jews to work the land. In turn, working the land would allow for: (1) the economic development of the Jewish state, (2) progress toward economic self-sufficiency, (3) the creation of the "ideal man," (4) the development of "ties to the land," and (5) the occupation of land and keeping others out. In addition, with water Israel could implement more fruitfully its policy of "population dispersal": spreading Jewish settlement throughout the country and, after 1967, the occupied territories, as well.

The importance of water to Arabs : Palestinians and "East Bankers"

Prior to 1948, the Arab population of Palestine constituted a largely agricultural society that worked and lived off the land.[127] Given that traditionally, agriculture was the principal economic activity, water, whether in the form of rainfall or surface flow, was vital to the livelihood of the Palestinian peasant. He was both tied to the land and dependent on water. Water was perceived as an extension of the land.[128]

As noted above, Zionist efforts at buying up land in Palestine during the first half of this century caused the gradual alienation of Arab peasants from their land. The establishment of the State of Israel in 1948 continued that process. In the perceptions of the Palestinians, they were being denied the land which they worked and hence, their livelihood, as well as the land which was their homeland, or *watan*. The combination of these two forms of denial was viewed as a threat to their survival.[129]

To the East Bank Arabs, water had a different significance. Prior to the establishment of the Kingdom of Jordan in 1946, the population of what was then called Transjordan was primarily nomadic or semi-nomadic.[130] Traditionally, to the bedouin, land *per se* is of no intrinsic value, since he views all land to be his and accessible to him. Nor does he recognize boundaries, demarcation lines, and the like. However, water obviously is very important to the nomadic way of life because movements are determined largely by the search for water and grazing-land for animals. Ideally, camps are set up in close proximity to water holes.

After the establishment of the Kingdom of Jordan, water was essential for the tasks of state-building and economic development in a predominantly desert environment. Agriculture had to be improved in order to feed the population, and potable water had to be provided. The sedentarization of nomadic populations accompanied the process of state-building, and this required water for domestic purposes, as well.

Following the first Arab–Israel War in 1948–49, the population of Jordan trebled. All resources of the country, which in any case were extremely limited, were strained. Moreover, the east Jordan Valley, which had previously been the home of roaming bedouins, was earmarked to become the settling-ground of the Palestinian refugees.[131] Water was essential for domestic consumption and the provision of sanitary living conditions. Furthermore, it was hoped that the Valley would eventually become the breadbasket of the kingdom; as noted above, it had potentially the most fertile land in the country. In order to become productive, however, irrigation water had to be made available.

Hence, the combination, in an arid climate, of the following three factors – acute population pressure, the demands of economic development, and the focus on the Jordan Valley for the settlement of refugees and the agricultural development of the country – has caused the East Bank Arabs to view access to water resources as essential to their continued survival.

3 Riparian disputes compared

As in the Jordan River basin, in the Euphrates, Indus, and Nile basins, there has been conflict among the riparian states over the allocation and utilization of the rivers' waters. All four riparian disputes are located in arid or semi-arid regions, where resource scarcity is a fact of life. In all four cases and for some or all of the riparians, dependence on the river system is great. The basin states have very important agricultural sectors; they depend on the river primarily for irrigation water. For at least some of the states in each basin, unimpeded access to the water resources is linked to national security concerns. As noted in chapter 1, basin-wide, integrated development has been advocated as the optimal means for sharing the waters of an international river, especially in situations of acute need. However, in none of the cases have the basin states elected this approach.

While the three cases share with the Jordan dispute certain basic similarities, there are significant differences in conditions and variables that account for the variation in outcomes. First, in the Nile basin, there is no protracted conflict over multiple issues among the riparian states as there is in the Jordan, Indus, and to a somewhat lesser extent, Euphrates basins. Second, in all but the Nile case, the upstream riparian is also the dominant power in the basin. In the Nile basin, the inverse is the case: the state furthest downstream is the dominant power. Third, agreement over access to the basin's waters has been achieved in two of the four cases, the Indus and Nile. However, in neither has the solution reached been optimal, in the sense advocated by planners, jurists (and implicitly, by liberal institutionalists, as well).

In this chapter, we highlight the variables that have affected state behavior in the three basins and elucidate the ways in which the different values attached to the variables have governed the riparian disputes.[1] Each in its individual historical context, we outline in broad strokes the environment of conflict and the conflict itself. In the concluding section, we reintroduce the conflict in the Jordan basin and draw comparisons among the four cases. We focus on the variables that make up our analytical framework: (1) resource need, (2) relative power, (3) character of riparian relations, and (4) efforts at

Table 3.1 *The river basins compared*

	Euphrates	Indus	Nile	Jordan
Area of basin	444,000 km	720,000 km	3,100,000 km	18,300 km
Discharge of river	31·8 bcm	97 bcm	84 bcm	1·2 bcm
Length of river	2,333 km	8,480 km (river and 7 tributaries)	6,400 km (White and Main Niles) 1,600 km (Blue Nile)	800 km
Number of riparians	3	2	2 (9)	4 (3 since 1967)
Status of agreements	None	Indus Waters Treaty 1960	Agreement for the full Utilization of the Nile Waters 1959	None
Mechanisms of cooperation	Tripartite technical commission that meets irregularly	Permanent Indus Commission	Permanent Joint Technical Commission	UN troops (UNTSO, UNMAC)

conflict resolution. The variations in outcomes in the river basins are assessed in terms of these four variables (see table 3.1).

Euphrates River basin

The Euphrates River rises in the mountains of southeastern Turkey and flows through the territories of Turkey, Syria, and Iraq before emptying into the Shatt al-Arab waterway.[2] (See map 3.1.) Twenty-eight percent of the basin lies in Turkey, the uppermost riparian, 17 percent in Syria, the middle riparian, and 40 percent in Iraq, the downstream riparian.[3]

The average annual discharge of the river is 31·8 bcm. 88 percent is generated within Turkey and virtually all of the remaining 12 percent in Syria. Iraq makes practically no contribution to the river flow.[4] Despite what may appear as an abundance of water, the beneficence of the river regime is upset by two characteristics of the river itself: flow varies considerably on a seasonal and annual basis, and historically, the river has been prone to regular and severe flooding.[5] Storage of spring floodwaters is the key to the problem of water resource management in the basin.

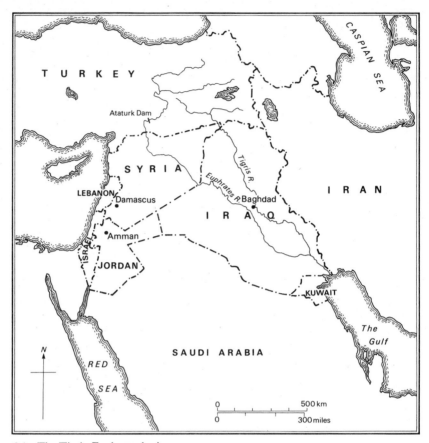

3.1 The Tigris–Euphrates basin

The Euphrates basin has an arid and semi-arid climate. Precipitation drops from 500 to 1,000 millimetres in the upper basin to less than 200 millimetres in southern Syria and Iraq.[6] Of the three riparians, Turkey is the best off in terms of water supply, and its average annual precipitation of 670 millimetres is adequate for rainfed agriculture. Nonetheless, the country suffers from irregular spatial and temporal distribution of water resources. The situation in Syria is far more serious. One-third of the country is steppe. More than half gets less than 250 millimetres of rainfall per year, and consists of desert and semi-desert regions. Less than 10 percent receives enough precipitation for rainfed agriculture. The Euphrates River alone represents as much as 86 percent of the water resources available to Syria.[7] In the case of Iraq, almost two-thirds of its total land area is desert and much of the country gets less than 125 millimetres of rainfall per year. Agricultural production in central and southern Iraq is highly dependent on the Tigris and Euphrates Rivers for irrigation water.[8]

For centuries, the Mesopotamian plain made large-scale use of the waters of the Euphrates, and as the downstream riparian, no harm was caused to those upstream.[9] In this century, Syria and Turkey showed little interest in the river until the onset of severe population pressure in the basin in the 1950s. By the mid-1960s, the two upstream states were devising unilateral projects to harness the Euphrates waters for irrigation and hydro-electric power production. Most significant was the construction of a dam at Tabqa in Syria (1968–73) and a series of dams in southeastern Anatolia (Turkey) – Keban (1965–73), Karakaya (1976–87), and Ataturk (1983–92).[10]

No doubt, utilization of the Euphrates waters upstream would have serious repercussions on projects downstream. The Syrian and Turkish projects promised to create a situation characterized by the twin problems of conflicting demands on scarce water resources, where demand exceeds supply, and depletion of the quantity and quality of water downstream because of upstream usage. A tripartite agreement on the distribution of the Euphrates waters was imperative. However, inter-state relations in the basin have proven to be a formidable obstacle to cooperation. Without delay, the issue of sharing water brought to the fore other sources of tension simmering between Turkey and Syria on the one hand, and Syria and Iraq on the other.

A first round of tripartite talks took place in 1965. They did not lead to an accord.[11] Turkey made agreement on the Euphrates waters conditional upon an inclusive agreement on the distribution of the waters of *all* rivers common to it and Syria. This put the latter in a difficult position because implicit in the proviso was the need for Syria to recognize Turkish sovereignty over Alexandretta (Hatay province), through which the Orontes River flows. This territory, ceded to Turkey by the French mandatory power in Syria on the eve of World War II, has remained a bone of contention between the two neighbors. Until today, successive Syrian regimes have demanded its return to Syrian sovereignty. Syria would not sign an agreement on the division of waters that flow through contested territory.[12]

In 1966, Syria and Iraq began a series of bilateral negotiations.[13] At this early stage, the contention between the two countries was of a technical nature, and concerned an appropriate distribution of the Euphrates waters. Given both its long history of large-scale exploitation of the river and its inferior riparian position in the basin, Iraq was anxious to protect its "established uses" and be able to extend irrigated agriculture in the future. As the classic downstream state, Iraq insisted on its claim to acquired rights to a fixed share of the river's discharge. Syria, however, rejected the Iraqi claim, arguing that potential needs had to be weighed against acquired rights. Representatives of the two states continued to meet every year for three years, and they discussed an apportionment that would give Iraq 59 percent of the river flow at the Syro-Iraqi border. Nonetheless, no agreement was formalized.[14]

In 1973, the Keban and Tabqa dams became operational. The filling of the reservoirs spelt a drastic reduction in flow to Syria and, especially, Iraq. In mid-1974, Iraq asked Syria to release an additional 200 mcm from Tabqa, to which the latter complied. On that occasion, the two riparians reached an agreement limiting the amount of water to be stored in the Tabqa reservoir and thereby guaranteeing Iraq's agricultural needs.[15] However, at the beginning of 1975, Iraq charged Syria with violating the agreement by reducing the flow, thus placing a rural population of three million at risk.[16] Indeed, the flooding of Lake Asad at the newly completed Euphrates High Dam at Tabqa deprived Iraq of part of the water it had previously received. Iraq issued a formal protest and took the matter to the Arab League. The Syrian Minister of the Euphrates Dam retorted that less than half the normal river flow had reached the Turkish–Syrian border that season.[17]

These events provoked a crisis in Syrian–Iraqi relations in 1975. Against the background of acute political and ideological tensions that had been festering since the inception of a B'athi regime in Baghdad in July 1968, the charges and counter-charges quickly reached a crescendo. Within no time, technical considerations seemed to fall by the wayside. The political rivalry over regional influence overshadowed all other mutual concerns.[18]

During April and May of 1975, there were several interventions by third parties. The Arab League, the government of Saudi Arabia, and President Sadat of Egypt undertook to mediate the conflict. However, each of these efforts came to naught.[19] With each stalemate, the crisis worsened. By the beginning of June, it was reported that Syria had transferred troops from its southern front to the Iraqi border, where allegedly, Iraqi forces were massing. The threat of war looming, Saudi Arabia made another attempt to defuse the crisis. This time, an understanding was reached. Syria announced in mid-August that it had accepted a Saudi proposal whereby Euphrates water would be shared between Syria and Iraq on a "proportional basis," in accordance with the amount of water reaching Syria from Turkey. Nonetheless, no agreement was signed and the water dispute remained unresolved.[20]

The political origins of the conflict between Syria and Iraq can be traced back to the B'athi seizure of power in Iraq in July 1968. The B'ath party had been in power in Syria since 1963, but in February 1966, the government of the "old guard" – the founding fathers of B'athism – was ousted by its dissenting younger members. Two years later, the "old guard" took power in Iraq. This posed a severe threat to the Syrian regime, which was struggling with a pro-"old guard" (and hence, pro-Iraqi B'ath) contingent at home. As long as the Syrian B'ath had not consolidated its grip over domestic forces, the competing tendency of a pan-Arab ideology in power in Iraq was perceived as an acute threat to the Syrian regime's continued survival. An impassioned propaganda war for "B'athi legitimacy" ensued, with each side making claims to its true B'athism, while leaving no stone unturned in an effort to undermine the authenticity of the other.[21] In this climate, neither regime could take a stand or make a move on any issue without it being viewed with deep suspicion by the other.

Not only did the conflict over water resources aggravate political tensions between the two downstream riparians, but it quickly proved to be a chessboard for the larger issues governing regional and inter-Arab politics. Until the consolidation of power by the al-Asad regime in Syria, the Euphrates issue was intimately linked to the B'athi contest for ideological hegemony. Once the Syrian–Iraqi relationship developed into a struggle for regional domination and recognition as the most "steadfast" Arab state in the aftermath of the 1973 Arab–Israeli war, the waters again proved to be an important playing card. To take but one example, Iraq had criticized what it perceived as Syrian peace overtures to Israel. Then, when Syria slowed down the flow of water toward Iraq in the spring of 1974 and again in 1975, Saddam Hussein charged Hafez al-Asad with doing so in retaliation for the criticisms of his "peace policy."[22]

Until today, no progress has been made at reaching a tripartite agreement on water-sharing in the basin, despite the fact that in 1980, all three riparians agreed to establish a technical commission for the exchange of information.[23] In 1984, Iraq agreed with Turkey to accept a minimum flow of 500 cubic metres per second, but Syria refused to negotiate at the time. Discussions between Syria and Turkey began in 1986 and are continuing. Some sources state that Turkey has signed a protocol with Syria, guaranteeing it 500 cubic metres per second, as well. The latter agreement, however, makes no reference to the earlier agreement with Iraq.[24]

Turkey, the upstream riparian, hopes to complete its massive water resource management schemes in southeastern Anatolia. These projects, commonly referred to by the acronym GAP (Guneydogu Anadolu Projesi [Southeast Anatolia Development Project]), could only be curtailed by a basin-wide accord.[25] The middle and downstream riparians, which would gain considerably from a water-sharing agreement, continue to have difficulty sitting at the same bargaining table, to say nothing of their inability to ally against the upstream riparian. The inter-state conflict serves as a profound constraint on all that is possible between them. Furthermore, there has been little outside encouragement, either regional or international, for basin-wide cooperation.[26]

Relative power in the basin is definitely in Turkey's favor. Not only is it in

Table 3.2 *Iraq's projected share of Euphrates water, 1986–2000+ (in mcm per year)*

	1986–90	1990–95	1995–2000	2000+
Estimated "natural flow" entering Iraq	33,460	33,460	33,460	33,460
Combined Turkish and Syrian use of water	4,109	13,460	24,562	28,987
Share remaining for Iraq	29,351	20,000	8,898	4,473

Source: Kolars and Mitchell, *Euphrates River*, p. 255.

the best riparian position, but also, it is economically and militarily the most powerful of the three states. Largely as a result, it has no interest in, and no material gain to reap from basin-wide cooperation. Moreover, its need for water, although important, is not nearly as great as that of Syria or Iraq downstream, and is confined to the southeastern corner of the country. (Nonetheless, its massive development project in the basin is being pursued in order to generate much-needed hydro-electric power, decentralize development, stop rural-to-urban migration, and appease the Kurdish population in the region.)[27] Syria is the smallest of the three riparians with, perhaps, the least economic development. Its riparian position, while superior to Iraq, is inferior to the most powerful state in the basin. No doubt, it would be interested in a bilateral agreement with Turkey. Of the three riparians, Iraq is in the least favorable position. It also is the most dependent upon the Euphrates River because of the extensive system of irrigated agriculture in the arid central and southern regions. This is despite the fact that the country has access to the abundant Tigris waters, as well.

The twin issues of recognition and legitimacy played a role in the riparian conflict in the early stages: between Turkey and Syria over Alexandretta, and between Syria and Iraq with regard to Bʿathi legitimacy. Since the mid-1970s, however, these concerns have been superseded by the highly personalistic contest between Syria and Iraq for political hegemony in the region, but more importantly, by Turkey's position of relative strength in the basin.

The conflict over the Euphrates waters remains unresolved. Although less dramatic than in the mid-1970s, the dispute is more critical today. The stakes are significantly bigger than in the past. The final stage of the Turkish South East Anatolia project is well underway and the planned withdrawal of as much as 14–17 bcm from the Euphrates River promises much hardship downstream.[28] Syria's ability to generate hydro-power and to extend irrigated agriculture will be curtailed by the depleted water levels. And Iraq, which has to contend with the water engineering schemes of both upstream states, will have to forfeit more than one-third of its intake from the Euphrates (see table 3.2). Not only will Iraq be hard-pressed to meet existing water consumption needs in its part of the basin, but also, it will not have at its disposal the large volumes of fresh water with which to reclaim its highly saline soils.[29]

Indus River basin

One of the largest river systems in the world, the Indus is shared by four states – Afghanistan, the People's Republic of China, India, and Pakistan – and is composed of the Indus River itself, five major tributaries, and two minor ones (see map 3.2). The headwaters of the system rise in Tibet and in the western Himalayas. India, including that part of Jammu and Kashmir under its administration, contains part of the headwaters of all five principal tributaries. None of the tributaries rise in Pakistan, but all except for one enter the country.[30]

Because of harsh topographical features and sparse settlement, the riparian conflict in the basin does not concern Afghanistan and China, but focuses upon the Punjab, the "five rivers" plain, that was divided by the 1947 partition boundary into West Punjab (Pakistan) and East Punjab (India). This densely populated, rich, agricultural region – the breadbasket of the subcontinent – is traversed by the Indus and its five main tributaries: the Jhelum, Chenab, Ravi, Beas, and Sutlej.[31] At the time of partition, the Punjab was criss-crossed by an extensive system of canals which had, for decades, provided irrigation water for approximately five million hectares of land.[32]

Except for the uppermost portions, the Indus basin is arid and semi-arid, with precipitation decreasing rapidly from north to south. The northern reaches of the Punjab plains receive 500 millimetres of rainfall per year, but most of the region receives no more than 250 millimetres. Rainfall is torrential and unreliable in the Pakistani Punjab, and increasingly so southwestwards. East Punjab is only slightly better off. Given the aridity of the basin, the Punjab rivers are of unrivalled importance as sources of water supply.

The combined annual discharge of the Indus and the five tributaries is 97 bcm.[33] Despite this impressive figure, there are drastic fluctuations in flow from month to month. Furthermore, the flow is most abundant during the summer (April–September), while the need for water is greatest in the autumn when the *kharif* (autumn-harvested) crops mature and the *rabi*

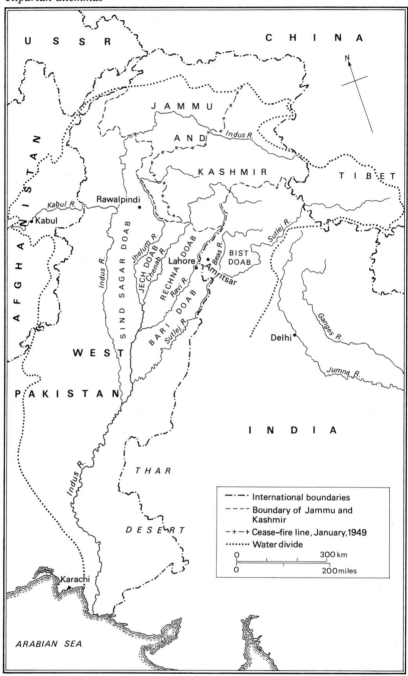

3.2 The Indus basin

(spring-harvested) crops are sown. The twin problems of seasonality and variability of flow can be solved only through the creation of storage.[34]

At the time of partition in 1947, more than eighteen million people lived in the Punjab, where agriculture was the pivot of the economy.[35] The Punjabis, of whom only 15 percent were urbanized, lived in an area no larger than 640 square kilometres. This high-density region was comprised of Muslims, Hindus, and Sikhs, who lived side-by-side while maintaining separate identities. In fact, the areas of highest densities coincided with the maximum communal mixture. Furthermore, the three communities had become, over the decades, highly dependent on the extensive irrigation system which had, by 1947, an established scheme of priorities to water resources.[36]

On the eve of independence, Muslims in the northwest and northeast of British India were strongly opposed to the idea of Hindu rule. The two religious groups could not agree on an administrative structure to succeed British rule. Eventually, a "two-states solution" was endorsed as the only hope to prevent civil war. Partition of the sub-continent took place on 15 August 1947. The international boundary between the newly constituted states of India and Pakistan was determined on the basis of confessionalism, since the immediate concern at the time was the separation of the two communities. The Punjab, with its high density and communal mix, was the area worst affected by partition. Mass migrations and colossal violence followed in the wake of the division of the region between India and Pakistan.[37]

Given that the boundary traversed the Punjab, it was inevitable that it would also cut across the Indus rivers and canal systems which had been developed under the conception of a single administration. India became the upper riparian with respect to the Upper Bari Doab Canal and the canal systems leading off from the Sutlej.[38] These waters became of central concern to Pakistan, as West Punjab had been heavily dependent on them well prior to partition. Moreover, the headwaters of none of the rivers of the Indus system rose in Pakistani territory; West Punjab became the lower riparian relative to East Punjab, and Pakistan relative to India.

The other major problem that resulted from the confessional conflict and partition of the sub-continent was the question of sovereignty over Kashmir and the allegiance of its population. This region, in the northern part of the basin, had a Muslim majority and a Hindu ruler. Two months after partition, the *Maharajah* acceded to India. The Muslim population rebelled. Indian and Pakistani forces intervened and heavy fighting ensued. And although the two sides accepted the cease-fire line proposed by the United Nations in December 1948, the dispute has continued, and invokes profound sentiments until today. Furthermore, the situation in Kashmir aggravated the water dispute enormously by giving India control over the Chenab and Jhelum rivers, which provide no irrigation water to India and very little to Jammu-Kashmir, but upon which West Punjab (and hence, all of West Pakistan) are heavily dependent.[39]

On 1 April 1948, less than four months after partition, India suddenly cut off the flow of water to Pakistan from the Upper Bari Doab and Dipalpur canal systems. This bellicose act deprived 5·5 percent of the sown area in West Pakistan of water at the critical time for sowing the *kharif* crops. It also deprived the city of Lahore of its prime source of municipal water. Whatever may have been the objective, India was implicitly asserting upstream riparian proprietary rights.[40] By the end of the month, after negotiations initiated by Pakistan, India restored the flow. And on 4 May, the two countries signed the Inter-Dominion Agreement.[41]

It is important to note, however, that India, as the upstream riparian, was in no hurry to make an agreement. Pakistan, on the other hand, was under pressure because of both its acute dependence on the Indus waters and its inferior riparian position. Moreover, because strategic advantage lay with India, Pakistan could not resort to force to reestablish usage. It had no alternative but to accept negotiations in which it held an unfavorable bargaining position.[42]

The agreement signed between the two riparians included the following stipulations: (a) India's rights to all of the waters in the eastern rivers (Sutlej, Beas, Ravi) were to be recognized, (b) India would give Pakistan time to develop alternative sources of water no longer available from the eastern rivers, and (c) Pakistan would pay a fee for the Indian waters supplied, until it could find replacement.[43] In August 1950, however, at a time when relations in the basin were particularly tense due to the migration of minorities, disposition of evacuee properties, occasional border incidents, and the unresolved Kashmir issue, Pakistan unilaterally declared the Agreement null and void.[44]

There were no new developments until David Lilienthal, former chairman of the Tennessee Valley Authority, became involved in the dispute in the spring of 1951. In an article he wrote after visiting the region, he emphasized Pakistan's absolute dependence on water, two-thirds of which originated in Kashmir: "No army, with bombs and shellfire, could devastate a land as thoroughly as Pakistan could be devastated by the simple expedient of India's permanently shutting off the sources of water that keep the fields and people of Pakistan alive."[45] Lilienthal echoed the functionalist approach when he advocated integrated development of the waters of the basin, and suggested that tensions could be reduced and problems solved if the two sides would agree to deal with one issue at a time. He believed that the water issue should be treated as a technical and engineering problem, rather than a political dispute. At Lilienthal's instigation, Eugene Black, then president of the International Bank for Reconstruction and Development (World Bank), announced that the Bank would be prepared to negotiate the Indus question.

India and Pakistan agreed to separate the water dispute from the Kashmir and other partition-related issues, and accepted the "good offices" of the Bank. However, both parties emphasized that they did not want an integrated system; India felt it could proceed with its own plans at less cost, and Pakistan did not want to be vulnerable to, nor dependent upon, India. Both countries insisted on controlling the works regulating their own water supply.[46]

Between May 1952 and September 1960, there were more-or-less continuous negotiations among the three parties. The concerns of both riparians hinged upon the need, not simply to preserve existing uses, but to satisfy demands for the extension of irrigation systems, as well. In February 1954, the World Bank released its proposal: the three western rivers (Indus, Jhelum, Chenab) were to be reserved for Pakistan's exclusive use, and the three eastern rivers (Ravi, Beas, Sutlej) for India's exclusive use. For a specified period, India would release from the three eastern rivers the historic withdrawal in Pakistan. During this transition period, link canals would be built in Pakistan to make transfers that would replace water supplies from India. The aim was to maximize benefits to both parties, while maintaining the minimum of dependence of one country on the other's good will.[47]

India accepted the Bank's plan in March 1954. Pakistan, however, was concerned about the seasonality of the flow; it feared it was not assured an adequate supply of water during the two critical periods of *rabi*-maturing and *kharif*-sowing on the one hand, and *kharif*-maturing and *rabi*-sowing on the other. Pakistan needed storage as well as replacement of water.[48] Negotiations were at an impasse from 1954 to 1958 due to this issue of storage facilities. Nonetheless, the Bank eventually recognized Pakistan's need, thus facilitating the latter's acceptance in December 1958 of the proposal for the division of the Indus waters. By 1960, six "friendly nations" had pledged grants and promised loans for construction of storage works.[49]

The Indus Waters Treaty was signed on 19 September 1960, and was based upon the World Bank's proposal of 1954: Pakistan had priority over the western rivers, India over the eastern rivers; 81 percent of the water was allocated to Pakistan, and the remaining 19 percent to India. Included in the treaty were stipulations for the building of storage reservoirs and link canals, and the establishment of a Permanent Indus Commission to oversee the implementation of the treaty. The Indus Basin Development Fund Agreement and the Loan Agreement were signed at the same time.

Two negotiating techniques played crucial roles in making possible the resolution of the water dispute. First, the riparian conflict was isolated from all other issues of discord between the two parties. Second, the final plan for the utilization of the Indus waters was formulated on the basis of *no interdependence* – the antithesis of integrated development and the institutionalist approach. It had become apparent that neither party trusted the other sufficiently to construct and operate a single integrated system; the concern for absolute sovereignty was paramount. In essence, the plan extended the process of partition; it resulted in the territorial division of the rivers.[50]

While conflicts over access to water resources had occurred prior to 1947 between East and West Punjab, the political partition of the basin changed radically the nature of riparian dispute. Water conflicts now engaged two independent, sovereign states. More important, however, the Indus waters issue was occasioned by the partition of the basin and hence, was derivative of the confessional conflict and power struggle that had, in the first place, provoked partition.[51] Superimposed on it was the deep bitterness between the two countries caused by the Kashmir dispute. Furthermore, in the aftermath of partition, all issues of mutual concern to India and Pakistan were colored by the antagonism and distrust that characterized their relationship. Why, then, were the adversaries able to resolve the riparian dispute, albeit in a sub-optimal fashion? What does the particular combination of variables in the Indus basin tell us about the outcome of conflict?

In terms of relative power resources, India was conspicuously better placed than Pakistan. It was in a superior riparian position and had strategic advantage by virtue of controlling the headwaters of the Indus and surrounding territory. Moreover, although it had plans to extend irrigated agriculture in its part of the basin, it was somewhat less dependent on the river system. India was immediately acknowledged in the international arena as the successor state of British India; this allowed it to behave more confidently *vis-à-vis* Pakistan and, in some circles, to perceive itself as having greater legitimacy.[52] Furthermore, the country had a relatively strong central government which, under the leadership of Nehru, exercised fairly effective control over the different regions from 1947 to 1960. This was despite the fact that various large religious groups were living within its borders, including sixty million Muslims; and the state, constituted as it is along secular, federative lines, can survive only by cultivating harmony among the communities. Herein lies a partial clue to India's regional behavior; its domestic structure is its Achilles heel. Undoubtedly, the proximity of a Muslim state organized along exclusively theological lines, and one which had rejected Indian hegemony outright, is perceived by India as a significant "structural political threat."[53] India's security concerns were aggravated by the arms build-up in Pakistan, made possible by the flow of cheap or free weapons from the United States as of 1954. This development added fuel to the already brewing power rivalry between the two neighbors. The perception of threat has caused India, despite its superior power position, to tread lightly in matters of inter-state concern, when those matters hinge upon highly sensitive issues such as confession and political allegiance, and reflect domestic vulnerabilities.

Pakistan's situation was more precarious. Because of its inferior riparian position and acute dependence on the Indus system, it perceived itself as highly vulnerable to and at the mercy of its adversary upstream. Moreover, it was a new state with a weak central government that, until the inception of military rule in 1958, had much difficulty exercising control over its rebellious regions and cultural groupings, and dominating their conflicting interests.[54] It also perceived the Indian state, as it was constituted, as a considerable structural political threat.

Agreement over the Indus waters was essential for Pakistan and somewhat less so for India. The positive intervention of the international community – its success at getting the stronger and less needy upstream state to sit at the bargaining table, and at obtaining Indian and Pakistani acceptance of the notion of separating the matter of sharing water from the larger conflict – proved to be the key to the resolution of the riparian dispute.[55] Equally important was the appreciation on the part of the mediator that cooperation via integrated development was unrealistic in this particular case, and that a solution through non-interdependence was both acceptable and not necessarily sub-optimal.

Nile River basin

The Nile basin is shared by nine sovereign states. Its vast catchment area, equivalent to one-tenth the size of the entire African continent, encompasses parts of Burundi, Rwanda, Tanzania, Kenya, Zaire, Uganda, Ethiopia, the Sudan, and Egypt.[56] The river system is composed of two major tributaries, the White Nile and the Blue Nile, which rise in Lake Victoria (Kenya, Rwanda, Tanzania, Uganda) and Lake Tana (Ethiopia), respectively. The two branches meet at Khartoum (Sudan) to form the main Nile, which continues northward through the Sudan and Egypt to the Mediterranean Sea (see map 3.3). All of the waters of the Nile derive from rainfall upon the Ethiopian plateau and hinterlands of the Equatorial lakes, and all riparian states except for Egypt, the furthest downstream, make some contribution to the river flow.

The average annual discharge of the Nile at Aswan is 84 bcm. However, as in the cases of the Euphrates and Indus systems, the pronounced seasonality

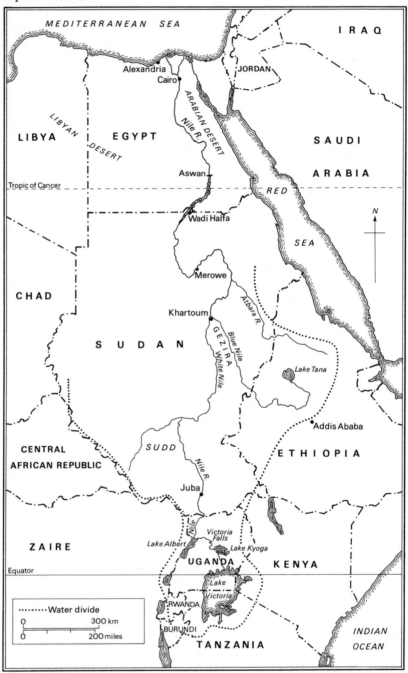

3.3 The Nile basin

of flow inhibits the maximum exploitation of water resources. The average volume of the Nile flood, like the rains at its source, is subject to acute fluctuations: more than 80 percent of the river's total discharge occurs from August to October, while nearly 20 percent is spread over the remaining nine months. Not only is the discharge seasonal, but also, much of it is untimely: abundant when need is relatively limited, and poor when need is great. Prior to the construction of the Aswan High Dam, the flooding of the river, coupled with the uneven temporal distribution of its flow, often caused untold hardship. By the end of the nineteenth century, it had become clear that the downstream states, to whom the Nile waters were of greatest concern, would have to create storage capacity as the only hope for harnessing the river and coping with its seasonal and unpredictable flow.[57]

Except for the East African plateau and the Ethiopian highlands, the Nile basin is arid throughout. From Uganda northwards, precipitation decreases rapidly from semi-aridity in the south, to extreme aridity in the north. The region from Merowe (Sudan) to Cairo is an "extremely arid zone."[58] In fact, for northern Sudan and Egypt, the Nile River is the *only* source of water for meeting consumption demand. That, coupled with the marked seasonal variation in river flow, causes the two downstream states to suffer the most from insufficient water in the very long and dry summer months.

Although there are nine riparian states in the Nile basin, it is only Egypt and the Sudan which, until today, have considerable need for its waters, and only they have been directly involved in the question of water rights. Rwanda, Burundi, and Zaire have little interest in the issue of water utilization in the basin; Kenya, Tanzania, and Uganda are more concerned with possible future use of the Equatorial Lakes they share (Victoria, Kyoga, and Albert); and Ethiopia, which occupies a very strategic position, has put off harnessing the abundant waters of the Blue Nile and, for the time being, uses the river as a "geopolitical bargaining chip" with its water-scarce downstream neighbors.[59] In contrast, the Sudan's dependence on the river system is great; Egypt's is absolute. The inhabitants of the Nile Valley rely exclusively on the river's waters for their survival. By 1987, the river was sustaining a population of 75 million in the two countries.[60]

As in the Jordan and Indus basins, and the Euphrates basin in Iraq, settlement in the Sudanese and Egyptian portions of the Nile basin is intimately associated with the river system. This is especially striking in the case of Egypt, where a population of almost 50 million is crammed into a habitable area of about 30,000 square kilometres, a narrow strip of land along the banks of the Nile and in the delta north of Cairo. Average density is 1,000 persons per square kilometre.[61]

Utilization of the river waters for agriculture in the Nile Valley has a long and colorful history, dating back some 7,000 years. The modern stage of river management and dam-building began in the middle of the last century. By the turn of the century, however, major socio-economic changes in the Egyptian countryside – most important among them, the spread of cotton cultivation (a summer crop) and the intensification of land use – brought to the fore the need for improved water resource management.[62] The need became increasingly pronounced in the first decades of this century, with the mounting pressures on water supply in Egypt and the Sudan, due to population increase and the extension of irrigated agriculture.[63] After World War I, the only possible solution to the unpredictability and untimeliness of the Nile flow was judged to be the development of an over-year storage capability. If Egypt and the Sudan had reservoirs to store the floodwaters of several years at a time, they would be better equipped to meet growing consumption demand.

As both downstream states had development plans for the river, it soon became imperative that they reach formal agreement on the allocation of the waters. The first Nile Waters Agreement was signed on 7 May 1929 between the Kingdom of Egypt and Great Britain, on behalf of the Sudan. By its terms, Egypt's "acquired rights" to the Nile waters were fixed at 48 bcm and the Sudan's at 4 bcm. Access to the entire flow of the main Nile from January to July was reserved for Egypt.[64] The distribution was not renegotiated until the 1950s, once Egypt stepped up its plans to build the Aswan High Dam.

Talks for a new allocation began in the fall of 1954. Egypt sought a substantial increase in its own share, basing its argument on its absolute dependence on irrigated agriculture, the fact that the Nile was its unique source of water, and its larger population and higher growth rate.[65] The Sudan, however, hoped to curb Egyptian demands and thereby assure its own future needs. On several occasions, bilateral negotiations were broken off and later resumed. The two riparians could not agree to a mutually acceptable apportionment. Moreover, as in the other cases of riparian dispute, albeit in a less pronounced fashion, issues external to the water question functioned as a perverse undercurrent to the negotiations. Regional politics and superpower rivalries brought pressure to bear on the Nile waters question, as did the nature of Sudano-Egyptian relations and the Sudan's perception of its permeability to Egyptian economic, military, and political interventions.

Because of Egypt's absolute dependence on the Nile waters and its inferior riparian position in the basin, one of the most persistent themes in its history has been the desire to secure the control, or at least the friendship, of those upstream.[66] As the classic downstream state, Egypt has had to seek formulae to prevent itself from becoming hostage to upstream states for its economic survival. With this end in view, major efforts have been directed at assuring its pre-eminence in the Sudan, at least. On occasion, it has exerted control over parts of that country and has advocated the political unification of the Nile Valley. Sudano-Egyptian unity would amount to a very strong entity in terms of size, population, and economic and political leverage. Hence, it would provide a formidable bulwark to unilateral actions upstream.

With the independence of the Sudan in January 1956, the idea of unity came to an end. Nonetheless, Sudanese perceptions of inferiority *vis-à-vis* its northern neighbor, despite a superior riparian position, disarmed it some-what in the Nile waters issue: "it could not unilaterally press its geographic advantage against the much stronger military power of Egypt."[67] Moreover, a new "ideological distance" had developed between the two riparians in the aftermath of the Suez Crisis and the deepening of Cold War politics in the Middle East. The Sudan, in the throes of domestic political turmoil, endorsed the anti-Communist Eisenhower Doctrine, while Nasir's Egypt forged economic and military links with the Soviet Union.[68] Relations deteriorated progressively until the fall of 1958 and the imposition of military rule in the Sudan, less than one month after the Soviet Union had made a formal offer to Egypt to help fund the Aswan High Dam.[69] Talks on a new allocation of the Nile waters were resumed soon after.

Egypt and the Sudan signed the Agreement for the Full Utilization of the Nile Waters on 8 November 1959. By its terms, Egypt's share was a total of 55·5 bcm and the Sudan's, 18·5 bcm. This represented a ratio of 3:1 in Egypt's favor, as opposed to the 1929 ratio of 12:1.[70] Implementation and supervision of the agreement was placed in the hands of a Permanent Joint Technical Commission (PJTC). For the most part, the agreement has been faithfully applied till now, the PJTC has met regularly, whatever the political climate, and both riparians have without exception received their designated shares.

Construction of the Aswan High Dam began in 1960 and was completed at the end of 1970, shortly after Abd al-Nasir's death. It was meant to be one giant project to provide over-year storage and adequate summer water for Egypt's commercial agriculture. It was also expected to provide the Sudan with enough additional water to increase its irrigated area threefold.[71]

Unlike in the Euphrates, Indus, and Jordan basins, the situation in the Nile basin can be considered, for the time being, a low-level conflict. This is due to a number of factors. First, only two of the nine riparian states have substantial, material interest in the river system, an interest founded upon acute dependence on its waters. Second, both states are the furthest downstream in the basin. Consequently, they accurately perceive their fates as being in the hands of those upstream, the logical site for new storage facilities. Third, the two most concerned states have a long history of contact. Much of this history has been punctuated by the domination of the weaker (upstream) by the stronger (downstream), and the resultant feelings of vulnerability on the one hand, and "hegemony" on the other. The first and second factors indicate that there is an identity of interests between the Sudan and Egypt *vis-à-vis* the (seven) upstream riparians and the Nile River. Because they share similar water-related security concerns, both have been anxious to assure their continued access to water. Egypt, with its absolutely inferior riparian position and most critical water situation, pushed for formalization of apportionment of the Nile waters. And the Sudan, given the third factor – relative power (viewed historically) – could not afford to ignore Egypt's economic needs and thereby undermine its own precarious stability. Nor could it extract much concrete advantage from its relatively strategic riparian position and slightly less critical water situation. Its power resources were virtually inconsequential compared to those of its downstream neighbor.[72] For all these reasons, the Sudan's perception of its interests has prompted it to work with Egypt, rather than without it.

Although it is accurate to describe the Nile waters issue as a low-level conflict, it is important to note that it has pronounced conflict potential. Threats emanate from two directions: (1) the highly strategic position of Ethiopia at the source of the Blue Nile, and (2) the absence of a basin-wide accord on water-sharing. Considering that by the late 1970s, both Egypt and the Sudan were approaching "the outer limits of what the existing system of seasonal and over-year storage facilities can provide," the gravity of these two conditions looms large.[73]

The Blue Nile is only one of eleven rivers rising in Ethiopia. It carries an average annual flow of fifty bcm to its confluence with the White and Main Niles at Khartoum and hence, represents 60 percent of the total discharge of the Nile system.[74] Indeed, "... Ethiopia holds both Egypt and the Sudan by the jugular."[75] Until recently, Ethiopia showed little interest in the hydraulic potential of the river. But as its population grows and food security declines, it will more than likely aim at harnessing the abundant waters of the Blue Nile. In fact, studies for a variety of storage, irrigation, and hydro-power projects along the river already exist.[76] Needless to say, Egypt and the Sudan have grounds for concern.

The ideal solution to this predicament is basin-wide cooperation. However, as in the other cases of riparian dispute, geopolitical susceptibilities often impede the optimal utilization of the waters of an international river system. Ethiopia has not made much effort to promote basin-wide accord because it sits astride a vast quantity of water which it could either exploit unilaterally for its own consumption, or use as a "bargaining chip" in its relations with the downstream states. The lacustrine states, Kenya, Tanzania, and Uganda, would be reluctant to enter into a basin-wide agreement since, given Egypt's superior might and acute need, they have little to gain and probably something to lose by an accord. Without a doubt, their lakes would be used as reservoirs for the Nile waters.[77] Only the Sudan and Egypt have considerable interest in a comprehensive agreement and only they have been lobbying for a renegotiation of the 1959 treaty.[78] Because of acute need and the fact that relative power favors the downstream riparian, these two states were able in the past to reach an agreement on water utilization in their part of the basin. But because of concerns external to the water issue, an all-inclusive Nile basin agreement has not been feasible until now.

Some comparisons

In all four cases of riparian dispute, the Euphrates, Indus, Nile, and Jordan, the need for access to water resources, for some or all of the basin states, is great. The Euphrates and Indus basins are both arid and semi-arid, and all riparians concerned are dependent on the rivers' resources, to a greater or lesser degree, for irrigation and hydro-power generation. The upstream riparians, Turkey and India, are somewhat less dependent than those downstream. The same is true for the Jordan basin after June 1967, once the two relatively well-watered upstream riparians lost sovereignty over the headwaters of the river. Prior to 1967, the waters of the Upper Jordan River were of little material concern to Lebanon and Syria; they were considered in much the same way as Ethiopia regards the Blue Nile – as a geopolitically strategic resource. But for Israel and the Kingdom of Jordan, the Jordan waters have always been intimately linked to state survival. The Nile basin is semi-arid and arid throughout, and the lower basin, which has been the locus of dispute, is an extremely arid zone. Utilization of the river in the upper basin is minimal. But for Egypt, the Nile is its unique source of water. The Kingdom of Jordan finds itself in a similar position *vis-à-vis* the Jordan–Yarmouk system.

In the Euphrates and Indus basins, and the Jordan basin after 1967, relative power is in the favor of the upstream state – Turkey, India, and Israel (on the Upper Jordan). As the upstream riparian, these states are in positions to exploit the river's resources unilaterally. Moreover, by virtue of their superior capabilities, they can do so with little fear of retaliation from their downstream neighbor(s). It is only when there is a formal water-sharing arrangement, as in the Indus basin, that unilateral activities can be inhibited. In the case of the Nile, the situation is reversed. The downstream state is not only the neediest in the basin, but also, the most powerful. Tampering with the river system upstream is checked by the threat of Egypt's superior power resources. The Sudan, for one, needs Egypt as much as it needs the Nile. In the Jordan basin in the 1960s, relative power was in the favor of Israel which, until June 1967, was the midstream riparian. Lebanon and Syria, at the sources of the river system, were not able to act as hegemons in the basin and divert the Jordan waters away from their foe, although they made a concerted effort to do so. Hence, in international river basins, the interest in cooperation on the part of the dominant power, irrespective of riparian position, is key.

In all but the Nile basin, inter-state relations are acrimonious and characterized by varying degrees of distrust, the perception of threat, and power struggle. In the three basins, there is something external to and independent of the immediate issue of access to water resources that tarnishes relations and functions as an obstacle to the optimal solution to riparian dispute. This is so, whether the external dynamic is a struggle for ideological and political hegemony as in the Euphrates case, a confessional conflict and power struggle as in the Indus, or a combination of these added to a conflict over land and fight for political recognition as in the Jordan. These identity-related external dynamics magnify the water dispute and extend it in scope. The water dispute serves as a chessboard on which the players confront each other on these larger issues and make their moves. The fact that the riparians are engaged in conflicts over *core values* deters them from collaborating in seemingly technical issues. "High politics" conflict impedes "low politics" cooperation.

Of the four cases of riparian dispute, two have been resolved. However, neither the conflict in the Indus basin, nor that in the Nile has been resolved in what is considered the optimal fashion – via integrated basin-wide cooperation. Nonetheless, in both cases, there were sufficient incentives for the parties to strike a bargain and adhere to it. In the Indus basin, there was positive and continuous involvement of a third party at a time when the upstream riparian, despite its superior power resources, was anxious to score points in the international arena and neutralize what it perceived as structural threats emanating from its embittered relations with Pakistan. The mediator was able to induce the upstream state, the key player in the basin, to cooperate. Besides, given the character of riparian relations, the realism of the solution proposed was irrefutable. In the Nile basin, it was the shared need for water resources coupled with the downstream state's overwhelming preponderance in virtually all spheres that provided the necessary impetus. Here, as well, a third party played an important role, at least in the initial stages; the World Bank had been instrumental in getting started the Sudano-Egyptian talks that culminated in the 1959 Agreement.[79]

In the Euphrates and Jordan basins, conflict over water resources persists. In the former, the most powerful state in the basin has no interest in negotiating water quotas. The middle and downstream states are locked into a power struggle that prevents them from lobbying together to assert their water needs and exert pressure on the upstream riparian. Moreover, there has been minimal input from the international community toward resolving this dispute. It is probably fair to say that if Turkey could be brought to the bargaining table and would promise substantial concessions, Syria and Iraq would agree to negotiate a water-sharing arrangement, despite their adversarial relations. This, however, was not the case in the mid-1970s, when the ideological conflict between Syria and Iraq was at its peak and the consumption needs of the riparians were not as great as they are today.

In the Jordan basin, as we shall see in the chapters that follow, riparian conflict has gone through two phases; in neither, has a formal accord been possible. In essence, the absence of cooperation has been due to both the distribution of power and the character of inter-state relations. In 1955, the Arab riparians decided to put off taking a final decision on the water-sharing plan sponsored by the United States. Syria, an upstream riparian and the most powerful of the concerned Arab states, had relatively little need for access to the Jordan waters. Hence, in response to the proposal for a functional arrangement in the basin, it insisted that it could not accept to cooperate with a state, the legitimacy of which the Arabs questioned. Withholding recognition, on the part of the most powerful and least needy riparian, foreclosed the potential for settlement. Eric Johnston, the US Government's "special envoy," believed that the Arabs would cast aside their determination to regain Palestine for the economic good of two basin states, Israel and Jordan. He failed to acknowledge that the conflict between the Arab states and Israel was one that engaged the identities and core values of both parties. Indeed, the prospects for functional cooperation were remote; there was little incentive for the Arab states to reach an agreement with Israel. In contrast, Israel was anxious to have an accord with the Arabs. That would amount to the formal recognition of Israel as a state in the Middle East with rights and needs. It would legitimize the *status quo* in the region and be a first step towards a comprehensive peace treaty. However, the stronger and less needy Arab riparians were wary of the political implications of a basin-wide agreement.

In the period since 1967, the ongoing Arab–Israeli conflict continues to make it very difficult for Israel and Jordan to cooperate formally. Nonetheless, because of both riparians' acute need for access to the Jordan waters, they have been able to engage in highly delimited, implicitly cooperative arrangements when there have been no known alternatives.

What distinguishes the conflict in the Jordan basin from the other riparian disputes discussed above is the very character of riparian relations and the constraints it places on foreign policy behavior. Although the conflict seems to be quite similar to that in the Indus basin, where a protracted political rivalry has tarnished relations for decades, it is important to note that for the most part, India and Pakistan did recognize each other as legitimate political entities. Moreover, they accepted that they shared certain basic needs that had to be met in one way or another. It was thanks to the positive involvement of an impartial mediator that there was a context in which both states perceived an equitable distribution of benefits and where there were sufficient inducements to bring them to the negotiating table. This has not been the case in the Jordan basin. In the final analysis, however, the fact of recognition did not promote the ideal solution to river basin development in the Indus Valley. The "high politics" conflict proved to be the chief obstacle to its realization.

PART II

The Jordan waters conflict

4 The Johnston mission to the Middle East (1953–1956)

In our discussion, in chapter 2, of the environment of conflict, we described the political landscape in the Jordan basin. We suggested that the roots of conflict over the waters of the river system lay in the convergence of two phenomena: (1) the fact of resource scarcity in Palestine, and (2) Zionist efforts to establish a Jewish national home in *Eretz Yisrael*, where there lived an indigenous Arab population. We then outlined the various efforts at land and water development in the Jordan basin from the beginning of Jewish immigration to Palestine until mid-century. We noted that immediately following the 1948–49 war, both Israel and Jordan experienced massive influxes of population. The resource bases of the two newly founded states were strained considerably.

In the aftermath of the war, the concurrence of three critical factors – (1) the absolute need of both Israel and Jordan to develop land and water resources, (2) the fact of water scarcity in the basin relative to needs, and (3) adversarial relations among the riparian states – extended the scope of the Arab–Jewish conflict and crystallized what was to become a central issue in the Jordan waters dispute: on what basis should the waters of the Jordan system be shared? How much water should go to each side, and according to what principle?

In this chapter, we focus on the first, and perhaps, most important episode of riparian dispute in the Jordan basin in the post-1949 period: the United States-sponsored Johnston mission to the Middle East. We describe this unique attempt at regional water development. Then, in an effort to understand the conduct of riparian dispute and the potential for cooperation among adversarial states, we analyze the experience of the mission in terms of the variables that guide state behavior and inform our study. This episode elucidates the difficulties inherent in efforts to resolve riparian dispute as a preliminary step to the resolution of a larger political rivalry, or even to de-link one from the other.

In the early 1950s, both Israel and Jordan were independently engaged in formulating and implementing national water schemes to develop their economies for the absorption of immigrants on the one hand, and refugees on the other. Throughout this period, there were recurrent hostile and retaliatory incidents across the Armistice Demarcation lines between Israel and its four Arab neighbors.[1] Clashes took place in the Demilitarized Zones (DMZ) that had been established by the Armistice Agreements at the end of the first Arab–Israel war (1949) in disputed territory along the Upper Jordan River and the southeastern shores of Lake Tiberias. At issue were different interpretations of the zones' legal status. Syria objected to Israel's pursuit of development projects in contested territory. The Kingdom of Jordan, which was, like Israel, highly dependent on the water resources of the basin, was especially concerned about possible harm to the flow of the Jordan River downstream as a result of Israeli activities upstream. The two controversial schemes in the northern portion of the basin were: (1) Israel's project to drain the Lake Huleh swamps, north of Lake Tiberias (1951), and (2) its project to divert part of the Jordan waters through a canal from Gesher Bnot Yaᶜacov [Jisr Banat Yaᶜqub, in Arabic] in 1953. Both were conceived as initial stages in the implementation of the country's Lowdermilk-Hays-inspired Seven Year Plan.

The United Nations became involved in these developments, largely through the Truce Supervision Organization (UNTSO) and Mixed Armistice Commissions (MAC), the apparati that had been set up after the war to keep the peace and investigate violations of the Armistice Agreements, but also by virtue of complaints lodged before the Security Council.

In 1951, and in accordance with a concession granted to it in 1934 by the British Mandatory Power, the Jewish Palestine Land Development Company (PLDC) began work on the Huleh project. The aim was to drain the lake and surrounding marshes, reclaim about 6,250 hectares (1 ha = 2·47 acres) of land for intensive cultivation, use the waters collected for irrigating other parts of the country, and eliminate the scourge of malaria in the immediate area. However, the project involved work on land in the central demilitarized zone, some of which was Arab-owned. Syria lodged several complaints before the MAC. It threatened to divert the sources of the Jordan at Banias, if Israel would not halt its work. There were frequent exchanges of fire between the two parties, culminating in a UN Security Council resolution on 18 May 1951, ordering a cease-fire and calling upon Israel to stop all activities at the site, in conformity with the decision of the UNTSO Chief-of-Staff. One month later, Israel received authorization to proceed with the project; the PLDC had found that it could relocate in the zone, and need not encroach upon Arab lands.[2]

This incident had indirect effects downstream. Shortly after the Huleh affair was resolved, the Kingdom of Jordan lodged a complaint before the Security Council. It charged that activities upstream were restricting the river flow to the lower valley and affecting water quality. In addition to the work at the new Huleh site, Israel had been periodically closing the sluice gates of the Jordan River at the southern tip of Lake Tiberias. As a result, the salinity of the flow downstream had increased to such an extent that it was impossible to irrigate the valley lands. With the economic life of the Jordan Valley thus in jeopardy, the Kingdom could not proceed with its own development projects, nor with the absorption and resettlement of Palestine refugees.[3] The United Nations Relief and Works Agency (UNRWA), which had been established in 1949 to provide a minimum of food and shelter for some 800,000 refugees, had been counting on settling the vast majority of its dependents on both banks of the Jordan River. Hence, the development potential of the valley in general, and access to water for irrigation in particular, were of immediate concern to UNRWA.[4]

The United States, as well, became interested in the development of the Jordan Valley. It did so for a variety of inter-related economic, ideological, political, and security reasons.[5] During this period of Cold War politics, Washington was deeply engaged in protecting what it considered as "power vacuums" from falling into the hands of Communist forces. Not only was the Middle East then considered a "vacuum," but a particularly strategic one given its immense pools of oil upon which much of western Europe was dependent. Moreover, in the Middle East, the United States Government observed with apprehension a gradual deterioration of the "free world" position, a growing distrust and suspicion on the part of the Arab states toward the United States, largely due to its support for Israel, and the rising tide of neutralism and nationalism. It sought to wage a two-pronged attack on the potential spread of Soviet influence to the region. On the one hand, it made plans to establish a strong regional defense alliance that would contain the Soviet Union, and it encouraged the Middle Eastern states to lend their support. The successive ideas for a Middle East Command and then a Middle East Defence Organization eventually materialized in the highly controversial Baghdad Pact (1955–58). On the other hand, and given that in official US circles it was believed that poverty provided fertile breeding-ground for communism, the American government prepared to wage a war on want. To curtail the spread of communism, it was necessary to improve standards of living and provide depressed and "susceptible" regions with economic development. The underdeveloped Arab states, with their increasingly nationalistic polities, and the disenchanted Palestine refugee population living in exile were considered prime targets. However, tensions in the Middle East, and especially between Arab and Israeli, were perceived as obstacles to social and economic development. To achieve the kind of progress the United States envisioned for the region, it was first necessary to orchestrate a rapprochement between the two parties and settle the Arab–Israeli conflict (see appendix 1). Finally, because of its hegemonic position in the international system and its role in the creation of Israel, the United States believed it had a responsibility to try to relieve tensions and solve the "Palestine Problem." Settling the refugees in neighboring Arab states was, in the Government's view, a prerequisite to both the prevention of the spread of communism and the resolution of the Arab–Israeli conflict.[6]

To this end, the United States encouraged UNRWA to investigate all possible schemes for the development of the Jordan Valley. However, the Lake Huleh and other DMZ episodes seemed to indicate that riparian water rights and area peace were intimately linked. This perception, which would prove to be most accurate, was enunciated in a Department of State Position Paper in May 1953: "It appears equally clear [to the US] that along with other outstanding issues of the Palestine dispute – compensation, repatriation, Jerusalem, boundaries – there is a fifth element, water, which must be considered as we approach a final settlement."[7]

The United States and UNRWA first became involved in a unilateral water plan for the Kingdom of Jordan, proposed by Mills Bunger, an American engineer with the US Technical Cooperation Agency (TCA) in Amman, that had been set up under Point Four of the Truman Doctrine and was active in assisting refugees. Bunger advocated a joint Syrian–Jordanian project to develop the Yarmouk waters by impounding them behind a 140-metre dam at Maqarin on the Syrian–Jordanian border and diverting water through a canal along the East Ghor of the Jordan River. It was a huge project, designed to provide water for the settlement of a minimum of 100,000 refugees on irrigable land in the valley, plus employment on the scheme itself and in ancillary industry.[8]

Both riparians were anxious to have the plan implemented: Jordan, because it would provide large-scale development that was sorely needed for the refugees and for the Jordanian economy as a whole; and Syria, because the power generation potential of the Maqarin Dam would go a long way to meet the needs of the country. Besides, the project was attractive for it circumvented the need to cooperate with Israel. And this was an extremely important consideration, especially in the aftermath of the assassination of Jordan's King Abdullah in July 1951. He had been suspected of negotiating secretly with Israeli personalities. In March 1953, UNRWA signed an agreement with Jordan to implement Bunger's project, and earmarked one-fifth of its budget for that purpose. In June, Syria and Jordan agreed formally to joint exploitation of the Yarmouk waters.[9] Work on the first stage began one month later.

These activities catalyzed an Israel Foreign Ministry interest in the Jordan waters issue at the inter-state level. It reacted in two ways. First, Government officials initiated a diplomatic campaign in Washington against the Bunger Plan, demanding recognition as party to the river's waters.[10] They suggested that the four riparian states discuss the possibility of integrating the water and power resources of the Jordan, Yarmouk, and Litani Rivers.[11] Second, the Government decided, in late July 1953, to activate the engineering proposal to divert the Upper Jordan River at Gesher Bnot Ya'acov in the Israel–Syria Demilitarized Zone: a preliminary step in the implementation of the national plan to transport water to the Negev desert. Work on the first stage of that project began on 2 September. Syria protested to the United Nations Security Council, and on 23 September, the UNTSO called upon Israel to halt its diversionary work at that site.[12]

Well before the developments in the summer of 1953 and despite the apparent enthusiasm for the Bunger Plan, the United States encouraged UNRWA to commission a thorough study of all previous plans for the utilization of the waters of the Jordan River and its tributaries. In 1952, UNRWA asked the Department of State to procure an engineering study for the unified development of the Jordan–Yarmouk River system.[13] It explained its *volte-face* thus: it wanted to be assured that the Bunger project was the most economical, and that the funds it was about to commit "would not be rendered nugatory by other projects undertaken by other interests in the same watershed."[14]

At the request of the State Department, the Tennessee Valley Authority assumed responsibility for conducting the study. It solicited the services of the engineering firm, Charles T. Main Inc. (Boston, Mass.), to work under its direction and formulate a broad plan, in general terms and disregarding political boundaries, for the effective and efficient use of water resources, emphasizing first, irrigation, and second, hydro-electric power production. Central to the idea of integrated regional planning was the aim to resettle about 200,000 Palestine refugees in the Jordan Valley. Alongside this aim was the expectation that the plan would bring economic development to the immediate region.

The Unified, or "Main," Plan was submitted to UNRWA and to the Government of the United States in August 1953, and to the governments of the riparian states one month later, coinciding with the American-initiated slow-down of work on the Syria–Jordan Yarmouk Project. The report suggested: (a) the construction of diversionary canals from the headwaters of the Jordan River (the Hasbani, Dan, and Banias) to irrigate the lands of the Upper Jordan basin, (b) the utilization of Lake Tiberias as a storage reservoir for the flood flows of the Jordan and Yarmouk Rivers, and (c) the laying of canals along the east and west sides of the Jordan River from Lake Tiberias to irrigate the lands of the lower valley (see map 4.1). It emphasized in-basin use of the Jordan waters, rejected the Bunger proposal to use the Maqarin Dam for irrigation, but endorsed it for power generation, and made no reference to the utilization of the Litani waters. The total quantity of water

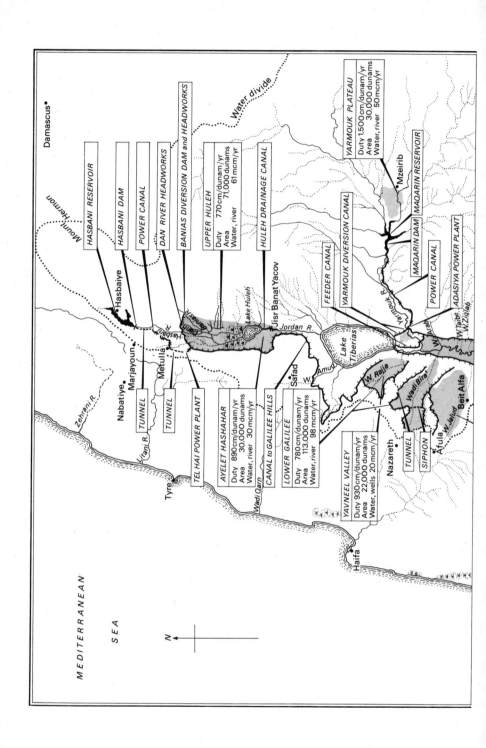

MEDITERRANEAN SEA

Damascus

Mount Hermon

Water divide

HASBANI RESERVOIR

HASBANI DAM

POWER CANAL

DAN RIVER HEADWORKS

BANIAS DIVERSION DAM and HEADWORKS

UPPER HULEH
Duty   770cm/dunam/yr
Area   71,000 dunams
Water, river   61 mcm/yr

HULEH DRAINAGE CANAL

YARMOUK PLATEAU
Duty   1,500cm/dunam/yr
Area   30,000 dunams
Water, river   50mcm/yr

YARMOUK DIVERSION CANAL

FEEDER CANAL

MAQARIN DAM

MAQARIN RESERVOIR

POWER CANAL

ADASIYA POWER PLANT

Mzeirib

Yarmouk R.

Hasbaiye

Hasbani R.

Banias R.

Dan R.

Lake Huleh

Jisr Banat Yacov

Jordan R.

Lake Tiberias

Nabatiye

Marjayoun

Metulla

Litani R.

Zehrani R.

TUNNEL

TUNNEL

TEL HAI POWER PLANT

AYELET HASHAHAR
Duty   890cm/dunam/yr
Area   30,000 dunams
Water, river   30mcm/yr

CANAL to GALILEE HILLS

LOWER GALILEE
Duty   780cm/dunam/yr
Area   113,000 dunams
Water, river   98 mcm/yr

Safad

Amud

W.

W. Rajja

Wadi Bira

Beit Alfa

Tyre

Wadi Qarn

YAVNEEL VALLEY
Duty   930cm/dunam/yr
Area   22,000 dunams
Water, wells   20mcm/yr

Nazareth

Afula

TUNNEL

SIPHON

W.Jalud

W.Taibe

W.Ziqlab

Haifa

N

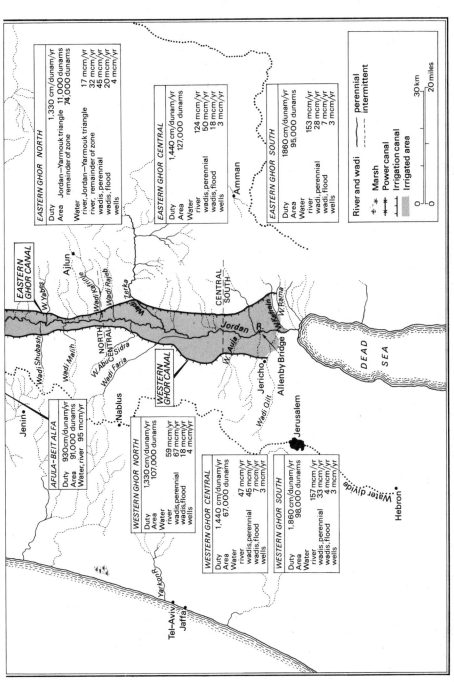

4.1 Plan of unified development of the Jordan Valley region, 1953

EASTERN GHOR NORTH

Duty	1,330 cm/dunam/yr	
Area	Jordan–Yarmouk triangle	11,000 dunams
	remainder of zone	74,000 dunams
Water		
river,Jordan–Yarmouk triangle		17 mcm/yr
river, remainder of zone		32 mcm/yr
wadis, perennial		45 mcm/yr
wadis, flood		20 mcm/yr
wells		4 mcm/yr

EASTERN GHOR CENTRAL

Duty	1,440 cm/dunam/yr
Area	127,000 dunams
Water	
river	124 mcm/yr
wadis, perennial	50 mcm/yr
wadis, flood	18 mcm/yr
wells	3 mcm/yr

EASTERN GHOR SOUTH

Duty	1860 cm/dunam/yr
Area	95,000 dunams
Water	
river	153 mcm/yr
wadi, perennial	28 mcm/yr
wadi, flood	7 mcm/yr
wells	3 mcm/yr

AFULA–BEIT ALFA

Duty	930cm/dunam/yr
Area	91,000 dunams
Water, river	95 mcm/yr

WESTERN GHOR NORTH

Duty	1,330 cm/dunam/yr
Area	107,000 dunams
Water	
river	59 mcm/yr
wadis, perennial	67 mcm/yr
wadis, flood	18 mcm/yr
wells	4 mcm/yr

WESTERN GHOR CENTRAL

Duty	1,440 cm/dunam/yr
Area	67,000 dunams
Water	
river	47 mcm/yr
wadis, perennial	45 mcm/yr
wadis, flood	7 mcm/yr
wells	3 mcm/yr

WESTERN GHOR SOUTH

Duty	1,860 cm/dunam/yr
Area	98,000 dunams
Water	
river	157 mcm/yr
wadis, perennial	33 mcm/yr
wadis, flood	4 mcm/yr
wells	3 mcm/yr

River and wadi ———— perennial
------- intermittent
Marsh
Power canal
Irrigation canal
Irrigated area

30 km
20 miles

EASTERN GHOR CANAL

WESTERN GHOR CANAL

Jenin
Tel-Aviv
Jaffa
Yarkon R.
Nablus
Ajlun
W. Yabes
Wadi Shubash
Wadi Maiih
W. Abu Sidra
Wadi Faria
Wadi Kufrinje
Wadi Rajeb
Zerka
Jordan R.
W. Auja
W. Qilt
W. Nukheila
W. Rama
Jericho
Allenby Bridge
Jerusalem
Hebron
Water divide
Amman
DEAD SEA
NORTH
CENTRAL
CENTRAL
SOUTH

Table 4.1. *Unified Plan: allocations*

	Quantity of water (mcm)	Land to be irrigated (ha)[a]
Israel	394	41,600
Jordan	774	49,000
Syria	45	3,000
Total	1,213	

[a] One hectare is equivalent to ten dunums; one dunum is equivalent to 1,000 square metres or approximately one-quarter of an acre.

in the Jordan basin was gauged at 1,213 mcm, and was to be allocated among the riparian states as shown in table 4.1. The average annual output of hydro-electric power was expected to be 210 million kilowatt-hours (kwh), and the estimated cost of the complete Unified Plan was $121 million, most of which was to be borne by the United States.[15] (See appendix 2.)

On 7 October 1953, President Eisenhower appointed Eric Johnston, then Chairman of the TCA's Advisory Board for International Development, "Personal Representative of the President" with the rank of ambassador, to carry out a mission to the Middle East. Johnston's mandate was to secure agreement from Israel, Jordan, Lebanon, and Syria on the development of the Jordan basin waters on a regional basis. The framework of the settlement was to include the following points: (1) the distribution of water should conform as closely as possible to the recommendations of the TVA report. As a minimum, Jordan should receive a substantially greater volume than it would from the unilateral development of the Yarmouk alone, and Israel should renounce all rights to divert for irrigation more than a specified volume of water from the Jordan River and tributaries; (2) Armistice line adjustments should be effected so that physical control over Lake Tiberias, the outlets from the lake, and the diversionary canal from the Yarmouk would not be exercised exclusively by Israel; (3) demilitarized zones in the Jordan Valley should be eliminated; and (4) the development of the Litani River must not be considered in the present context.[16] Eisenhower's special envoy was accorded full latitude to advocate variations in the TVA plan within the above terms of reference, and was instructed to use future levels of economic and military aid, plus UNRWA contributions, as bargaining chips with the riparian states.[17] The Johnston mediation effort was conducted in four rounds of negotiations over a two-year period. His first visit to the basin states was scheduled to begin in Beirut on 22 October 1953.

Round one

Two episodes cast a dark shadow over Johnston's visit. First, there was the Israeli armed attack on three Jordanian villages – Qibya, Budros, and Shuqba – that resulted in the deaths of over fifty civilians and incited Jordanian passions more than had any other cross-border attack.[18] Second, the United States Secretary of State, John Foster Dulles, announced on 20 October that his government was withholding funds earmarked for Israel because it had failed to stop work at the Bnot Ya'acov site, in violation of the decision of the UNTSO Chief of Staff. The funds would be deferred as long as Israel was acting in defiance of that decision and unilaterally diverting the Jordan River in the DMZ.[19] Israel stopped the work at the site one week later. No doubt, the riparians' perceptions of the Johnston mission on the eve of its arrival in the region were colored by these events and their antecedents.

Three elements characterized the Arab attitude. First, the mission was perceived as yet another indication of the American Government's pro-Israel bias.[20] For one, Eric Johnston's personal credentials as an impartial mediator were viewed with much suspicion: it had become known that he was a vice-chairman of the American Christian Palestine Committee, a pro-Zionist philanthropic organization.[21] Second, given the Arabs' perception of America's stance, they were skeptical about its avowed intentions. American efforts were seen, not as a humanitarian gesture to improve socio-economic conditions throughout the Jordan basin, but rather as an attempt to promote collaboration with Israel and seduce the Arabs into recognizing the Jewish state.[22] Third, the Arab riparians were deeply resentful of the use of economic aid as bait with which to secure basin-wide agreement. Moreover, the threat of withholding aid would not overcome the "emotional aversion to doing business with Israel."[23] In sum, of paramount concern to the Arabs in consideration of the Johnston mission at this stage was their commitment to non-cooperation with and non-recognition of the State of Israel. Their initial response to the project for unified development was an unqualified rejection.

Israel's response was less clear-cut. In official circles, opinions were divided. On the one hand, the mission was perceived as an opening for direct negotiations with the Arabs, eventually leading to peace treaties.[24] Partisan to this view was Moshe Sharett, then Foreign Minister and head of Israel's delegation to the Johnston mission. He believed that "regional co-operation was desirable, both for the optimal use of limited water and as a possible breakthrough to a peace settlement..."[25] But the TVA plan, as it stood, was viewed as damaging to Israel's interests and perceived rights; it would take water away from the country and its national projects.[26] The general reaction of the press was hostile. *Davar*, the organ of the *Histadrut*, the General Federation of Labor, wrote on 22 October: "the plan...is designed to sabotage the Israeli Plan for the exploitation of all water resources in Israel. Its transparent purpose is to hamstring Israel and transfer the control over its water to foreigners..."[27] Nonetheless, the possibility for peace with their neighbors was a strong incentive for the more moderate elements in government to seriously consider a basin-wide scheme.

From 22 October to 3 November, Ambassador Johnston shuttled among the capitals of the four riparian states and Egypt, with the aim to encourage political leaders to consider favorably the principle of unified regional water development.[28] Government officials in the Arab capitals reiterated that the Arabs did not want to participate in an American program that would assist Israel.[29] There could be no cooperation with the enemy, either economic or political, direct or indirect. Moreover, Jordan was anxious to have the Yarmouk Project implemented, and Syria demanded full recognition of its status in the DMZ.[30]

Eric Johnston arrived in Tel-Aviv on 28 October, the day the United States reinstated economic aid and the day after Israel had published its own Seven-Year Plan.[31] Moshe Sharett insisted on inclusion of the Litani River in any regional scheme, the utilization of Jordan waters outside the basin, and direct negotiations with the Arab riparians. Moreover, Israel would not relinquish sovereignty in exchange for economic aid.[32] Johnston responded that his government was not prepared to consider the inclusion of the Lebanese river, as it was outside the watershed in question, nor was it realistic to hope for direct negotiations, given the political climate in the basin.[33]

In his report to the President on the results of his mission's first visit to the Middle East, Eisenhower's special envoy stated that all four riparians, plus Egypt, had expressed serious reservations. Nonetheless, they had indicated a willingness to consider the proposals contained in the TVA plan and to meet again for more discussions on the specifics of a regional project. In accordance with their amenability to the idea of unified development, he ranked the states, from most to least, thus: Egypt, Israel, Lebanon, Syria, Jordan.[34]

Throughout the fall and winter of 1953–54, while the Arabs and Israelis were studying the plan and formulating counter-proposals, DMZ-related issues dominated regional affairs and UN concerns. Soon after Johnston's departure from the Middle East in November, Israel's ambassador to the UN announced that if an agreement on a regional plan could not be reached within the next two to three years, his country would have to proceed with its own plans to divert water southward from the Bnot Ya'acov site. In the meantime, it would continue the project within its own sovereign territory.[35] Although it had agreed to call a temporary halt to that part of the project located in disputed territory, it maintained that Syria's pressure on the UN was the unjustified act of a hostile neighbor, "bent upon Israel's economic strangulation" – "a single phase of its bitter political and economic warfare..."[36] The Government's position was that "there shall be no Syrian control of Jordan River waters..."[37] Israel insisted that it was the only country in the basin in a position to prevent the Jordan River waters from being wasted.[38]

At the Arab League Council meetings in January 1954, a technical commission was set up to study the Unified Plan. The Committee of Arab Experts, led by Mohamed Ahmed Salim, an Egyptian engineer, was composed of politicians and technicians from Egypt, Jordan, Lebanon, and Syria. After the Committee's first meeting in January, Mahmoud Riad of Egypt's Ministry of War reported that the Arab states did not want to reject a regional scheme outright. Nonetheless, they could not accept it as it stood, since "Israel would have complete control of the waters on which Jordan would be dependent..."[39] Not only was it politically undesirable to store waters needed by Jordan in a lake controlled by Israel, but also, as the water of Lake Tiberias had a far higher salt content than that of the Yarmouk, it was foolhardy to mix the two; the salinity of irrigation water for the Lower Jordan Valley would increase as a result. Instead, Yarmouk waters should be stored in a reservoir on the Yarmouk, as suggested in the Bunger proposals. The Committee expressed several other objections. Israel should not be allowed to use Jordan waters outside the watershed. As a basin-wide plan, water must be allocated and utilized to satisfy the needs of that circumscribed area alone. Furthermore, water requirements in the Jordan Valley had been underestimated; Israel's allotment was too high, Jordan's and Syria's too low. Moreover, Lebanon had been excluded altogether from the project, although a tributary of the Jordan, the Hasbani River, rose in its territory.[40]

In the Arab Plan, published in March 1954, the Committee outlined its counter-proposal. The main features were the following: (1) the use of the Upper Jordan and Hasbani Rivers for irrigation and power, (2) the construction of two storage dams on the Yarmouk (at Maqarin and Adasiya) to generate power and irrigate Jordan Valley lands in Jordanian territory, (3) the rejection of Lake Tiberias as the principal storage site for surplus Yarmouk waters, (4) the utilization of the Lower Jordan, south of Lake Tiberias, and its tributaries, for the irrigation of the Jordan Valley, (5) allocation of a modest water supply to Lebanon, and (6) international supervision over the distribution of water in the basin.[41] (See appendix 3.) The allocation of water proposed is outlined in table 4.2. Israel would get about 20 percent of the waters of the Jordan system, as opposed to 33 percent in the Main Plan, and Syria's allocation would increase threefold.

The Government of Israel had been studying the Main Plan and devising a counter-proposal, as well. Government-appointed experts expressed their

Table 4.2. *Arab Plan : allocations*

	Quantity of water (mcm)	Land to be irrigated (ha)
Israel	270	23,400
Jordan	911	49,000
Syria	120	11,900
Lebanon	32	3,500
Total	1,333	

disagreement with the Plan's principal conclusions: "We are at a loss to understand ... why, in a true regional program, the use of the Litani River in Lebanon has been completely omitted ... "[42] Without its inclusion, the needs of none of the riparian states would be satisfied; with its inclusion, all needs could be met. Moreover, recommendations concerning allocations and irrigable area were flawed. For one, the quantity of water allotted to the Kingdom of Jordan was extravagant.[43] Conversely, only about one-quarter of the river flow would be left for the use of Israel, "a quantity so small as to be utterly out of proportion to any reasonable minimum to be allocated ... "[44] In fact, there was a difference of 281 mcm per annum between the water resources which Israel believed it would ultimately be able to obtain from the completion of its long-term unilateral development program and those which would be available to it according to the TVA study. Thus, American embassy officials in Tel-Aviv reported that: "the difference ... is of such a large magnitude that the Israel Government would consider that its participation in a multilateral program as now outlined would constitute a severe blow to its economic development plans and its aspirations to provide an economic basis for future large-scale immigration."[45] Hence Moshe Sharett's comment to Eric Johnston in the fall 1953, that Israel's attitude toward the unified proposal would be determined in large part by the distribution of the Jordan waters and by the possibility for the inclusion of the Litani waters in the scheme.

There were other matters of concern to the Israeli team. Among them, the report employed outmoded doctrines, such as exclusive within-basin use of water, to support the suggested allocations. Besides, the limitations imposed by these doctrines resulted in both the non-utilization of important quantities of water which could reasonably be included within the scheme, as well as the neglect of the development needs of the Negev region.[46]

The Government then commissioned John S. Cotton, former advisor on the planning of Israel's National Water Carrier system, to prepare a "truly regional scheme," incorporating the criticisms and suggestions outlined

Table 4.3. *Cotton Plan: allocations*

	Quantity of water (mcm)	Land to be irrigated (ha)
Israel	1,290	179,000
Jordan	575	43,000
Syria	30	3,000
Lebanon	450·7	35,000
Total	2,345·7	

above. The Cotton Plan, approved by the Israeli cabinet in early June, had as its guiding principle the aim "to provide for the full irrigation of all irrigable lands in the Kingdom of Jordan...[and] all irrigable areas in Southern Lebanon as well as Syrian lands in the Upper Jordan basin, leaving Israel all the surplus water from the Jordan–Yarmouk System and the Litani flow."[47] The project included the diversion of the Litani River in Lebanon into the Jordan system. And it envisaged separating Jordan's irrigation network from Israel's by constructing reservoirs and dams in Jordan to collect the major part of Yarmouk waters for Jordan's use. John Cotton recommended the resumption of the Bnot Ya'acov project, including the laying of a canal that would conduct a part of the water leaving the power station to a reservoir to be constructed at Battauf, north of the city of Nazareth. Two other canals were proposed: one, to transport water to the northern Negev, the other, from Lake Tiberias to the Beisan Valley.[48] The Litani would provide fresh water to Lake Tiberias, to compensate for the increased salinity caused by the diversion of the Upper Jordan River. The total volume of water to be shared was twice that in the Main Plan and the irrigated area was three times as large. The allocation of water to Israel was increased more than threefold; Jordan's allocation was cut by 25 percent, and Syria's, by 30 percent (see table 4.3). The Plan assumed a sevenfold increase in power production and a fourfold increase in the total cost. As with all previous projects for the water resources of Palestine/Israel, the Cotton Plan asserted Israel's sovereign right to use its share of the Jordan waters wherever it wished, within the territory of the State (see appendix 4).

The two counter-proposals, the Arab Plan and the Cotton Plan, became the "bargaining postures" for the second round of negotiations with Eisenhower's "Personal Representative" in June 1954.[49]

Round two

On the eve of Eric Johnston's second visit to the Middle East, tensions between Israel and the Arab states were running high. Throughout June, there had been numerous shooting incidents across the Israel–Jordan Armistice lines, culminating at the end of the month in the outbreak of fighting in Jerusalem.[50] There were border incidents, as well, with Syria and with Lebanon, and Egypt and Israel quarrelled over freedom of navigation in the Suez Canal and Straits of Tiran. Moreover, both Shishakli of Syria and Naguib of Egypt had recently been ousted from power. "An atmosphere of internal dissension prevailed in all the countries of the region."[51] Nonetheless, Johnston was anxious to proceed with his mission, and obtain "agreement in principle" to the Unified Plan.

Meetings began with the Arab Committee in Cairo on 13 June. The Arab Plan was discussed and special consideration was given to four crucial points: (1) allocation of water: it was agreed, in principle, that quantities allocated to the riparian states would approximate the Unified Plan; (2) extra-basin usage: the Arabs continued to adhere to their official position that water must not be transported outside the basin, despite Johnston's insistence that it would be an impossible "selling job" to convince Israel to agree to extra-basin use limitations;[52] (3) storage: the Committee pressed for maximum storage on the Yarmouk, with only flood waters diverted into Lake Tiberias, stating that this was essential for the security of Jordan. Otherwise, with major storage in Lake Tiberias, Israel would be in a position to cut off the Kingdom's water supply. Johnston agreed in principle to two reservoirs for the river's waters; (4) international supervision: the Arabs wanted a fairly elaborate mechanism of control over various aspects of the regional project, once agreement on Jordan Valley development had been reached.

In a telegram to the Department of State on the eve of his departure for Israel, Eric Johnston concluded thus: "I leave Cairo much encouraged at the prospect of obtaining Arab cooperation in integrated valley development."[53] He knew, however, that this would not entail direct cooperation with Israel.

Negotiations in Jerusalem began on 20 June. The Israeli team pushed for acceptance of the Cotton Plan and urged the inclusion of the Litani waters in a "genuinely regional scheme." Johnston rejected the Plan outright, because of the political and hydrologic realities in the Jordan basin.[54] He would concede to Israel's demand for extra-basin usage, despite Arab objections, but on the issue of the Litani, he would not budge. By the end of the talks three days later, Israel had abandoned its insistence on inclusion of Lebanon's national river.[55]

Other aspects of an integrated scheme remained to be resolved. On the question of the division of the waters, Israel would not agree to its allocation as per the Main Plan, claiming that the figure of 394 mcm was at least 20 percent short of the country's needs. As for storage sites, it rejected the use of Lake Tiberias as a reservoir for Yarmouk waters to be released to the Arabs.[56] It did not want a central reservoir within its territory to be outside its control. Nor was international supervision in the basin an attractive proposition: Israel was reluctant to accept arrangements which it feared would impinge upon its sovereignty. It would only agree to minimal controls at a technical level.

Johnston tried to convince the Israeli team that a water-sharing agreement with the Arabs would "clear the political air," and for that reason alone, it was important to make concessions.[57] He urged the team to accept three principles: (1) a prior claim to water lay with the Kingdom of Jordan for the resettlement of refugees, (2) Lake Tiberias would be used as common storage, and (3) a neutral body would supervise the distribution of water *in situ*. Israel had a negative response to the first two principles, and a highly qualified positive one to the third.[58]

In a memorandum on the status of Jordan Valley negotiations after Johnston's departure from the region, the situation was described as hopeful. Although no agreement had been reached, both sides had indicated acceptance of the principle of unified development. Johnston was optimistic that the differences could be reconciled. The most difficult issue outstanding was the division of the waters. His task at this point was to formulate a new proposal on allocations that would be acceptable to both sides.[59]

Round three

During the fall of 1954, the results of soil tests and a hydrological survey of Jordan, conducted by the American engineering firms, Baker and Harza, at the request of the Jordanian government and the US TCA, were made available to Ambassador Johnston. Although not directly related to his mission, the study provided data which proved helpful for the task of securing agreement to the unified development of the Jordan Valley.[60] Baker and Harza found that there was more cultivable land in the Jordanian portion of the Valley than had been thought, but that the water duty, the amount of water required per unit of land to produce crops, was less than previous estimates had indicated. This information enabled Johnston to revise his figures and offer Israel considerably more water than he had in June 1954.

The third round of talks began in Israel on 27 January 1955. Three outstanding issues remained to be resolved since Johnston's prior visit. First, there was the question of water allocations. The Main Plan had allocated 394 mcm to Israel. At the second meeting, Israel requested 462 mcm. By virtue of the Baker–Harza findings, Johnston was now in a position to offer Israel 446 mcm, or 95 percent of what it had asked for. Second, there was the matter of the use of Lake Tiberias as an international reservoir, in addition to some storage on the Yarmouk River. Third, there was the type of administration that would oversee the functioning of the unified scheme.[61]

Johnston presented Israel with his new offer on the first day of talks. That afternoon, Prime Minister Sharett announced that his team had decided to reject it; the figure of 462 mcm was only a part of what they had requested. Israel wanted a total of 568 mcm, in fact. Furthermore, despite the technical advantages, his country could not accept the proposed use of Lake Tiberias as an international reservoir, precisely because of "international circumstances"; this was perceived to be threatening to the state. Security concerns, as elaborated by Sharett, lay at the forefront of Israel's position:

> We have serious grounds to fear that this will involve us in complications and will open the way for endangering our very vital interests... We are a young state. We are a small state. We are a state hemmed in by enemies on all sides. It is quite natural that we should be particularly jealous in safeguarding our territorial integrity and the completeness of our sovereign rights.

Moreover, if Lake Tiberias were to be used as an international reservoir, "it is inevitable that in due course... it should lead to the creation of territorial claims, claims to the change of boundaries..." This was something that must be avoided at all costs, since "the territorial integrity and full possession and exercise of [their] sovereign rights are of supreme importance in our national life, and there can be no compromise on that."[62]

Soon after Sharett's impassioned speech, it became clear to Johnston from the discussion that ensued, that Israel wanted not only an allocation of 568 mcm for itself and no international storage in Lake Tiberias, but also, no water for Jordan, either from the Upper Jordan River or from the lake. All water for the Kingdom would have to be drawn from the Yarmouk River, while a portion of that water, no less than 40 mcm, would be allocated to Israel.[63] Furthermore, from the total of 568 mcm, Israel planned to divert at least 240 mcm to the Negev.

Johnston expressed consternation at Israel's expectations and formulation of its needs. A member of his team reacted by saying that obviously, "the presumption on the part of Israel is that the Jordan is not an international river."[64] This matter was debated at great length, and on several occasions the talks nearly broke off. For the duration of his stay in Israel, the twin issues of water allocation and Lake Tiberias engaged the attention of the two negotiating teams.[65]

On 30 January, Eric Johnston made a statement to the Israeli committee in which he emphasized that the United States could not sponsor a plan which did not include the use of Lake Tiberias as the international reservoir, since it was the most efficient and economical site for storing Jordan and Yarmouk waters.[66] Furthermore, he stressed that Jordan needed approximately 760 mcm per annum, and that could be met only by drawing about 540 mcm from the Yarmouk River and Lake Tiberias. Having said this, Johnston proposed a new division of the waters:

Lebanon	35 mcm	
Syria	132 mcm	
Jordan	540 mcm	(280 mcm from the Yarmouk; 260 mcm from Lake Tiberias, 100 mcm of which would be Yarmouk water stored in the lake)
Israel	430 mcm	(plus an additional 62 mcm from the Huleh drainage project = 492 mcm)[67]

The Israeli team balked at the new proposal. In its "Comments on Ambassador Johnston's Statement of 30 January 1955," it complained that the allocations for the Arabs were increasing all the time; it appeared that Johnston was aiming to satisfy the requirements of the Arab countries first.[68] These allegations were made despite the fact that Israel was now being promised over 40 percent of the waters of the entire drainage system, and that the Johnston mission had been taking into consideration the needs of the Arab states within the basin, while in the case of Israel and at its insistence, extra-basin usage was being weighed, as well. The team added that Israel's need to absorb large numbers of Jewish immigrants was no less pressing than the resettlement of Arab refugees in Arab countries. As for the utilization of Lake Tiberias, it reiterated its earlier position that that would be acceptable only if there was direct cooperation between the Arabs and Israel, or if the Litani River were included in the regional scheme.[69] It then outlined a counter-proposal to Johnston's offer of the day before:

Lebanon	35 mcm	
Syria	112 mcm	
Jordan	322 mcm	(from the Yarmouk River, plus an additional 270 mcm from perennial flows inside the country)
Israel	451 mcm	(40 mcm from the Yarmouk River, 411 mcm from the Upper Jordan River, in addition to the 62 mcm from the Huleh scheme)

In essence, Israel was insisting on the Jordan River for Israel and the Yarmouk for Jordan and Syria, minus Israel's historic and anticipated uses from the latter river. The two parties were at a stalemate, and in his "Statement to the Israeli Committee on 31 January," Johnston beseeched the team to reconsider his amended proposal and show some flexibility and goodwill.[70]

From there, Eisenhower's envoy went on to Cairo to meet with the Arab committee. By the end of the talks on 7 February, two formulae had been proposed for the division of the waters. Both were acceptable to Johnston. The committee members were to transmit these proposals to their respective governments for decision. They were:

    i. The immediate allocation of the total estimated supply, thus:

Lebanon	35 mcm
Syria	132 mcm
Jordan	520 mcm
Israel	the remainder (equivalent to 400+ mcm)

    ii. immediate partial allocations, thus:

Lebanon	35 mcm
Syria	132 mcm
Jordan	375 mcm
Israel	350 mcm

(leaving approximately 200 mcm to be divided between Jordan and Israel after a three-year period)

On the question of storage, the Arabs agreed in principle to the use of Lake Tiberias, but insisted on greater security storage on the Yarmouk than economy alone would justify.[71]

After the Cairo meetings, Johnston remarked that while his team had tried to insist upon the technical aspects of the Jordan Valley plan whenever confronted with objections or counter-proposals, the matter was quickly moving into the political sphere. He anticipated that political factors would dictate the final decisions.[72]

In an effort to urge acceptance of one of the two proposals, Johnston proceeded to the riparian capitals. Recent political developments in the Arab world threatened to rock his initiative. The controversial Baghdad Pact was on the immediate agenda, sharply dividing the Arab regimes. In Syria, Faris al-Khouri's pro-Iraq government had recently been brought down and was replaced by Sabri al-Asali's, with marked pro-Egyptian tendencies. And in Lebanon, President Camille Chamoun was supporting the policies of Nuri al-Saʿid of Iraq: pro-Baghdad Pact and hostility to arrangements with Israel.

Johnston's reception in the Arab capitals reflected these events and positions. The Jordanian government, reassured somewhat by the results of the Baker–Harza survey and by the relative calm along its border with Israel, was anxious for arrangements that would promise economic development. In Syria, an official announcement reiterated the government's support for the results of the Cairo talks. But in Lebanon, calls for non-cooperation with the American mission and unilateral exploitation of the Hasbani River threatened to undo all that had been accomplished.[73]

Nonetheless, at a meeting with the Council of Arab Foreign Ministers in Beirut on 19 February, Johnston managed to secure a tentative agreement that set forth the points on which substantive accord had thus far been reached. It included the following:

(1) Storage

Water for the Arabs from the Jordan and Yarmouk Rivers would be stored and regulated primarily through reservoir facilities to be constructed on the Yarmouk, in addition to some storage in Lake Tiberias. Johnston would recommend that the United States contribute $21,600,000 toward the construction of a storage dam on the Yarmouk for Syria and Jordan. Flood waters exceeding the storage capacity and irrigation needs would be spilled into Lake Tiberias for release to Jordan. And arrangements concerning the control of the waters would in no way alter existing territorial rights and claims.

(2) Division of waters

Jordan – 537 mcm from the Jordan and Yarmouk Rivers (plus internal sources of wells, springs, and wadis within the Kingdom)

Syria – 132 mcm from the Banias, Jordan and Yarmouk Rivers

Lebanon – 35 mcm from the Hasbani

(3) Supervision

A neutral body, acceptable to all parties, would be established to oversee the withdrawals and release of water.[74]

While Johnston was negotiating with the Arabs, the Israeli team had modified its formula on the division of the waters. The principle they adopted was the following: the Jordan River for Israel, the Yarmouk River for the Arabs; Israel would give the Arabs a specific quantity of water from the Jordan, and the Arabs would do likewise for Israel from the Yarmouk. The question remained, how much would Israel release and how much would it accept.[75] The Israeli team was no longer rejecting Arab access to Jordan waters from Lake Tiberias. It would accept the release of 50 mcm from the lake for Jordan, and perhaps an additional 50 mcm under very stringent conditions.

However, the Arab team wanted 131 mcm for Jordan from Lake Tiberias. Johnston asked Israel to withdraw the conditions on the additional 50 mcm. He would try to persuade the Arabs to reduce their claims to 100 mcm, but no less.[76]

It was during this crucial negotiating session (21–23 February) that Johnston presented the Israelis with a proposal suggested by Arthur Gardiner, and which became known as the "Gardiner Formula" of the Revised Unified Plan: Syria would get 20 mcm from the Banias, 22 mcm from the Jordan, and 90 mcm from the Yarmouk. Lebanon would get 35 mcm from the Hasbani. The Kingdom of Jordan would get all that remained from the Yarmouk, and Israel, all that remained form the Jordan. The Kingdom would release for Israel 25 mcm from the Yarmouk, and Israel would release for the Kingdom 100 mcm from the Jordan. Of that 100 mcm, Israel could include 30 mcm from the saline springs in Lake Tiberias. To this Johnston added that he would try to get an additional 15 mcm from the Yarmouk for Israel. However, if not successful, the Israelis would be obliged to accept the Gardiner Formula as is.[77] Thus ended the third round of talks in February 1955 (see table 4.4 and figure 4.1).

Reviewing the results of his negotiations, Johnston told UN officials that Syria had "inferentially agreed to permit the Israelis to withdraw water from the Jordan River at Jisr Banat Ya῾qub," and the Arab states generally had agreed to "look the other way at Israel's withdrawal of Jordan water from the basin, so long as the total quantity Israel diverts is held within agreed limits."[78] In Israel, however, there was much caustic debate over the Jordan River issue.[79] As far as Johnston could tell, the polity was almost equally divided between those who wanted to take the river, making no deal of any kind, on the theory that no one would stop them, and those who wanted to settle the problem by peaceful means.[80] Johnston announced that he would not reopen negotiations unless Israel presented him with "a firm and reasonable offer which he [could] take to the Arabs"; one that was "reasonably close to the position reached with the Arabs in Beirut in February 1955."[81]

In mid-June, Israel's ambassador to the United Nations, Abba Eban, informed Johnston that his country would be prepared to release up to 75 mcm from the Upper Jordan River for Jordan, and would agree to the creation of additional storage space in Lake Tiberias for the conservation of Yarmouk flood flows.[82] Israel was anxious for a settlement of the Jordan waters question, one way or another; strong domestic forces were pressing the Government to resume work at Bnot Ya῾acov before July. One month later, a "Draft Memorandum of Understanding" was signed in Washington by Israeli and American representatives. It incorporated the terms of the Revised Unified Plan, with water allocations as suggested by the "Gardiner Formula." The purpose of the memorandum was "to set forth the elements of the understanding... subject to final approval by the Governments of Israel and the United States."[83] With a propitious offer from the Israelis in hand, Johnston made plans to return to the Middle East.

As the Government of Israel's position was improving, the Arabs' was rapidly deteriorating. The stiffening of their attitude *vis-à-vis* cooperation with Israel was, in part, a reaction to the Israeli raid against Egyptian military posts in the Gaza Strip and the conclusion of the controversial Baghdad Pact,

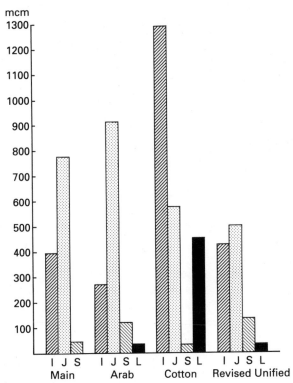

Figure 4.1   Development plans compared: allocations

Table 4.4. *Development plans compared : allocations (mcm per year)*

	Main	Arab	Cotton	Revised Unified
Israel	394	270	1,290	*c.* 425
Jordan	774	911	575	*c.* 500
Syria	45	120	30	132
Lebanon		32	450·7	32

both in February 1955, and the heightening of clashes along the demarcation lines throughout the summer months. It was, as well, the result of the intensification of inter-Arab conflict over this and other issues.

In Lebanon, the Parliament voted on 26 July to reject the Johnston Plan categorically. The Government insisted that the project favored Israel and that approval of the Plan meant collaboration with the enemy.[84] In Jordan, where political turmoil and the politicization of the disgruntled refugee population were on the increase, the original perception of the Johnston mission had resurfaced: clearly, the plan was designed to liquidate the refugee problem rather than to allow the refugees their right to repatriation. The government was urged to develop the resources lying within the boundaries of the country and not cooperate with Israel, even at the expense of significantly more water.[85]

On the eve of Ambassador Johnston's fourth visit to the Middle East, the Arab stance did not augur well. Hostile demonstrations in the riparian capitals were coupled with official statements that a plan could only be accepted under the auspices and with the approval of the (eight) Arab League states, represented by their foreign ministers at a conference in Cairo. Thus, the Jordan waters question would remain linked to the Palestine Problem. It would also be more difficult to exploit inter-Arab differences and impose a settlement with Israel on the Arabs.[86]

Round four

Eric Johnston returned to the Middle East on 25 August 1955. His intention was to secure agreement finally from all the states concerned to the Revised Unified Plan for the Jordan Valley. His task was made especially difficult by the fact that old fears had resurfaced and were now being fueled by an untimely speech made by the American Secretary of State, John Foster Dulles. Before the Council on Foreign Relations on 26 August, Dulles announced that in order to secure a lasting and stable peace in the Middle East, the United States would: (1) pay adequate compensation to the Arab refugees, (2) underwrite some of the expense for a regional water development project to further the development of the area's economy, and (3) guarantee new and permanent political boundaries which would replace the old Armistice lines.[87] In effect, he was pushing for a comprehensive Arab–Israeli political settlement at the same time as advocating acceptance of the Johnston Plan.

The Arab states, led by Syria, denounced Dulles' proposals as an attempt to legitimize a situation which they did not accept. His statement fed their suspicions that the Johnston mission was a trap to secure Arab recognition of the State of Israel. It placed the Jordan Valley Plan within a political context that made its acceptance untenable. Johnston now had to try to undo the damage done and convince the Arabs that, in fact, his program would require no political accommodation with Israel, and that it involved no change in the political status of the area. But the argument that the program had only one purpose, to irrigate the lands of the Jordan Valley so that they would produce crops and support people, fell on skeptical ears.

At his meetings with the Ministerial Committee of Jordan (25–28 August),

Ambassador Johnston said that of the four riparians, the Kingdom had the most to gain from his Plan. He then announced that he was reducing Jordan's share of water by 40 mcm and increasing Israel's by 15 mcm, claiming that since not all the irrigable land in the Jordan Valley would be irrigated at any one time, there were, overall, fewer hectares requiring an allocation of water.[88] In effect, Jordan was being offered all of the Yarmouk waters minus 90 mcm to Syria and 40 mcm (25 + 15) to Israel, plus 100 mcm from the Jordan River at Lake Tiberias, giving it a total of 470 mcm (370 + 100) from the river system.[89]

The Jordanian Committee members were taken aback by the new proposal that reduced Jordan's irrigable land area and gave the country less water. This was especially perplexing, given that the Baker–Harza data – 51,300 hectares of irrigable land in the Jordan Valley – which Eric Johnston had been abiding by and defending for months, was said to be the most authoritative.[90] They were very suspicious of Johnston's argumentation in support of this change, and believed that it represented no more than a concession to Israel.

The political implications of the Jordan Valley Plan continued to weigh heavily on the Arab states. Virtually all elements of the project were now being called into question. At the third Ministerial Committee Meeting, the Arab team balked at Israeli usage of Yarmouk water to irrigate the Triangle, and suggested the use of Lake Tiberias water instead.[91] Furthermore, in Jordan, popular disapproval of the Plan made it an extremely difficult program to sell to the public, especially now that the country would be getting even less water than had been allocated to it in the Beirut Memorandum.[92]

At an informal meeting on the last day of Johnston's stay in the Kingdom, the Prime Minister told him that his country would be prepared to support the proposals on economic grounds only, if: (a) the dam on the Yarmouk River at the Maqarin site would be built to allow for a future increase in dam height and capacity, (b) a greater amount of water from the Upper Jordan River would be released to Jordan from Lake Tiberias, and (c) more specific guarantees would be given as to the actions to be taken in the event of violations. However, he insisted that a political decision would have to be taken in concert with the other Arab League states, and that the project must be purely economic in objective. There could be no political accommodation in the area.[93]

In a comment to the Secretary of State, Eisenhower's envoy described his perception of the interests of and constraints upon Jordan thus: "In my judgement, the Hashemite Kingdom of Jordan seriously wants the project but it must surmount several difficulties. On the one hand, these involve the substance of the proposals and internal and public relations problems, while on the other, they relate to Jordan's ability to enlist the support of the other Arab countries... The Jordanian cabinet appears willing to try to isolate the project from the question of a general political accommodation in the area and secure the support of Lebanon, Syria, and Egypt."[94]

From Amman, Johnston went on to Cairo, Damascus, and Beirut to make a final appeal to Arab leaders and technicians to support the Jordan Valley project. In all three capitals, he met with stern objections. At the meeting with the Arab Technical Committee in Beirut on 8 September, Johnston presented his latest offer, the Revised Unified Plan. It differed from the Beirut tentative agreement on three issues: (1) Johnston was now recommending that a dam with a capacity of 300 mcm be built on the Yarmouk River, and that Jordan and Syria would have the right to increase it further, at their own expense; (2) instead of deciding now on the usage of Lake Tiberias for the storage of Yarmouk floodwater, a final decision would be deferred for five years, during which time other possible sites for more economical storage would be investigated; (3) the amount of Upper Jordan water from Lake Tiberias to the Kingdom of Jordan was reduced from about 140 mcm to 100 mcm, thereby decreasing Jordan's total water supply from 760 mcm (as per the Main Plan) to 720 mcm.[95] To compensate for the decrease in its allocation, Jordan would have access to 30 mcm from the saline springs lying at the bottom of the lake. Despite profound reservations, the Technical Committee decided to approve the Revised Unified Plan. In late September, it recommended it to the Arab League Political Committee.[96]

According to members of Johnston's team at the point discussions were concluded, "there was in effect virtual agreement as to the wording of the plan which on the one side the Arab states would sign, and by separate document the Israelis would sign. The extent of agreement was such at the time that there were nearly five pages of identical understanding with regard to water allocation, storage and the international control authority... The only actual disagreement which had existed at that time of a technical nature related to a small difference on the water quantity and quality to be assigned to Israel and Jordan."[97] No final understanding was reached on precise allocations.

The Political Committee of the Arab League, composed of the Foreign Ministers of (eight) Arab states, met in October and debated the issue for four days. It decided not to veto the Unified Plan outright, but rather, to try to "play for time"; it referred the Plan back to the Technical Committee for further study. On 11 October, the Arab News Agency in Cairo issued the following statement from the Political Committee:

Representatives of the Arab countries concerned... have studied the Arab Plan [!] for the exploitation of the waters of the River Jordan and its tributaries...

They have found that despite the efforts exerted there remain certain important points which need further study. It has, therefore, been decided to instruct the Experts' Committee to continue their task until a decision is reached which would safeguard Arab interests.[98]

Jordan was anxious for the implementation of the Unified Plan since it was in great need of access to the water resources of the river system. Lebanon had consistently rejected any basin-wide water project, but it was not as influential as Syria given its inferior power position both within the basin and among the Arab states. Although there was some difference of opinion on this issue in Syria, domestic political instability was such that no party was prepared to take the risk and support even a technical arrangement with the enemy. There was an implicit consensus that there could be no cooperation, or semblance of cooperation, with Israel. In contrast, Egypt had consistently supported the idea of unified development. However, given that it was not a riparian state, there was a structural limitation on the extent to which it could enjoin the Arab riparians to accept the Plan.[99] It is also possible that ʿAbd al-Nasir was less inclined to use his influence in this regard, in view of the escalating tensions along the Armistice demarcation lines, the conclusion of the Baghdad Pact – to which he was deeply opposed – and the American refusal, in the summer of 1955, to sell Egypt arms on a favorable basis.

Nonetheless, after the Arab League meetings in October, ʿAbd al-Nasir told Ambassador Johnston that he thought Arab acceptance of the project would eventually be forthcoming, and asked for some time to bring the Arab states into line on a water agreement.[100] When Israel's Foreign Minister Moshe Sharett learnt of this request, he announced that he would give Nasir until the end of February 1956.[101] After that, Israel would feel free to resume work on the Bnot Yaʿacov project if by then a regional water scheme had not been accepted. But portentous developments in the region served to lessen the chances for riparian agreement.

In the summer of 1955, Egypt, unable to obtain arms from the West on terms it could meet, turned to the Soviet Union. In September, it accepted an offer from the Soviets to supply it with arms. The deal enhanced ʿAbd al-Nasir's prestige in the Arab world, but it weakened his position in the West and aroused the profound concern of Israel. It was clear, much to the chagrin of the Eisenhower Administration and despite its efforts, that the Soviet Union had managed to establish influence in the Middle East and with Nasir especially. Israel, fearing that the arms deal would give Egypt technical superiority, embarked upon its own search for more weapons. Mutual fears incited an arms race and the multiplication of border incidents.[102]

Also indicative of the rapid deterioration of Arab–Israeli relations was the growing influence of the "activist" line in Israel's military and foreign policy, and the replacement of Moshe Sharett by David Ben-Gurion as prime minister in 1956. Representing the "pacifist" line, Sharett favored non-aggressive conciliatory attitudes which could lead to peace. Ben-Gurion, however, believed that Israel should always retaliate with force against Arab acts of hostility or breaches of the Armistice.[103] In this highly volatile environment, one act of violence led to another.

Nor were the Israel–Syria or the Israel–Jordan demarcation lines spared increased tensions. Repeated announcements by Israeli officials, throughout the winter months, of plans to implement the Bnot Yaʿacov project were perceived by the Arab riparians as a pressure tactic. The Syrian government, believing these statements to be threats of aggression, also threatened to take unilateral action; it would resort to force, either by firing on the diversion site or by cutting off the river flow nearby.[104] The Bnot Yaʿacov project had emerged as a potential *casus belli* between the Arab states and Israel. Washington, in an attempt to defuse the worsening tensions in the region, pleaded with Syria to accept the Revised Unified Plan. But the plea was regarded with deep suspicion.

The first of March passed without Israel resuming work at Bnot Yaʿacov. Nonetheless, the situation had already deteriorated to the point at which, as in the words of the Foreign Minister of Lebanon, "no Arab Government could now support the Jordan Valley Plan and remain in office."[105] President Nasir himself was pessimistic about the short-range prospects for the regional water scheme. There was no question about its technical, engineering aspects. However, Arab politicians were against it on political grounds. The problem rested primarily with Syria and its complex domestic politics. Although a new cabinet with pro-Egyptian tendencies had recently been formed, there had also emerged a strong opposition Bʿathist faction in Parliament, which was hostile to unified development.[106] Besides, all political parties in the country had agreed that no action could be taken in favor of the Johnston Plan.[107] In fact, as far as the Arabs were concerned, the concept of unified development, as embodied in the Jordan Valley Plan, had been completely abandoned.[108]

In the spring of 1956, UN and US Government officials summed up the Arab attitudes to the Johnston Plan thus: The Jordanian government was still very anxious to have the plan put into effect, despite there being some internal opposition to it. Nasir of Egypt favored the plan and would push it if he felt that the situation was appropriate. But the Syrian and Lebanese governments were bitterly opposed.[109] At the end of March, the Arab League Political Committee reconvened to discuss the Jordan waters issue. Again, the foreign ministers failed to reach agreement.[110]

Throughout the summer of 1956, the situation in the central Middle East deteriorated rapidly. Tensions mounted and severe clashes ensued along the Armistice demarcation lines. Jordan perceived the conduct by Israel of military exercises along the "border" as provocation; it began to negotiate for Iraqi troops to reinforce the Arab Legion in the event of further hostilities.[111] In July, John Foster Dulles, wary of the Egyptian president's courtship with the Soviet bloc and his increasingly neutralist policies, suddenly withdrew his government's offer to help finance the Aswan High Dam. Nasir responded by nationalizing the Suez Canal, thus provoking (or providing the justification for) the Suez Crisis and Sinai war – the tripartite, British–French–Israeli aggression against Egypt.[112] With Israel and Egypt at war by the end of October, there was no more talk of a Jordan Valley plan.

The mission interpreted

Despite the fact that formal agreement to a regional water scheme was not reached, both the Arabs and the Israelis had accepted the Revised Unified Plan at a technical level. Moreover, Israel and Jordan, the two riparians most dependent upon the Jordan waters and most in need of a basin-wide accord, independently and tacitly abided by the allocations prescribed in the Plan in their water utilization from 1956 to 1967.[113] For both countries, the material advantages of the plan were not only indisputable but also, far superior to any other unilateral or regional scheme proposed. In fact, the Johnston Plan became the *de facto* discussion point and measuring rod for all subsequent efforts at developing the Jordan waters.

The experience of the Johnston mission elucidates the fact that profound geopolitical and security-related concerns, emanating from historical circumstance and the character of relations in the basin, often dominate the seemingly technical issue of allocating water resources. As we have seen in other cases of riparian dispute in adversarial settings, such concerns tend to impinge upon the abilities of states to elect the ideal solution to resource scarcity. In essence, the economic–developmental needs of some or all of the basin states fall victim to the inter-state conflict.

The unresolved "question of Palestine" lay at the heart of all interactions and governed all that was possible between Arab and Israeli. In the immediate post-1948 period, the humiliated Arab states sought to oust (what they referred to as) the "Zionist entity" from Arab soil and return Palestine to its indigenous inhabitants. Much of Arab political discourse at the time focused on the loss of Palestine and its implications; and the need to understand and reverse the defeat became one of the major defining concerns of Arabism, Arab nationalism, and inter-Arab politics.[114] The State of Israel was perceived as a foreign intrusion and a western imperialist construct. Dealings with the illegitimate state were viewed as treasonous. For Zionists, however, the memory of ethnic and religious persecution in central Europe was vivid. Palestine's new immigrants were determined to preserve the territorial and ethnic integrity of the Jewish homeland within secure borders. Arab acts of aggression were interpreted as attempts at its annihilation. For the young state, the perception of threat from an exceedingly hostile environment defined its security concerns. Moshe Sharett described the psychological underpinnings of much of his government's behavior thus:

> We have to ensure our survival against the very heavy odds with which we are grappling, in the face of the pressure upon us of the countries by which we are surrounded, a pressure which is to this day inexorably hostile. We are *hemmed in* [emphasis my own] here, by decrees of providence, within this narrow strip of land on the eastern shore of the Mediterranean not so richly endowed with national wealth.[115]

It is not enough to say that the vital interests of Israel and the Arab states were at odds; in fact, the very identity and *raison d'être* of one were contested by the other. (While Israel did not contest the legitimacy of the Arab states, it did not recognize the national aspirations of the Palestinians.) Moreover, the organizing ideologies of both were defined, in part, with reference to the other. Withholding recognition because of a perception of questioned legitimacy was part and parcel of the political conflict. Israel was anxious to have formal accords with the Arab states since that would imply explicit recognition and acceptance of a Jewish state in historic Palestine; hence, the end to external threats to its survival. For the Arabs, however, Israel had no apparent legitimacy; it had been established through conquest and deceit. Furthermore, recognition of what was perceived as an illegitimate political entity was equivalent to forsaking the struggle to regain Palestine and accepting the *status quo* in the aftermath of the 1948–49 War; in other words, a repudiation of one of the most important "binding agents" of the "Arab nation" in the modern period. Whether out of profound commitment to a central defining concern of Arabism or because of a narcissistic preoccupation with political survival, no single Arab government dared to engage its country in a process that would spell the formal acceptance of the Jewish state within the post-1949 boundary lines.

It was this highly charged psychological environment that was treated as an abstraction by the Eisenhower Administration in its attempt to resolve some of the tensions in the central Middle East. The visceral sentiments at play in the Arab–Israeli conflict were viewed as obstacles to cooperation. Rather than confront them, Washington, in the fashion suggested by political functionalists, tried to brush them aside.

In order to understand why the Johnston mission failed to achieve its objectives, it is necessary to analyze the Jordan waters issue in terms of the four variables, or dynamics of state behavior, that compose the framework of this study: (1) resource need, (2) character of riparian relations, (3) relative power in the basin, and (4) attempts at conflict resolution. As in the other cases of riparian dispute treated in the preceding chapter, these variables and the weights assigned to them informed the positions taken by the riparian states with regard to a regional water project.

As we recall from our discussion of the environment of conflict, the greatest portion of the Jordan basin lies within the territories of Israel and Jordan. Of the four riparian states, these two are the most arid and the most dependent on the river system. In Jordan, the need for water management as a means to promote state-building and achieve economic development was recognized as early as in the 1930s, well before the establishment of the State of Israel. But after the 1948–49 War and the influx of nearly half a million refugees, the absorptive capacity of this resource-poor country was strained to the breaking-point. The Jordan Valley was the only region appropriate for settlement and agricultural development. However, the Kingdom, 80 percent of which is desert, had only one river – the Yarmouk – with which to irrigate its cultivable land. In fact, the continued survival of the Jordanian state was dependent upon unimpeded access to the waters of the Jordan–Yarmouk system.[116]

Israel's water situation was no more attractive. Although slightly less arid than its neighbor, it was increasingly dependent on access to fresh water to meet the agricultural and developmental needs of a burgeoning economy and a rapidly growing immigrant population. Government policy aimed to extend irrigated agriculture and settlement throughout the country. As noted in chapter 2, this objective was fundamental to the ideological foundations of the State, as well as to its security concerns. Economic capability, ideology, and security were all inter-related and closely linked to the need for access to water resources. In his own definition of security, David Ben-Gurion illuminates the perceived link thus:

the scope of our defence... does not depend on our army alone... Israel can have no security without immigration... Security means the settlement and peopling of the empty areas in north and south... the establishment of industries throughout the country; the development of agriculture in all suitable areas; and the building of an expanding (self-sufficient) economy... Security means economic independence...[117]

Moshe Sharett described this link, as well, and elucidated unequivocally the primacy of water resources in the continued survival of the Jewish state:

Water for Israel is not a luxury; it is not just a desirable and helpful addition to our system of natural resources. *Water is life itself.* It is bread for the nation – and not only bread. Without large irrigation works we will not reach high production levels, to balance the economy and to achieve economic independence. And without irrigation we will not create an agriculture worthy of the name... and without agriculture – and especially a developed, progressive agriculture – we will not be a nation rooted in its land, sure of its survival, stable in its character, controlling all opportunities of production with material and spiritual resources... [118]

For Jordan and for Israel, therefore, the river system was intimately bound up with state survival. For Syria and for Lebanon, however, it was more or less incidental. Syria did make use of a very small portion of the Yarmouk waters to irrigate the Hauran region in the southern part of the country, and could have reaped significant benefits in terms of hydro-electric power production had a dam been built on the Yarmouk River. In addition, Syrian farms in the DMZ were irrigated with water from the Upper Jordan River. But in terms of the country's overall water balance, the Jordan system was dwarfed by the mighty Euphrates River and tributaries in the north and the east. Relatively well-watered Lebanon had little material use for the Jordan system. While a small portion of the southern part of the country was irrigated by the Hasbani tributary, the Litani River was a far richer asset. Lebanon's interest in the Jordan waters issue was largely due to the inherent political implications and ramifications. The same was true for Syria, albeit to a slightly lesser extent. Given that the Jordan waters were regarded by the upstream states in much the same way as Ethiopia regards the Blue Nile – as a geopolitically strategic resource and not as an essential element of state survival – Lebanon and Syria, like Ethiopia *vis-à-vis* Egypt and the Sudan, had little incentive to strike a bargain with Israel over their utilization. This, however, was not the case with Jordan.

Despite the pressing need in Israel and in Jordan for a regional scheme, the character of relations in the basin, derivative of historical circumstance, made its realization unfeasible. Riparian relations and the way in which they influenced the outcome of Eric Johnston's mission can be analyzed in terms of three inter-related variables: (1) recognition and legitimacy, (2) perceptions, and (3) security concerns.

It is probably correct to say that withholding recognition of the State of Israel was the immediate reason for the non-committal response of the Arab Political Committee to the Revised Unified Plan in October 1955. The Arabs clearly understood that recognizing a country's right to water resources was an explicit recognition of that country's right to exist.[119] This fact could not be dodged, not even by Johnston's insistence that the Unified Plan did not require the Arabs to deal directly with Israel. The Plan did involve the storage of Yarmouk waters in Lake Tiberias, that is, in territory under Israeli jurisdiction. It also stipulated the need for the Arabs to release Yarmouk water for Israeli use and for Israel to release Jordan water for Arab use. Whether these arrangements were carried out directly or through a third party was academic; they were tantamount to formal acceptance of the other and its rights as a political entity. But non-recognition of the Jewish state within the territory defined by the 1949 Armistice demarcation lines was one of the central organizing principles of Pan-Arabism. All Arab states had, at the very least, to pay lip service to this precept.

Arab concern for the political implications of a basin-wide scheme was reiterated throughout the two years and four rounds of mediation efforts. This concern was magnified when border incidents were at their peak in terms of frequency and intensity. The Arab states were reminded that by cooperating in a regional development project, they would be contributing to the strengthening of the Jewish state. Obviously, that was contrary to their vital interests; in fact, it was perceived as sowing the seeds of their own undoing. Moreover, given their avowed commitment to regain Palestine, they could not logically accept a plan, the objective of which was to settle Palestinian refugees outside Palestine. Nonetheless, Arab concern for the political implications diminished when the material advantages to be reaped from regional development were blatantly clear. Lebanon's concern never subsided. But the Kingdom of Jordan, which had initially been vehemently opposed to the Johnston Plan, had become, by the second round of talks, the most favorably disposed of the Arab riparians. No doubt, it had the most to gain. Furthermore, the Arab Technical Committee, keenly aware of the material benefits of the proposed scheme, approved it on a technical basis. However, it could not accept it on political grounds.

At the time, non-recognition of Israel was the foremost element in the regional political behavior of Syria, the strongest of the Arab riparian states. ʿAbd al-Nasir, of course, understood this, but he also grasped the extent to which the Unified Plan would serve the development needs of Jordan. For these reasons and with the *dénouement* of the Johnston mission, he recommended that the Arab states and Israel go ahead with those parts of the Plan that could be pursued independently and did not require cooperative arrangements.[120] Israeli General Moshe Dayan had made a similar proposal at the beginning of negotiations in 1953. He thought that rather than have water projects on a regional basis, a more realistic solution would be to give the Jordan River to Israel and the Yarmouk River to the Kingdom of Jordan. Each side would then have access to about half the water of the Jordan system and would neither be dependent upon nor need to deal with the other.[121] This proposed solution was, in fact, quite similar to that followed in the Indus basin. And in essence, a combination of Nasir's and Dayan's suggestions is what prevailed between the two downstream riparians in the Jordan basin from 1956 to June 1967, without formal accords.

No doubt, Arab non-recognition of Israel was a major preoccupation of the Israeli political establishment. Although Israel's negotiating team had been very obstinate with regard to the country's water rights, the view that a formal agreement on water sharing could mean a major breakthrough in the Arab–Israeli deadlock had become, by the spring of 1955, a strong incentive to temper its position. The "pacifist line" in the Government was prepared to make a few relatively minor concessions in exchange for peace. But mutual fears and suspicions lessened the chances for a successful agreement.

Arab perceptions of Israel's interests influenced the Arabs' attitude toward unified development and sharpened their security concerns. The issue of intra-basin versus extra-basin usage of the Jordan waters is a case in point. The Arab states were very apprehensive about Israel's intention to carry water from the Jordan system outside the watershed and to the Negev. It was not so much that some of this was "Arab water," from tributaries originating in Lebanon and Syria, nor even that this was contrary to the Arabs' understanding of international law. Most significant, from the Arab point of view, was that the water would be used to extend and improve the economic development of Israel and make possible the absorption of more Jewish immigrants throughout the country. In sum, the Arabs could not support a project that would strengthen their enemy. Hence, as a means to protect themselves, they tried, albeit unsuccessfully, to have the principle of extra-basin usage rejected. Also because of security concerns, the Arab team contested the use of Lake Tiberias as a common reservoir. The Arab states could not depend on the goodwill of their enemy to release the water so crucial to their survival.

Israel's perceptions of its needs, its security, and the interests of its neighbors also influenced its attitude toward a regional scheme. In a speech during the third round of talks with Eric Johnston, Prime Minister Moshe Sharett expressed this vital relationship in no uncertain terms:

what is to you [the US Government] just one item and not a very high one on the world agenda [water resource development of the Jordan basin] is to us our whole life, our whole existence, our whole future... The problem which is the subject of our discussion is the very essence of our life... A good part of it [the land of Israel] is arid, some of it permanently so ... But our most fundamental problem is how best to utilise the extremely limited soil resources of the country in order to produce as much as possible of the food we need. We can only do it by irrigating as large a proportion of the fertile area as possible...

Now you have that little river called the Jordan, which is part of our ancient history, and which is one of the historic and geographical symbols of our country. You know what kind of stream it is, very limited. Every drop of its water is precious, every drop of it is part of our future.

Moreover, the country had to be developed to provide a haven for increasing numbers of Jews fleeing persecution:

We don't know yet what the future holds in store for this country or for our people, scattered as it is in lands near and far. Things that may happen any day in certain countries of North Africa may completely transform the position here. We consider those people as living on the brink of a volcano. A day may come when they will need this country very badly, when escaping to this country will be to them their only salvation...Without drawing an unnecessarily dark picture of the situation and the prospects, we have been taught by bitter experience to expect and to be ready for the worst. That is a problem which always preys on our minds.

But even with the population that we have at present, we must cultivate and irrigate a lot more than we do today, to enable us to feel more balanced in our economic life and not expose ourselves to the danger of being starved out in a crisis.[122]

In the Jordan basin, as in most international settings, historical conditions have spawned particular types of interstate relations. It is the distinctive character of these relations and perceptions that have defined the security environment of the riparian states and influenced their regional behavior.

In addition to riparian relations, relative power resources in the basin influenced the outcome of the Johnston mission. In terms of riparian position, relative power was in the favor of Lebanon and Syria; the tributaries of the Jordan system rose within their territories. In theory, these two countries could have obstructed a regional water-sharing scheme simply by diverting the headwaters of the Jordan River and disrupting the flow downstream. In fact, the Syrian Government had threatened on several occasions to re-route the Banias River through Arab territory.[123] However, these were no more than idle threats. The growing military capability of the State of Israel, backed by Western arms and assistance, gave the Arabs pause. ʿAbd al-Nasir, for one, was anxious not to provoke Israel; he knew that the Arab armies were no match for the Israel Defence Forces (IDF).[124] And the Syrian leadership understood that diverting the headwaters would surely lead to war.

Far more significant about the role of relative power in riparian conflict was the way in which the outcome of the Johnston negotiations reflected the asymmetry of power in the basin. Of the three Arab riparian states, Syria was by far the strongest. When the Political Committee of the Arab League met in October to discuss the Revised Unified Plan, it was the Syrian objection that held sway. As for Jordan, severe domestic and regional constraints allowed it no alternative but to accept the Syrian position, despite its acute need for water for socio-economic development. King Hussein, himself, had pointed out that even the semblance of cooperation with Israel would amount to his "political suicide" because of the growing instability in his country.[125] The Palestine refugees were becoming increasingly politicized and demanding their "right to return"; and Suleiman Nabulsi's opposition National Socialist Party, the only licensed political party in the country and an increasingly influential one, had rejected the Plan unequivocally and was pressuring the King to do likewise. In its view, the Johnston Plan was a political project and not an economic one. Its principal objective was to orchestrate cooperation between the Arabs and Israel, and eliminate the refugee problem.[126]

In the regional sphere, as well, the Kingdom was severely constrained. It was a relatively weak state with the means of defending only very limited interests. Its resource base was poor, institutional framework underdeveloped, communal structure fragmented, and allegiance to central power uncertain. Furthermore, the country was kept afloat by huge foreign (British) subsidies, and until 1956, its army, the Arab Legion, was headed by British officers.[127] Domestic constraints impinged upon the state's international behavior. Hence, much as Jordan was interested in the Unified Plan, it could not, as the Prime Minister had pointed out, "take a favorable decision without consulting its fellow Arab states."[128] Furthermore, despite Egyptian involvement in the Johnston negotiations and ʿAbd al-Nasir's influential position in the Arab world, Egypt's leader could do little to sway Syria. By the summer of 1955, the three borders with Israel were the scenes of heightened tensions and almost daily incidents.

Moreover, unlike the Indus basin dispute, the role of the third party in the Jordan waters issue and the manner in which it attempted to resolve the conflict did not lend itself to a positive outcome. As noted above, the Arab states perceived a strong pro-Israel bias in the American Administration and were, as a result, wary of its intentions. The United States had been involved in the creation of the Jewish state and had been lending it material and ideological support since 1948. Currying Arab favor in the 1950s was viewed as an attempt to win over the Arab states in the context of Cold War politics, and not as an indication of support for their organizing principles. Furthermore, the appointment of Eric Johnston as "personal representative" of President Eisenhower was suspect. Johnston was not considered an impartial mediator. In fact, in private conversations, certain members of the Arab Technical Committee confessed that at times, they felt that Johnston was negotiating for Israel. He employed threats to get the Arabs to cooperate with their enemy.[129] The Arabs could not help but feel that the aim of the unified project was to freeze the *status quo* in the basin and secure Arab acquiescence to a political situation which they, with growing bitterness and solidarity, rejected.[130]

The Arab states, and especially Jordan, did want access to water resources, but they did not want to cooperate with Israel in the absence of an overall political settlement. The Jordan waters issue could not be considered outside the context of relations in the basin, and those relations were part and parcel of the larger political conflict. Moreover, the dispute over the Jordan waters was a manifestation of an inter-state conflict which persisted within a very particular context of non-recognition. In part, it was the central feature of non-recognition that rendered unfeasible the proposed solution to riparian dispute. The most powerful and, in terms of the Jordan waters, least needy of the Arab states would not acquiesce to cooperative involvement with a state, the legitimacy of which it did not recognize. Without Syria's accord, the other Arab riparians could not accept basin-wide cooperation, no matter how badly they may have needed it. In essence, because the larger political rivalry engaged historically formed *core values*, the adversaries were reluctant to allow collaboration, even in technical matters. This was especially true when collaboration was not considered essential, as was the case with Lebanon and Syria *vis-à-vis* the Jordan waters. For them, the larger Arab–Israeli conflict took precedence over any material benefit that could possibly accrue as a result of cooperation with the enemy.

In contrast, the riparian states in the Indus basin were eventually able to divorce the water dispute from other contentious issue areas. This was despite the fact that the political rivalry between India and Pakistan engaged core values, as well. As we recall, the creation and *raison d'être* of Pakistan was the result of ethnic and religious strife in the Indian sub-continent prior to Partition. Nonetheless, the two states did, for the most part, recognize each other's right to exist.

Furthermore, the realism of the solution proposed to water development in the Indus basin was indisputable. Acknowledging that the two parties did not trust each other enough to share water in a fashion that would require almost daily cooperative interactions, the World Bank drew up a plan to divide the Indus system in two, in such a way that there would be no inter-dependence in the basin and hence, no cause for discord. The third party had understood the context of relations in the basin. Its solution to water development reflected this context and, therefore, made it more acceptable to the riparians.[131]

In the case of the Jordan basin dispute, the inverse was attempted. The third party sought to use water resources as a medium by which parties would have tangible evidence that things were " getting done," and that their material situations would continue to improve if only the inter-state conflict were resolved. The third party did not propose a solution to water development that was in keeping with the character of relations in the basin. As noted above, there were both Arab and Israeli officials who had thought that a more realistic solution to water development in the Jordan basin would be the separation of the system into two independent parts, so that Arabs and Israelis would not have to interact on such a crucial issue. However, the United States Government rejected this suggestion; it saw water-sharing as the gateway to peace and cooperation. The Eisenhower Administration, echoing the functionalist theory of spillover, hoped that "... by regional economic development people in the area will begin to talk with each other and eventually this would lead to better relations for all."[132] Formal agreement to water-sharing was never reached.

Nonetheless, access to the waters of the river system was absolutely essential for Israel and Jordan. Following the Johnston negotiations, both states independently pursued those projects within their territories that did not involve cooperation, and respected the idea of the Jordan River for Israel and the Yarmouk for Jordan. In effect, a solution somewhat similar to that in the Indus basin was pursued by the most needy riparian states, in the absence of a formal accord. It was adhered to throughout the turbulent sixties, until the outbreak of the June War.

5 Perception and misperception: the Jordan waters crisis (1964) and the onset of war

The combination of relative power resources and the fact of inter-state conflict over core values influenced the outcome of Eric Johnston's efforts in the Jordan basin. No doubt, cognitive dynamics would continue to guide the foreign policy behavior of the riparian states, and the objective environment, or more specifically, the distribution of power, would establish outcomes.

In this chapter, we discuss the Jordan waters crisis of 1964 and the deterioration of relations in the central Middle East that led up to the outbreak of the third Arab–Israel war. Our primary concern is to highlight the complexity of inter-state relations in the region, and the perceptions and security concerns that emanated from them. The aim is to understand the way in which cognitive variables influenced the decision-making and regional behavior of the Arab states and Israel. First, we outline the developments that provoked the Jordan waters crisis and other critical events of the period. Then, we analyze the foreign policy behavior of the states in question, in terms of their different perceptions of themselves and the environment. Finally, we evaluate the cognitive dynamics in relation to outcomes in the Middle East in 1964 and 1967.

Before proceeding, two points of clarification must be made. First, while the Jordan waters crisis and the 1967 war were two distinct crises in a protracted conflict, we believe that the former can be considered as one of several conflict spirals that, either directly or indirectly, provoked the latter. Second, in the pages that follow, we discuss developments that had much to do with the outbreak of war, but had little or no apparent relationship to the conflict over water resources. The reason for this is twofold. First, as our principal concern in this chapter is to illuminate the importance of perceptions in directing behavior, the period from 1964 to June 1967 provides fascinating cognitive material on the foreign policy behavior of the states in question. Second, the geopolitical outcome of the 1967 war proved to be a major turning-point in the conflict over the Jordan waters.

In the atmosphere of renewed hostility in the central Middle East, precipitated by the Sinai–Suez War, both Israel and Jordan reverted to their pre-Johnston mission unilateral plans to tap the water resources of the

115

Jordan River system. Jordan embarked upon the Ionides–MacDonald scheme to extend an irrigation canal from the Yarmouk River, southward along the eastern Ghor of the Jordan Valley. Israel proceeded with its Ten Year Plan and the integration of all the water resources of the country into a comprehensive country-wide network, the National Water Carrier.[1] (See map 5.1.)

The East Ghor Canal project was a Jordanian venture, carried out in cooperation with Syria as per their June 1953 agreement, and financed jointly by the governments of the United States and Jordan. Work on the project began in August 1958.[2] It consisted of a seventy-kilometre main canal which, in the initial stages, would tap approximately 123 mcm of water per year from the Yarmouk River to irrigate 12,000 hectares of cultivable land, and eventually 35,000 hectares, along the eastern slopes of the Jordan Valley. From its diversion point ten kilometres northeast of the confluence of the Yarmouk and Jordan Rivers, the canal would traverse and tap the Zarqa River, an unshared tributary of the Jordan, as well as seven intervening wadis, or seasonal streams. Later stages of the project included plans to construct storage reservoirs: at Mukheiba, east of Adasiya in the Yarmouk gorge, to hold up winter floodwaters and allow for the extension of the East Ghor canal almost to the Dead Sea; and at Maqarin, on the Jordan–Syria border, to impound winter flows and control their release for irrigation, as well as for hydro-electric power to be shared by the two countries. Moreover, a feeder canal would be laid, linking the East Ghor canal with a West Ghor canal. United States' support for the project was based on the fact that the amount of water to be diverted conformed with the quantities assigned to the Kingdom under the Unified Plan (1955).[3]

The aim of the project was to extend irrigated agriculture, double (and eventually, triple) yields, and provide employment in this small, arid, resource-poor country, threatened by an explosive population growth (approximately 2·8 percent per annum), yet heavily dependent upon agriculture as the principal source of economic sustenance.[4] By June 1963, the first three stages of the project were completed. The canal was diverting more than 123 mcm of fresh water from the Yarmouk River annually.[5]

Since the debacle of the Johnston mission, the Government of Israel had been proceeding with work on the National Water Carrier system, having relocated the diversion point of Upper Jordan waters away from Bnot Ya'acov in contested territory. The system's main conduit, a 112-kilometre series of canals, tunnels, and giant pipelines, extended from Eshed Kinrot on the northwestern shore of Lake Tiberias, down to Rosh Ha'ayin east of Tel-Aviv, the terminal of the National Water Carrier. By the mid-1960s, the southern end of the main conduit would be linked to the existing Yarkon–Negev pipelines, thus bringing Jordan water to the coastal plain and

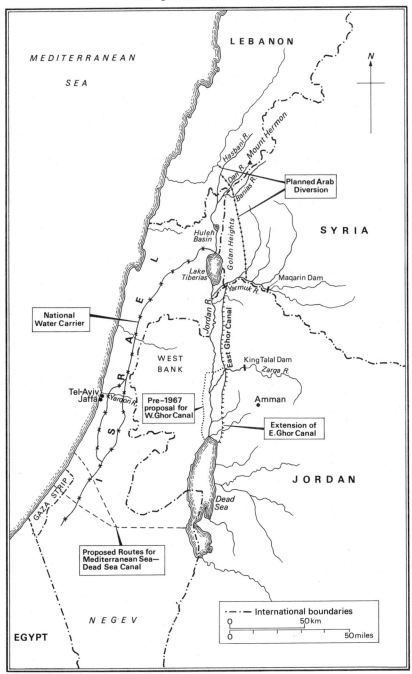

5.1   The Jordan basin: major existing and proposed projects

the Negev desert region.[6] In the initial stages, the system would carry 150–180 mcm of water per annum. In the final stages, aimed for 1970, 320 mcm of Jordan water would be drawn from Lake Tiberias, thereby increasing Israel's water supply by approximately one-fifth. The aims of the scheme were threefold: (1) to coordinate the several existing and planned parts of the country's water distribution system, (2) to extend irrigation further southward in the Negev by augmenting the existing water projects with a flow of water from the Upper Jordan, and (3) to stabilize the water economy of the central coastal plain. To complete its work, Israel sought funding from the United States, and argued that as in the case of Jordan's East Ghor Canal project, the National Water Carrier scheme remained within the limits of the Johnston stipulations.[7]

In June 1959, the Government of Israel publicized its plans to pump fresh water from Lake Tiberias and transport it southward, outside the Jordan basin.[8] The Arab states, and especially those directly concerned, reacted vociferously to this project. They perceived it as a violation of the rights of the Arab riparians and of those living within the basin, a violation of international law, and a profound threat to the security and survival of the Arab states. After a lull of almost four years, since the breakdown of the Johnston mission, the issues which had plagued water development in the Jordan basin prior to and during Johnston's efforts resurfaced and were sharpened. By 1967, the Arab states and Israel were at war. The Jordan waters question had exacerbated the tensions in the region that eventually led to military confrontation and a radical transformation of the geopolitical map of the central Middle East.

The beginning of Arab summitry

Soon after details of Israel's National Water Carrier project became known, the Arab League Council revived the Technical Committee that had been formed during the Johnston mission, and mandated it to study the project and recommend a course of action.[9] Despite Arab protests, Israel was determined to implement the scheme: Moshe Dayan, then Chief-of-Staff and *Mapai* candidate to the fourth *Knesset* (Israel's Parliament), announced in October 1959 that the next government would divert the Jordan waters to the Negev, with or without Arab agreement. Levi Eshkol, designated Minister of Finance in the new government, declared that the diversion had become a "top priority project"; its first stage would be completed by 1964.[10]

The Kingdom of Jordan, most dependent of the Arab riparians on the waters of the Jordan River and most likely to suffer from a depletion of fresh water in Lake Tiberias, made a strong plea for concerted action to prevent the execution of the Israeli project. Two possible responses were put forward and deliberated by the Arab states: (1) divert the Hasbani and Banias headwaters northward into Lebanon and Syria, to obstruct their access to Israel, and/or (2) take military measures to deny Israel Upper Jordan water and thereby, provoke a confrontation. Egypt, Jordan, and Lebanon supported the first proposal.[11] The Syrian Bᶜath Party, which opposed the Arab diversion scheme as an evasion of the "duty" to fight Israel in order to recover Palestine, advocated the second. No other Arab state espoused the military response.

In November 1960, the Technical Committee submitted a proposal to the Arab League. It called for the diversion of the Hasbani inside Lebanon, the channelling of its surplus waters to the Banias in Syria, and the diversion of the surplus waters of the Banias to the Yarmouk for the benefit of Jordan (see map 5.2). The Arab League adopted the plan. The Syrian Bᶜath Party attacked it as a demonstration of cowardice. Israel's Foreign Minister Golda Meir warned that any move by the Arab countries to divert the headwaters of the Jordan River would constitute "an outright attack on one of Israel's means of livelihood"; it would be regarded as "a threat to peace."[12]

Despite the fact that the Arab League had adopted the diversion plan, the matter remained at an impasse until 1964. For four years, the Arab states, both within and without the Arab League framework, debated the question of an appropriate response to the National Water Carrier. Numerous meetings were convened, a variety of resolutions were passed and threats voiced to frustrate Israel's plans, either by diversion or by force of arms. There was agreement on the injurious effects the water project would have on the Arabs.[13] In the economic sphere, agricultural development in Jordan would suffer considerably. By diverting water from the Upper Jordan River, Lake Tiberias would be denied the addition of fresh water necessary to reduce its salt content. Hence, water flowing out of the lake into the Lower Jordan to irrigate the Valley lands would remain too saline for use. From a legal and political point of view, as well, the project was unacceptable. First, by diverting water outside the basin before the needs of the entire basin had been met, the National Water Carrier project was a violation of international law and the rights of the inhabitants of the basin.[14] Second, the diversion contravened the rights of the Arabs, in whose territory the Jordan River originated. Finally, it represented a profound security threat; by virtue of developing the Negev desert region, the National Water Carrier would enhance Israel's economic potential and industrial power, and would make possible the absorption of far greater numbers of Jewish immigrants. The result would be a stronger state in economic, military, and demographic terms. Not only was a strong enemy state, in and of itself, a threat to the

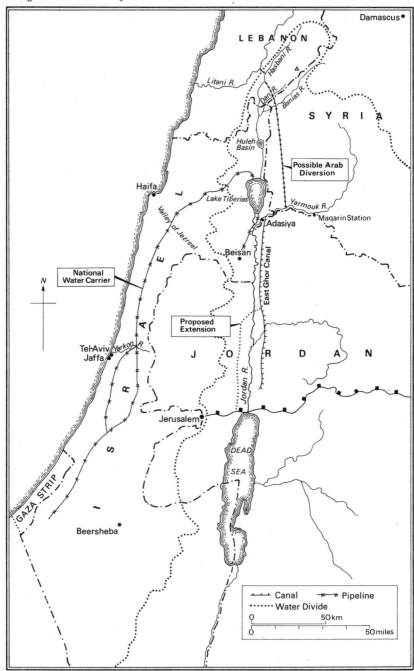

5.2   The Jordan basin: unilateral development schemes by Israel and Jordan

security of the Arabs, but also, it was assumed that a stronger Israel would be favorably disposed to territorial expansion.[15]

While they concurred on the evils of the National Water Carrier project, Arab leaders could not agree on a uniform strategy to adopt. Their indecisiveness reflected prevailing inter-Arab rivalries. Instead of precipitating unified action, the Jordan waters issue added fuel to the friction among Arab regimes. Rather than endorse and implement an effective pan-Arab policy to defend their avowed interests, Arab leaders engaged in mutual recriminations and biting invective concerning weakness in the face of Israel's threat to carry Jordan waters southward and cowardice with regard to the "Palestine Question."[16] The outcome, at least until the mid-1960s, was that none of the decisions, resolutions, or threats were put into effect.

In January 1961, the Government of Israel announced that it had given a big financial boost to the National Water Carrier project so that the first stage could be completed by 1964.[17] In April, the Council of the Arab Chiefs-of-Staff met and made recommendations to the Arab League, based on its assessment of the distribution of power in the region: (1) the Arab armies should be built up so that they could eventually take unified action against Israel, (2) a joint general command of the forces of the Arab states should be formed without further delay, and (3) the Jordan headwaters should be diverted.[18] The Defence Council of the Arab League endorsed these recommendations, ratified the Arab diversion plan, and agreed to the use of force to prevent Israel from transporting Upper Jordan waters southward.[19] Nonetheless, the debate over the two conflicting positions – immediate war, or its deferral – continued unresolved.

ʿAbd al-Nasir tried to convince the other Arab leaders that the time was not ripe to fight Israel. He knew from President Kennedy that the United States would support Israel if the Arabs launched an attack because of its water project.[20] Nor could the Arabs count on Russian support. Moreover, he insisted that the Arab states were not yet strong enough to face the enemy in a military confrontation. The Egyptian President had no intention of abandoning the idea of fighting Israel, but he would act upon it only when he felt certain that the Arabs were ready, and not before.[21]

As the first stage of the National Water Carrier neared completion and the transfer of water to the Negev was imminent, President Nasir, challenged by the persistent Syrian (and Jordanian) accusations of laxity, called a summit conference of the Arab Kings and Heads of State. At this first in a series of conferences, in Cairo, from 13 to 17 January 1964, Arab leaders sought to breach the stalemate by adopting a uniform position and policy on the Jordan waters question. Inter-Arab disputes – among them, the acrimonious break-up of the Syria–Egypt union in 1961 – had been preventing the Arab regimes from effectively resisting what they referred to as "aggressive expansionist ambitions threatening all Arabs alike."[22]

According to the Secretary-General of the Arab League, ʿAbd al-Khaliq Hassunah, the summit conference was a success. It had "purified the Arab atmosphere" and demonstrated Arab solidarity. Moreover, several important resolutions were passed.[23] Most significant among them were those that outlined practical measures to resist "the existing Zionist danger."

Although the conference proceedings remained secret, it became known that several matters had been decided upon. First, a plan to divert the Jordan headwaters would be implemented. To that end, a special fund and department would be set up at the Arab League to supervise the plan, and a budget of $17·5 million would be allocated for its execution. A committee of experts would be formed, the Authority to Exploit the Waters of the Jordan River and its Tributaries, and charged with designing and supervising the construction of a number of engineering works in Lebanon, Syria, and Jordan, and later, with exploiting the waters of the Jordan tributaries in the Arab states.[24] It was expected that the diversion would be operational within eighteen months. Second, a joint Arab military command would be established under Egyptian leadership to defend the diversion works from possible (Israeli) aggression. The Arab states would contribute a sum of $42 million to set up the unified command and reinforce the armies of Jordan, Lebanon, and Syria. Third, the Arab leaders pledged to end inter-Arab differences and consolidate their relations. Moreover, they agreed to organize their political and economic affairs with other states in the international community on the basis of the attitude those states adopted to the Jordan waters issue and to the "Palestine Question," in general.[25]

It soon became clear, however, that the show of strength and solidarity, trumpeted by the Arab League and the media services of the Arab states, was illusory. Syria was disappointed with the decisions taken at the conference. The regime doubted that the application of the resolutions would foil "the Zionist project," which posed "a threat to the very existence of the Arabs as a nation." It wanted a decisive war with Israel.[26] To this end, it called upon the Arab governments to act immediately to establish and support a joint military command. As far as the Syrian leadership was concerned, "this command [is] the effective means of destroying the plot to rob the Arab waters. It is the means capable of liberating the usurped homeland from the colonialist Zionist occupation."

The reaction of the Israeli press to the first summit varied with regard to political persuasion, but for the most part, there was a consensus on three points. First, no matter the concrete results of the conference, the fact that it had taken place and that several resolutions had been accepted unanimously constituted a victory for Nasir's initiative.[27] Second, it was obvious that the

Arabs were still united in their hatred of Israel. The resolutions indicated that they were simply waiting for the day when they would be ready to fight Israel. Hence, the decision not to go to war was *not* an expression of the desire for peace.[28] Third, Syria posed the greatest concern, since it was not satisfied with the outcome of the conference and had reserved for itself freedom of action. Moreover, it was not convinced, as were the other Arab states, that it could not face Israel in a military confrontation. Israel was wary of Syrian moves that could drag other Arab states into a war.[29]

The Israeli Premier and Defence Minister, Levi Eshkol, announced that his country would resist "unilateral and illegal steps" by the Arab states, and would act to safeguard its "vital rights."[30] Israel would pump from Lake Tiberias within the limits of the quantities allotted to it under the Johnston Plan. Israel had full right to carry out its project in accordance with principles of international law. Furthermore, the Arab riparian states were each drawing water from the Jordan system, but they wanted to prevent Israel from drawing its own share. He concluded, saying that "the Arabs' argument is not about water but is an argument which denies Israel's right to exist."[31]

In May, five months after the first Arab summit, Israel began test pumpings through the National Water Carrier's main conduit.[32] The Government announced that it was carrying out military maneuvers around the sites of the project. In response, the Assistant Secretary-General of the Arab League, Sayyid Nawfal, announced that "victory is in the hands of the Arabs, the sole owners of the usurped right. They are bound to carry out their duty, speed up the implementation of their legitimate defensive plan until they achieve its goal..."[33] Syria's reaction to the news was not so fervent. It urged the Arab states, once again, to abandon their idleness and implement the resolutions to resist Israel's plans.[34]

A second Arab summit conference was held, in September 1964 in Alexandria. Its purpose was to chart the next phase of the "struggle." Several important decisions were taken. First, work on the Arab diversion scheme was to begin at the end of the month; contractors were given orders to start on those projects that were ready for execution.[35] Second, and in accordance with the diversion scheme, a dam would be constructed at Mukheiba on the Yarmouk River along the Syria–Jordan border, and would be linked by tunnel to the East Ghor Canal. It would have a storage capacity of 200 mcm of water, which would come from the Yarmouk as well as from the diverted Banias and Hasbani tributaries.[36] Third, aggression against any one Arab country would be considered as aggression against all. Hence, Arab leaders were instructed that as the work on the diversion scheme proceeded, their armed forces should remain in a state of alert, ready to repel attacks.[37] Fourth, the Palestine Liberation Organization (PLO) was established to represent the Palestine Arab people and defend their interests. And a military wing, the Palestine Liberation Army (PLA), was to be formed from among the refugees and would operate under the aegis of the joint Arab command.[38]

Again, official communiques on the summit conference were laudatory. ʿAbd al-Khaliq Hassunah announced that the Arab states had unanimously defined the "national cause" as that of "liberating Palestine from Zionist imperialism." To achieve their final goal, they had committed themselves to pursuing a joint plan of action.[39] Jordan's King Hussein stated that, "a new and important phase has now begun, namely the phase of serious unified work and the determination to achieve clear and defined aims."[40] He expressed the belief that the future would fulfill all Arab aspirations and that the Arab states would remove all obstacles in their path.

Despite public affirmations of confidence, serious differences had emerged in Alexandria. Military preparations and collective action were issues of contention between Egypt and Syria, but also, between Egypt on the one hand, and Jordan, Lebanon, and Syria on the other.[41] The controversy revolved around Nasir's idea to have the forces of the Egyptian-led joint military command stationed in the Arab riparian states, allegedly as a precautionary measure against possible Israeli aggression once work on the diversion had begun. Lebanon, Syria, and Jordan categorically refused to accept Egyptian-led troops on their soil.[42] Rejecting Egyptian attempts to act as a regional hegemon, the Arab riparians were suspicious of Nasir's proposal. But while they did not want to accept foreign troops, nor would they begin work on the diversion until they had received adequate military guarantees.[43]

The other major source of contention was Syria's avowed determination to fight Israel, with no further delay. The Syrian leadership was demanding that a definite date be set for "serious action to recover the usurped homeland."[44] This was truly a curious position, given that Syria insisted that the diversionary works within its territory required military protection from outside. Nonetheless, the regime was pressing for war. And the media services asserted that, "the [Syrian] Arab masses today feel that they are capable of fighting the battle and winning victory..."[45]

Both issues – the Egyptian request and the Syrian demand – were rejected by the second summit conference. However, they continued to be sources of dispute among the rival Arab states and exposed the myth of Arab unity.

Arab unity breaks down

Within six weeks of the commencement of work on the Arab diversion project, both Syrian and Israeli radio reported a border clash between the two countries. Each side accused the other of initiating the confrontation.[46] Israel announced that Syria's pretext was the building of a road on a strip of land in contested territory in the region of the Dan River, two metres from the Israel–Syria border. Syria maintained that Israel's pretext was the work on the diversion scheme, but more importantly, fear of Syria's commitment and tenacity. Whatever the truth of the matter, the clash was the first in a series of military responses to rival water projects and conflicting political–economic aims and interests.

With regard to the utilization of the Jordan waters, threats and counter-threats among the basin states were a recurrent theme during this period. Israel's Premier Levi Eshkol stated that, "water is a question of life for Israel." Hence, any attempt to prevent Israel from using the part of the Jordan River waters due to it in accordance with the Unified Plan would be considered a violation, not simply of the country's borders, but of its right to exist.[47] He warned his Arab neighbors not to be drawn into a dangerous adventure over the Jordan system, for "Israel would act to ensure that the waters continue to flow" into its territory. While tampering with the country's water supply could incite a military showdown, Israel felt confident of its power resources: it could "rely on the strength of its defence forces" and on the promises made by the United States to support it on the water question.[48]

Cairo radio scoffed at Eshkol's statements: "Israel's threats are vain and hollow... because in the calculations governing the balance of power in the Middle East, Israel does not count as a Power, and because, in the calculations governing the entities of the area, Israel does not count as an entity." Moreover, even if Israel were to try to obstruct the implementation of the Arab projects, "the Arab nation... has drawn up... plans capable of securing victory against the Israeli conspiracies of theft and aggression."[49] The Arabs were determined, "to deprive the snake of Arab blood which it has sucked."[50] At the end of December 1964, Damascus announced that the diversion of water from the Hasbani tributary in Lebanon to the Banias in Syria had just begun.[51]

Throughout the first half of 1965, the Arab diversion was the cardinal political issue of inter-state relations in the Middle East. In keeping with its policy to consolidate its military strength in an effort to deter the Arab regimes, Israel made important purchases of arms from Europe and the United States. Arab statesmen continued to hold conferences in which they reviewed the achievements of past meetings and reaffirmed earlier decisions.[52] And the media services continued to expound Arab steadfastness and determination, unity and solidarity, conviction and fearlessness.[53]

Clashes along the Israel–Syria border continued during the spring and summer months. Each time the scenario was the same. Israel accused Syria of

125

having fired on Israelis working near the Dan springs, southeast of the Bnot Ya῾acov bridge. And Syria charged that Israeli forces had hit Syrian workers and equipment at the site of the headwaters diversion project. By the third clash, in August, tensions had escalated to the point that both sides brought in their air forces.[54]

Military confrontation in the diversion area had two immediate effects. First, the ruling B῾ath Party in Syria was prompted to accuse the Arabs, once again, of laxness in the face of the "Israeli challenge."[55] It appeared that the plans to deny Israel the waters of the Upper Jordan River and repel aggression had been shelved. And Syria was left alone, without the backing of the joint Arab commitments and without the protection of a unified command. The regime called on the Arab states to activate the decisions taken at the summit conferences. Second, the clashes reawakened the Arab debate between those in favor and those against immediate war.

῾Abd al-Nasir's response to the B῾athis' proddings was candid and firm. First, the unified command could not carry out its duties to the full, because "the Arab countries [are] afraid of one another" and would not allow inter-Arab military forces to enter their territories to defend them in time of need.[56] More specifically, he said, Egypt had been ready to send aircraft to Syria when Israel opened fire on the worksite in May, but Damascus would not provide an airbase. Second, the suggestion to wage war against Israel was sheer folly: "how can we talk about attacking when we are unable to defend ourselves?"[57] The Syrian regime could not even protect a few of its tractors from Israeli gunfire, yet it was clamoring for the elimination of the enemy state and seemed to be convinced that it was capable of such a feat. Nasir accused the B῾ath Party of having "reduced the liberation of Palestine to claptrap and bravado."[58]

But the bitter rivalry between Nasir and the Syrian B῾ath was not the only fissure in the unified Arab front. Other serious rifts had developed, beginning with Tunisian President Habib Bourguiba's statement in the spring of 1965, calling for recognition of, negotiations and peaceful coexistence with the State of Israel. Because of the collective Arab position asserting the illegitimacy and hence, non-recognition of the Jewish state, Bourguiba's proposal was perceived as treason. Moreover, it defied and counteracted Arab assertions of unity and solidarity. At a meeting in April, the representatives of the Arab Kings and Presidents unanimously agreed to "reject any call for recognition, peace or coexistence with regard to Israel which, with the help of imperialism, has seized a part of the Arab homeland and expelled its people..."[59] Bourguiba was isolated. A vindictive slander campaign began between Egypt and Tunisia, and soon after, between Syria and Tunisia as well.

The Bourguiba affair triggered other latent inter-Arab differences. For one, open hostility emerged between the Palestine Liberation Organization and the Jordanian regime. Ahmed al-Shuqayri, the leader of the PLO, publicly accused the Kingdom – the host country of the largest number of refugees – of doing nothing concrete in support of the Palestine Arabs.[60] Instead, he charged the regime with trying to dominate the PLO and weaken the Palestinians. Activities which the Organization had intended to carry out were prohibited, the Palestinians were refused military training, and the front-line villages could not be armed. For al-Shuqayri, the most closely implicated Arab state was aloof to the "Palestine Question" and the role of the PLO. King Hussein, however, was responding to perceived structural political threats. He feared the growing strength and popularity of the PLO in Jordanian territory. Besides, he knew that the presence of organized, politicized, and armed Palestinians precipitated clashes along the already troublesome western frontier.[61]

As for border incidents during this period, they increased in number and intensity. In addition to ongoing clashes between Israel and Syria, there were confrontations along the Israel–Jordan frontier. More often than not, water installations were targets of attack. Israel radio announced that there had been several attempts to sabotage the National Water Carrier system.[62] It was believed that the raids were carried out by members of *al-Fatah*, a military wing of the PLO, operating from bases inside Jordan. The Jordanian government had been asked repeatedly to take measures to halt the incursions and prevent the "establishment of bases and the training of terrorists" on its territory. But since infiltrations had recurred, the Government of Israel was retaliating. Thus, it aimed to make clear to its neighbors that, "infiltrators and saboteurs [will] not be permitted to cross the border";[63] "there would be no calm on the Jordanian side as long as there was no calm on the Israeli side."[64] Despite stern warnings and swift retaliations, tension continued to reign along the armistice lines.

Whither the diversion scheme?

By mid-summer, there were rumors that work had stopped at the diversion site in Syria. And a Beirut newspaper reported that the Lebanese government had halted the diversionary work in its country, as well, because the funds allocated for that purpose had run out.[65] It intimated that the same was true in both Jordan and Syria. Amman radio, however, insisted that work on the Mukheiba dam would begin in August.[66] One month later, representatives of the Arab Kings and Presidents met for a third summit conference.

Again, eulogistic commentaries on the conference were aired by the media services of Arab states. Not only had the previous resolutions been reaffirmed, but also, the controversial issues of military protection for the diversion operations and the deployment of the joint forces had apparently been settled.[67] Moreover, short- and long-term plans to confront Israel and eventually liberate Palestine had been agreed upon. Cairo radio was optimistic: "with all this in mind, we can conclude that the rifts and contradictions which have appeared ... in the Arab world recently ... have not been able to hamper the river diversion plans or smother the spirit of Arab summits."[68] Contrary to official declarations, it was soon confirmed by less sanguine sources that, in fact, diversionary work had ceased. Hassanein Haykal announced that the Syrian regime, demonstrating a lack of "psychological readiness," abandoned the project after it had had to face Israel "in small local skirmishes."[69] Levi Eshkol asserted that, "with remarkable firmness and ability, the Israel Defence Forces foiled the beginning of the water diversion scheme in the neighboring countries ..."[70]

Furthermore, the question of military deployment had not been resolved satisfactorily. According to both Haykal and Shuqayri, Jordan opposed the entry of Iraqi and Saudi troops onto its soil, and the Government of Lebanon did likewise with regard to Syrian troops. The diversion sites remained unprotected.[71] Amman protested vehemently against these allegations. King Hussein announced that work on the Mukheiba dam was underway and that the Jordanian army was "fully prepared to protect the installations ... with their blood and souls."[72] Prime Minister Wasfi al-Tal added that, if the diversion should require protection by "our Arab brothers," the joint command was authorized to move units to any place it saw fit.[73] The truth of the matter was that the Arab diversion scheme had fallen by the wayside; inter-Arab issues were proving to be more important than water issues or, more correctly, larger Arab–Israeli issues.

Although inter-Arab relations were turbulent and Arab assertions confusing, the Israeli leadership perceived that war was imminent. High-ranking Government officials expressed the belief that Arab leaders were preparing to fight Israel, even if at times, they adopted public postures of restraint.[74] The aim was to camouflage their real intentions. This being the case, Israel would continue to consolidate its military strength in an effort to deter confrontation. But if necessary, stated Eshkol, "we shall not hesitate ... to defend our State, our citizens, our borders, and the sources of our life."[75] As tensions in the region escalated throughout the autumn of 1965 and the winter of 1966, this perception gained in importance. In the spring, Eshkol announced that in anticipation of "serious military tests," his government was doing everything possible to strengthen the fighting capacity of its Defence Forces (IDF) and fill the gaps that still existed in its arms supply.[76] The Israeli Premier did not fail to add, however, that his country's principal aim in the region remained the advancement of peace.

Peace, however, was not on the agenda. During the winter of 1966, there was a major American arms sale to Israel. The United States Government insisted, to the disbelief of the Arab states, that its intention was to maintain a power balance in the Middle East.[77] Then in February, there was a *coup d'état* in Syria. The Bᶜathi government of Amin al-Hafez was overthrown by Salah Jadid and the dissenting wing of the Bᶜath Party. The new regime promised to be more radical in its positions and policies. It said little of Arab unity and much of revolution, vilified Arab conservatives and moderates unsparingly, and stepped up border tension with Israel.[78]

By spring, Syria and Jordan were engaged in a fierce mudslinging campaign. The Bᶜathi government accused the "agent Jordanian reactionaries" of cooperating with Israel against Syria by massing troops along Syria's southern border, while Israel did likewise along the southwestern front.[79] Amman retorted that Damascus was guilty of collaborating with the enemy. It denounced the new Syrian regime as "a gang of saboteurs and terrorists who cloaked their Marxist theories with national slogans."[80] The semblance of Arab unity was rapidly foundering.

As if to aggravate an already perverse situation, King Faysal of Saudi Arabia, supported by Jordan's King Hussein and supposedly, the United States as well, began to promote the idea of establishing an Islamic Pact of all Muslim states. The avowed aim was to bring the countries together, regardless of their political systems, in a solidarity conference at Mecca, with more permanent arrangements to follow.[81] However, because of Faysal's courtship of the more conservative regimes and his acceptance of American arms and the establishment of British military bases, Nasir believed that the Saudi monarch had important undeclared objectives: (1) to have the more radical states outnumbered in the Pact, in an effort to resist the "evils of socialist revolution and Soviet influence," and (2) to restore foreign involvement and "protection" in the region, by placing the Arab countries within the spheres of imperialist influence. For Nasir and his followers, all this was reminiscent of the Eisenhower Doctrine and Baghdad Pact. Moreover, by serving the interests of Britain and the United States rather than Arab unity, it made a mockery of the "Palestine Question" – the "first Arab question."[82] In Nasir's view, the idea had to be opposed outright.

In this atmosphere of suspicion, polarization, and chicanery, the Egyptian leader saw no point to the convocation of a fourth summit conference, due to be held in Algeria in September 1966. Instead of achieving Arab unity "for the sake of Palestine," all that the summit conferences had achieved thus far was "the unity of reaction against the Arab revolutionary forces and the unity of reaction with colonialism."[83] Nasir announced that he would not attend the meeting, and suggested that it be postponed until there could be "some sort of coexistence" among the Arab regimes, especially when matters were of mutual concern.

In response to Nasir's call, the Saudi Government stated that it would freeze all its commitments to the organizations formed by the conferences until the fourth summit was held.[84] Jordan followed suit. By the beginning of 1967, the two monarchies were boycotting the Authority for the Jordan Headwaters, the Palestine Liberation Organization, and the Unified Military Command.

As the objective situation deteriorated, the mudslinging between the "revolutionaries" and "reactionaries" intensified: Egypt, the PLO, and Syria versus Saudi Arabia and Jordan. Moreover, clashes between Israel and Syria were stepped up. In mid-July (1966), Israel's air force hit the diversion works on the Banias–Yarmouk canal in Syria, near the northern shore of Lake Tiberias.[85] An air battle ensued. Israel reported that the raid was in retaliation for several sabotage operations in which its civilians had been wounded, and property and equipment damaged.[86] The Government believed that the operations had been conducted by Palestinian *fedaʾiyin*, proceeding from Syrian territory. One month later, there was a second dogfight, this time, over Lake Tiberias.[87] Two Syrian planes were shot down. The Syrian Foreign Ministry accused Israel of using *fedaʾiyin* incursions as an excuse to justify a pre-planned, large-scale aggression.[88] But *al-Thawrah*, the Bʿath press, expressed the view that Israeli attacks were prompted by the perception of threat; they were proof that Syria had become "a real strategic danger to imperialist interests, the Zionist base and the agent reaction."[89] Indeed, it was only a matter of time before Syria would eliminate Israel, as it had resolved, in a "decisive, popular war."

Arif's Iraq and Bourguiba's Tunisia also expressed the view that the Israeli raids had been premeditated.[90] They were part of a military plan to destroy the work-in-progress on the Jordan tributaries and launch a surprise war on the unprepared Arabs. The two regimes independently urged the Arab states to end their differences, from which only Israel benefited, and face the common enemy together. ʿAbd al-Nasir announced that he was prepared to coordinate with the Syrian Government, so that they could "stand in the face of aggression as one front."[91] In November, the two regimes signed a Mutual Defence Pact.[92]

Levi Eshkol, in a speech before the Knesset, warned Syria that if acts of sabotage and murder in Israeli territory continued, his country "would act to curb them" and would "choose the suitable time and means" to do so, "in accordance with its right to self defence."[93] He stated that the gravity of the recent acts of sabotage justified direct military action against Syria. But for the time being, Israel would exercise restraint and use diplomatic channels to prevent an escalation of tensions in the region. A few days later, however, he called on settlers in the border zone "to increase their preparedness."[94]

In November, Israeli forces launched a fierce attack on villages in the

Hebron district of the West Bank, ostensibly in retaliation for infiltrations from Jordan.[95] The raid prompted violent demonstrations on the West Bank, demanding an end to the Hashemite regime, which had consistently refused to arm the inhabitants of front-line villages and support the PLO. The Jordanian government responded with massive arrests and the forced shut-down of PLO offices. Egypt and Syria lashed out at the "agent regime" in Amman, accusing it of collusion with Zionism and imperialism, against the "Arab nation."[96] They were convinced that King Hussein was cooperating surreptitiously with Israel in an effort to liquidate the *fedaʾiyin*. The slander campaign between the "revolutionaries" and the "reactionaries" continued into the new year.

In the winter of 1967, the Jordanian government announced that work on the nearly forgotten Mukheiba Dam project was proceeding.[97] Soon after, the Authority for the Exploitation of the Waters of the Jordan River and Tributaries made it known that the diversion scheme was not progressing as scheduled.[98] Work had started on various parts of the project and then came to a standstill. Other parts had not begun at all. Moreover, financial obligations had not been met.

In April, tensions erupted along the Israel–Syria border, once again. Syria fired on Israelis cultivating land in contested territory in the demilitarized zone, and shelled border settlements. Israel downed six Syrian MiG fighters.[99] Levi Eshkol announced that by retaliating, his country was exercising its right and duty to defend itself against repeated attempts to violate its sovereignty. He warned the Syrian leaders that "the miscalculation they were making regarding the extent of [our] patience was very dangerous for them."[100]

Jordan accused Egypt and the Unified Arab Command of having abandoned Syria. Amman taunted the Egyptian leader, saying that his non-response was proof of the emptiness of his declarations.[101] For his part, Nasir announced that despite the military alliance, he was not in a position to defend Syria, since the latter continued to refuse to have Egyptian planes stationed on its soil. Nasir could not support Syria in an air clash with Israel from Egyptian territory.[102]

Throughout April, there were repeated complaints to the Mixed Armistice Commission of cross-border violations. Israel accused Syria of firing on settlements in the DMZ, and Syria accused Israel of crossing the armistice lines. At the end of the month, a water pumping station in northern Israel was destroyed in what was assumed to be another *fedaʾiyin* operation.[103] Again, Eshkol issued a stern warning: "Israel views with extreme gravity the recent acts of sabotage in its territory and, if there is no way out, will be forced to take suitable retaliatory measures against the sabotage nests ... "[104]

The situation along the Israel–Syria armistice lines remained volatile, and skirmishes continued. By mid-May, the Syrian government announced that enemy troops were concentrating along its southwestern border. The Egyptian leadership declared a state of emergency for its armed forces.[105] Cairo radio, somewhat less sensitive to the gravity of the situation and sounding a bit like its Syrian counterpart, made the following statement: "We challenge you, Eshkol, to try all your weapons. Put them to the test; they will spell Israel's death and annihilation."[106]

For Damascus as for Cairo, the successive provocative statements made by Israeli officials laid bare the intention to attack Syria, and this intention was confirmed by Soviet intelligence reports.[107] Nonetheless, the Bᶜathi regime responded confidently that the enemy's plans were doomed, because "the revolutionary front is impregnable."[108] Damascus radio invited Israel to choose the time for its own defeat.[109]

In what later proved to be a decisive move in the unfolding of events, ᶜAbd al-Nasir demanded, on 18 May 1967, the immediate and total evacuation of the United Nations Emergency Forces stationed in the Sinai Peninsula. Then, expecting this would deter Israel from launching a punitive attack on Syria, he had the Egyptian army take up positions in the Sinai and along the border with Israel. Within a few days of this threatening move, Nasir, responding to the taunts and challenges of the Hashemite regime in Jordan, announced that he was closing the Straits of Tiran to Israeli ships and to all ships carrying strategic cargo to Israel. Tel-Aviv responded, saying that any interference with the freedom of shipping in the Gulf of Eilat and in the Straits constituted an act of aggression against Israel; and Nasir's aggression "endangers Israel's existence."[110]

At the end of May, Jordan and Egypt signed a defence pact, and Jordan gave permission for Iraqi and Saudi troops to enter its territory. The Israeli government affirmed that it would intervene if the *status quo* were violated by the entry of troops into Jordan: "Along with ᶜAbd al-Nasir's aggression in the south, this step will leave no alternative for Israel..."[111]

By 5 June, fierce fighting broke out between Egyptian and Israeli forces. Within no time, all states of the central Middle East were involved in this, the third Arab–Israel war.[112]

Cognitive dynamics

The turn of events in the Middle East during the 1960s dramatizes once again the symbolic character of Palestine/Israel, and the importance of that symbol to the states in the region and to their interactions. The conflict of interests that developed as a result of rival claims to the land and resources of Palestine/Israel functioned both as a mechanism regulating inter-state relations and as a significant part of the ideological content of the parties. It acted as a principal agent for defining national identity and social solidarity on the one hand, and images of the enemy on the other.

Moreover, the Jordan waters crisis elucidates the geopolitical and security concerns of the Arab states and Israel, and how those concerns were brought to the fore by (the possibility of) man-made structural changes to the natural environment; changes which could affect power resources, strategic advantage, and regional political patterns. Because of the scarcity of water resources in the central Middle East, water augmentation systems were essential for enhancing the economic and political capabilities of states. But as political relations in the general region were conflictual, improved capabilities would strain them yet further. Israel's National Water Carrier project and the Arabs' diversion scheme are cases in point. Not only did they encapsulate the protracted conflict, but also, they foreshadowed significant changes to power relations between adversaries.[113] Hence, each party perceived the rival scheme as a profound security threat. The Arabs referred to the National Water Carrier as a project which was "no less dangerous than the establishment of Israel in 1948"; it represented "aggressive expansionist interests" and was a "threat to the very existence of the Arabs as a nation."[114] Israeli Government officials spoke of the possible consequences of the Arabs' project in hyperbolic terms, drawing analogies between water and life-blood. In essence, the diversion scheme did not concern water resources; it was a project to "deny Israel's right to exist."[115] Because the projects were perceived as representations of the hostile aims of the enemy, both were treated as military targets.[116]

To understand the regional behavior of the Arab states and Israel during the period leading up to the 1967 War, we must first analyze the character of inter-state relations. We begin with a brief examination of inter-Arab relations. Then, we take a closer look at the ways in which state actors, both Arab and Israeli, perceived their environment. As noted in chapter 2, it is on the basis of the actor's image of his milieu that decisions are formulated and policy implemented. Through systematic textual analysis of speeches, editorials, and radio broadcasts from the period under review, we sketch the psychological environment in the central Middle East by highlighting perceptions of aims and interest, legitimacy, threat, and relative power, all in relation to the security concerns of the states in question. Finally, we analyze the outcomes of regional behavior, this time with reference to the operational environment, the actual situation in which policy has been executed. We note that the success or failure of policy is contingent upon a realistic assessment of the environment.

Central to any discussion of inter-Arab relations is the political ideal of Arab unity: the common assumption among Arabs that they constitute a single nation that ought to be united.[117] For whatever reasons, the myth of single-nationhood has constituted a principal binding agent of the Arab states. It is to this ideal that Arab regimes have felt they must express loyalty. Moreover, the idea of Arab unity has taken on the aura of a sacred symbol or ritual. Thus, violation of the idea is taboo; it is tantamount to apostasy, treason, and the like. While to uphold it connotes devotion, rectitude, honor, and steadfastness. Among the various concerns of the pan-Arab ideology that have demanded solidarity is the unresolved "Question of Palestine." A unified and uncompromising attitude toward the State of Israel has been required of all true members of the "Arab Nation."[118]

Another important element that colored inter-Arab relations in the decade leading up to the 1967 War was the issue of Egyptian leadership. Because of its superior power resources – in terms of human capital, idea-of-the-state, institutional structure, and military capacity – Egypt had consistently conducted itself as a regional great power, with influence and interests throughout the area. However, the pursuit of its hegemonic position created tensions between it and other rising powers: Saudi Arabia, because of its oil wealth and favorable relations with the West, and to a lesser extent, Syria after 1963, because of the ideology of Bʿathism, which posed as a more radical alternative to Nasir's "Arab Socialism." In essence, inter-Arab rivalries were challenges to, or attempts to challenge, the regional hegemony of Egypt and ʿAbd al-Nasir. The ritually symbolic "Question of Palestine" played a secondary, albeit important, role in these rivalries. It functioned, more-or-less, as a propagandistic symbol, the loyalty to which rival Arab states competed over in their efforts to appear the most courageous, the most committed. In an atmosphere provided by the pan-Arab idea, mistrusting Arab states exploited opportunities to embarrass their rivals on issues directly or indirectly linked to Palestine. One of the most significant rivalries of the period, that between Egypt and Syria, illustrates these dynamics.

Between 1961 and 1966, the Syrian leadership wavered between two positions: challenging Egypt's hegemony and castigating Nasir and his political influence on the one hand, and emulating his policies and seeking his protection on the other. The traditional wing of the Bʿath Party, in power from 1963 to 1966, preached the idea of Arab unity and especially, unity among socialist regimes. ʿAbd Al-Nasir used the formula of Arab unity, as well, and in part because of his dominant position in the region, he was able to use it more effectively than did the Bʿath. Disheartened, the Syrian regime reacted by trying consistently to outdo Nasir in militancy on nationalist and "revolutionary" issues. It did not have much success. However, the new regime of "radical" Bʿathis (1966–) "was free of the 'unity complex' of its predecessors and felt no embarrassment over the fact that they were not prepared to accept Egyptian leadership. They said little of Arab unity, and much of revolution. They intensified the leftist postures of the previous regime, redoubling its castigation of the Arab conservatives and moderates and stepping up border tension with Israel."[119] The combination of the Bᶜath Party's reckless behavior and Nasir's attempts to act as a regional hegemon drew the Arabs into a very costly war with Israel.

Despite the demands of Arab unity, the Arab states, in fact, were not unified in their attitude on policy toward Israel. Well into the Jordan waters crisis, there were lengthy debates among Arab leaders on whether to instigate a military confrontation as advocated by Syria, or rather, follow Nasir's advice and build up their armed forces in preparation for war at some later date. With regard to Israel's National Water Carrier, there was a consensus that the project should be brought to a halt because of its economic and political ramifications to the detriment of the Arabs. A diversion scheme was conceived to impair Israel's objectives in water development. The Syrian leadership, however, did not believe that diverting the Jordan headwaters was sufficient to thwart Israel's intentions. In its official discourse, at least, the regime was determined to fight the enemy and put a final halt to "Zionist aggression." In an interview in 1965, Major-General Amin al-Hafiz, the head of Syria's National Revolutionary Command Council, expressed the official position of his government thus:

Our target is Israel as a State. We accept nothing short of the removal of its existence which is a threat to the Arab homeland from the Gulf to the Ocean...We wish the others were as serious as we are when it comes to the question of Palestine.[120]

One year later, as the situation in the region was deteriorating rapidly, the Bᶜath Party reiterated its stance: "we have very simply and clearly resolved...to destroy Israel with a decisive popular war."[121]

ᶜAbd al-Nasir was also hostile to the presence of a Jewish state in Palestine, but at least until May 1967, he was far more prudent than the Bᶜathis in his attitude and assessment of relative capabilities in the region. He maintained that the Arabs' final aim was "the liberation of Palestine from Zionist imperialism" and the repatriation of the Palestine Arabs. Nonetheless, he was convinced that the Arab states were not strong enough to face Israel militarily.[122] He suggested that the Arabs had to first build up their armed forces so that they could initiate a confrontation and win. Furthermore, he felt that a war for the liberation of Palestine was unthinkable as long as the Arab states were divided.

Throughout the period under review, the Arab states could not enunciate a defined objective, consistent with their capabilities and representative of a collective interest. Largely because of their own internal divisions, they were unable to decide whether their policy should aim at destroying the State of Israel or simply at containing it. In the absence of more substantive forms of policy, the Arab leaders often resorted to sentiment or simplistic propaganda, rather than unified, reasoned strategy.

Nonetheless, the Government of Israel claimed to be very concerned about Arab unity, the formation of an Arab Joint Command and the Palestine Liberation Organization, ʿAbd al-Nasir's influence, and Syria's hard-line position. It was convinced that Arab declarations were sincere; the Arab states were bent on Israel's destruction. Government officials pointed to a three-pronged Arab strategy against the Jewish state: (1) building a military force, (2) conducting an international campaign to harm Israel's prestige and position, and (3) implementing a program aimed at sabotaging Israel's development through boycotts, theft of water, and other similar measures.[123] Israel was not relieved by the majority decision at the first Arab summit conference not to wage war. The Arabs were merely trying to play for time in order to build up their fighting capacity in preparation for total war. Despite their internal bickerings, the Arab states were united in their hatred of Israel.[124] The only significant difference among them was that the Syrian regime, which by 1966 had assumed the role of spearhead in the campaign against Israel, believed that war should be declared immediately.

The fear that Israel's continued survival was threatened – what Michael Brecher has referred to as the Holocaust syndrome[125] – was expressed time and again during the period under review. The object of fear was, primarily, the President of Egypt. Unlike the Syrian Heads of State, ʿAbd al-Nasir was a recognized, respected, and highly influential *zaʿim* – a true leader in the Arab world, backed by a relatively strong state with substantial power resources. Moreover, he had a reputation for getting things done. In contrast, Syria was in a more-or-less constant state of internal political and economic turmoil. It did behave provocatively, but because of its relatively poor resource base and weak leadership, it could not back up its threats effectively. Hence, it was not as great a source of concern to Israel until the more radical Bʿathis seized power in 1966, costly sabotage operations across the Israel–Syria border were stepped up, and Nasir came to the regime's defence.

The perception of threat from a hostile environment was so acute that the Israeli leadership spoke in terms of a possible resurgence of the likes of Nazism. In May 1963, well before the beginning of Arab summitry, Prime Minister David Ben-Gurion wrote of his fears for his people in a letter to President Kennedy:

For many years the civilized world did not take seriously Hitler's statement that one of his aims was the world-wide extermination of the Jewish people. I have no doubt that a similar thing might happen to Jews in Israel if Nasser succeeded in defeating our army...[126]

Invoking the horrors of the past and equating the Arabs with the Jews' erstwhile persecutors was not uncommon, nor was it reserved for hard-line government officials. On the eve of war in 1967, *Ma͑ariv*, one of the largest mass-circulation tabloids in Israel, referred to the Arabs as "those who openly threaten to complete Hitler's work."[127]

Israel's aims emanated from its appreciation of its security environment. On the one hand, the state was determined to develop the water resources that passed through its territory and increase the country's economic potential. To that end, the Government insisted that it would resist unilateral and illegal steps by the Arab states to deny Israel Upper Jordan waters, and would act to safeguard the country's vital rights and needs. On the other hand, Israel would continue to strengthen its defensive and deterrent power in an effort to ward off hostile threats.

However, the military build-up in Israel and massive arms purchases from Europe and the United States were viewed by the Arab states, not as a response to perceived threats, but rather, as preparation for aggression. Israel's efforts to bolster its security through the accumulation of power were interpreted by the Arabs as a threat to their own security.[128] Hence, the perception of threat to core values was at the forefront of both Israel's and the Arab states' regional behavior. Not only the development of the Negev desert, but also the very existence of a Jewish state in Palestine were viewed as profound threats to the security of the Arabs. The establishment of the State of Israel was considered "the main danger."[129] The Syrian leadership – whether conservative politicians and their military allies (1961–63), or the B͑athists later (1963–66, 1966–) – was more outspoken in this attitude than any of the other Arab regimes. In its public statements, it consistently referred to the "Zionist threat to the Arab existence."[130] Nor was this view openly contested by other Arab leaders, except for Bourguiba.

It was not simply that the Arab states felt threatened by the presence of Israel on their borders, but more importantly, they did not recognize the legitimacy of a Jewish state in Palestine. As noted above, this was the official Arab position. It was evoked at the three summit conferences and bandied about by the media services. Israel was perceived as an "imperialist occupation force in an Arab land."[131] The Syrian press reported that the Arabs regarded Israel as "an aggressive entity whose existence they reject in all circumstances."[132] And Cairo radio, in response to Israel's threats to put a stop to the Arab diversion scheme, commented that Israel did not count as a power in the Middle East; it did not even count as an entity.[133]

The Government of Israel, in turn, did not recognize the existence of a Palestinian people with rights to nationhood. Accordingly, it did not recognize the historic claims of the Palestine Arabs to the land of Palestine, nor, after 1956, the right of the refugees to return to their homes. Thus, the

Palestinian national movement was perceived as illegitimate. In sum, therefore, the inter-state conflict engaged two nationalist movements, each struggling for its right to national identity and national existence, while denying the adversary these same rights. A principled non-recognition – the result of a shared perception of the "other" as illegitimate – marked the conflict at a very basic level.

Perceptions of the "other" and of the "self" are influenced by the context in which actors find themselves. Context is supplied by the situation, which includes historical circumstance, norms and values, as well as immediate concerns and deeply rooted expectations.[134] The focus on perceptions in the study of international politics aims to elucidate the links between the cognitive dynamics of state actors and decision-making, foreign policy, inter-state conflict, and the like. Authors proceed from the twin assumptions that "every decision-maker is in part a prisoner of beliefs and expectations that inevitably shape his definition of reality," and that beliefs and expectations condition behavior.[135] Using psychological theories of cognition and/or content analysis of speeches and statements, analysts study the belief system of individuals or states, their perceptions and images of themselves and of the "other."[136]

Several of the findings of this body of literature are immediately relevant to our examination of Arab and Israeli perceptions during the period leading up to the 1967 war. First, there is the notion of a "closed belief system" or "cognitive rigidity." Once an image of the "other" is developed, actors adhere undeviatingly to it, and information about the "other," whether ambiguous or even discrepant, is assimilated to that image. The "other" is viewed in a rigid, simplistic, and mechanical fashion; it is always the same, always predictable, always suspect.[137]

Second, images of the enemy often are highly ideological and conform to a Manichean world view. There is a "psychological god–devil axis" in attitudes: actors demonstrate a diabolical enemy-image and a morally innocent self-image. The self/group is idealized, the adversary is demonized, and all struggles other than those in which the self/group is engaged are devalued.[138] This tendency, which has been discussed extensively in studies on the concept of ideology and ideological discourse, can take on religious proportions, characterized by the polarization of good and evil, pure and impure, identity and non-identity.[139] Ideology can be defined as a complex of ideas or notions that are considered by the subject as an interpretation of the world or of his/her own situation, and which represents for him/her the absolute truth.[140] This belief system both influences and justifies the behavior of the subject; it is the structure within which he operates and through which he promotes his own interests.

Third, characteristic of an ideology or closed belief system is the tendency to perceive with distortions. This is the case, given that ideology transforms the categories and notions used by the thinking process in keeping with a particular perspective. By virtue of its rigidity, partiality, and egocentricity, the subject's interpretation of the environment is not realistic. And behavior, based upon an inaccurate appreciation of a concrete situation, can yield unanticipated outcomes.

Through textual analysis of speeches and broadcasts from the period under review, the above elements come to the fore. The first two, cognitive rigidity and the Manichean character of perceptions, can be illustrated by means of a cursory examination of the language used by the Arabs and the Israelis to describe the "self" and the "other." The third element, the tendency to distortion, can be demonstrated by a study of language, as well as by outlining perceptions of relative power in the region and their relationship to the outcomes of foreign policy behavior in the 1960s.

In official statements and reports from media services of Arab countries of the central Middle East over a six-year period (1961–67), the State of Israel was repeatedly referred to as "imperialist" and "colonialist": pejorative terms, connoting activities which, in this day and age, are frowned upon by the international community. Israel was "an imperialist occupation force in an Arab land."[141] Zionism, the unifying ideology of the Jewish state, was equated with imperialism and colonialism. Even worse, Israel was considered a stooge for imperialism: "imperialist and exploiting forces ... back Zionist imperialism in Arab Palestine and use Israel as a military base for aggression against the Arab homeland."[142] The State was also referred to as a "racist aggressive base," an "aggressive stronghold in Palestine." Not only was it belligerent, but it was depicted as criminal and conspiratorial as well, with regard to both its nature and its intentions: it was "the gangster state inside Palestine," engaged in a "plot ... to rob Arab waters."[143] Nor was Israel spared dehumanization. It was stripped of its human qualities and given the attributes of an animal: "Zionist imperialism [was] crouching on the soil of Arab Palestine."[144] On one occasion, the demonization was blatant. The enemy was described as "a snake which had sucked Arab blood."[145]

In contrast, the Arabs spoke of themselves in laudatory terms. The Syrian regime and media services constantly referred to their people as "the struggling Arab masses," as if they represented an organized, popular force fighting oppression. They were considered "revolutionary" masses, engaged in a struggle to turn back the tides of imperialism and colonialism in the Middle East, by "liberating the usurped homeland." Arab aims were extolled: the "sublime Arab interests" represented a "legitimate defence against the Zionist aggression upon the Arab land and water."[146] The twin elements of liberation and defense were prominent in Arab discussions of their intentions. Moreover, terms commonly associated with religious belief and practice were employed regularly, drawing sharp contrasts with images of the enemy. The dutiful Arab masses were ready to make "any *sacrifice* for the sake of destroying the Zionist plot... to rob Arab waters."[147] And the Palestine Arab people had "a *sacred* right to the liberation of their homeland from Zionist colonization."[148] [Emphasis, my own.] In this battle, depicted as one between good and evil, revolution and reaction, the Arab League considered the Palestine Liberation Organization "a vanguard of the joint Arab struggle," while Damascus regarded the Syrian people as "the vanguard of Arab forces to face all challenges..."[149]

However, the more the radical Bʿathi regime spoke sloppily of revolution and the imminent destruction of Israel, and the more it engaged in reckless behavior along its borders, the more its official discourse demonstrated self-deception and distortion. Syria regarded itself as "the pillar of the revolutionary movement in freeing the Arab homeland from every form of imperialist domination."[150] Moreover, it considered that "the revolutionary front [is] impregnable."

A perusal of official Israel Government statements and reports from the national media services also provides evidence of the State's image of itself and of the "other." Compared to the Arab regimes and especially to Syria, Israel resorted to a more rational–legal discourse. Instances of the dehumanization and demonization of the enemy through the use of language tend to be less frequent in public pronouncements, and in general, more subtle than was the case with the Arabs. Nonetheless, they do occur. One instance, not characterized by its subtlety, equates the Arabs with a ghoulish historical figure, who masterminded and proceeded to implement a plan to annihilate the Jews. The Arabs were referred to by the Israeli press as "those who openly threaten to complete Hitler's work."[151] Other allusions were made to the inhuman nature of the enemy: infiltrators into Israeli territory were described as proceeding from "nests," as if they were insects, snakes, or birds of prey.[152] The Arabs were perceived as having criminal, evil intentions. Their long-term goal was to eliminate the Jewish state. In the short-term, they were trying to ensnare it: Nasir and the Arabs were "tightening the ring around Israel."[153]

Israel's perception of itself, on the other hand, is brought to the fore through the persistence of self-confident statements and self-righteous assertions. The state's fighting forces were consistently referred to in the most eulogistic terms. The Israel Defence Forces (IDF) operated "with remarkable firmness and ability," and were deployed "in accordance with the best rules of military science."[154] They were inspired, not only by heroism, but by the "Jewish tradition of devotion to duty, the pioneer spirit, and daring," as well.[155] Israel Government officials invariably demonstrated firmness and equanimity in their public pronouncements, even when the political situation in the region had reached crisis proportions and war was deemed inevitable. The State spoke dispassionately of its intentions: "It was...made clear to the neighboring states that infiltrators and saboteurs will not be permitted to cross the border."[156] On the eve of war, Levi Eshkol announced self-assuredly that his country would "foil all plans to divert the headwaters of the Jordan River and it will make sure that the Red Sea is kept open to shipping." Moreover, "we have laid down the principle that we will choose the time, the place, and the means to counter the aggressor."[157]

The State was both confident of its power resources and convinced of the justice and legality of its interests and intentions. Nonetheless, it sought to promote an image of itself as a pacific, yet *besieged* nation, forced, against its will, to build up its military capability. As noted above, the Arabs were "tightening the ring" around Israel. The implication was that threats to its survival from an exceedingly hostile environment allowed it no alternative but to prepare for war. Nonetheless, in keeping with its avowed peaceful aims and moral stature, it would continue to take great pains not to resort to force. At the height of cross-border clashes in 1966, Eshkol announced that the recent acts of sabotage "justified direct military action against Syria," but for the time being, Israel was exercising restraint and using diplomatic channels in an effort "to prevent an escalation of events in this region."[158] On the eve of war, the view that Israel was a beleaguered nation, caught between the devil and the deep blue sea, was pervasive among the policy elite: "Today we are facing a battle which has been imposed on us." (Eshkol.)[159]

We have no alternative but to answer the challenge forced upon us, because the problem is not freedom of navigation, the challenge is the existence of the State of Israel, and this is a war for that very existence. (Chief-of-Staff, Yitzhak Rabin)[160]

Defence Minister Moshe Dayan asserted: "We have no invasion aims. Our only target is to foil the Arab armies' aim of invading our country."[161]

The polarization of good and evil, highlighted in the preceding examination of the Arabs' and Israelis' images of themselves and the other, has been interpreted by Finlay *et al.* in a manner which is both enlightening and appropriate:

Through identifying an enemy and portraying him as the incarnation of evil, the individual – or the nation-state – assumes a posture of self-righteousness. In effect this means transcending the threat by elevating the self to a position of superiority, moral or otherwise. Accordingly, justice, truth, and other virtues which are praiseworthy, self-justifying, and self-glorifying are on "our" side almost automatically. Such assumptions tend to produce grandiose feelings of power, invulnerability, and strength *vis-à-vis* the enemy, even though such conclusions may be unwarranted...However, self-righteousness also is a means of reducing stress, of protecting the self against threats, of satisfying needs for security or emotional release and catharsis; it is a method of reducing inner conflicts by displacing them onto external scapegoats.[162]

This brings us to the last cognitive dynamic to be considered – perceptions of relative power in the region – and its relationship to the outcome of foreign policy behavior.

As noted above, the State of Israel expressed confidence with regard to both the strength of its defense forces and support from the great powers. It was convinced that relative power was in its favor:[163] "We have the power not only to halt aggression but also to defeat the armies of the enemy in their territory."[164] However, it was concerned about the military alliance between Egypt and Syria, formed in November 1966. Egypt was far and away the most powerful of Israel's Arab enemies. Haunted by fear, the State sought to pursue the will-o'-the-wisp of absolute security. For over a decade, it had been engaged in a major effort to build up and consolidate its military capability.

ʿAbd al-Nasir, as well, was convinced that relative power in the region was in Israel's favor. Not only was its military capability superior to that of the combined Arab armies, but also, the state enjoyed widespread international recognition and support. The United States, for one, was perceived to be firmly behind Israel.[165] Nasir knew that the Arabs could not face Israel on the battlefield, and for that reason, he considered Syria's call for immediate war sheer folly.[166] But while he was cautious, at least until mid-May 1967, he was also confident that in the long-run, the Arabs would be victorious. In the short-run, however, they would have to build up their armed forces.

In contrast, the Syrian Bʿath Party's perception of relative power in the region was confused. While it insisted that the diversion works in its territory required military protection from outside – an implicit recognition of inferior capability – it consistently demanded war with Israel. Furthermore, it claimed that not only did it stand at the "vanguard of Arab forces," but also, the "Arab masses" felt "capable of fighting the battle and winning victory…"[167] The regime's official discourse was imbued with arrogant self-confidence and expressions of infallibility. The persistent refrain was that it was only a matter of time before Syria (and the Arabs) would destroy Israel:[168]

Syria has become a cause of worry to them [Israel and imperialism] as a result of its surge of serious constructive work…

The Syria of the revolution is not the Syria of old. It is the Syria whose Army taught the aggressors hard lessons: Israel, imperialism, and their lackeys will not remain in this land because the Arab people and Army know what to do about Israel and imperialism.[169]

With the radical Bᶜathis in power (1966–), this oratorical "style" conjured up visions of grandeur, often tending toward delirium:

Syria's methods have become a real strategic danger to imperialist interests, the Zionist base and the agent reaction. [Syria today] is the force that has been able to overcome and to crush all plots aiming at distracting it from construction. This is the force that has been able to base its economy on accurate plans which enable it to improve its economic potentialities in a way which continuously strengthens its military capabilities. Syria today is the force that has been able to change and direct all Arab conditions and to begin preparation of the atmosphere of Arab struggle by an effective coming together among the Arab progressive forces...

Israel realises that the revolutionary logic which emanates from Syria and establishes itself everywhere reveals its pure imperialist nature and role... Israel also realises that the question between itself and the overwhelming logic which strengthens the siege around it and which threatens to eliminate it has become only a matter of time.[170]

The Bᶜath Party's public posturing displayed a tendency to self-deception and ideological distortion for which the comment from Finlay *et al.*, quoted above, provides a partial explanation.

The Arab media services, for the most part, demonstrated an appreciation of reality not unlike that of the Syrian regime. They too boldly expressed the conviction that the Arabs were ready to fight Israel and capable of winning. As far as they were concerned, relative power resources in the region were not in Israel's favor.[171] On the eve of war, the Egyptian press asserted defiantly that the Arabs would do more than simply defeat the enemy; they would "teach it a lesson":

Israel will not... escape punishment... If Israel now tries to set the region on fire, then it is definite that Israel itself will be completely destroyed in this fire, which will surround it on all sides...[172]

In the same vein, Cairo radio challenged not only the enemy state, but its presumed allies, as well:

Eshkol, Rabin, agents, imperialists, we await you on the frontier; we wait with death for Israel, with death for the rule of agents and for all American and British interests in Arab oil.[173]

Needless to say, the outcome of events in the region was not one that the Arab states had bargained for. In June 1967, after only six days of fighting, they were dealt a tremendous blow. The Israel Defence Forces (IDF) captured the Syrian Golan Heights and the Egyptian Sinai Peninsula. They wrested the West Bank and East Jerusalem from Jordan and the Gaza Strip from Egypt. Once again, thousands of Palestine Arab refugees poured into the neighboring states, and especially into Jordan. Moreover, the precious headwaters of the Jordan system which, in theory, had given Lebanon and

Syria riparian advantage in the basin, were no longer accessible to the Arab states; the Upper Jordan River now flowed, almost exclusively, within Israel and territory controlled by Israel.

Israel's assessment of relative power was appropriate. So was ʿAbd al-Nasir's, at least in the short-run. The Egyptian leader, however, was entangled in regional commitments and power struggles that prevented him from following his instincts to avoid war. In an effort to maintain his leadership in the Arab world, he committed himself to Syria's defense in the fall of 1966. Once he had done so, he was bound to face the consequences of the Bʿath Party's reckless behavior along its border with Israel. Again to demonstrate courage and preserve his leadership in the face of repeated taunts and challenges from the conservative regimes, he threatened Israel in the spring of 1967 and thereby escalated tensions in the region. In no time, Nasir and his Arab rivals found themselves in a disastrous situation, with neither real military strength nor effective international support. And while in 1964, the Arabs collectively had failed to prevent Israel from using the disputed Jordan waters for its own purposes, in 1967 they "failed not only to back up their provocative military challenge to Israel, but even to defend themselves minimally against her response."[174] In terms of military capability, Israel was the hegemonic power in the region.

PART III

The Jordan basin since 1967

6 Water and development in Israel and Jordan

After six days of fighting, the geopolitical map of the central Middle East changed dramatically. By occupying the Sinai Peninsula, Gaza Strip, West Bank, Golan Heights, and East Jerusalem, Israel more than trebled the territory it controlled. The new territorial configuration of the region represented a remarkable strategic improvement for Israel. Its land boundaries had shrunk by about 25 percent, while its shoreline more than doubled. In the south, Egyptian forces had been pushed back across the desert to the opposite side of the Gulf of Suez. In the north, Israeli forces had captured the high ground over Syria, thus bringing them within 24 kilometres of the Damascus–Amman highway. And in the center of the country, the cease-fire line was pushed eastward beyond the West Bank, to the Jordan River.[1] (See map 6.1.)

Israel's gains were also impressive insofar as water resources were concerned. By occupying the Syrian Golan Heights, it controlled the headwaters of the Banias tributary. The only remaining northern source of the Jordan system outside Israel's command was the Hasbani tributary, rising in southeastern Lebanon. (By 1978, however, the state had gained much influence in that region. And since the 1982 invasion of Lebanon, Israeli forces have maintained effective control over the south and thus, of the Hasbani tributary, as well.) In terms of the Jordan River proper, it was in the advantageous position of upstream riparian in the basin.

In addition, Israel achieved substantial gains on the West Bank. The rich groundwater sources of that territory fell within its jurisdiction. Well before 1967, the state had become dependent upon the waters of the Yarqon-Taninim aquifer, in the western portion of the West Bank. As of the mid-1950s, between one-quarter and one-third of Israeli water consumption has originated in rainfall over the western slopes of the West Bank and has been drawn, by drilling inside the "Green Line" – the 1949 Armistice Demarcation line – from the same aquifer system that contains the water reserves for the West Bank.[2] While Israel did have access to these subterranean sources prior to 1967 by virtue of the fact that the waters flow naturally westward toward the Coastal Plain, occupation has allowed it to

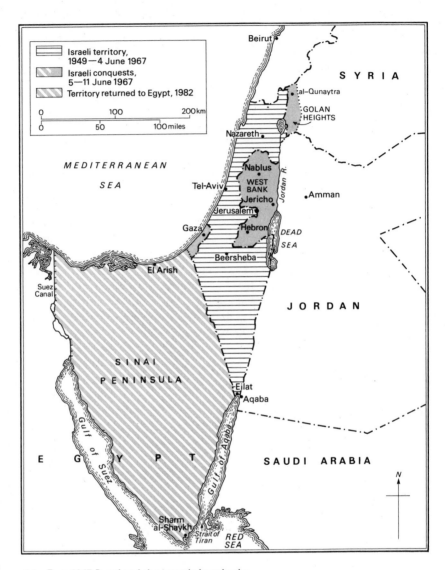

6.1   Post-1967 Israel and the occupied territories

monitor their utilization within the West Bank proper, and thereby ensure that they remain available for Israeli consumption.

Israel's gains were the Arabs' losses. Of the three Arab riparian states, the Kingdom of Jordan suffered the worst blow. It lost the West Bank and hence, one-third of its population and its richest agricultural land. Although this territory had made up only 6 percent of the kingdom's total area, it had accounted for as much as 45 percent of its Gross National Product in 1966, one-quarter of its cultivated area, and almost 60 percent of its agricultural output.[3] Jordan also lost East Jerusalem, which was not only a religious symbol, but the focus of its tourist industry, as well. It "gained" an additional 300,000 Palestinian refugees from the West Bank and Gaza Strip. Virtually overnight, the state's total population swelled to three times what it had been in 1948.[4] National production plummeted, investment was frozen, and basic infrastructural services were badly overburdened. There were severe pressures upon the Jordanian government to alleviate the country's growing social and economic ills. In terms of water resources, Jordan's situation changed significantly, as well. Israel now occupied 20 percent (about 12 km) of the northern bank of the Yarmouk River as opposed to 10 percent (6 km) before the war.[5] This proximity has placed severe constraints upon Jordan's ability to exploit that resource – the kingdom's only abundant source of fresh water – as it had planned.

Having lost their superior riparian positions, Lebanon and Syria were no longer considered party to the Upper Jordan waters. (Syria, however, retained its upstream status on the Yarmouk and so, became involved in discussions over the apportionment of its waters in the late 1970s and again, in the late 1980s.) Neutralized, both withdrew from the resource dispute that had plagued the basin. Along with Egypt, which had suffered a devastating blow, they turned their attention to the military, territorial, and psychological defeat they had just undergone.[6]

Since 1967, the riparian dispute has changed dramatically. No longer is the Arabs' aim politically motivated: to keep water away from the Israelis in order to frustrate the socio-economic development of their society. Jordan has come to accept, at least tacitly, the new geopolitical setting as "infrastructural fact." Given the objective reality, the kingdom's principal goal is a technical one: to secure a just allocation of the waters of the Jordan–Yarmouk basin.[7] Indeed, the riparian dispute has entered a pragmatic, technocratic water management phase. Highly specific issues are of concern to both parties, with the need to maximize access to increasingly scarce water resources being paramount.

In the remaining chapters of this study, we focus primarily on Israel and Jordan. The conflict over the Jordan waters now engaged the states which, since mid-century, had been the most deeply concerned with and dependent upon the river system. The two adversaries would compete with each other for access to the waters of the basin. Our discussion of this period begins by describing the development of water resources in Israel and in Jordan. We delineate the profound resource constraints faced by the two countries and the various efforts made to meet growing consumption demand.

Israel

In the cases of both Israel and Jordan, the late 1960s was a turning-point in agricultural development and water utilization. Israel's National Water Carrier was completed in 1964 and Jordan's East Ghor Canal entered into operation in 1966. Both projects were considered essential for the long-term development of their respective states, and both had gone through lengthy gestation periods, harking back to the 1944/48 Lowdermilk–Hays proposal on the one hand, and to 1939 and Michael Ionides' report, on the other.

Until 1964, water planning in Israel revolved around the idea of diverting northern resources southward. A state enterprise had been planned and was being implemented to carry out three primary directives that had, as noted in chapter 2, important ideological components: agricultural development, population dispersal, and development of arid regions. In this first phase, economic constraints had minor effect on water planning: "Water had to be made accessible in order to develop the country, and so it was."[8] Between 1950 and 1970, water utilization increased from 17 to 95 percent of total resource potential, and the irrigated area expanded more than six times. Population nearly tripled in size, while water consumption of all sectors combined witnessed a sixfold increase. Needless to say, agriculture was, and continues to be, the major consumer, hovering between 70 and 80 percent of total consumption.[9]

In the second phase of water planning, however, Israel had to face several problems attendant to a changed situation. By the mid-1960s, the country's sustainable annual water yield – the fixed quantity of water available on a yearly basis – then equivalent to an average of 1·5–1·6 billion cubic metres (bcm), had been almost totally utilized. In the early 1970s, consumption exceeded the sustainable annual yield, and over-pumping, which supplied the additional resources, began to seriously endanger the long-term water balance.[10] The natural resources of conventional water were used up. For the first time, the state was forced to deal with the problem of shortage.

Rather than modify the ideological objectives of resource planning or change consumption patterns in keeping with the new situation of scarcity, Israel has engaged in a variety of specialized projects, aiming to close the gap between consumption and supply by focusing on, *faute de mieux*, "unconventional" water resources or approaches. There have been projects to intercept intermittent flood flows, reclaim sewage water, increase rainfall through cloud-seeding, replenish aquifers to protect them from saline water seepage and depletion of water levels, and desalinate water on a very small scale for the industrial sector.[11] Of these, the most significant additions to net supply capacity have been achieved through sewage reclamation and secondarily, the controlled mining of aquifers.[12] (See table 6.1.)

Despite the additions to national water supply provided by the implementation of such projects, Israel has been pumping more water than it had since the 1970s. Hydrologists maintain that a minimum of 200 mcm have been overpumped on a yearly basis, resulting in a water deficit in 1991 of 2 bcm, equivalent to one entire year's water supply. It is only thanks to some degree of groundwater replenishment that the deficit is not superior to what it actually is.[13]

Hardest hit by overpumping is the Coastal Plain aquifer, Israel's second most abundant source of groundwater. Water levels in the aquifer have been lowered considerably, creating depressions of the water table in certain areas of as much as several metres below sea level. And the salinity of the water supply has increased markedly in the over-exploited parts of the basin. A similar trend is observed in the Yarqon-Taninim aquifer (West Bank), as well. Exploitation of that reservoir exceeds its estimated safe yield by 35–40 mcm.[14] In an effort to counteract these effects and improve the hydrological situation of the subterranean reservoirs, Mekorot, Israel's national water authority, has been artificially recharging water into the depleted aquifers. The water used to replenish the Coastal Plain aquifer, for example, derives from Lake Tiberias (via the National Water Carrier).[15]

As the quality and supply constraints on resource development intensified, beginning in the mid-1970s, the government feared that irrigation water to agriculture would have to be cut. Domestic and industrial consumption could not be curtailed significantly, especially since they represent fairly inelastic demands which increase with population growth and the rise in living standards. But cutting irrigation water promised to be an extremely difficult alternative, given the pre-eminence of the agricultural sector and its powerful, well-represented interests.[16]

To avoid having to take drastic measures while allowing the sector to remain productive, efforts have been made to improve the efficient utilization of water in agriculture via drip irrigation, for example, and other methods whereby water use per unit of product could be reduced.[17] Nevertheless, in order to satisfy urban and industrial demands, agricultural consumption of water had to be cut for the first time in 1986. The eventual need to resort to such a move had been anticipated ten years earlier.[18]

From 1988 to 1991, there were three consecutive years of drought in the

Table 6.1. Israel: distribution of water supply by source and quality 1984/85, 2000 (mcm per year)[a]

	1984/85				2000			
	Fresh	Brackish	Irrigation	Total	Fresh	Brackish	Irrigation	Total
Groundwater	1,205	135	—	1,340	955	160	—	1,115
Jordan River	580	—	—	580	620	—	—	620
Yarmouk River	100–140	—	—	100–140	100–140	—	—	100–140[b]
Floodwater	15	10	15	40	30	—	50	80
Wastewater	30	—	80	110	—	—	—	275–345
Losses	−60	—	—	−60	−40	—	—	−40
Total supply	1,870–1,910			2,110–2,150	1,665–1,705			2,150–2,260

[a] In this table, fresh water refers to water in which salinity does not exceed 400 milligrams (mg) per litre chlorides. In brackish water, salinity does exceed that amount. Irrigation water is composed of recycled wastewater and floodwater.

[b] The estimate for the supply of water to Israel from the Yarmouk River in the year 2000 assumes that a dam on the river will not have been built before that date.

Source: adapted from Schwarz, "Israeli Water Sector"; Naff, "Jordan Basin"; AMER; interviews.

Table 6.2. *Israel: resource supply and population growth projections,*
1991–2020

Year	Population (in millions)	Water consumption (mcm per year)[a]	Renewable fresh water supply (mcm per year)
1991	4·4	2,100–2,200	1,950
2010	6·0		2,060[c]
2015–2020	6·3	2,800–2,900	
2020	6·4[b]		

[a] Including Golan Heights and Jewish settlements in the West Bank.
[b] Immigration of Soviet Jews during the 1990s will increase the 2020 population figure by about 1 million.
[c] Excluding West Bank and Gaza Strip.
Source: Naff, "Jordan Basin"; AMER; Schwarz, "Israeli Water Sector."

Jordan basin. During the 1990–91 rainy season, for example, precipitation in Israel totalled 1·3 bcm, compared with an average of 1·7 bcm and with water consumption that peaked at 2·1 bcm in 1988 and averages 1·9 bcm.[19] There had been so little rainfall, in fact, that the level of Lake Tiberias reached an all-time low. Not only was there hardly any pumping of water from the lake through the National Water Carrier, but also, there was virtually no recharging of the coastal aquifer. Each year since the beginning of the drought – since 1986 in fact – the water commissioner had to cut back the allocation to agriculture. While the cutback was a mere 10 percent in 1986, it rose to 37 percent in 1990.[20] Indeed, over the years the sector has been receiving a diminishing share of the total water supply: 77 percent in 1960, 68 percent in 1989. Given the resource supply constraints and population growth projections, these trends are bound to continue.[21] (See table 6.2.)

Israel's water problems appear to be less severe when considered within a regional context. In fact, it is outside the immediate Jordan system that members of the Israeli "water establishment" have been extending their gaze as the only solution to a pending water crisis.[22] In 1986, Tel-Aviv University, with the support of the Armand Hammer Fund for Economic Cooperation in the Middle East, published a study, detailing the ways in which the major rivers of the central Middle East – the Jordan, Litani, Nile, and Yarmouk – could be shared to the advantage of all states and territories of the region.[23] This highly imaginative study has historical precedents. As we recall, European Zionists at the Paris Peace Conference in 1919 requested that the borders of the Jewish state include the Litani River. And during the early stages of negotiations with Eric Johnston in the 1950s, the Israeli team insisted that the Lebanese national river be included in the basin-wide development scheme.[24] Moreover, while Egypt, Israel, and the United States were discussing the framework of a bilateral peace treaty at the end of the 1970s, then President Anwar Sadat proposed to pump Nile water across the Sinai desert into Israel.

Jordan

For the Kingdom of Jordan, there has been virtually no alternative to ameliorating the agricultural potential of the country other than by concentrating on the Jordan Valley, which constitutes a mere 0·6 percent of the state's land area. The Yarmouk River on the northern border, and with an average annual stream flow of 438 mcm under "normal" climatic conditions and prior to diversions, is the only abundant source of fresh water available.

As noted in chapter 2, the poverty of the country's resource potential was recognized as early as in the 1930s, when the idea was put forward to extend a canal from the Yarmouk River southward along the eastern Ghor of the Jordan Valley. Since the completion of its first phase in the sixties, the East Ghor Canal has remained the centerpiece of Jordan's efforts at agricultural development.

In the aftermath of the 1967 war and until the decimation of the Palestinian resistance in Jordan in 1970–71, water and agricultural development in the kingdom suffered a severe setback. On the one hand, the Valley was virtually depopulated of its 60,000 pre-war population. On the other hand, the main canal had been hit and knocked out of service on four separate occasions between June 1967 and August 1971. And the twin-pipe inlet to the canal from the Yarmouk-Adasiyeh diversion tunnel was damaged by shelling in 1969.[25] With the return to calm in the fall of 1971, the government's national planning team focused on the Jordan Valley as the priority area. Of the total of 44,000 irrigable hectares of farmland in all of Jordan, 30,000 are in the Valley.[26] It was deemed the only region where food production could be increased and large-scale employment provided.

In 1972, the Government of Jordan established a Jordan Valley Commission to oversee the social and economic development of the Valley.[27] That same year, the first in a series of comprehensive development projects was proposed. It included harnessing the Zarqa River and side wadis, to irrigate land below the extension of the East Ghor Canal.[28] A follow-up, the Jordan Valley Development Plan, 1975–1982, was later prepared to incorporate both the activities of the earlier three-year plan (stage one projects) and a scheme for the construction of the Maqarin Dam on the Yarmouk River (stage two).

In 1978, the eighteen-kilometre extension of the East Ghor Canal was completed. The total irrigated capacity of the Valley reached approximately 24,000 hectares, representing an increase of about 130 percent over the corresponding figure for 1966. The country's export performance, compared with its food imports, improved considerably.[29] To date, the canal, renamed the King Abdullah Canal in 1987, has been lengthened three times; it is now 110 kilometres long, covers the entire length of the Valley, and can provide irrigation water for 28,800 hectares of land.[30] Jordanian hydrologists anticipate that if additional water sources are harnessed, the remaining hectares suitable for irrigated agriculture in the valley could be developed by the year 2000.[31]

Since the late 1970s and the beginning of serious water shortages, the country's only remaining hope has been the construction of a dam on the Yarmouk River which, as we recall, Jordan had been wanting since the 1950s. Creating storage would solve the problem of Jordan's inability to capture the winter flow of the Yarmouk, and facilitate meeting current and anticipated demand for water for a few decades, at least. Impounding those waters and regulating their distribution would make possible the extension of the irrigated area in the Jordan Valley, the increase in agricultural production, and the provision of badly needed potable water for the country's rapidly growing urban population.[32] The project received considerable support from bilateral and multilateral donors. But the government of the United States, which was to make the largest loan, required that "riparian issues" be resolved between Jordan and Syria, and Jordan and Israel, before the funds would be made available.[33] As we shall see in the last chapter, riparian agreement was not forthcoming, and the construction of the Maqarin Dam and later, a revised version of it – the considerably smaller Unity (al-Wahdah) Dam – was postponed indefinitely. Thus, Jordan is able to utilize no more than 120–140 mcm of Yarmouk water annually, equivalent to roughly one-third of the river's total discharge.[34] (See map. 6.2.)

In the absence of a dam on the Yarmouk, Jordan has been proceeding with other smaller scale projects, such as raising the King Talal Dam on the Zarqa River, extending the King Abdullah Canal to reach the northern tip of the Dead Sea, and groundwater exploration in the Southern Ghors and Wadi Araba. Each of these projects, however, has come up against serious limitations. The Zarqa River, for one, has been described as "an environmental disaster." Not only is it terribly polluted, but during the summer months, its flow consists almost entirely of sewage effluent. Studies show that the water in the reservoir on the river is suitable only for salt-tolerant crops.[35] Second, although the King Abdullah Canal is the main lifeline for most irrigation projects in the Jordan Valley and southern Ghors, the flow in the southern extension is a mere trickle. For more than a decade,

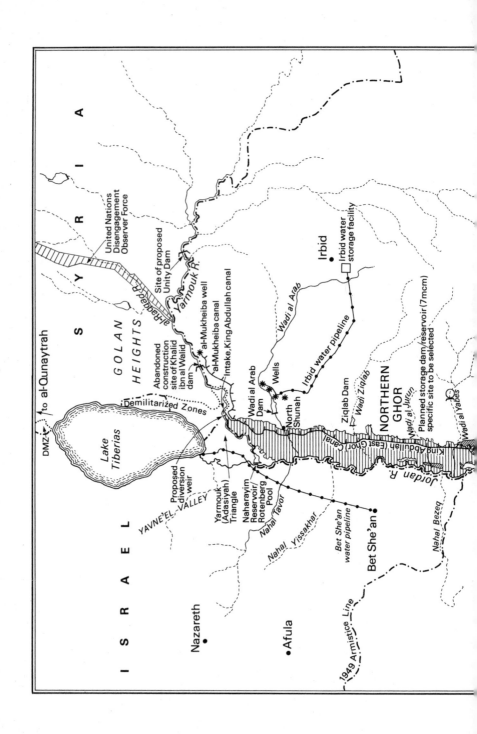

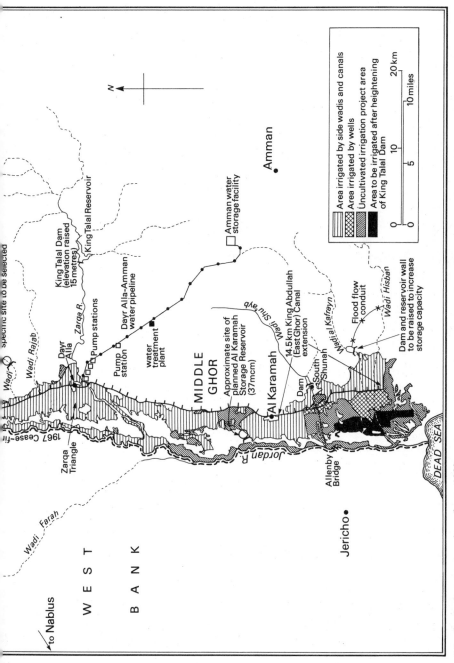

6.2 Jordan's water supply and use, 1989

Israel has prevented Jordan from cleaning out the intake to the canal when it fills up with silt and sediment. In the mid-1980s, the United States Government mediated an agreement on this matter between the two states. Nonetheless, restrictions on Jordanian maintenance work are reimposed periodically.[36] As for groundwater, supplies are limited and, as in Israel, their quality is subject to deterioration due to over-exploitation and seepage of wastes. In the Azraq and Disi basins, for example, withdrawals have been exceeding safe yields for more than a decade; as a result, water levels have dropped by 3–5 and 8 metres respectively, and salinity has increased considerably. Currently, groundwater is extracted at the level of 110 percent of total available renewable supplies.[37] Moreover, while non-renewable groundwater is fairly abundant in the south – in the Qa Disi aquifer, for example – it is more than 300 kilometres from the major population centers in the north, and hence, transportation costs would be considerable. Groundwater has been found in other parts of the country, but in general, the water resources still to be developed are meagre.[38]

Jordan's population has been growing at the rate of 3·7 percent per annum and is expected to continue to do so during the next two decades. Thus, in twenty years, the population will more than double, from 3·2 million in 1990 to 6·8 million in 2010.[39] If living standards are to remain the same, domestic water demand will double over the twenty-year period, as well. However, any rise in living standards will lead to even greater demands on the water supply. And given that there remain at least 7,000 hectares of land to develop in the Jordan Valley alone, agricultural demand will increase, as well. No doubt, because of high population growth and the trend toward increasing urbanization, demands for water by all sectors are bound to grow, causing considerable deficits to the resource base (see tables 6.3 and 6.4).

In Jordan today, both urban and rural areas are subject to water rationing. Moreover, as in the case of Israel, the country has had to reallocate water from agriculture to municipal and industrial uses, in an effort to meet growing demand. The government has also been trying to improve the delivery system of water by, among other things, adopting drip irrigation as quickly as possible.[40] There has been some experimentation with non-conventional sources of water, such as wastewater reuse, desalination of sea or brackish waters, cloudseeding, and the like. However, these technologies tend to engage very high costs, and especially since the Gulf War of 1991 and the decimation of the Jordanian economy, funds have been in very short supply.

Because net additions to supply are limited, Jordan, like Israel, has been considering possibilities to "import" water from outside the immediate region. In 1982, the Kingdom weighed the feasibility of a project to convey about 160 mcm of water per year from the Euphrates River in Iraq to

Table 6.3. *Kingdom of Jordan : projected water demand and supply,*
1990–2020 (mcm)

	Demand			Supply
	M and I[a]	Agriculture	Total	Safe yields
1990	200	520	740	730
2000	300	750	1,045	862
2010	400	1,010	1,410	850
2020	620	1,530	2,150	850

[a] Municipal and Industrial.
Source : Abu-Taleb *et al.,* "Water Resources," p. 15 and "Jordan River Basin,"
p. 126.

Table 6.4. *Kingdom of Jordan : projected water deficit, 1990–2005 (mcm)*

	1990	1995	2000	2005
Water demand	740	890	1,045	1,200
Water supply	730	862	862	862
Net annual deficit	10	28	183	338

Source : Abu-Taleb *et al.,* "Jordan River Basin," p. 122.

Jordan's northern plateau, a distance of 590 kilometres. The project, however, has been shelved. Not only was the capital cost forbidding – estimated at approximately $2 billion in 1982 – but also, it was feared that in the turbulent political climate of the Middle East, the pipeline could be a target of sabotage.[41] From 1986 through 1991, Turkey's President Turgut Ozal was championing the concept of a "peace pipeline." The proposed project would have consisted of two pipelines to transport water from the Seyhan and Ceyhan rivers in Turkey southward to Syria, Jordan, Saudi Arabia, and other Gulf states.[42]

Conclusion

Together, Jordan and Israel have been consuming about 108 percent of their total usable water supplies.[43] In order to curtail the persistent shortages and put a stop to over-exploitation of subterranean sources, both states would have to engage in remedial actions such as restructuring their economies,

Table 6.5. *Water projects in Israel and Jordan and their outcomes,*
1950–1990

Beneficiary	Year	Project	Outcome
Israel	1951	Drainage of Lake Huleh swamps	Completed
	1953	Diversionary canal from Lake Tiberias (Gesher Bnot Ya'acov)	Completed, having relocated diversion point
	1959–64	National Water Carrier	Completed
	1960s	Lake Tiberias as reservoir	Completed
Jordan (and Syria)	1953	Bunger Plan to develop Yarmouk	Thwarted by US-sponsored "Unified" Plan
Jordan	1958–66	East Ghor Main Canal	First 3 stages completed
	1960s	Mukheiba Dam	Work stopped (1967) by military intervention
Arab riparians[a]	1964	Arab diversion	Work stopped (1966)
Jordan	1972–82	Jordan Valley Development Stages 1 and 2	
		(a) Extension of East Ghor Canal	Completed
(and Syria)	1976–81	(b) Maqarin Dam	Thwarted by failure to reach agreement
	1987–90	Unity Dam	Thwarted

[a] Lebanon, Syria, and Jordan.
Source: compiled by author.

drastically reducing irrigated agriculture, revising existing crop patterns, and employing greater efficiency through stringent application of water-saving technologies.

Indeed, both basin-wide and regional water sharing, in conjunction with radically revamping national economies, conservation methods, and consumption patterns, would be the answer to the critical problem of scarcity in the Jordan basin. In terms of both geography and economic efficiency, this would represent the ideal solution to the satisfaction of competing needs and conflicting interests (see table 6.5).

7 Riparian relations and the perception of conflict

In this chapter, we shift the focus back to the cognitive variables at play in the Jordan basin. We begin by discussing the relationship that has developed between Israel and Jordan since 1967. To evaluate the potential for cooperation among adversarial states, we link Jordan's attitude toward its avowed enemy to three factors: (1) relative power or, more specifically, Israel's overwhelming (military) capability, (2) a long, shared border with Israel and hence, both geographic proximity and a number of common problems, and (3) acute need for unimpeded access to shared water supplies. In light of the geopolitical environment in the central Middle East, domestic needs and national interest have encouraged Jordan to seek a highly delimited, yet implicitly cooperative, relationship with Israel. Next, we consider the contrasting impressions of Israelis and Jordanians with regard to the persistence of riparian dispute. We highlight the salience in perceptions of both resource need and relative power, and provide an explanation for the variation in perceptions not unlike that for cooperation in international river basins.

Israel and Jordan: challenges and constraints

In order to make sense of the very particular relationship that has developed between Jordan and Israel, it would be necessary first to analyze each of the two states in terms of their strengths and weaknesses, internal and external constraints. Because such an exercise would take us well beyond the subject matter of this book, we will restrict ourselves to a few critical points of comparison. First, as we recall, the idea of the state in Jordan is weakly developed.[1] The kingdom is vulnerable to challenges and interference from within and without. Internal threats emanate from the weakness of national sentiment and, especially in the past, from the Palestinian refugees. External threats emanate from Israel and from stronger, more radical Arab states. As one Jordanian pointed out: "King Hussein is very constrained because he is sitting on top of a powder keg – a large Palestinian population. And he knows that if he misbehaves, Israel will move in."[2] The fragile foundations of the state and resultant threats to it translate into profound constraints upon the regime's maneuverability both domestically and internationally.

By and large, the Jordanian regime has been able to deal efficiently with internal threats to its institutions and establish a fairly effective machinery of governance, backed by an able military and a highly efficient intelligence organization, even in the absence of a strong idea of the state.[3] However, it is primarily from the external environment that threats persist. The state has been the object of verbal threats and mobilizations from Egypt, Iraq, Syria, and even Saudi Arabia.[4] The Hashemite regime is neither Arab socialist, nor clearly Arab nationalist. On the one hand, its attitude toward Israel has consistently been relatively moderate. On the other hand, its forceful elimination of the Palestinian resistance in Jordan in 1970 was considered reprehensible.[5] While the King had overcome the physical threat to his monarchy, he did so at a heavy political cost. Not only did his regime become the mortal enemy of Palestinian nationalists, but also, it was dangerously isolated in the Arab world for several years. Syria and Iraq closed their borders with Jordan, Kuwait and Libya suspended annual subsidies to the regime, and relations with Egypt and Tunisia deteriorated markedly. Not only had the regime always displayed a strong tendency to conservatism and alliance with the West, but also, it became clear that Hussein had an ambiguous relationship with Palestinian nationalism – one of the "organizing ideologies" of Arabism.[6]

Threats from Israel are of two forms. On the one hand, there is the military challenge. Jordan perceives that Israel, or at least the right-wing *Likud* bloc, is tempted to annex the East Bank and would do so with the slightest provocation.[7] To recall the candid words of one Jordanian interviewed, "[King Hussein] knows that if he misbehaves, Israel will move in."[8] The feeling is that Israel would like to have the East Bank of the Jordan River as a buffer zone of many miles of desert between itself and Iraq.[9] On the other hand, Jordan faces a political challenge insofar as there have been repeated insinuations and outright assertions from members of the Israeli political establishment that the East Bank should be, or already is, a Palestinian state. Hence, a second Palestinian state – on the West Bank – would be superfluous. To document this position, Jordanians call attention to an article entitled, "A Strategy for Israel in the Nineteen Eighties," written by an Israeli journalist and former Foreign Ministry employee:[10]

Jordan is in reality Palestinian, ruled by a Transjordanian bedouin minority, but most of the army, and certainly the bureaucracy is now Palestinian. As a matter of fact, Amman is as Palestinian as Nablus...

There is no chance that Jordan will continue to exist in its present structure for a long time and Israel's policy both in war and in peace ought to be directed at the liquidation of Jordan under the present regime and the transfer of power to the Palestinian majority. Changing the regime east of the river will also cause the termination of the problem of the territories densely populated with Arabs west of the Jordan...

The argument that the Kingdom of Jordan is a Palestinian state was reiterated recently by one of the more "hawkish" members of the *Likud* party.[11]

In the case of Israel, the idea of the state and its organizing ideology remain very strong in the eyes of the vast majority of its citizens.[12] Moreover, while external threats to the idea of the state do exist, they have become less of an objective concern since 1967. Nonetheless, the state continues to evoke the potential threat that emanates from some (or all) of the Arab regimes. Indeed, because of Israel's widely recognized military and technological superiority in the region, such threats have been effectively contained. The experience of the 1967 war made this reality all too blatant for those Arab states which had previously spoken arrogantly and nonchalantly of their intentions to eliminate the Jewish state from their midsts.[13] Since their military defeat, such talk has been removed from the official discourse.

Second, in terms of its physical base, the Kingdom of Jordan faces considerable constraints as well. Jordan is a poor country in terms of investment capital, entrepreneurship, raw materials, and agricultural productivity. One of the major and persistent problems it faces is that it cannot feed itself. Agriculture provides subsistence for only 60 percent of the population; less than one-tenth of the land is cultivated and foodstuffs remain the primary import item.[14] In addition, the country does not produce a single bullet, to say nothing of the weapons it requires.

While Israel, like Jordan, lacks important natural resources such as water, minerals, and extensive cultivable land, it has managed to build up an impressive industrial infrastructure and to produce a variety of goods of high quality. The local arms industry provides one such example. According to one study, Israel was the world's seventh largest arms exporter in 1980; its weapons shipments were equivalent to 40 percent of the country's total exports and were the largest single export item.[15] In addition, the state is believed to have nuclear capability. Needless to say, Israel has fared much better than Jordan in this domain.

Without going into further detail, it should be evident that Israel's power resources are far superior to those of Jordan. One need only consider the strength of national sentiment within Israeli Jewish society, the impressive military capability of the state and its alliance with America to substantiate this broad assertion.

Two factors characterize Jordan's regional status. On the one hand, survival is its main and most exacting objective.[16] On the other hand, relative power is not in its favor, either *vis-à-vis* Israel or the neighboring Arab states. This particular context has prompted Jordan to seek international relations which, if they cannot allay its precarious situation, then at least do not exacerbate it. Because of both the power constraints upon the Kingdom and its critical need for access to scarce water resources, it has tried to maintain, in the aftermath of the 1967 defeat, a non-confrontational relationship with Israel.

Pax in belli

In fact, there have been, over the years, numerous incidences of both implicit and explicit cooperation between the two states. In a fascinating piece of investigative journalism, the former editor of Israel's *Ma'ariv* newspaper outlines a fourteen-year history of direct talks between the two official enemies.[17] Providing dates, places, participants, and subject matter, Moshe Zak begins in 1963 and the first meeting in London between King Hussein and an emissary of then Prime Minister Levi Eshkol. His account ends in 1977, when the *Likud* bloc came to power, Prime Minister Menachem Begin refused to meet King Hussein, and the Jordanian monarch, himself, no longer saw any point to further discussions. Zak maintains that as of 1970, contacts led to explicitly cooperative arrangements.

Most prominent, of course, was the support lent to King Hussein by Israel during Black September (1970). As he was finalizing his plans to decimate the PLO in Jordan, the king apparently sought guarantees from both Israel and the United States. Via a message to then Foreign Minister Abba Eban, conveyed through the American government, Hussein asked for Israel's assurance that: (1) it would not take advantage of the fact that the king would have to thin out his forces on the western border, and (2) it would assist Jordan in the event that neighboring (Arab) states rallied to the PLO's side.[18] In fact, as the Jordanian army was proceeding with the king's orders to eliminate the *feda'iyin*, Syria invaded northern Jordan with 200 tanks.[19] In response, and with the assurance that the United States and Israel were firmly behind him, Hussein had his airforce attack and rout the Syrian contingents. Israel had accepted to intervene against Syria, if necessary.[20]

Also significant is the fact that since July 1967 and throughout the 1973 war, the bridges linking the East Bank and the occupied West Bank remained open, thus ensuring ongoing economic and cultural links between the two sides.[21] Furthermore, a few incidences related to water resources have been resolved, either through contacts with the United States or through long and laborious negotiations with the United Nations Mixed Armistice Commission. In 1969, for example, Jordan received Israel's agreement, through United States' mediation, to repair the East Ghor Canal after it had been bombarded by Israeli forces.[22] And in 1985, after two and one-half years of negotiations through the Mixed Armistice Commission, Jordan was given permission by Israel to clear a sandbar that had formed in the Yarmouk River and had been blocking the intake of the East Ghor Canal and hence, the past flow of river water to Jordan.[23]

This relationship, appropriately referred to by Ian Lustick as an "adversarial partnership," has been variously explained.[24] One very astute Jordanian clarified it thus: When issues arise of mutual concern and manifest an "overriding practical imperative," the two adversaries are prepared to meet and seek resolution of the matter. As noted, meetings take place either through the mediation of the United States or the Mixed Armistice Commission. Issues such as access to water resources, pollution in the Gulf of Aqaba, or the "open bridges" policy are considered "essential elements of Jordanian survival." In such cases of overwhelming importance, Jordan is prepared to deal with the enemy. Thus, there is *de facto* cooperation between the two states on a very small number of issues. However, this does not imply political recognition of the other. These are technical, practical problems that must be solved for the survival of both countries, and the arrangements that proceed from them are purely utilitarian.[25]

For the most part, Jordanians interviewed agreed that the kingdom is severely constrained by the power imbalance in the region. Jordan knows that it poses no threat to Israel, precisely because it lacks military strength and unswerving international backing – the very attributes that Israel seems to possess in full measure. No doubt, Jordan fears Israel's military might and international status.[26] It also fears, as noted above, that branch of Zionism that calls for the incorporation of the East Bank into the Jewish state. Israel could overrun the country with little difficulty. In fact, in the words of one interviewee, "the proximity of these two countries is so worrisome to Jordan."[27] As a result of this political, psychological, and geographical context, Hussein tries to maintain a non-volatile relationship with his powerful neighbor: "it's best for Jordan not to say too much, to keep quiet, and thereby, not to rock the boat."[28]

In their own explanations for this very particular relationship, the Israelis interviewed noted that there is an "identity of interests" between the two states.[29] Both are concerned to contain the Palestinians and prevent the establishment of an independent Palestinian state on their borders. Both share indispensable water resources. Such commonalities provide incentives for cooperation. Moreover, some Israelis found significant that King Hussein was part of a Jordanian tradition of accommodation with Israel; a tradition which began in the 1940s, with the king's grandfather, Abdallah.[30] Others argued, more convincingly, that the Jordanian regime was prepared to live in peace with Israel, but not to make blatant concessions. It could not accept a formal peace with Israel, although it may want to, because Jordan is a weak state and has more radical regimes, such as Syria, on its back.[31] Nonetheless, most interviewees did concede that one of the primary reasons for the implicit cooperation between the two enemies is the fact that King Hussein realizes that he cannot fight Israel: "he knows he ought to behave."[32]

No matter what, the Kingdom of Jordan is and wants to remain a part of the Arab camp. Besides, it has never been in a position to take independent stands on issues that are regarded as crucial to the "Arab nation" and central to its organizing ideologies. At the same time, and because of its particular constraints, it must not provoke its powerful neighbor. Therefore, it has had to find a *modus vivendi* with Israel that conforms to its own fundamental needs and interests, and perceptions of the environment.

Based on both our understanding of the strengths and weaknesses of the respective states and the diverse interpretations of the "adversarial partnership," we conclude that state behavior in international affairs is strongly influenced by the interplay between the state's interests and its perceptions: perceptions of its own needs, security, and capabilities, and perceptions of other states' interests, intentions, and capabilities. Given its perceptions of itself and of the other, the state calculates whether: (a) it should cooperate, (b) the failure to cooperate would cause it harm, (c) it can act independently and unilaterally, (d) it can actively oppose the other. Having made its calculus, Jordan considers it to be in its national interest not to cooperate formally, but also not to "rock the boat." Because of its needs, constraints, and relative power resources, its attitude toward Israel since 1967 has been a combination of highly delimited, implicit cooperation and, out of loyalty to Arabism and its organizing principles, public invective.[33] Jordan has sought a kind of *pax in belli* with Israel, as the only hope for its continued survival.

In sum, the relationship that has developed over the years between the two adversaries has been shaped by Israel's overwhelming military preponderance, a long shared border and, as a result, a number of common concerns – not least among them, access to scarce water resources. When there has been cooperation between Israel and Jordan, it has concerned technical matters in response to overriding practical imperatives. In all cases, the cooperative arrangements have been perceived as indispensable and unavoidable. Without them, domestic needs could not be satisfied, hence, threats to national security could result. In the specific case of water, access to shared supplies is considered vital to continued survival. Thus, among adversarial states in an international river basin, engaged in a protracted conflict, instances of functional cooperation do not necessarily imply the end or diminution of political rivalry, or even of dispute over water resources.[34]

Divergent perceptions

In fact, there is a fundamental discrepancy in the respective perceptions of Jordanians and Israelis with regard to the persistence of water conflict in the

Jordan basin since 1967. How can we explain this discrepancy? How is it that an issue of concern to two (or more) states may be viewed by one as a source of conflict, while not by the other? Stated differently, what determines whether or not a state perceives a dimension of its international relations as conflictual?

When asked about the persistence of riparian dispute, all Jordanians interviewed were categorical. Each insisted that a conflict over water resources continues to exist. Some maintained that as long as the two parties cannot sit down together, there is conflict.[35] Others said that as long as Jordan does not have a dam on the Yarmouk River, conflict persists. This is so, because water is the only source of food security in the kingdom, and the Yarmouk is the only large body of fresh water available.[36] Still others claimed that as long as the two states share important water resources and face critical shortages, at the same time as both are determined to increase their development potential substantially, there is bound to be conflict.[37]

However, what has changed since 1967 is, according to most Jordanians interviewed, the way in which a conflict over water manifests itself – its "shape and form." No longer is it a "public issue" of "grand proportions," engaging people's unswerving attention, as was the case in the mid-fifties and mid-sixties.[38] Rather, it has become a "silent war" between Israel and Jordan; each recognizes the other's right to a proportion of the basin waters, but they differ on the quantities involved.[39]

This change has taken place for a variety of reasons. First, the water issue was submerged by other events and more pressing concerns in the aftermaths of the 1967 defeat and the so-called "Arab victory" in 1973. Essentially, attention turned to the newly occupied Arab territories.[40] Second, the Jordan River itself, which has been both a religious and an ideological symbol for Arabs and Jews alike, has receded in importance. Not only had the Arabs lost sovereign control over its northern headwaters, but also, as we recall, the water in the river's southern reaches has become increasingly saline. Today, the Lower Jordan is no more than a drainage ditch, and its waters can be used for the irrigation of very few types of crops.[41] Smaller shared bodies of water, such as subterranean sources and the Yarmouk tributary, have since gained in importance. Third, Israel has adopted a new approach to water development. Since the 1982 invasion of Lebanon, it has sought to examine water resources within a regional context and is less concerned with individual rivers. As noted in the previous chapter, Israel would like to have access to the Litani and Nile Rivers. It would like to set up multinational water projects with Arab states, using Israeli know-how and Arab water.[42] Fourth, the Kingdom of Jordan, the only remaining Arab riparian on the Jordan River proper, has come to recognize that *vis-à-vis* Israel, its hands are tied. There is little it can do to prevent its more powerful neighbor from carrying out its water-related plans and utilizing the waters they share as it chooses and in the quantities it is able to draw off.[43]

Besides having become a "silent war," the conflict has extended in scope insofar as virtually all sources of water have been drawn in. Conflict manifests itself as one of physical "proximity of protagonists" not merely to surface run-off, but to underground reserves, as well.[44] The major issues involved are: (1) exploitation of the Yarmouk waters, (2) the unsatisfactorily resolved question of a dam on the Yarmouk, (3) the subterranean sources of the West Bank, and (4) the subterranean sources in Wadi Araba, south of the Dead Sea. Before exploring these areas of conflict in the following chapter, we now consider Israeli perceptions.

In contrast to Jordanians, those Israelis interviewed held one of two positions: they maintained either that there no longer is a conflict over water resources in the basin, or that there is only "potential conflict." Three high-ranking officials in the "water establishment" agreed that "points of tension" do arise, because both countries are so dry and there is an acute imbalance in the region between soils and water supply. Nonetheless, such disagreements are of "minor significance." Besides, there exist effective mechanisms, such as third party intervention, for "ironing out" potentially conflictual issues.[45]

Most Israelis went even further. They stated that, on the contrary, there is a "fair amount of cooperation" between the two parties.[46] One of the examples cited was the following: not only do Israel and Jordan abide more-or-less by the stipulations of the 1955 Johnston Plan, but also, Jordan keeps very strictly to the shares of Yarmouk water allocated to Israel, even if it suffers as a result.[47] Furthermore, the two states have been able to conclude cooperative arrangements, because there exists an "identity of interests" between them, especially *vis-à-vis* the major issues concerning water resources and development.[48] One interviewee claimed that generally speaking, the water dispute between Israel and Jordan has been solved. This has come about because the parties separated the riparian dispute from the larger political conflict, as had been the case in the Indus basin.[49]

With regard to potential conflict, one Israeli remarked that in the late 1970s and early 1980s, the Maqarin Dam and Med-Dead canal projects had been serious candidates. However, both were laid aside. He added that groundwater in the Arava (Wadi ʿAraba), where Israel and Jordan share aquifers, may well become a source of conflict in the future. In that arid region, as we shall see in the following chapter, both states engage in subterranean pumping without any coordination between them and at the risk of endangering the quality of that unique water supply. Moreover, they are likely to increase their pumping activities in the south, as scarcity becomes an even more pressing problem.[50] Finally, several of those Israelis interviewed conceded that the rich groundwater reserves of the West Bank, upon which the State of Israel is dependent, would become a source of intense conflict, if the question of self-rule for the occupied territories emerged as a seriously debated political issue in the region.[51]

Why is it that Israelis and Jordanians diverge in their perceptions of an ongoing conflict over water resources in the basin? Why do Jordanians perceive conflict wherever there are shared bodies of water, while Israelis perceive conflict only on the West Bank?

Just as the combination of resource need and relative power determines the possibility for cooperation in international river basins, so does it explain the variation in perception of the conflict potential of any particular issue. States have different perceptions of the nature and extent of their adversarial relationships. This is especially the case when there is an obvious asymmetry of power between foes. The stronger state may not perceive conflict at all, but this is largely due to the fact that relative power is in its favor. It can achieve its aims by virtue of its superior power resources – via influence, force, "rank," technology, or simply by instilling fear. Under the circumstances, weaker states are often cowed into compliance and potential challengers are neutralized. Hence, there is little reason for the stronger state to perceive conflict.

The weaker state, however, does perceive conflict. Since the asymmetry of power is not in its favor, it is not in a position to achieve its aims and satisfy its needs in an optimal fashion. Its capabilities are inferior to those of its adversary. In effect, it has little alternative but to accept a *modus vivendi* dictated by the stronger. Hence, conflict does exist. Nonetheless, it is not actively played out, since the weaker state does not perceive itself to be capable of altering the *status quo*. Because of the constraints upon it, it is in the weaker state's interest not to incite open conflict. Stated otherwise, when a state's interests are being blocked, but the state does not perceive itself to be in a position to alter the situation by eliminating or even reducing the blockage, or it perceives the potential costs of doing so as outweighing the benefits, overt conflict is unlikely to emerge.

Interestingly enough, several of the Jordanians interviewed described the Kingdom's ability to deal with water-related issues in ways that corroborate this hypothesis. Each statement alludes to the significance of the power equation in states' perceptions and regional behavior:[52]

There is very little that Jordan can do about what Israel does to its water supply. It can yell and scream, call the Mixed Armistice Commission, or go to the United Nations Security Council. But these measures, in essence, are of little use. Basically, Israel does what it wants, and Jordan simply tries to survive the blows.[53]

The regime does not perceive itself to be in a position to take strong action to rectify wrongs. It has very little leverage in the region and in the international community.

Moreover, the proximity of Israel is so worrisome to Jordan. Hence it is thought best not to say too much, to keep quiet, and not "rock the boat." So, when Israel does something that impinges upon Jordanian rights and/or resources, Jordan often lets these things go unnoticed for the sake of preventing a flare-up. Jordan realizes that it is not in a position to retaliate.[54]

The Arab attitude in the post-1967 period is, "if we cannot retrieve Nablus and Hebron, how can we get back the waters?" Jordan does not have the military capability. Israel knows that Jordan is weak and so, it can encroach upon it. There is not much that Arabs can do to stop the Israelis from changing the character of the land (and its water resources) in the Jordan basin and occupied territories.[55]

In Jordan's perception, a water conflict persists because, with Israel's superior might, it can impose its interests in the basin. The absence of power parity, with Jordan as the losing party, causes the Kingdom to view the matter as one of conflict.[56]

Indeed, the above statements and the condition they portray are reminiscent of the Athenians' assertion to the Melians during the Peloponnesian War: "...the strong do what they can and the weak suffer what they must."[57]

As we have noted, the Kingdom of Jordan is severely constrained in the region. Generally speaking, it has limited means to satisfy its needs and interests. No doubt, physical proximity to Israel has profoundly influenced Jordan's regional behavior. Furthermore, the country's water situation has become increasingly critical since the mid-1970s. Given Israel's superior power resources, Jordan assumes, rightly or wrongly, that it is virtually at Israel's mercy insofar as common water supplies are concerned. Hence, all shared bodies of water are perceived as sources of conflict.

For the most part, Israel is in a better position to meet its needs and exploit water resources. Unlike Jordan, there is only one source of water that Israel views as having conflict potential – the subterranean supplies of the West Bank – and that is because the ruling political establishment claims that denying Israel access to that source would pose a threat to its national security.

In sum, therefore, the perception of conflict over water resources is linked to two factors: (1) the state's relative power resources, and (2) its need for unimpeded access to the water supply in question. If the security of a state could be threatened by denial of access to a particular body of water, the latter would be considered a (potential) source of conflict. In contrast, when the security of a state cannot be so threatened, either because the water resources are not vital and indispensable, or else, the state is hegemonic in the basin insofar as power and capabilities are concerned, the very same body of water will not be considered a potential source of conflict.

8 Riparian disputes since 1967

In order to substantiate the argument about the perception of conflict, we explore, in this chapter, the four areas of actual or potential conflict in the Jordan basin since 1967. They are: (1) the question of a dam on the Yarmouk, (2) exploitation of the Yarmouk waters, (3) the subterranean sources in Wadi Araba (ha-Arava) and, (4) the subterranean sources of the West Bank. As in the preceding chapters, our discussion highlights, where appropriate, those variables that influence riparian dispute and determine its outcome.

We find that in none of the four areas has relative power favored the Jordanians or the Palestine Arabs. On the contrary, it has favored Israel, or, as in the case of the Maqarin Dam, a combination of Israel and Syria. In only one of the four areas, the West Bank, can the water resources in question be considered essential for the survival of the State of Israel. (And in part for this reason, Israel is acutely concerned about the future status of this territory.) Hence the perception that this constitutes a source of conflict with the Arabs. In contrast, in at least two and possibly three of the areas, the waters are fundamental to the security concerns of Arabs. Impounding the winter flow of the Yarmouk River behind a dam continues to be indispensable for the Kingdom of Jordan. Moreover, for there to be economic growth and development on the West Bank, let alone a viable (Palestinian) state, there would have to be imports of water from outside the region, if the territory's rich aquifer system cannot be tapped locally. Finally, in all four areas, it is the persistence of inter-state conflict that has inhibited the optimal development of water resources and thwarted the satisfaction of the needs of riparians. This has been a constant throughout the history of the Jordan waters dispute.

Dam-building on the Yarmouk River

As noted in chapter 6, the development of the Jordan Valley had become, by the mid-1970s, a high priority for the Jordanian government. The aim was to meet the socio-economic needs of the country's rapidly growing population. Improving agricultural production and the overall quality of life through the extension of the irrigated area, the development of hydro-electric power, and

171

the provision of storage for municipal and industrial water uses, figured significantly in Stage II of the Jordan Valley project. As the centerpiece of the scheme, the idea of impounding the Yarmouk waters behind a dam, straddling the river at the Maqarin site – first advocated by Mills Bunger in the early 1950s and adopted by the UNRWA in 1953 for a short period prior to the Johnston mission – was revived enthusiastically by the Jordanian authorities.[1] In 1976, Jordan and Syria renegotiated and agreed to amend their 1953 treaty on joint exploitation of the Yarmouk waters.[2] Thus began the campaign to realize the Maqarin project, initially planned as a Jordanian–Syrian irrigation and hydro-electric scheme for the benefit of both sides of the common border.

The Carter administration in Washington immediately took an interest in the project. As with the Johnston mission, the United States perceived regional water development as a stepping stone to regional peace, given that projects would require multilateral cooperation in the use of water resources.[3] In 1976, it financed a feasibility study of Jordan Valley irrigation through dam-building and utilizing Yarmouk waters. It then undertook to help finance the Maqarin project.

Israel reacted strongly to the revival of the Maqarin project, and referred to it as "a return to the struggle over the waters."[4] It demanded recognition as a party to the Yarmouk waters, as it had with the Bunger Plan in the fifties. Two matters were of especial concern to the government. First, it wanted a guarantee that Jewish settlements in the Yarmouk Triangle could continue to draw water from the river in accordance with past use. Second, if there were going to be modifications in water distribution from the river, it would want to reopen a dialogue on some of the technicalities of the Johnston plan pertaining to Yarmouk water.[5]

The plan for Unified Development (1955) had made allowances for an allocation of at least 70 mcm (with some parties claiming that it was as much as 150 mcm) to the West Ghor of the Jordan Valley via a feeder canal from the Yarmouk River.[6] Hence, Israel served to gain considerably from a reconsideration of the plan now that it occupied the West Bank. Israel argued that if Jordan and Syria were to go ahead with their dam project, its allocation of Yarmouk water would have to be reevaluated. It maintained that it would have rights to all the water reaching the West Bank, in addition to that which had been earmarked originally for the West Ghor Canal. Military occupation bestowed rights of sovereignty and resource exploitation.

Again, water development in the Jordan basin brought into focus the larger inter-state conflict and some of the basic issues that were at its core: (1) control over land and, as its extension, control over water resources, and (2) recognition and legitimacy of control. The question arose as to whom belonged the Yarmouk water quotas which, according to the Johnston Plan, were to be diverted from the Jordan Valley flats east and west of the river: to Israel, which now administered the western Jordan Valley, or to the Arabs, from whom the land was captured in 1967. The Johnston Plan had recognized the Arabs' entitlement to these quotas because of their intended purpose – refugee rehabilitation.

Jordan, Syria, and the United States perceived in Israel's reaction to the Maqarin project an implicit demand for additional water resources to facilitate its settlement plans in occupied territory.[7] Washington's response at this initial juncture was categorical: it did not accept that Yarmouk waters be used for the implementation of an extensive Jewish settlement program in the Jordan Valley. This it conveyed to the Government of Israel, and went further to express its reservations regarding Israel's standing as a sovereign power in "Judea and Samaria." These were considered conquered territories under military occupation; they were not legally incorporated parts of the State.[8] However, before proceeding with discussions, all parties awaited the results of the American-financed feasibility study, carried out by the Harza Overseas Engineering Company, one of the two firms which, in the mid-1950s, had drawn up the project for the Kingdom of Jordan for the utilization of the Jordan and Yarmouk Rivers.[9]

Among the various recommendations made by Harza in 1978 was the construction of a 170-metre-high dam, reservoir, and powerplant at the Maqarin site, with a total volume of 320 mcm and a useful storage capacity of 275 mcm.[10] An allowance of between 17 and 25 mcm of Yarmouk River water, depending on whether or not a diversion dam could be built at Adasiye, was to be released annually to meet the acquired needs of the Yarmouk Triangle. At the time of carrying out the study, the total cost of the proposed project was estimated at $432 million. Eighteen months later, when the project was being discussed in the US Congress, the estimated cost had risen to about $650 million and was likely to continue rising.[11] The office of the President announced that it would seek appropriations from Congress for a total support of $150 million over a three-year period, provided that the project proceeded as planned.

At a session of Congress devoted to foreign assistance disbursements for fiscal year 1979, two major provisos were attached to Washington's decision to support the Maqarin scheme. First, United States' participation was dependent upon Jordan having obtained firm commitments from other sources for the balance of the financing of the project. Second, the United States had to be assured that "the interests of all the riparian states on the question of water sharing downstream have been taken into consideration. This will involve firm understandings with and between Israel and Jordan, as well as the continued cooperation of Syria..."[12]

Since Israel was the downstream riparian on the Yarmouk River, the availability of water for the Yarmouk Triangle (and perhaps for the West Bank as well) had to be addressed. Impounding Yarmouk flow in the Maqarin reservoir would impact upon the downstream availability of water. Thus, Jordan had to reach agreement with Israel on water allocations and structures. Jordan also had to reach agreement with Syria, since water that would be stored in the dam originates in the upper reaches of the Yarmouk River in Syria, and one side of the dam would be constructed on Syrian territory.[13]

At least in the short-term, the first proviso was straightforward. At a meeting held in October 1979, financial commitments for the balance of the project were earmarked or tentatively pledged by seven other donors.[14] However, it was the second proviso that would prove to be *the* stumbling block to the entire scheme.

Initially, Syria was anxious to have the Maqarin project implemented; it stood to gain the bulk of the limited amount of hydro-electric power (15 megawatts) generated at the damsite.[15] Nonetheless, given that four of the five sources of the Yarmouk River rose in Syria and that some 48 mcm of those waters were to be diverted into the Maqarin reservoir, an important question remained to be settled: to what degree did Syria intend to utilize the upstream sources for domestic purposes, thereby affecting downstream water supplies?

A United States' Government staff study mission to the region at the end of 1978 reported that it was not clear how much water the Syrians would be taking from the Yarmouk tributaries. Their ultimate decision on water uses remained an "important imponderable."[16] Two years later, and despite continuous discussions helped along by the shuttle diplomacy of former United States Assistant Secretary of State Philip Habib, there was still some doubt as to how much water the Syrians wished to utilize rather than have flow into the Maqarin reservoir.[17]

Israel's official position *vis-à-vis* the project was that it too wished to be cooperative. However, it did have certain riparian concerns.[18] Of primary interest was the impact of the dam on Israel's own perceived water needs. The government required precise information and firm guarantees on two main issues: (1) the size and capacity of the dam to be built, and (2) the quantities of water that would be released from the dam for the Yarmouk Triangle and for the West Bank.[19]

Since the critical matter for Israel was water allocations and their destinations downstream of the dams, it was necessarily anxious to know about the structural design and capacity of the dams to be built.[20] As to allocations for the Triangle, Jordan's opening position was 17 mcm of Yarmouk water, in keeping with the lesser of the two figures proposed in Harza's 1978 feasibility study. Israel rejected that figure and insisted on a minimum of 40 mcm, as it had during the third round of the Johnston mission talks. As a compromise, the United States proposed an allocation of 25 mcm, which Israel already had access to by virtue of "historic use" in the Triangle. Besides, this was the figure stipulated in Johnston's Revised Unified Plan and which Israel had apparently agreed to by signing the Draft Memorandum of Understanding in July 1955.[21] Israel, however, was claiming an option on an additional quantity of water for prospective irrigation schemes.[22]

In these initial stages, little progress was made in building greater understanding between Israel and Jordan. The major point of friction remained the Jordan Valley on both sides of the river where, in terms of geography, the two countries and the West Bank shared surface flow and, in part, subterranean waters as well. Israel's concerns stemmed from the fact that the usable capacities of the principal surface resource, the Jordan River, and its natural storage reservoir, Lake Tiberias, were already exploited. Moreover, groundwater basins in the western valley were being pumped annually to limits just short of net depletion and irreversible deterioration.[23] There was little expectation of discovering new aquifers with significant yields. The government of Israel maintained that a reduction in water flowing from the Yarmouk to the Jordan would automatically result in further local drilling of West Bank aquifers, some of which carry water to within Israel's pre-1967 lines. Thus, Israel would have access to less water.[24] Conversely, the more water available to the West Bank, the fewer additional underground drillings there to affect Israel's supply. Hence, the government believed it had a legitimate right to seek agreement with Jordan on the amount of water which would flow to the West Bank.

Be that as it may, the Kingdom of Jordan insisted that it would not support the extension of Jewish settlement in occupied territory.[25] Furthermore, it had become increasingly concerned about the link that was being drawn between its own vital needs and Israeli needs in occupied territory, especially since at the talks among Israel, Egypt, and the United States over the question of West Bank–Gaza Strip autonomy, coinciding with the discussions over the Yarmouk waters, Israel had insisted on retaining control over the territory's water supply.[26] The indirect talks between Israel and Jordan, mediated by Philip Habib, provoked much dispute over the politically sensitive issue of Israel's avowed responsibility to negotiate suitable future water supplies for the West Bank and Gaza Strip.

Because the two riparians could not work out a mutually acceptable division of the Yarmouk waters, the United States Government Economic Support Fund appropriation of $50 million, originally programmed for the Maqarin Dam, could not be allocated either for fiscal year 1979 or for the following year.[27]

In the meantime, the need for a dam on the Yarmouk River was gaining in importance. Less than two-thirds of Jordan's exploitable water potential had been harnessed by 1979.[28] The kingdom continued to produce no more than 20 percent of its food requirements. Moreover, Amman and surrounding areas were experiencing severe water shortages; some districts, in fact, received piped water only once a week.[29] Not only had the groundwater servicing the urban complex become increasingly polluted, but also the aquifers themselves were limited in supply. By 1980, the amount of potable water available to the urban areas was only about one-half of what was desirable to sustain adequate health conditions.[30] Thus, the Maqarin Dam, which had originally been intended as an exclusively agricultural and hydro-power scheme, would now be necessary for the diversion of drinking water to the major cities as well.

As time passed, the United States remained interested in supporting the scheme for its intrinsic value as the solution to Jordan's difficult water situation and as a potential "gateway to peace" in the region.[31] Nonetheless, congressional opinion reflected increasing concern over the rising cost of the project as its schedule slipped and its viability became less certain, given the serious political issues involved.[32] The Foreign Assistance budget for fiscal year 1981 was passed without the inclusion of a request for financing the Maqarin Dam.

In the spring of 1980, however, the *New York Times* reported that Israel and Jordan were discussing the division of the Yarmouk waters fairly successfully, using the "good offices" of the United States. According to both American and Israeli officials, the negotiations were entering "advanced stages."[33] Around the same time, relations between Jordan and Syria, which had been reestablished only four years before, suddenly took a nosedive. Severe domestic turmoil and fierce internal opposition characterized Hafez al-Asad's regime in the late 1970s and early 1980s.[34] The Syrian leadership accused Jordan of lending covert support to the Muslim Brotherhood in Syria in order to destabilize the regime. Asad struck back by massing troops along the Jordanian border and threatening to invade.[35] The Iran–Iraq War followed, with Syria supporting the former and Jordan, the latter.

In this atmosphere of renewed tension, there was no prospect of reaching agreement on riparian issues. The bilateral talks, mediated by Philip Habib, bogged down and soon after, came to a complete halt. According to high-ranking Jordanian officials, the Syrians would not respond to any overtures concerning a water-sharing plan.[36] And in 1981, the United States Department of State announced that it would not seek new funds from Congress for the scheme until there were improved political conditions in the region.[37] Jordan's inability to reach agreement with Syria became the immediate cause of the indefinite postponement of the much needed dam.

In the final analysis and according to those interviewed, the Maqarin scheme could not be implemented primarily because of Syria's rejectionist position.[38] Syria would not approve a project that entailed any form of cooperation with Israel.[39] Its position had not changed significantly since the breakdown of the Johnston mission in 1955; then as now, it was not prepared to support even a technical arrangement with the enemy, no matter how urgent. Besides, the Maqarin project was largely for Jordan's benefit. (Syria may have acted otherwise had it been the principal beneficiary and had its need for the project been indispensable.) Nor did the leadership want to engage in a scheme that would be located within reach of Israeli artillery.[40] It was acutely aware from past experience that hydraulic installations were tempting military targets in conflict situations. The construction of the Mukheiba (or Khalid ibn al-Walid) Dam on the Yarmouk River had been stopped by Israeli military intervention in June 1967. The preliminary work on the Arab diversion scheme in Syrian territory succumbed to Israeli gunfire during the mid-1960s. And Jordan's East Ghor Canal had been knocked out of service on four separate occasions between 1967 and 1971.[41] Undoubtedly, Hafez al-Asad was also profoundly concerned about the sophisticated installations on the Euphrates River in the north of the country.[42] (See map 8.1.)

With regard to Israel and Jordan, it is likely that, given their ability on several occasions to conclude technical arrangements when deemed imperative, they would have been able to do so this time as well, had there been no need to involve Syria.[43] Needless to say, Israel would have driven a hard bargain. It is our personal conjecture that Jordan would have conceded eventually to the 40 mcm for the Yarmouk Triangle and perhaps a symbolic allocation for the West Bank, as well, despite its official non-recognition of Israeli sovereignty over the territories. It is important to recall that impounding the Yarmouk waters behind a dam remained, as of the mid-1970s, the *only* solution to the Kingdom's precarious water situation. The unfortunate combination of Jordan's critical need for water, its unfavorable geographic position by virtue of having no natural storage on the Yarmouk, and its inferior power resources compel the regime to engage in cooperative arrangements with Israel which may be viewed by some as politically compromising, but are considered by the Kingdom as vital for its continued survival.

As we have seen in previous chapters, domestic needs often fall victim to inter-state conflict. In the particular case of the Jordan basin, the aim to develop water resources in an effort to meet the socio-economic needs of the riparians brought to the fore those issues that characterized their political rivalry: (1) control over land and resources, (2) legitimacy and recognition of control, (3) identity and allegiance of populations. There could be virtually

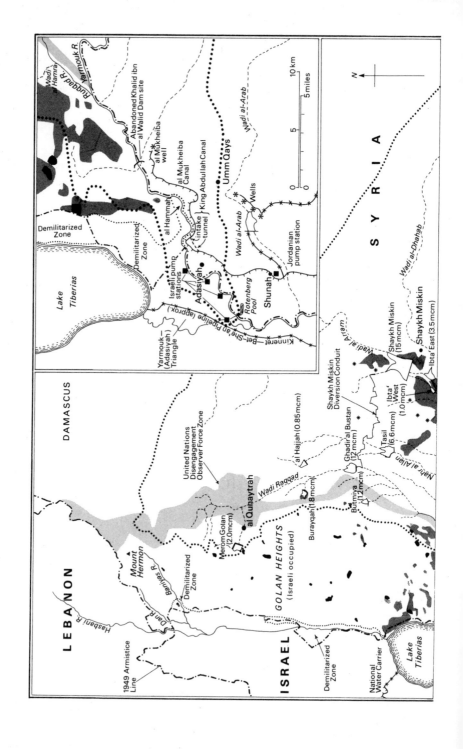

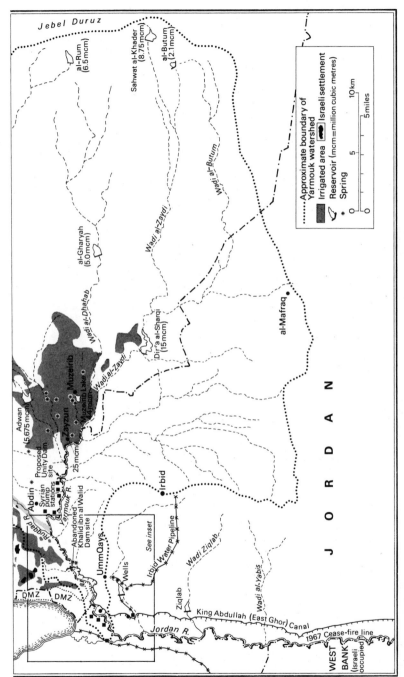

8.1 Yarmouk River watershed

no dealings between riparian states and no development efforts in the basin without reference to the larger regional conflict.

Moreover, the experience of the Maqarin Dam project, as with earlier schemes, elucidates the proposition that regional conflict exacerbates the water problems of states by virtue of the fact that it impedes the optimal resolution of water disputes in an international river basin. Accordingly, an end to riparian dispute requires the prior resolution of the political conflict and not vice versa. This finding refutes the position and efforts of the United States Government. The latter consistently believed, in the mid-1950s as in the late 1970s, that cooperation among adversaries was possible in areas of mutual concern and that solving the water problems of states would contribute to peace. American administrations devoted much time and energy to promoting this view. In fact, in the Jordan basin, regional development of water resources could not be realized *precisely* because of the inter-state conflict. The latter would have to be resolved before the former could be successfully implemented.

In recent years, yet another attempt has been made at having a dam built on the Yarmouk River. At the initiative of Jordan, a treaty was signed between it and Syria in September 1987.[44] Jordan badly needed access to more water. Syria wanted to reduce its political isolation and consolidate its southern flank. Both wanted to improve their diplomatic relations. Nonetheless, to secure an agreement, Jordan had to make major concessions. By the terms of the treaty, a dam of about one-half the size of the proposed Maqarin dam would be built near the former site. Syria would be allowed to build a series of 24 dams upstream, in addition to receiving most, if not all, of the electricity generated by the Unity (*al-Wahdah*) dam.

The Harza engineering firm was commissioned by the United States Agency for International Development to conduct a feasibility study of the project. In its report, it insisted that because of intensive water utilization upstream, the dam could have a capacity of no more than 225 mcm of water. Of this, 50 mcm would be transported directly to the Amman/Zarqa urban area to provide for domestic consumption.

Jordan petitioned the World Bank to help finance the project, estimated at $400 million, and inspire confidence among other potential donors. The Bank, however, made its involvement conditional upon securing the agreement of all riparians to the project itself, as well as to the exchange of information about water usage.

The United States Department of State conducted low level "quiet inquiries" in 1988. Shortly thereafter, Secretary of State James Baker appointed Richard Armitrage mediator between Israel and Jordan.[45] Until there was an improvement in its relations with Syria, the United States would engage in no mediation effort with that country. Negotiations took place from September 1989 to 20 August 1990 and the Iraqi invasion of Kuwait. Since the Gulf crisis and the collapse of the Jordanian economy, there have been no new attempts to resurrect the dam project.

Exploiting the Yarmouk waters

In the absence of a dam on the Yarmouk, Syria continues to divert water upstream for its extensive irrigation projects, and Israel diverts to Lake Tiberias as much of the winter flow as climatic factors and the lake's storage capacity permit. Yarmouk water stored in Israel's natural reservoir can then be used for internal consumption.[46]

The river's winter flow amounts to some 300 mcm per annum, or approximately two-thirds of total discharge under "normal" climatic conditions and prior to diversions.[47] According to Israeli sources, a small pumping station was built on the Yarmouk in 1975–76, and for several years, "a few tens" of mcm were diverted annually to Lake Tiberias. The declared assumption of the Israeli government was that this withdrawal would not be long-lasting; it was initiated because water was "going to waste," while Israel could make use of it until such time as artificial storage were created on the river.[48] Publicly, officials insist that Israel does not lay claims to this source. It is simply taking advantage of its favorable geographic position for the time being, and improving its water budget as well.[49]

In the mid-1980s, informed sources suggested, Israel was diverting substantially more than "a few tens" of mcm to Lake Tiberias. Artificial storage on the Yarmouk had still not been built. Besides, Lake Tiberias had the capacity to store some 180 mcm from the Yarmouk River alone.[50] According to our estimates, based on interviews, Israel was diverting approximately 100 mcm of Yarmouk winter flow to its natural reservoir on a yearly basis during the first half of the 1980s. This was in addition to the 25 mcm that it gets during the summer months for the Yarmouk Triangle, in accordance with historical right and the stipulations of the Johnston Plan.[51] Hence, of a total discharge of about 450 mcm, Israel was exploiting more than 25 percent, as opposed to the 5 percent suggested by Eric Johnston. No doubt, withdrawals from the river are dependent upon prevailing climatic conditions. According to one source, Israel's withdrawal fell to 80–85 mcm during the recent years of drought (1987–91).[52]

A favorable geographic position has allowed Israel to store and exploit the Yarmouk winter flow. Apart from creating artificial storage – itself fraught with difficulties – there is virtually nothing that Jordan can do to prevent the Israeli diversion. Surely, the combination of Israel's superior geographic and topographic position, and Jordan's inability to reach an agreement with the other riparians concerning the building of a dam on the Yarmouk, is a source of humiliation for the kingdom. Besides, it confirms the latter's perception of an asymmetry of power in the basin, in favor of its upstream and downstream neighbors.

No doubt for Jordan, the Yarmouk is considered a source of conflict. The river is the only major body of water available to the kingdom. In contrast, Israel's dependence on the river's waters is limited; it amounts to no more than 6 percent of the country's total available supply. Despite Jordan's overriding dependence, it has no storage capacity. As long as this remains the case, Israel can continue to extract part of the winter flow, store it in its own natural reservoir, and use it for domestic consumption. And Syria can continue to withdraw increasing amounts of water upstream for its own irrigation projects. In effect, Jordan's hands are tied.

Wadi ʿAraba/ha-Arava

This region, which extends from some fifty kilometres south of the Dead Sea to the Gulf of Aqaba on both sides of the international boundary, is very arid. The only water available for agricultural purposes can be found in subterranean basins, some of which are common to Israel and Jordan. Being a largely desert region, fertile land is limited, as is the potential for extensive economic development.

Both Israel and Jordan have been implementing a variety of agricultural schemes on their respective sides of the border. Both have been irrigating land by pumping groundwater from the aquifers that they share. Since there is no coordination of activities, pumping is competitive. The combination of competitive pumping and the fact that the rate of aquifer recharge in this region is limited, has resulted in the rapid depletion of groundwater supplies and their increasing salinity.[53]

To date, no technical agreements over these waters have been sought by either side. Neither party perceives the supplies to be nearly as significant – in terms of quality, quantity, and exploitability – as the Yarmouk waters, for example. As long as these subterranean sources are not perceived to be essential for survival, cooperative arrangements are not sought. But it is likely that in the future, as the demand for water increases with population growth and socio-economic development, Wadi ʿAraba groundwater may gain in importance to both Jordanians and Israelis. As we have seen with other cases, once resources come to be considered essential to the development concerns of states, cooperation may be solicited.

In the absence of coordination, the outcome of competitive groundwater pumping turns on relative power in the basin, or more precisely, "who can dig deeper to take the maximum amount of water from the aquifer."[54]

Because of its superior technology and know-how, Israel invariably "comes out on top."

As noted in the previous chapter, the Arab view since 1967 is that the conflict over water has extended, insofar as "virtually all sources of water are drawn in." Moreover, the conflict is perceived as one of "protagonist proximity not simply to run-off, but even to underground reserves." Because of the asymmetry of power in the basin, coupled with Arab perceptions in the post-1967 period, the limited groundwater supplies of Wadi ʿAraba are considered a source of conflict with Israel, and one that is likely to increase in importance. Conversely, because relative power is in its favor, Israel denies the importance of these southern aquifers and their conflict potential.

To both Arabs and Israelis, however, there are certain subterranean sources that are considered of paramount importance and essential to national survival. These are the rich groundwater reserves of the West Bank, the territory which the State of Israel refers to by its Biblical names, Judea and Samaria.

West Bank groundwater

It appears equally clear [to the United States] that along with other outstanding issues of the Palestine dispute – compensation, repatriation, Jerusalem, boundaries – there is a fifth element, water, which must be considered as we approach a final settlement.

US Department of State, Position Paper, May 1953[55]

The role played by West Bank water resources in the larger water dispute in the Jordan basin since 1967 can be illuminated through a review of Israel's water supply and consumption practices. As noted in chapter 6, the average sustainable annual water yield in pre-1967 Israel was approximately 1·6 bcm, about 60 percent of which derived from groundwater. As of the mid-1980s, exploitation of fresh water had reached 1·9 bcm, of which roughly 1·2 bcm – or three-fifths of total renewable water potential – were of subterranean origin.[56]

The critical point about the groundwater sources upon which the State of Israel is dependent, is their location and direction of flow. Of the three main aquifer groups, only one is located in Israel proper, beneath the coastal plain. This is the second most abundant of the three groups. The remaining two originate in occupied territory. The Yarqon-Taninim aquifer, the most abundant, extends from north to south along the western foothills of the West Bank (see map 8.2). Its natural recharge flows in a westerly direction across the "Green Line," the 1949 United Nations Armistice Demarcation line, into Israel's coastal plain. The least abundant – those aquifer groups in the northern part of the West Bank – drain an area across the "Green Line," as well, and discharge into the Bet She'an and Jezreʿel Valleys. Both the

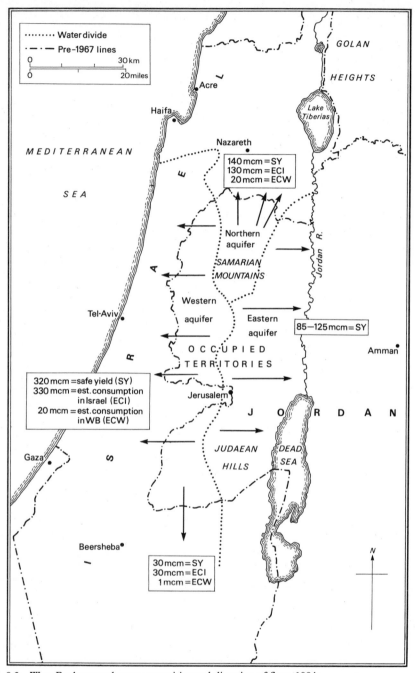

8.2   West Bank groundwater: quantities and direction of flow, 1984

western and northern basins can be tapped from either side of the "Green Line." However, only 5 percent of the combined recharge area of the two water tables is located in Israel proper.[57] Another group of aquifers, the smallest of the West Bank water tables, forms the eastern drainage basin. Its waters do not traverse the Armistice Demarcation line and hence, cannot be exploited outside the territory. Its flow discharges into the Jordan Valley.[58] (See table 8.1.) From table 8.1, we note that approximately 40 percent of the groundwater upon which the State of Israel is dependent and one-quarter of its sustainable annual water yield originate in occupied territory. These facts highlight the perceived importance of the West Bank for the security and development concerns of Israel. They suggest, as well, why West Bank water has been a source of conflict between the Arabs and Israelis since 1967.

The water resources of the West Bank can be divided into two categories: (1) surface run-off, including river and stream flow and (2) groundwater. There is considerable variation in published discharge figures, ranging from a total of about 650 mcm to as much as 900 mcm.[59] No matter which of the figures one considers, what is significant about total availability is that the consumption of water by the Arab population of the West Bank in the 1980s, and this we shall see in greater detail below, has not been allowed to exceed 125 mcm, that is, 14–18 percent of total availability.[60] Hence, the remainder, of between 525 to 775 mcm, minus that which is lost to evaporation or surface run-off before it can be utilized, represents the amount that can be exploited by the non-Arab population and/or beyond the territory of the West Bank.

Both prior to and since 1967, agriculture on the West Bank has been mostly rainfed. Until the mid-1960s, the limited irrigated agriculture that existed was largely dependent upon spring water. Nonetheless, by June 1967, the total output of wells, on the western slopes and in the Jordan Valley, was 38 mcm.[61]

Since 1967 and the Israeli occupation of the West Bank and Gaza Strip, local development of water resources has been strictly controlled. The primary aim has been to protect the precarious water balance of the State of Israel within the "Green Line." To reiterate, about 40 percent of the groundwater which Israel consumes and one-quarter of the state's sustainable annual water yield originates in rainfall over the western slopes of the West Bank, and is drawn by drilling inside pre-1967 Israel proper from the same aquifer system that contains the water reserves for the West Bank.[62] Hence, from the point of view of Israel and its security concerns, it is imperative to minimize local utilization of West Bank aquifers, and impede their over-exploitation and resultant salinization. Excessive pumping of subterranean sources causes a drop in the water table which, in turn, invites salt water encroachment.[63]

Table 8.1 *Principal aquifers in Israel and West Bank*

	Drainage area (km²)	Direction of flow	Safe yield (mcm per year)
Israel			
Coastal plain	1,800	west	240–300
West Bank			
Western basin	1,600	west	335
Northern basin	590	north/northeast	130–140
Eastern basin	2,021	east/southeast	85–125

Source : Schwarz, "Water Resources"; "Israeli Water Sector."

Although figures vary considerably, the absolute limit on West Bank water use – that is, the sustainable annual yield minus that which is lost to evaporation or surface run-off – is, according to one study, about 615 mcm.[64] However, it has been reported that in the spring of 1990, the combined allocations for West Bank Arabs, Jewish settlers, and the amount reaching Israel was estimated at 807 mcm per year. This represents an annual water deficit in the territory of almost 200 mcm, due to the over-exploitation of the western and northeastern basins.[65]

By 1982, over-exploitation had led to a drop in the water table at a rate of 0·3–0·4 metres per annum in the western basin and about two metres in part of the northeastern basin.[66] This constitutes a grave potential danger to the continued intensive utilization of groundwater. In fact, one source estimates that by 1994, the two basins will have lost approximately one-third of their water tables. Furthermore, over-pumping will increase the salinity of the entire aquifer system of the West Bank.[67]

Because of the delicate hydrodynamic balance between fresh and saline water bodies, coupled with the inexorable growth of Israeli water consumption, as outlined in chapter 6, water resources must be protected. That being the case, the current Israeli political establishment deems it necessary to prevent substantial economic development of the Arab sector of the West Bank, so that rainfall, which seeps into the ground and replenishes the western and northeastern aquifers, would continue to flow across the "Green Line" where it is tapped by an elaborate system of wells between Haifa and Tel-Aviv.

Israel's water resources are administered by the Israeli Water Commission at whose head there is a commissioner, subject to the authority of the Minister of Agriculture. The other main components of the Water Commission Administration are Mekorot, Israel's national water authority, and

Table 8.2 *Water consumption on West Bank by sector (mcm per year)*

	Agriculture	M & I[a]	Total
1968	75	5	80
1981	90–100	14	104–114
1990	100	25	125

[a] Municipal and industrial.
Source: Kahan, *Agriculture and Water*, p. 25; AMER.

Table 8.3 *Water consumption in Israel by sector (mcm per year)*

	Municipal	Industrial	Agriculture	Total
1979/80	375	90	1,235	1,700
1982/83	401	103	1,255	1,759
1983/84	419	103	1,356	1,878
1984/85	422	109	1,389	1,920
1985/86	450	103	1,434	1,987

Source: State of Israel, *Statistical Abstract* 1987.

Tahal, the Water Planning for Israel Company. Mekorot is responsible for the construction of irrigation and water supply projects, and Tahal, for the overall planning and design of water development projects. Since July 1967, the water resources of the Occupied Territories have gradually been integrated into the Israeli water system, and now are under the direct control of the Water Commission.[68] In an effort to protect the quantity and quality of the water resources consumed in Israel proper, the policy set forth by the commissioner allows West Bank Arabs a total consumption of 125 mcm per annum,[69] plus a small margin of growth in personal use (see tables 8.2 and 8.3).

Stringent measures have been adopted to ensure that this policy is respected. First, no wells can be drilled on the West Bank without permission from the Civil Administration, Tahal and Mekorot. No Palestinian Arab individual or village has received permission to drill a new well for agricultural purposes since July 1967, nor repair one that is close to an Israeli well.[70] Sinking wells on the mountain ridge, the location of the Yarqon-Taninim aquifer, is strictly forbidden.[71] Occasionally, permission is granted for the drilling of wells destined for domestic use. With regard to Arab requests, Israel's Water Commissioner, Meir Ben-Meir, has been quoted as saying: " If their demand is for drinking water, we must say yes... We do say

187

yes. But we are not going to stop irrigating our orchards so they can plant new ones."[72] Second, for the agricultural activities of West Bank Arabs, only "existing uses" of water are recognized; the term refers to uses which existed in 1967–68.[73] Thus, water allocations to Arab agriculture have remained frozen at their 1968 figure of 100 mcm, with a slight margin for growth.[74] Third, the technology for deep-drilling and rock-drilling – that which would be required in the western basin, at least – remains in Israeli hands. Fourth, West Bank Arabs are not allowed to use water for agricultural purposes after four o'clock in the afternoon.[75] Fifth, strict limits are placed on the amount of water that can be pumped annually from each well. Meters fixed to wells monitor the amounts extracted. In 1983, the total quantity of well water permitted to the Arab population did not exceed the 1967 level of 38 mcm.[76] Finally, whereas the water utilized by Jewish settlers is heavily subsidized by the state, West Bank Palestinians receive no subsidy at all.[77] They pay a higher price per cubic metre of water than do the settlers. It has been estimated that in 1990, Palestinians were paying as much as six times more for water than the settlers.[78] The effectiveness of these measures gains in significance when Arab utilization of West Bank water is compared with that of the Israeli population.

While Palestinian Arabs have been prevented from sinking new wells for agriculture, Mekorot drilled thirty-six wells on the West Bank between July 1967 and 1989 for the domestic and irrigation needs of Jewish settlements. Of these, at least twenty are in the Jordan Valley and ten on the mountainous western fringe.[79] And unlike Arab wells, which rarely exceed depths of 100 metres, those drilled by Mekorot are between 200 and 750 metres deep.[80] Greater depths allow for superior output and water quality. While Arab extractions have remained fixed at their 1968 level of 38 mcm, Jewish settlements, in the early 1980s, were consuming close to 50 percent of the total amount of water pumped on the West Bank.[81] By 1987, the unequal distribution of water resources had sharpened yet further. *Le Monde* reported that West Bank Arabs were receiving barely more than 20 percent of the total volume of water pumped from the West Bank.[82] According to another source, Palestinians were receiving 17 percent of West Bank water at the end of the decade (see tables 8.4 and 8.5). Moreover, it has been reported that, in their projections for the year 2000, the Israeli water authorities plan to allot some 150 mcm for the West Bank population, who will then number well over one million, and 110 mcm for the expected 100,000 Israeli settlers.[83] These figures represent a ten times greater per capita water allocation for Jewish settlers than for West Bank Palestinians.

Competition over scarce resources on the West Bank manifests itself not solely in the implementation of stringent measures to control water usage, but also, through the effects that these measures have had on Arab

Table 8.4 *West Bank aquifers : consumers and degree of consumption, 1990*
(*percentages*)

	West Bank Arabs	Israel	Settlers
Western basin	5	95	
Northeastern basin	15	85 +	
Southeastern basin	64		28

Source : Schwarz, "Israeli Water Sector"; AMER.

Table 8.5 *Consumption of West Bank water, 1988/89*

Consumer	Population	Quantity Consumed (mcm per year)
Israelis (inside "Green Line")	4,200,000	560
Settlers (excluding East Jerusalem)	70,000	40–50
West Bank Arabs	1,000,000	125

Source : Kolars, "Course of Water"; USG/DS; AMER.

agriculture. To take one example, it has been noted that where well-drilling for Jewish settlements is carried out in close proximity to Palestinian springs or wells, the result has been a marked decline in the output of the springs and a lowering of the water level in the wells.[84] This is due largely to the fact that, with superior technology in hand, Mekorot drills deep wells after extensive geological surveying, in contrast to Palestinian farmers who drill shallower wells in convenient locations.[85] The deeper the well (and the more geologically sound its location), the more abundant its water supply and the better equipped it is to resist contamination, salt water intrusion, and the harsh effects of drought. In addition, when two wells are located within the effective radius of each other, the deeper one tends to milk the water supply of the shallower one. When this is coupled with absence or sparseness of rainfall, the shallower well is gradually sucked dry.

Of the 200,000 hectares of cultivated land on the West Bank, in the early 1980s, roughly 13,000 hectares (or 6 percent) were under irrigation. (See table 8.6.) According to a report by Tahal, there remain approximately 53,500 hectares of potentially irrigable land. An additional 200 mcm of water would be required to bring this land under irrigation.[86] However, as the water resources of the territory are already almost fully committed, such development cannot take place. The Israeli water establishment contends

Table 8.6 *West Bank: Cultivated and Irrigated Area by Population, 1980*

	Total	Arabs	Jews
Land area	560,000 ha		
Cultivated area	200,000 ha	190,000 ha	9,030 ha
as % of total cultivated area		95%	4·5%
Irrigated area	13,000 ha	4,873 ha	8,127 ha
as % of total irrigated area		37%	62%
as % of own cultivated area		2·5%	90%

Source: USG/DS; Kahan, *Agriculture and Water*; AMER.

that the West Bank suffers from acute water shortage, more so than does Israel proper.[87]

It is true that there is more irrigable land on the West Bank than water currently available for new uses. And with that criterion in mind, it is reasonable for analysts to argue that the future development of the territories is "totally dependent upon imports of water from outside sources."[88] What is equally true, however, is that a large portion of the West Bank water supply is exploited beyond the territory's frontiers. Hence, if that, or even part of that which is currently tapped outside the region were made available to the local population, there would be the resources with which to irrigate the remaining irrigable land. Indeed, all of the West Bank's current and even anticipated future needs could be met if the waters of the western basin alone were available for local consumption.[89] In other words, it is only because of the highly inequitable distribution of its water resources that the West Bank can be considered "water poor"; in fact, there is no absolute shortage.

Nonetheless, it is important to remember that the waters of the western basin drain naturally toward Israel's coastal plain. They do not respect boundaries nor Armistice Demarcation lines. Nor are there any clearly defined international laws prohibiting the exploitation of groundwater across political frontiers.[90] In addition, it is both easier and less costly to tap the western aquifers from Israel proper, because the topography inside the "Green Line" is less mountainous and less rocky than on the other side. It involves neither long-range drilling nor rock-drilling. Furthermore, because the State of Israel has immediate access to some of the most sophisticated techniques in water usage and exercises sovereign control over the Territories, it can extract water from any of the West Bank aquifers long before and more efficiently than the local Arab population. As one Israeli expert on water affairs has pointed out: "The West Bank cannot use the water that underlies its territory because Israel is more advanced in using water, and they use the waters of the Yarqon-Taninim aquifer first."[91]

As we have seen in chapter 7, the question of access to West Bank water is the only water-related issue that Israel perceives as a source of conflict between itself and the Arabs. The combination of Israel's acute dependence on the water supply in occupied territory and the Arab population's historical right to its land and resources inevitably provokes competition and conflict.[92] Given that groundwater represents some 60 percent of the total water consumption of the State of Israel, and that about 40 percent of this source originates on the West Bank, the significance of the territory's water resources is indisputable. Without access to the rich groundwater supplies of the West Bank, Israel would be denied about one-quarter of the water it consumes.

This combination of factors exposes one of the major reasons why Israel will not easily rescind control over the territory. Because of the perceived links between the water resources of the West Bank and the survival of the State of Israel, accepting an independent Palestinian state on the West Bank and hence, relinquishing control of the territory's resources, is interpreted by some as equivalent to an act of national suicide:

Though it is the security imperative for Israel's retaining control of these areas [Judea and Samaria] that is usually discussed, the retention of control of their water resources is no less vital to its continued existence. Israel draws more water from their two main aquifers...than it gets from the Jordan River Basin. Only unified, controlled management of the water resources of the entire area west of the Jordan River can prevent water seeping in and causing irreparable damage...

Israel's final control of these areas is not negotiable. For if the Arabs were free to tap the aquifers to their hearts' desire, they could turn Israel's coastal plain into a desert.[93]

Understandably therefore, a former water commissioner has referred to the water issue as a "time bomb" that would eventually demolish any political arrangements with regard to the future status of the Occupied Territories, unless they included a satisfactory solution to struggles for access to and control over water resources.[94]

9 Conclusion: the conduct of riparian dispute and the potential for cooperation in international river basins

Having analyzed the conflict over the waters of the Jordan River basin from its inception to the present day and drawn comparisons with other cases of riparian dispute in protracted conflict settings, three tasks remain in our inquiry. First, we answer the questions posed in the introduction, in light of the historical record. Second, we evaluate the four variables, or dynamics of state behavior, in terms of the role each has played and the importance of that role in promoting or impeding cooperation. Finally, we refine our argument on the potential for cooperation in international river basins, highlighting the relative persuasiveness of realism and liberal institutionalism.

Conflict and cooperation explained

In the specific case of the Jordan basin, how has the larger political conflict shaped the various efforts to find a negotiated solution to the water dispute?

Over the course of the history of the water dispute, and given the intense hostility between Israel and the Arab states, the primary concern of the parties in considering possibilities for cooperation has been with the issue of relative, and sometimes even absolute, gains. As neo-realists and some neo-liberal institutionalists would expect, neither side has been willing to engage in any activity that could help the adversary become stronger. Specifically, because water is an essential input for growth and development, each side has remained fearful that an agreement for sharing water resources might leave it much weaker at some later date.

In the Jordan basin, the concern for the distribution of gains has been far more important in its bearing on the potential for cooperation than has the intensity or protractedness of the political conflict, for example, or even the issue of non-recognition. In other words, it was not so much that the (Arab) states could not cooperate in sharing water resources because they denied the legitimacy of "the other," but rather, if they would share water and not try to exploit the maximum unilaterally, irrespective of the other's rights and claims, they would be contributing to improving the capabilities of "the other." Doing so could backfire somewhere down the road.

192

One of the major concerns of the Arabs with regard to the plan for the unified development of the Jordan system was the issue of intra-basin versus extra-basin usage of the waters.[1] The Arabs were apprehensive about Israel's intention to transport Jordan water to the Negev desert in the south, outside the basin. It was not so much that this was "Arab water," from tributaries originating in Lebanon and Syria, nor even that the plan contravened international legal principles. Most significant about Israel's project, from the Arab point of view, was that this water would be used to promote the economic development of Israel and the absorption of more Jewish immigrants throughout the country. In sum, the Arabs would not support a project that would strengthen their enemy. To protect themselves, they sought to have the principle of extra-basin usage rejected.

Israel was also deeply concerned about relative gains. It contested Eric Johnston's proposal that Lake Tiberias, which lies within Israeli territory and divides the river system into the Upper and Lower Jordan, be used as an international reservoir for storing water, a portion of which would be used directly by Israel, while another portion would be released by Israel for Arab use.[2] Israel feared that this would guarantee the Arabs future claims to Upper Jordan water and could even encourage demands for territorial changes. One way or another, Israel perceived that the Arabs would gain substantially – and Israel would lose – if it were to concede this.

The concern for relative gains was brought to the fore, again, in the late 1970s and early 1980s, over the issue of Jordan's wish to have a dam built at Maqarin on the Yarmouk River.[3] As we recall, Israel's initial reaction to the project was that it wanted to revive the terms of the earlier "Johnston Plan," since provisions had been made in the plan for a quantity of Yarmouk water to be allocated to the western portion of the Jordan Valley – the West Bank – once a dam were built on the river. Now that Israel exercised control over the territory and plans for building a dam on the Yarmouk were being discussed, it was interested in receiving that share. It did not want the quantity that had previously been allocated to the West Bank to remain on the East Bank and contribute to the East Bank's resource potential simply because the territory was no longer in Jordanian hands. However, Jordan was concerned about the distribution of gains as well. It did not want an allocation to be made to the West Bank from the Yarmouk River, because it knew that the water would be used to extend Jewish settlement in occupied territory and develop the Jewish economy.

As we shall see in the following section, the overall significance of the larger political conflict, including the concern for relative (and/or absolute) gains, receded in importance *only* when the failure to come to agreement could have had devastating consequences.[4] Specifically, this has occurred when one party or the other, but especially the most needy, was sure to experience substantial material gains by sharing resources cooperatively.

When a riparian dispute co-exists with a larger inter-state conflict, is it reasonable to aim to resolve the former as the first step to resolution of the latter? In other words, is the functionalist argument feasible: can we expect to achieve overall political cooperation among hostile states via an ongoing process of task-based arrangements for the satisfaction of shared interests? Similarly, is the neo-liberal argument, about the efficacy of international institutions in promoting cooperation by binding states in "a long-term multilevel game," convincing? More generally, if regime formation is indeed the answer to conflict, how, and under what conditions, can it be achieved? In the history of the dispute over the Jordan waters, there were attempts on two occasions to promote functional arrangements and establish a "regime" for sharing water resources in the basin. In the cases of both the Unified Development Plan in the 1950s and the Maqarin Dam scheme at the end of the 1970s, the United States' Government lent support to the projects in the hope that they would be catalysts to peace in the region.[5] It expected this would happen in the fashion suggested by the functionalists: ongoing practical cooperation in issues of mutual concern would blur animosities by virtue of a new perception of shared needs, eventually leading to overall political cooperation. However, US-sponsored efforts were not successful. On neither occasion was the context one in which *all* parties perceived an equitable distribution of benefits – what Grieco refers to as "a balanced achievement of gains"[6] – nor were there sufficient inducements to bring all parties to the bargaining table. To date, functional arrangements in the Jordan basin have been possible between Israel and only one of the three Arab riparians – Jordan. Nonetheless, they have been exceedingly fragile and limited to one specific task. Before explaining why these two states have been able to achieve limited cooperation, we must first look more closely at the failure to establish regimes in the basin.

If we borrow the language of game theory and consider the functionalist formula as one of iterative games, we note that each player, but especially the one who has the least to lose, can refuse to play any particular game. That is a truism of the game. In the Jordan basin, it was this veto power of the strongest and least needy that resulted in the breakdown of efforts to achieve functional cooperation. More correctly, the player – Syria in the mid-1950s, for example – exercised its veto power because it perceived the payoff structure of the game mediated by Eric Johnston to be incompatible with cooperation. In its assessment of its national preferences, the strongest and least needy player believed that the costs of cooperating outweighed the benefits. Stated otherwise, the lack of mutual interest in the basin foreclosed the possibility of regime-creation.[7] No doubt, and as the neo-functionalists have pointed out, the absence of ideological consensus and agreement of any sort between the parties to the conflict served as an added deterrent to cooperation.

Eric Johnston's lengthy mediation effort was fraught with difficulties. Throughout the negotiating process, there was constant disagreement over water allocations and their destinations, as well as conflicting views of rights, needs, and international legal precedents. Of the four riparians, Israel and Jordan had the greatest need for the Jordan waters. Lebanon and Syria, on the other hand, could have used a portion of the waters for domestic purposes, but given their favorable position as upstream riparians and the fact that they each had other relatively abundant national rivers, they considered the river system primarily as a geopolitically strategic resource *vis-à-vis* Israel, downstream. Nonetheless, both sides eventually admitted that the plan was acceptable on technical grounds. The Arab League, however, was against it for political reasons.[8] And Jordan, the most needy of the Arab riparians, had no clout in inter-Arab politics. The mediation effort came to a halt.

Especially during the years prior to the war of June 1967, the "Question of Palestine" lay at the heart of all interactions and governed all that was possible between Arab and Israeli. As some of the cognitive approaches to the study of cooperation rightly point out, "historically situated" states respond to their environment in light of their very particular normative and ideational constraints. To wit, preferences are linked to the objective environment, as well as to the "psychomilieu."[9] In the Jordan basin, neither party could treat the possibility of sharing water as a straightforward, unambiguous issue. Implicit in water-use arrangements was formal acceptance of "the other" and its rights as a political entity. However, withholding recognition because of questioned legitimacy was part and parcel of the Arab–Israeli conflict. The combination of the nature of the political conflict, the concern for relative gains, and the Arabs' perception that as a collectivity, they had little to gain materially and much to lose politically from a water-sharing scheme with Israel prevented the more powerful Arab states from accepting a regime in the basin.

Again, in the early 1980s, efforts to achieve functional cooperation – this time, on the Yarmouk River – came to nought because of the veto of the stronger Arab riparian (which was also the least needy of the three concerned states) and its perception of the payoff structure. Syria would not approve the Maqarin Dam project, since it would entail cooperation with Israel and would be located within reach of Israeli artillery. Syria's strained relations with Jordan at the time served as another deterrent to cooperation. Moreover, being the upstream riparian, Syria was in the most advantageous position. There could be no cooperation in the basin without its acquiescence, unless it was coerced by a militarily stronger downstream state or third party. This is true of international river basins, in general.

As in the case of the Johnston mission, the Maqarin Dam issue indicates that regional political conflict exacerbates the water problems of states in arid regions, by virtue of the fact that it impedes the "optimal" resolution of riparian disputes. In the Jordan basin, regimes for the distribution and management of water resources could not be realized, in part, because of the cognitive variables at play in the larger conflict. As the neo-functionalists intimate, regimes do not materialize when political conflict engages visceral concerns, as elaborated in the Arab–Israeli confrontation, that would necessarily be ignored by functional cooperation. In the Jordan basin, to any but the most needy state, cooperation would have been too costly: there were not sufficient inducements to renege on basic organizing principles to achieve what a functional arrangement had to offer. The "shadow of the future" was forbidding: anticipated long-term political losses outweighed immediate material gains. Indeed, the optimal resolution of riparian dispute requires, at the outset, the resolution of the larger political conflict and not vice versa.

The way in which the dispute over the Indus waters was resolved substantiates this argument, as well. Soon after the World Bank became involved in trying to negotiate a water-sharing agreement between India and Pakistan, it realized that because of the historically conditioned framework, it was not going to reach a cooperative solution to the riparian dispute. The mediator anticipated that either or both players would use its/their veto power and refuse to play the game because of the perception of an unfavorable payoff structure. In fact, both parties emphasized that they did not want an integrated system of water utilization. This being the case, the Bank aimed to resolve the dispute via non-cooperation. In practice, this meant that the river system was divided into two parts – one for India, one for Pakistan. There was to be no interdependence and no interaction. Essentially, this solution was the antithesis of that proposed by the functionalists.

Given the experiences in resolving riparian dispute in both the Jordan and the Indus basins, the realist critics of functionalism are correct: states that are adversaries in the "high politics" of war and diplomacy do not allow extensive collaboration in the sphere of "low politics," centered around economic and welfare issues. In fact, the spillover effect runs in the opposite direction to that suggested by Mitrany: economic and welfare collaboration is retarded by "high politics" conflicts between states. Thus, it is hard to escape the conclusion that prior agreements to cooperate, or at least a predisposition to cooperation, must precede regime formation. Once in place, international institutions may indeed be effective in promoting further cooperation, as suggested by neo-liberals, but they will not be established unless there is some mutuality of interests, and the political climate is one of mutual recognition and a degree of shared ideological or philosophical commitment – what the neo-functionalists refer to as "value complementarity." Similarly, epistemic communities may advance cooperation among states, but here too, their efficacy relies upon prior decisions by states to cooperate. Moreover, they can be instrumental only when national decision-makers are willing to give scientific elites access to the policy process.[10] These conditions, of course, have not prevailed in the Jordan River basin.

Related to the question above and to the functionalist argument, is it possible to de-link issues when a riparian dispute co-exists with a protracted political conflict, so that the former could be resolved without reference to the latter?

The response to the preceding question would suggest that here too, our answer must tend toward the negative. Throughout the history of the Jordan waters conflict, the riparian dispute has been intimately bound up with the larger political rivalry. Both have been treated as one and the same by the riparian states. More correctly, the riparian dispute has been regarded as a manifestation, or dimension, of the Arab–Israeli conflict. To take one example, we recall that during the initial stages of the Johnston mission, the Arabs, as a collectivity, insisted that they would deal with the water issue only within the context of a larger political settlement with Israel. Israel, on the other hand, was anxious to use regional water-sharing as a means to acquire bilateral peace treaties with the Arab states.[11]

Especially when the context of relations is one of non-recognition, as in the Jordan basin and the Euphrates basin between Syria and Iraq, and/or acute hostility, including the case of the Indus basin, states will not elect to cooperate on most issues, if they can get away with it. They would not choose to renege on their political positions and ideological commitments; they would have to be forced to do so, in one way or another, as we will argue in our response to the next question. The failure to resolve the riparian dispute in the Jordan basin indicates that the neo-liberal institutionalists are correct in their (essentially neo-realist) prediction: when relations among states approximate a series of zero-sum games, not only is de-linking exceedingly difficult, but also, linkages may in fact impede cooperation.[12]

In the 1950s, the Eisenhower Administration did what the functionalists suggest: it treated the highly charged psychological environment in the central Middle East as an abstraction in its attempts to resolve some of the tensions in the region. Since these sentiments were viewed as obstacles to cooperation, rather than confront them, it sought to brush them aside. However, the Arabs and Israelis could not do likewise. Historically formed

197

cognitive factors and (conflicting) organizing principles have influenced the ways in which they interact.

Needless to say, states do seek to satisfy their domestic needs and national interests. What is more important to understand, though, is that interests emerge within the context of a particular belief system and historical experience. This, both neo-realists and neo-liberals, in general, fail to take sufficient account of.[13] Indeed, national interests and foreign policy behavior are responses to environmental constraints that are normative and ideational in nature, as well as being structural and material.[14] They are not based simply on a rational calculus of utility maximization.

The solution reached to the Indus waters dispute highlights this point. There, the mediation effort was quite successful because the third party took into consideration the context of relations in the basin, and understood that historically formed values and beliefs were bound to affect outcomes. The matter at hand was *not* a straightforward, unambiguous issue of sharing water resources. Because of the particular context, very strong inducements to cooperate would be essential. Nonetheless, it was only with a non-cooperative and hence, in narrowly defined game-theoretic terms, sub-optimal solution, that issues could be de-linked.[15]

How, then, can we explain that states engaged in a protracted political conflict have been able, on occasion, to come to arrangements – not unlike "tacit" or "implicit" regimes[16] – for sharing, managing, and developing water resources? What characterizes these occasions? Moreover, do such arrangements have more general implications for political relations and the potential for peace?

When technical cooperation has been achieved in international river basins (and hence, it appears that issues have been de-linked), the arrangements concluded are of a particular sort. To the contracting parties, they are perceived as both vital and indispensable, for they are bound up, in one way or another, with the states' security concerns. In the case of riparian dispute, the factor that will almost invariably lead states to seek technical collaboration is that of acute need for water resources and/or dependence upon a specific, shared body of water. The failure to establish a water-sharing regime would be considered threatening to the state's continued survival. Moreover, in situations where need is coupled with relatively inferior power resources, the interest in a regime is especially keen. Indeed, both (international) systemic and (domestic) political–economic conditions influence the desirability of cooperation. The example of Israel and Jordan is instructive in this regard.

As noted, after the breakdown of the Johnston mission talks in 1955, both Israel and Jordan followed, more-or-less, the guidelines of the Unified Plan with regard to water allocations from the Jordan system, in the absence of an agreement. Until June 1967, Jordan was releasing the quantity of water suggested by the plan from the Yarmouk River for Israeli usage, and Israel was releasing Upper Jordan water into the Lower Jordan after having diverted the quantity allocated to it in the plan.[17] Both countries were highly dependent on the river system; neither could do without it. For Israel, the Jordan system represented one-third of the country's total annual consumption of water; for Jordan, it accounted for more than two-thirds. Both countries, but especially the latter, had been anxious for a basin-wide agreement to the Unified Plan.

For the same reason, Jordan was anxious to reach agreement with Israel and Syria to construct the Maqarin, and later, the Unity, Dam.[18] To reiterate, the Yarmouk River is Jordan's only abundant source of surface flow. However, about one-third of its total discharge cannot be exploited by the Kingdom, since there are no storage facilities on the river to capture and impound the winter flow.

In contrast, if a riparian state is not in need of access to the water supply, and/or, relative to the other basin states, it has superior power resources – including military capability and riparian position – it will have little, if any, incentive to conclude technical arrangements and establish a regime. In the 1950s, neither Lebanon nor Syria had much use for the waters of the Jordan system. For this reason, they were not favorable toward the Unified Plan. And, given that Syria was the most powerful Arab riparian and one of the more influential Arab states, its interests prevailed. Had Lebanon and Syria been dependent on the Jordan waters, they may have been more inclined toward the Unified Plan and striking a bargain, even with the enemy. No doubt, as the upstream states in the basin, they may have tried, as in fact they did in the mid-1960s, to utilize their superior riparian positions and exploit the Jordan waters unilaterally, irrespective of downstream needs. The outcome of their efforts to divert the waters of the river system demonstrates that, despite their advantageous riparian position, they were not able to behave as hegemons in the basin.[19] By that time, the distribution of power was not in their favor, but in that of Israel, the midstream state.

The centrality of both need and relative power in the quest for cooperation and the potential for regime formation in river basins is illustrated by the Euphrates case, as well. Of the three riparian states, Turkey has absolute advantage. In addition to being the upstream riparian, it also is militarily the strongest. Given its hegemonic status in the basin, there is no good reason why it should support the creation of a water regime with Syria and Iraq. Without a regime, it is able to enjoy the maximum advantage; with a regime, its maneuverability would be constrained. No doubt, Syria and Iraq could gain considerably from a basin-wide accord.[20]

Hence, insofar as international river basins are concerned, we do not find

199

cooperative arrangements where threats to security – in the form of resource need – do not inhere, and where they are not advocated or imposed by a hegemon. This insight is brought out repeatedly in examinations of transboundary resource disputes. As noted in our discussion of riparian conflict in the Jordan basin since 1967, Israel and Jordan are currently engaged in competitive groundwater pumping in the Wadi ᶜAraba (ha-Arava), a desert region south of the Dead Sea. Neither side considers the quantities involved, nor its dependence upon them, important enough to warrant technical cooperation. Nonetheless, as demand for water increases, Jordan, because of its acute need and relatively inferior capabilities, may seek the creation of a·regime in this region. However, its success will depend either on the inclination of Israel, if the *status quo* in the basin prevails, or on that of an influential/hegemonic third party.

Finally, when technical arrangements are established among adversarial states in river basins in arid regions, these have no implications for the end to political conflict. In fact, they are considered by the riparians as single-play games: specific to the task and limited in scope. Contrary to the predictions of functionalists and the underlying assumptions of some neo-liberals, neither player makes an effort to enmesh his opponent in an ongoing process of interaction.[21] Issue-linkage is not possible, nor is the provision of side-payments.[22] Implicit in the single-play game is defection from any other possible game, be it coterminous or subsequent. Thus, there is no "shadow of the future" and no potential for binding people together in a multi-level game.[23] To wit, in the international river basins we have studied, the very few instances of technical cooperation and "tacit" regime formation were responses to overriding practical imperatives; they were perceived as indispensable and unavoidable. These highly delimited, highly specific arrangements have no conflict resolution potential. Indeed, the neo-functionalists are correct: spillover is not automatic, for it is on the basis of a variety of considerations – national interests, broadly defined – that states decide whether or not to allow cooperation in one domain to spill over into another.[24]

What determines whether a state perceives a dimension of its international relations as conflictual? When a particular issue concerns two (or more) states, how can we explain that one may consider it a source of conflict, while the other(s) may not?

In our discussion of riparian disputes in the Jordan basin since the 1967 war, we noted that the Kingdom of Jordan has identified three distinct areas of ongoing or anticipated conflict over water resources with Israel. It insists that on the Yarmouk River, in Wadi ᶜAraba, and on the West Bank, Arabs and Israelis continue to compete, directly or indirectly, for access to scarce water resources. Israel contests this position. It maintains that, by and large, conflict over water in the Jordan basin has long been resolved. There remains, however, only one area of potential conflict, and that concerns the abundant subterranean water supply of the West Bank.[25]

We contend that, just as the combination of resource need and relative power determines the possibility for cooperation in international river basins in arid regions, so does it explain the variation in perception of the conflict potential of any particular issue. Where threats to national security – in the form of denial of access to vital water resources – inhere in a geopolitical setting, the concerned state is likely to view that source of water as having acute conflict potential. In contrast, where threats do not inhere, either because the water supply in question is not considered vital and indispensable, or else the state is hegemonic in the basin and hence, has the means to satisfy its perceived needs and interests, the very same water supply will not be viewed as a (possible) source of conflict.

The Kingdom of Jordan perceives virtually every shared body of water as a source of conflict with Israel. As noted in chapter 6, the country's water situation became critical by the mid-1970s, by virtue of an overburdened demand schedule, severe supply constraints, and the diminishing quality of existing sources, all in the face of a high population growth rate. Coupled with Jordan's pressing need for water is its relatively inferior status in the basin. To reiterate, in terms of power resources, the country is severely constrained; it has limited means to satisfy its needs and interests. Observers note that, given its geopolitical environment, mere survival is its principal and most exacting objective.[26] If physical proximity to the adversary, which also happens to be hegemonic in the immediate region, is perceived as a source of conflict, and has, throughout the history of the Arab–Israeli confrontation, profoundly influenced Jordan's regional behavior, then undoubtedly, shared bodies of water would be perceived in like fashion as well.

In contrast, Israel has been the hegemonic power in the Jordan basin since the mid-1960s. In addition to its impressive military capability, it has, by and large, the material resources with which to achieve many of its (non-political) objectives. In terms of technological *materiel* and expertise, industrial development, and financial support, it ranks higher than its immediate Arab neighbors. With its superior power resources, it can exploit any shared body of water in a favorable manner. In theory, it can deny access to other parties, as well. For this reason, Israel does not perceive water as an ongoing source of conflict with Jordan, except in one, very particular case.

In the last chapter of this book, we noted that Israel's acute dependence on the groundwater supply of the West Bank accounts for the official Israeli position that continued, unimpeded access to that source is crucial for national security and survival. As long as the *status quo* persists and Israel remains hegemonic both in the occupied territories and in the central Middle East, there is no reason to fear for that critical source. However, the dominant conservative view is that if Israel loses or rescinds political and military control of the West Bank, more than one-quarter of the country's water supply, and hence its national security, would be threatened. Besides, the state cannot be assured that it will remain hegemonic. At some future date, Israel may no longer be in a position to utilize its power resources to avert threats to its security.

Dynamics of state behavior

Before concluding, we must reconsider the four principal variables and elucidate what we have learnt about the roles they play in the evolution of riparian dispute and their importance in promoting or impeding cooperation in international river basins. The variables are: (1) the character of riparian relations, or, the impact of the larger political conflict, (2) resource need/dependence, (3) relative power, and (4) efforts at conflict resolution and third party involvement.

In the Jordan, Indus, and Euphrates basins, the fact of a larger political conflict between at least two of the riparians has served as a disincentive to cooperation, especially since, in all cases, the conflict implicates the core values of states. Reluctance to cooperate with an adversary in seemingly technical matters is, as realists point out, a reflection of their "high politics" conflict.

No doubt, the persistence of political conflict may influence the course and evolution of riparian dispute, and even – as in the case of the Indus basin – the type of solution reached. It is abundantly clear from the history of the Jordan waters conflict, that decision-making and foreign-policy behavior are conditioned by cognitive dynamics: inter-state relations, core values, organizing principles, and perceptions of the "other" and of the environment. True, in the Euphrates basin, for example, the intense hostility between Hafez al-Asad of Syria and Saddam Hussein of Iraq has prevented the two states, which are in inferior power positions relative to Turkey, from allying against the upstream riparian.[27] However, in none of the riparian disputes we have studied has the outcome been determined by the political conflict.

In the Jordan basin and to the states most dependent on the river system, the political conflict, and the related concern for the distribution of gains, recedes in importance when the material benefits to be reaped from a regime loom large.[28] To ensure their survival, water-scarce Israel and Jordan have been prepared to "set aside" the Arab–Israeli conflict on a few occasions characterized by pronounced mutual interests. In contrast, in the 1950s, for example, access to the Jordan waters was not a domestic concern for Lebanon and Syria. The two upstream states used the larger political conflict as the justification for non-cooperation.

While the fact of resource need and dependence will prompt states to seek cooperative arrangements, the distribution of power in the basin will influence both the desire for a regime as well as its creation. To take the Euphrates case as an example, it is important to understand that irrespective of the political rivalry between Syria and Iraq, a water-sharing regime in the basin will not take shape, no matter how badly the two downstream states may need one, as long as Turkey, with its hegemonic status both geographically and militarily, does not want one and is not forced to accept one. Being the upstream riparian, Turkey has no need and no desire to share the Euphrates waters.

The case of the Nile basin provides an instructive example of the importance of this combination of factors, as well. There, the most water-dependent state is also the most powerful. With its superior capabilities, Egypt has been able to make its vital needs felt. A regime has been established, with Egypt as the main beneficiary.

In the Indus basin, the hegemonic and less needy state was eventually induced to seek a solution to the riparian dispute. The positive and tireless efforts of an impartial third party at an opportune historical moment, and its appreciation of the context of relations, brought pressure to bear on India.

The potential for cooperation

In sum, in the international river basins we have studied, a variant of the theory of hegemonic stability holds true. In all cases, outcomes reflect the distribution of power. Cooperation is not achieved unless the dominant power in the basin accepts it, or has been induced to do so by an external power. Moreover, the hegemon will take the lead in establishing a regime or accept regime change, and will enforce compliance to the regime, only if it serves to gain as a result.[29] In the absence of coercion from outside, this occurs in river basins *only* if: (1) the dominant power's relationship to the water resources in question is one of critical need, linked to its national security concerns, and (2) it is not the upstream riparian. Cooperation in international river basins is brought about by hegemonic powers.

Based on the experiences in four international river basins, the central argument of our study can be restated thus: when a riparian dispute in an arid region unfolds within the context of a more comprehensive political conflict, the former cannot be effectively isolated from the latter. Limited agreement on sharing water resources cannot be attained, largely because the least needy and/or most powerful state will derive little benefit from cooperating and relinquishing its most favorable position. Instead, it will use the political conflict and implicitly, the concern for relative gains, as its justification for non-cooperation. In contrast, the neediest and least powerful riparian will seek a cooperative arrangement, despite the larger conflict, because it has little, if any, alternative. When it is successful – and this happens only when the dominant power in the basin has been induced to cooperate for one reason or another – the arrangement is specific to the task and cannot be viewed as an avenue toward political settlement.

Appendix 1 US involvement in water development in the Jordan basin

The danger to world peace in the Middle East is clear to us all. The unrelenting antagonism between the Arab states and Israel is invitation to mischief by the Kremlin. No one can say how swiftly or in what direction the flame of open war between Arab and Jew might spread. But no one can doubt that the strategists of Communism would be quick to fan the flame. Chaos is their ally.

...

Much of American foreign economic policy today is premised on the assumption that healthy social progress is the most effective antidote to the Communist virus, which, in common with its bacteriological cousins, strikes hardest at run-down, poorly nourished systems. For this reason, we have undertaken a global effort to help less-advanced peoples help themselves toward a better and more rewarding life. But in the Middle East, the continuing tension between Israel and her Arab neighbors is a massive barrier to economic development and the kind of progress we believe the people of the region must and can achieve.

...

Until there is rapprochement between the nations of the region, social progress is going to be slow. Until there is progress, mass discontent will not abate, but swell. While the discontent persists, the ground remains fertile for the seeds of Communism. They are being sown there now.

...

> From the text of a lecture by Eric Johnston at Cornell University, 6 May 1954; US Information Service Daily News Bulletin, vol. 6, no. 88, copy in *INA* 3688/9, "masa u-matan im johnston"

US objectives and policy with respect to the Near East

General considerations

The Near East is of great strategic political and economic importance to the free world. The area contains the greatest petroleum resources in the world; essential locations for strategic bases in any world conflict against Communism; the Suez Canal; and natural defensive barriers. It also contains Holy Places of the Christian, Jewish, and Moslem worlds, and thereby exerts religious and cultural influences affecting people everywhere. The security interests of the US would be critically endangered if the Near East should fall under Soviet influence or control.

Appendix 1

Current conditions and trends in the Near East are inimical to Western interests. During recent years the prestige and position of the West have declined. The nations of the Near East are determined to assert their independence and are suspicious of outside interest in their affairs.

...

Efforts to prevent the loss of the Near East will require increasing responsibility, initiative, and leadership by the US in the area.

...

The rate of economic growth and distribution of its benefits are among the important factors affecting internal stability, popular and leadership attitudes toward the Free World and Communism, and the maintenance of governments free of Communist control or influence. It is in the US interests to help guide the social and economic pressures for revolutionary change into channels leading to healthy economic growth while maintaining and improving political stability.

Supplementary statement of policy on the Arab–Israel problem

General considerations

During the past year tensions have increased between the Arab states and Israel, and the Soviet Union has stepped up its activities in the Near East. The point has been reached where new means should be sought to alleviate the situation, not only because of the seriousness of the Arab–Israeli problem per se, but in order to preclude the danger of the loss of the Near East by the West.

Course of action

Seek by all appropriate means to secure an agreed and equitable division of the waters of the Jordan River system between Israel and the interested Arab states and the establishment of an international control authority. Take such steps as may be feasible to ensure that neither party prejudices the allocation of the available waters by an international control authority. Link the development of the Jordan Valley to Arab refugee resettlement to the maximum extent practicable.

> The extracts above are from the Statement of Policy by the National Security Council, Washington, 23 July 1954; *FRUS* vol. 9, no. 219, pp. 525–36

Appendix 2 The unified development of the water resources of the Jordan Valley region

The project was prepared at the request of the United Nations under the direction of the Tennessee Valley Authority by Charles T. Main, Inc. (Boston Mass., 1953). It is an engineering office study based upon materials, reports, and data made available to the Tennessee Valley Authority, and done without field investigations. The following is a summary of its main features.

First, the essence of the report has been described thus:

As a problem of engineering the most economic and the quickest way to get the most use from the waters of the Jordan River system requires better organisation of the headwaters on the Hasbani and in the Huleh area to serve the lands by gravity flow within that part of the Jordan watershed and use of Lake Tiberias as a storage reservoir for the flood flows of the Jordan and Yarmouk Rivers. From Lake Tiberias these waters would be made available by gravity flow to irrigate lands on the east and west sides of the Jordan Valley to the south ... Use of the natural reservoir afforded by Lake Tiberias takes advantage of an asset already at hand; there is no known alternative site, at any cost, for a reservoir that would effectively regulate and store the flood flows of the Jordan and its main tributary, the Yarmouk... Thus the report describes the elements of an efficient arrangement of water supply within the watershed of the Jordan River system. It does not consider political factors or attempt to set this system into the national boundaries now prevailing.

> From letter submitted by Gordon Clapp, Chairman of the Board, TVA, to the Director of UNRWA; beginning of report

Second, the report suggests the following distribution of water for the irrigation of land areas:

    394 mcm to irrigate 416,000 dunum in Israel
    774 mcm to irrigate 490,000 dunum in Jordan
    45 mcm to irrigate 30,000 dunum in Syria

The total quantity of water in the Jordan basin is assumed to be 1,123 mcm, and the total irrigable area, 936,000 dunum.

Among the works envisaged by the project, the most important include the following:

(1)   construction of dam on upper Hasbani River for storing its surplus water

(2) diversion of waters of Banias, Dan, and Hasbani Rivers to a canal that would convey waters to irrigate lands on the western side of the Jordan River as far south as the Jezreel Valley

(3) diversion of the Yarmouk River into the East Ghor Canal and into Lake Tiberias, where its waters would be stored with that of the Jordan River to be used to irrigate cultivable land in the Ghor

(4) construction of two main canals, one east of the Jordan River and the other west of the river, to carry water southward, as far as just north of the Dead Sea

(5) draining of Huleh marshes and clearing them for agriculture

(6) construction of a canal to carry water from behind the Hasbani dam, and a power station near Tel Hai to use the irrigation water for hydro-electric power generation

(7) construction of hydro-electric power facilities on the Yarmouk River, including a dam at Maqarin, a power canal, and a power house near Adasiya

Two major projects for the generation of hydro-electric power are envisaged, providing a total estimated average annual output of 210 million kilowatt hours.

Project	Location	Average annual output
Tel Hai plant	Hasbani River	76 million kWh
Adasiya plant	Yarmouk River	134 million kWh

Finally, the estimated cost of the entire plan, excluding raising the Maqarin dam, is $121 million.

Appendix 3 The Arabs' Plan for development of water resources in the Jordan Valley

A summary of the plan can be found in *The Egyptian Economic and Political Review*, vol. 2, no. 2 (October 1955), pp. 42–46.

The Arab Technical Committee believes it is practically impossible to propose a plan for the development of water resources in the valley of the Jordan River and its tributaries on the basis of disregarding the political boundaries between countries falling in the valleys of these rivers. The project for development of waters of these rivers must therefore take into consideration the existing boundaries between the countries providing irrigation to all arable land actually around the sources and in the valleys of these rivers within the boundaries of each country.

Main features of the plan

(1) utilization of Yarmouk River water for irrigation and hydro-electric power production:
    the waters should be developed through storage in the river basin, for the benefit of both Jordan and Syria according to the Agreement Pact signed by them (4 June 1953);
    there should be no storage of Yarmouk waters in Lake Tiberias because, (a) the lake and its shores are in Israeli territory, (b) average salinity of Lake Tiberias is much higher than that of the Yarmouk, (c) evaporation losses in Lake Tiberias are very high;
    a storage dam should be constructed on the Yarmouk River either at Maqarin or at Wadi Khaled, for both power production and irrigation;
    the available draft (of 360 mcm) could be utilized for irrigation thus:
        Syria – 80 mcm to irrigate upstream of dam
                10 mcm to irrigate in the Yarmouk Valley between the dam site and Adasiya
        Jordan – 270 mcm to irrigate the East Ghor via East Ghor Canal;
    construction of diversionary dam and power plant on the Yarmouk River near Adasiya, linked by canal to the dam site upstream;

both power plants, at Maqarin and at Adasiya, are to be used for the benefit of Syria and Jordan

(2) Allocation of water for irrigation

Lebanon – 32 mcm to irrigate 35,000 dunum in Hasbani River Valley

Syria – 120 mcm to irrigate 119,000 dunum in Banias River Valley, al-Boteiha, Yarmouk Plateau, Yarmouk Valley

Israel – 270 mcm to irrigate 234,000 dunum in Upper Huleh, Ayelet Hashahar, Yavneel Valley, Yarmouk Triangle, west of West Ghor

Jordan – 911 mcm to irrigate 490,000 dunum in East Ghor and West Ghor;

Jordan River and tributaries north of Lake Tiberias to be used for irrigation in Lebanon, Israel and Syria;

Hasbani River to be used for hydro-electric power generation for Lebanon; therefore, construction of a storage dam, irrigation canal, and power station on the Hasbani River;

construction of irrigation canals on left and right side of Banias River for irrigation of Syrian lands

Appendix 4 The Cotton plan for the development and utilization of the water resources of the Jordan and Litani River basins

The following is drawn from a report on the Cotton Plan in the National Archives of the State of Israel, Foreign Ministry document (Record Group 93), box 3688, file 2.

Main features of Plan:

(1) a comprehensive plan – not limited to resources of the hydrographic basin, "but includes all resources which can be beneficially integrated into a regional plan"

(2) achieves an irrigated area (2,600,000 dunum) almost three times that of the Main Plan (940,000 dunum)

(3) allocation of full quantity of water required for irrigation of all the irrigable areas within the Jordan, Litani, and Yarmouk basins; only the excess water would be allocated for the Coastal Plain and southern regions of Israel

Inclusion of Litani River

A diversion of surplus water of the Litani would in no way handicap irrigation development in Lebanon, while the hydro-power potential could be considerably increased... Such a development must not be considered as a diversion of a natural resource of an Arab state for the benefit of Israel; it should rather be defined as the conveyance of this resource, through Israel territory, for the common benefit of the Arab basin states and Israel.

Allocation of water
  1,290 mcm of water to irrigate 1,790,000 dunum (179,000 ha) in Israel
  575 mcm   to irrigate   430,000 dunum in Jordan
  450·7 mcm   to irrigate   350,000 dunum in Lebanon
  30 mcm   to irrigate   30,000 dunum in Syria

Power generation
  1,400 million kWh per year.

Capital cost of plan
  c. $470 million

Appendix 5 Annex II: Water-related matters

from the *Treaty of Peace between the State of Israel and the Hashemite Kingdom of Jordan*, 26 October 1994

[copies provided to the author by the embassies of the Kingdom of Jordan and the State of Israel, Washington, D.C.]

Pursuant to Article 6 of the Treaty, Israel and Jordan agreed on the following Articles on water related matters:

Article I: Allocation

1. Water from the Yarmouk River
   a. Summer period – 15th May to 15th October of each year. Israel pumps (12) MCM and Jordan gets the rest of the flow.
   b. Winter period – 16th October to 14th May of each year. Israel pumps (13) MCM and Jordan is entitled to the rest of the flow subject to provisions outlined herein below.
       Jordan concedes to Israel pumping an additional (20) MCM from the Yarmouk in winter in return for Israel conceding to transferring to Jordan during the summer period the quantity specified in paragraphs (2.a) below from the Jordan River.
   c. In order that waste of water will be minimized, Israel and Jordan may use, downstream of point 121/Adassiya Diversion, excess flood water that is not usable and will evidently go to waste unused.
2. Water from the Jordan River
   a. Summer period – 15th May to 15th October of each year.
       In return for the additional water that Jordan concedes to Israel in winter in accordance with paragraph (1.b) above, Israel concedes to transfer to Jordan in the summer period (20) MCM from the Jordan River directly upstream from Deganya gates on the river. Jordan shall pay the operation and

maintenance cost of such transfer through existing systems (not including capital cost) and shall bear the total cost of any new transmission system. A separate protocol shall regulate this transfer.

b. Winter period – 16th October to 14th May of each year. Jordan is entitled to store for its use a minimum average of (20) MCM of the floods in the Jordan River south of its confluence with the Yarmouk (as outlined in Article II). Excess floods that are not usable and that will otherwise be wasted can be utilised for the benefit of the two Parties including pumped storage off the course of the river.

c. In addition to the above, Israel is entitled to maintain its current uses of the Jordan River waters between its confluence with the Yarmouk and its confluence with Tirat Zvi/Wadi Yabis. Jordan is entitled to an annual quantity equivalent to that of Israel, provided, however, that Jordan's use will not harm the quantity or quality of the above Israeli uses. The Joint Water Committee (outlined in Article VI) will survey existing uses for documentation and prevention of appreciable harm.

d. Jordan is entitled to an annual quantity of (10) MCM of desalinated water from the desalination of about (20) MCM of saline springs now diverted to the Jordan River. Israel will explore the possibility of financing the operation and maintenance cost of the supply to Jordan of this desalinated water (not including capital cost). Until the desalination facilities are operational, and upon the entry into force of the Treaty, Israel will supply Jordan (10) MCM of Jordan River water from the same location as in (2.a) above, outside the summer period and during dates Jordan selects, subject to the maximum capacity of transmission.

3. Additional Water
    Israel and Jordan shall cooperate in finding sources for the supply to Jordan of an additional quantity of 50 MCM/year of water to drinkable standards. To this end, the Joint Water Committee will develop, within one year from the entry into force of the Treaty, a plan for the supply to Jordan of the abovementioned additional water. This plan will be forwarded to the respective governments for discussion and decision.

4. Operation and Maintenance
    a. Operation and maintenance of the systems on Israeli territory that supply Jordan with water, and their electricity supply, shall be Israel's responsibility. The operation and maintenance of

the new systems that serve only Jordan will be contracted at Jordan's expense to authorities of companies selected by Jordan.

b. Israel will guarantee easy unhindered access of personnel and equipment to such new systems for operation and maintenance. This subject will be further detailed in the agreements to be signed between Israel and the authorities or companies selected by Jordan.

Article II: Storage

1. Israel and Jordan shall cooperate to build a diversion/storage dam on the Yarmouk River directly downstream of the point 121/Adassiya Diversion. The purpose is to improve the diversion efficiency into the King Abdullah Canal of the water allocation of the Hashemite Kingdom of Jordan, and possibly for the diversion of Israel's allocation of the river water. Other purposes can be mutually agreed.

2. Israel and Jordan shall cooperate to build a system of water storage on the Jordan River, along their common boundary, between its confluence with the Yarmouk River and its confluence with Tirat Zvi/Wadi Yabis, in order to implement the provision of paragraph (2.b) of Article I above. The storage system can also be made to accommodate more floods; Israel may use up to (3) MCM/year of added storage capacity.

3. Other storage reservoirs can be discussed and agreed upon mutually.

Article III: Water quality and protection

1. Israel and Jordan each undertake to protect, within their own jurisdiction, the shared waters of the Jordan and Yarmouk Rivers, and Arava/Araba groundwater, against any pollution, contamination, harm or unauthorized withdrawals of each other's allocation.

2. For this purpose, Israel and Jordan will jointly monitor the quality of water along their boundary, by use of jointly established monitoring stations to be operated under the guidance of the Joint Water Committee.

3. Israel and Jordan will each prohibit the disposal of municipal and industrial wastewater into the course of the Yarmouk or the Jordan Rivers before they are treated to standards allowing their

unrestricted agricultural use. Implementation of this prohibition shall be completed within three years from the entry into force of the Treaty.

4. The quality of water supplied from one country to the other at any given location shall be equivalent to the quality of the water used from the same location by the supplying country.

5. Saline springs currently diverted to the Jordan River are earmarked for desalination within four years. Both countries shall cooperate to ensure that the resulting brine will not be disposed of in the Jordan River or in any of its tributaries.

6. Israel and Jordan will each protect water systems in its own territory, supplying water to the other, against any pollution, contamination, harm or unauthorised withdrawal of each other's allocations.

Article IV: Groundwater in Emek ha'Arava/Wadi Araba

1. In accordance with the provisions of this Treaty, some wells drilled and used by Israel along with their associated systems fall on the Jordanian side of the borders. These wells and systems are under Jordan's sovereignty. Israel shall retain the use of these wells and systems in the quantity and quality detailed in Appendix 1, that shall be jointly prepared by 31st December, 1994. Neither country shall take, nor cause to be taken, any measure that may appreciably reduce the yields or quality of these wells and systems.

2. Throughout the period of Israel's use of these wells and systems, replacement of any well that may fail among them shall be licensed by Jordan in accordance with the laws and regulations then in effect. For this purpose, the failed well shall be treated as though it was drilled under license from the competent Jordanian authority at the time of its drilling. Israel shall supply Jordan with the log of each of the wells and the technical information about it to be kept on record. The replacement well shall be connected to the Israeli electricity and water systems.

3. Israel may increase the abstraction rate from wells and systems in Jordan by up to 10 MCM/year above the yields referred to in paragraph 1 above, subject to a determination by the Joint Water Committee that this undertaking is hydrogeologically feasible and does not harm existing Jordanian uses. Such increase is to be carried out within five years from the entry into force of the Treaty.

4. Operation and Maintenance
   a. Operation and maintenance of the wells and systems on Jordanian territory that supply Israel with water, and their

electricity supply shall be Jordan's responsibility. The operation and maintenance of these wells and systems will be contracted at Israel's expense to authorities or companies selected by Israel.

b. Jordan will guarantee easy unhindered access of personnel and equipment to such wells and systems for operation and maintenance. This subject will be further detailed in the agreements to be signed between Jordan and the authorities or companies selected by Israel.

Article V: Notification and agreement

1. Artificial changes in or of the course of the Jordan and Yarmouk Rivers can only be made by mutual agreement.
2. Each country undertakes to notify the other, six months ahead of time, of any intended projects which are likely to change the flow of either of the above rivers along their common boundary, or the quality of such flow. The subject will be discussed in the Joint Water Committee with the aim of preventing harm and mitigating adverse impacts such projects may cause.

Article VI: Co-operation

1. Israel and Jordan undertake to exchange relevant data on water resources through the Joint Water Committee.
2. Israel and Jordan shall co-operate in developing plans for purposes of increasing water supplies and improving water use efficiency, within the context of bilateral, regional or international co-operation.

Article VII: Joint Water Committee

1. For the purpose of the implementation of this Annex, the Parties will establish a Joint Water Committee comprised of three members from each country.
2. The Joint Water Committee will, with the approval of the respective governments, specify its work procedures, the frequency of its meetings, and the details of its scope of work. The Committee may invite experts and/or advisors as may be required.
3. The Committee may form, as it deems necessary, a number of specialized sub-committees and assign them technical tasks. In this

context, it is agreed that these sub-committees will include a northern sub-committee and a southern sub-committee, for the management on the ground of the mutual water resources in these sectors.

Notes

1 Introduction: conflict and cooperation in international river basins

1. A river basin, catchment area, or watershed refers to the area within which rainfall drains into a given stream. This includes land area, the river and its tributaries, and groundwater resources.
2. Ludwick A. Teclaff, *The River Basin in History and Law* (The Hague: Martinus Nijhoff, 1967), p. 3.
3. Common property resources have the same characteristics as public goods – jointness of supply and non-excludability – except that use of the resource by one unit does detract from the benefits enjoyed by the other(s). For a discussion of international river basins as common property resources see, David LeMarquand, *International Rivers: the Politics of Cooperation* (Vancouver, B.C.: Westwater Research Centre, University of British Columbia, 1977). For a discussion of the principal characteristics of the ideal collective good see, among others, Duncan Snidal, "Public Goods, Property Rights, and Political Organizations," *International Studies Quarterly* no. 23 (December 1979), pp. 532–66.
4. John Waterbury, "Dynamics of Basin-wide Cooperation in the Utilization of the Euphrates" (paper prepared for the conference: The Economic Development of Syria: Problems, Progress, and Prospects, Damascus, 6–7 January 1990), p. 1.
5. On the internationalization of river basins and its advantages see C. B. Bourne, "The Development of International Water Resources: the Drainage Basin Approach," *The Canadian Bar Review* vol. 47, no. 1 (March 1969), pp. 62–82; A. H. Garretson, R. D. Hayton, C. J. Olmstead, and Richard R. Baxter (eds.), *The Law of International Drainage Basins* (Dobbs Ferry: Oceana Publications, 1967); Albert Lepawsky, "International Development of River Resources," *International Affairs* vol. 39 (1963), pp. 533–50; Teclaff, *The River Basin*.

    The development of the river basin as a unit has been widely advocated by planners, politicians and jurists, and has been adopted as policy and implemented in multi-national agreements in numerous basins. By 1965, the concept of joint development had been implemented, in one form or another, in agreements regarding the Rio Grande (1944), Lake Titicaca (1957), Mekong (1957), Nile (1959), Indus (1960), Uruguay (1960), Colombia (1961), Senegal

(1963), Niger (1963), and Lake Chad (1964). Teclaff, *The River Basin*, pp. 200–01.

6. There is a vast literature on conflict over natural resources. See, among others, Ruth W. Arad, Uzi B. Arad, Rachel McCulloch, Jose Piñera, and Ann L. Hollick, *Sharing Global Resources* (Council on Foreign Relations, McGraw-Hill Book Co., 1979); N. Choucri and R. North, *Nations in Conflict* (San Francisco: W. H. Freeman, 1975); Geoffrey Kemp, "Scarcity and Strategy," *Foreign Affairs* (January 1978), pp. 396–414; Ronnie D. Lipschutz, *When Nations Clash: Raw Materials, Ideology, and Foreign Policy* (Cambridge, Mass.: Ballinger Publishing Co., 1989); R. North, "Toward a Framework for the Analysis of Scarcity and Conflict," *International Studies Quarterly* vol. 21, no. 4 (December 1977); Arthur H. Westing (ed.), *Global Resources and International Conflict: Environmental Factors in Strategic Policy and Action* (Oxford: Oxford University Press, 1986).

7. See, among others, Robert Gilpin, *War and Change in World Politics* (Cambridge: Cambridge University Press, 1981); Hans Morgenthau, *Politics among Nations*, 4th edition (New York: Knopf, 1966), first published in 1948; Kenneth Waltz, *Man, the State and War* (New York: Columbia University Press, 1959).

8. See, Garrett Hardin, "The Tragedy of the Commons," *Science* 162 (1968).

9. For studies of conflict over the waters of international river basins see, among others, Garrettson, *The Law*; Malin Falkenmark, "Fresh Waters as a Factor in Strategic Policy and Action" in Westing (ed.), *Global Resources*, pp. 85–113; LeMarquand, *International Rivers*; Lepawsky, "International Development"; Col. Roy L. Thompson, "Fresh Water Scarcity: Implications for Conflict – an overview" (paper prepared for the conference on Scarce Resources and International Conflict, International Security Studies Program, The Fletcher School of Law and Diplomacy, Tufts University, 4–6 May 1977); Thompson, "Water as a Source of Conflict," *Strategic Review* vol. 6, no. 2 (spring 1978), pp. 62–72. For domestic conflicts see, Arthur Maass, *Muddy Waters: The Army Engineers and the Nation's Rivers* (Cambridge, Mass.: Harvard University Press, 1951); W. R. D. Sewell, "The Columbia River Treaty: Some Lessons and Implications," *Canadian Geographer* vol. 10, no. 3 (1966).

10. From, Edward Azar, Paul Jureidini, and Ronald McLaurin, "Protracted Social Conflict: Theory and Practice in the Middle East," *Journal of Palestine Studies* vol. 8, no. 1 (1978), p. 50. See, as well, Edward Azar: "Protracted International Conflicts: Ten Propositions," *International Interactions* vol. 12, no. 1 (1985), pp. 59–70. For the relationship of protracted conflicts to crises see, Michael Brecher, "International Crises and Protracted Conflicts," *International Interactions* vol. 11, nos. 3–4 (1984), pp. 237–97; Michael Brecher and Jonathan Wilkenfeld, "Protracted Conflicts and Crises" in Brecher and Wilkenfeld, *Crisis, Conflict and Instability* (New York: Pergamon Press, 1989), pp. 127–40.

Examples of protracted conflicts, apart from the Arab–Israeli case are those between the two Koreas, China and the Soviet Union, Pakistan and India.

11. Studies of the Jordan waters conflict prior to the 1967 war abound. Studies of

the conflict since 1967 are rare; those that do exist, focus primarily on the West Bank. There have been a few doctoral theses on the subject as well. For the period prior to 1967 see, Basheer Khalil Nijim, "The Indus, Nile, and Jordan: International Rivers and Factors in Conflict Potential" (Indiana University, 1969); Mohamad Ali al-Saadi, "The Jordan River Dispute: a Case Study in International Conflicts" (University of Massachusetts, 1969); for the periods prior to and since 1967 see, Miriam R. Lowi, "The Politics of Water under Conditions of Scarcity and Conflict: the Jordan River and Riparian States" (Princeton University, 1990); David Merkle Wishart, "The Political Economy of Conflict over Water Rights in the Jordan Valley from 1890 to the Present" (University of Illinois at Urbana-Champaign, 1985). For book-length studies on the pre-1967 Jordan conflict in foreign languages see, among others, Ali Muhamad Ali, *Nahr al-Urdun wal-Muʾamara al-Sahyuniya* [The Jordan River and the Zionist Conspiracy] (Cairo: al-Dar al-Qawmiya, n.d.), in Arabic; Simha Blass, *Mei Meriva u-Maʿas* [Water in Strife and Action] (Israel: Masada Ltd., 1973), in Hebrew; A.-M. Goichon, *L'Eau, Problème Vital de la Région du Jourdain* (Brussels: Centre pour l'Etude des Problèmes du Monde Musulman Contemporain, 1964); Abd al-Hafiz Muhamad, *al-Nahr illadi Wahada al-Arab Nahr al-Urdun al-Xalid, w-Mashariʿ al-Tahwil* [The River which United the Arabs, the Jordan River, and Development Projects] (Cairo, 1964), in Arabic; Yoram Nimrod, *Mei Meriva* [Angry Waters: Controversy over the Jordan River] (Givat Haviva: Center for Arabic and Afro-Asian Studies, 1966), in Hebrew. Despite the numerous volumes devoted to this riparian dispute, there have been few attempts to analyze it (and its relationship to the large political conflict) within a theoretical framework. See in this regard, Thomas Naff and Ruth Matson (eds.), *Water in the Middle East: Conflict or Cooperation?* (Boulder, Colo.: Westview Press, 1984).

12. Because unitary development of the river basin is considered optimal, that pattern of development should be treated as the goal which states strive for. Nonetheless, it is important to note that unitary development is an ideal type; in fact, it is rarely achieved. The author is grateful to Dr. Steven Lintner for highlighting this point (personal communication, 15 February 1992).

13. In this book, we use the term "liberal institutionalism" to refer to the various tendencies within the evolution of postwar liberal international theory that stress the impact that institutions may have on political behavior and outcomes in world affairs. While this emphasis is common to functionalists, neo-functionalists, interdependence theorists, regime theorists, and neo-liberal institutionalists, we recognize that there are significant differences among them. For a most useful discussion of the varieties of perspectives within this school of thought see, Mark W. Zacher and Richard A. Matthew, "Liberal International Theory: Common Threads, Divergent Strands" in Charles Kegley (ed.), *Controversies in International Relations Theory: Realism and the Neoliberal Challenge* (New York: St Martin's Press, 1995).

14. Robert O. Keohane, *After Hegemony: Cooperation and Discord in the World Political Economy* (Princeton: Princeton University Press, 1984), p. 27.

15. Andrew Moravcsik, "Liberalism and International Relations Theory," Working Paper no. 92–6, Center for International Affairs, Harvard University (October 1992), p. 11.

16. Classical realist works include: Raymond Aron, *Peace and War: A Theory of International Relations*, trans. Richard Howard and Annette Baker Fox (Garden City, N.Y.: Doubleday & Co., 1966); E. H. Carr, *The Twenty Years' Crisis, 1919–1939: An Introduction to the Study of International Relations* (New York: Harper Torchbooks, 1964); Morgenthau, *Politics among Nations*. Neorealist works include: Robert Gilpin, *US Power and the Multinational Corporation: The Political Economy of Foreign Direct Investment* (New York: Basic Books, 1975); Gilpin, *War and Change*; Gilpin, *The Political Economy of International Relations* (Princeton: Princeton University Press, 1987); Waltz, *Man*; Waltz, *Theory of International Politics* (Reading, Mass.: Addison-Wesley, 1979).

17. Joseph M. Grieco, *Cooperation among Nations: Europe, America, and Non-Tariff Barriers to Trade* (Ithaca, N.Y.: Cornell University Press, 1990), p. 38.

18. *Ibid.* p. 39.

19. Robert Gilpin, "The Richness of the Tradition of Political Realism" in Robert O. Keohane (ed.), *Neorealism and its Critics* (New York: Columbia University Press, 1986), p. 305.

20. Waltz, *International Politics*, p. 105.

21. Grieco, *Cooperation*, p. 28; Duncan Snidal, "Relative Gains and the Pattern of International Cooperation," *American Political Science Review* vol. 85, no. 3 (September 1991), pp. 702–26. Robert Powell qualifies the neo-realist assertion about the concern for relative gains, claiming that only when "the constraints defining the system create opportunities for one state to turn relative gains to its advantage and to the disadvantage of other states" would this concern be important and, therefore, cooperation inhibited. "Absolute and Relative Gains in International Relations Theory," *American Political Science Review* vol. 84, no. 4 (December 1991), p. 1,315.

22. Grieco, *Cooperation*, p. 47.

23. Gilpin, *US Power*, pp. 34–36; Stephen D. Krasner, "Global Communications and National Power: Life on the Pareto Frontier," *World Politics* 43 (April 1991), p. 366.

24. Grieco (*Cooperation*, p. 10) notes that realists view states in anarchy as "defensive positionalists": given their core interest in survival, states are preoccupied with their relative capabilities and relative status. Defensive-state positionalism thus creates the relative gains problem for cooperation. It is important to add, however, that realists are equally concerned about absolute gains, if there exists the possibility that overall gains may strengthen a potential adversary.

25. For functionalist theory see, David Mitrany, *A Working Peace System* (Chicago: Quadrangle Books, 1966 [first published in 1943]) and *The Functional Theory of Politics* (New York: St. Martin's Press, 1975); J. P. Sewell, *Functionalism and World Politics* (Princeton: Princeton University Press, 1966). For neo-functionalism see, Ernst Haas, *The Uniting of Europe: Political, Social, and Economic*

Forces, 1950–1957 (Stanford: Stanford University Press, 1958); *Beyond the Nation-State: Functionalism and International Organization* (Stanford: Stanford University Press, 1964); Leon Lindberg and Stuart Scheingold (eds.), *Regional Integration: Theory and Research* (Cambridge: Harvard University Press, 1971); Joseph Nye, *Peace in Parts: Integration and Conflict in Regional Organization* (Boston: Little, Brown, & Co., 1971). For interdependence theory see, Robert Keohane and Joseph Nye, *Power and Interdependence: World Politics in Transition* (Boston: Little, Brown, & Co., 1977).

26. The major neo-liberal institutionalist works include: Robert Axelrod, *The Evolution of Cooperation* (New York: Basic Books, 1984); Robert Axelrod and Robert Keohane, "Achieving Cooperation under Anarchy: Strategies and Institutions" in Kenneth Oye (ed.), *Cooperation under Anarchy* (Princeton: Princeton University Press, 1986), pp. 226–54; Robert O. Keohane, *After Hegemony*; Keohane, *International Institutions and State Power: Essays in International Relations Theory* (Boulder, Colo.: Westview Press, 1989).
27. Keohane, *After Hegemony*, p. 7.
28. Axelrod, *Evolution of Cooperation*; Axelrod and Keohane, "Achieving Cooperation."
29. Grieco, *Cooperation*, p. 48.
30. Gilpin, *War and Change*; see, as well, note 16 of this chapter.
31. The theory links tangible state capabilities to behavior. It is a model in which outcomes reflect the relative power of actors. Robert Keohane, "The Theory of Hegemonic Stability and Changes in International Economic Regimes, 1967–1977" in Ole Holsti, Randolph M. Siverson, and Alexander L. George (eds.), *Change in the International System* (Boulder, Colo.: Westview Press, 1980), pp. 131–62; Keohane, *After Hegemony*, p. 31. The theory derives from Charles P. Kindleberger, *The World in Depression, 1929–1939* (Berkeley: University of California Press, 1974).
32. Needless to say, realists are also concerned about cheating; otherwise, they would not be so insistent about the need for mechanisms that enforce compliance to rules of behavior.
33. Among these we would include, for example: Norman Angell, *The Great Illusion: A Study of the Relation of Military Power in Nations to their Economic and Social Advantage* (New York: G. P. Putnam, 1911); Helen Milner, "The Assumption of Anarchy in International Relations Theory: a Critique," *Review of International Studies* no. 17 (1991), pp. 67–85; Mitrany, *Working Peace*; Oran Young, *International Cooperation: Building Regimes for Natural Resources and the Environment* (Ithaca and London: Cornell University Press, 1989); Mark W. Zacher, "The Decaying Pillars of the Westphalian Temple: Implications for International Order and Governance" in James N. Rosenau and Ernst-Otto Czempiel (eds.): *Governance without Government: Order and Change in World Politics* (Cambridge: Cambridge University Press, 1992).
34. Mitrany, *Working Peace*, pp. 26–27, 38.
35. *Ibid.* pp. 97–98.
36. *Ibid.* pp. 48, 58.

37. Nye, *Peace in Parts*, p. 81; E. Haas, "The 'Uniting of Europe' and the Uniting of Latin America," *Journal of Common Market Studies* vol. 5 (June 1967), p. 324.
38. Haas, *Beyond the Nation-State*, p. 48.
39. Nye, *Peace in Parts*, pp. 83–84, 85.
40. Robert O. Keohane, "Neoliberal Institutionalism: A Perspective on World Politics" in Keohane, *International Institutions*, pp. 2–3, 10; Keohane, *After Hegemony*, p. 6.
41. Keohane, *International Institutions*, p. 18, fn. 20.
42. Keohane, *After Hegemony*.
43. The concept of regime has been defined in various ways. See, for example, S. Krasner, "Structural Causes and Regime Consequences: Regimes as Intervening Variables" in Stephen Krasner (ed.), *International Regimes* (Ithaca, N.Y.: Cornell University Press, 1983), pp. 61–91; Donald Puchala and Raymond Hopkins, "International Regimes: Lessons from Inductive Analysis" in Krasner (ed.), pp. 1–21; Oran Young, *Resource Regimes: Natural Resources and Social Institutions* (Berkeley: University of California Press, 1982), p. 20; and "International Regimes: Problems of Concept Formation," *World Politics* no. 32 (April 1980), pp. 331–35. For a provocative critique see, Susan Strange, "Cave! Hic Dragones: a Critique of Regime Analysis" in Krasner (ed.), pp. 337–54.
44. Robert Keohane, "Multilateralism: An Agenda for Research," *International Journal* vol. 45, no. 4 (autumn 1990), p. 734.
45. Peter M. Haas, *Saving the Mediterranean: the Politics of International Environmental Cooperation* (New York: Columbia University Press, 1990), p. 55. For earlier uses of the term and other, similar terms see, Haas, p. 55 fn. 22.
46. *Ibid.* pp. 183–85.
47. Kenneth Oye, "Explaining Cooperation under Anarchy: Hypotheses and Strategies" in Oye (ed.), *Cooperation under Anarchy*, p. 15.
48. Consider the following description of the strategy followed to reach multinational agreement to the Mediterranean Action Plan:

> Negotiations were broken down into iterated games. The progressive development of the various Med Plan components through a process of a great number of meetings and interim agreements provided participating states with gradually increasing competence and confidence in the negotiating process... Besides the payments they received from participating, delegates stood to gain in future exchanges as well. UNEP deliberately set out to lead the Mediterranean states down the slippery slope to more binding environmental commitments.... Haas, *Saving the Mediterranean*, p. 184

49. "By binding people together in a long-term, multilevel game, organizations increase the number and importance of future interactions, and thereby promote the emergence of cooperation among groups too large to interact individually." Axelrod, *Evolution of Cooperation*, p. 131; See, as well, Axelrod and Keohane in Oye (ed.), "Achieving Cooperation."
50. Helen Milner raises a similar point with regard to Haas (*Saving the Mediterranean*), in her review article, "International Theories of Cooperation among

Nations: Strengths and Weaknesses," *World Politics* vol. 44, no. 3 (April 1992), pp. 479–80. The existence of (regimes and) epistemic communities indicates prior agreements to cooperate. Thus, it is those prior agreements that require explanation.

51. Keohane, "Multilateralism," p. 741.
52. Moravcsik, "Liberalism and International Relations Theory," p. 35.
53. Keohane, "Multi-lateralism," pp. 744–45.
54. *Ibid.*; Keohane, *After Hegemony*, pp. 105–06, 258–59; Charles Lipson, "Why are Some International Agreements Informal?" *International Organization* vol. 45, no. 4 (autumn 1991), pp. 508–14. On the importance of reputation in deterrence theory see, among others, Robert Jervis, "Deterrence and Perception," *International Security* 7 (winter 1982/83); Thomas Schelling, *Arms and Influence* (New Haven: Yale University Press, 1966).
55. It is important to note that the water-sharing plan of the late 1970s was highly restrictive in nature. It involved basin-wide coordination because that was the only way Jordan's water problems could be resolved. Compared with the earlier period, the United States Government showed few signs of visionary idealism. Nonetheless, it was anxious to assist in the normalization of relations among Israel, Jordan, and Syria by promoting agreement on a technical problem. The author is grateful to a former United States Government official for this insight (personal communication, 24 February 1992).
56. The term "ideational" refers to the products or creations of the human mind.
57. See, Lipschutz, *When Nations Clash*. The author's central thesis is that the foreign policy behavior of industrialized states, with regard to access to strategic resources, is determined by both material and "ideal" interests.
58. Kenneth Oye inadvertently highlights one of the major flaws in the neo-liberal argument when he notes that, in general, cooperation is a prerequisite of regime creation. "Explaining Cooperation under Anarchy: Hypotheses and Strategies" in Oye (ed.), *Cooperation under Anarchy*, p. 21.
59. Oran Young identifies three broad types of regimes: (1) tacit, implicit, or spontaneous, (2) negotiated, and (3) imposed. *International Cooperation*, pp. 84–89.
60. On the importance of geographic variables in the political behavior of states see, Jean Gottmann, *La Politique des états et leur géographie* (Paris: Colin, 1952); Halford J. Mackinder, "The Geographical Pivot of History," *Geographic Journal* vol. 23 (1904), pp. 431–44; Harold and Margaret Sprout, "Environmental Factors in the Study of International Politics," *Journal of Conflict Resolution* vol. 1, no. 4 (December 1957), pp. 309–28; Nicholas Spykman, *The Geography of the Peace* (New York: Harcourt Brace, 1944).
61. It became apparent from our research in the Middle East that the chief concerns of the riparians in the Jordan basin have revolved around each of these variables, to varying degrees and at different times. In the three other cases of riparian dispute, most, if not all, of these variables have come into play as well.
62. See, note 16 of this chapter.
63. It is on the basis of their perceptions of the environment that states formulate

policy and take action. See chapter 5, for a study, through the analysis of texts, of the psychological environment in the Middle East in the 1960s, with a focus on actors' perceptions. On the role of perceptions in international politics see, among others, Robert Jervis, *Perception and Misperception in International Politics* (Princeton: Princeton University Press, 1976); Harold and Margaret Sprout, "Geography and International Politics in an Era of Revolutionary Change," *Journal of Conflict Resolution* vol. 4, no. 1 (1960); Arthur A. Stein, "When Misperception Matters," *World Politics* vol. 34, no. 4 (July 1982). On perceptions in the Arab–Israeli conflict see, among others, Wm. Eckhardt, "Arab–Israeli Perceptions of the Middle East Conflict," *Peace Research* vol. 6, no. 3 (1974); Yehoshafat Harkabi, *Arab Attitudes toward Israel* (New York: Hart Publishing Co., 1972); D. Heradstveit, *The Arab–Israeli Conflict : Psychological Obstacles to Peace* (Oslo: Universitetsforlaget, 1979); Ralph White, "Misperception in the Arab–Israeli Conflict," *Journal of Social Issues* vol. 33, no. 1 (1977).

64. On the politics of mediation see, among others, Oran Young, *The Intermediaries : Third Parties in International Crises* (Princeton: Princeton University Press, 1968). For its application to the Arab–Israeli conflict see, Saadia Touval, *The Peace Brokers : Mediators in the Arab–Israeli Conflict, 1948–1979* (Princeton: Princeton University Press, 1982).

65. Note that of the four variables, only resource need is specific to riparian issues, although it can be subsumed under the very broad category of state's interests. The remaining three variables can be linked to a variety of theoretical literatures in the study of international politics. Relative power is reminiscent of realism, hegemonic stability theory, and "power analysis" in general. Riparian relations shares commonalities with cognitive and cultural approaches to the study of behavior, and conflict resolution ties in with the vast literature on the politics of mediation.

66. See, note 49 of this chapter. The "cooperation under anarchy" literature makes the claim that altering the environment in which states interact can increase incentives to cooperate. This is done by: (1) lengthening the "shadow of the future" – the promise that parties will continue to meet over the indefinite future, (2) increasing the transparency of state action, by providing information and reducing uncertainty, and (3) altering the "payoff structure," or parties' preferences or assessments of their national interests. (Axelrod, *Evolution of Cooperation*; Oye (ed.), *Cooperation under Anarchy*.) For other works in international relations theory that build upon microeconomics and the prisoners' dilemma paradigm see, for example, Snidal, "Relative Gains"; Michael Taylor, *Anarchy and Cooperation* (New York: Wiley, 1976); R. Harrison Wagner, "The Theory of Games and the Problem of International Cooperation," *American Political Science Review* vol. 77, no. 2 (June 1983).

2   The environment of conflict in the Jordan basin

1. *Man–Milieu Relationship Hypotheses in the Context of International Politics* (Center of International Studies, Princeton University, 1956); "Environmental

Factors in the Study of International Politics," *Journal of Conflict Resolution* vol. 1, no. 4 (December 1957), pp. 309–28. See, as well, *An Ecological Paradigm for the Study of International Politics* (Princeton: Center for International Studies, 1968), monograph no. 30; "Geography and International Politics in an Era of Revolutionary Change," *Journal of Conflict Resolution* vol. 4, no. 1 (1960); *Towards a Politics of the Planet Earth* (New York: Van Nostrand Reinhold Co., 1971).

2. Following in the tradition of the Sprouts, Robert North has written that environmental factors play a role in human behavior insofar as they act as "constraints on the possible." ("Toward a Framework for the Analysis of Scarcity and Conflict," *International Studies Quarterly* vol. 21, no. 4, [December 1977], p. 572.) David Orr has a similar formulation: the natural environment should be portrayed as "a matrix of possibilities which condition but do not determine outcomes." ("Modernization and Conflict: Second Image Implications of Scarcity," *International Studies Quarterly* vol. 21, no. 4 [December 1977], p. 596.)

3. See, among others, Halford J. Mackinder, "The Geographical Pivot of History," *Geographical Journal* vol. 23 (1904), pp. 431–44; *Democratic Ideals and Reality* (New York: Henry Holt, 1919); Nicholas J. Spykman, *The Geography of the Peace* (New York: Harcourt Brace, 1944).

4. Moshe Inbar and Jacob O. Maos, "Water Resource Planning and Development in the Northern Jordan Valley," *Water International* vol. 9 (1984), p. 19.

5. Efraim Orni and Elisha Efrat, *Geography of Israel* (Jerusalem: Israel Universities Press, 1971), p. 15. About one-third of the Arava Valley lies in Israel, the remainder lies in Jordan.

6. *Ibid.* p. 151.

7. *Ibid.* p. 27.

8. *Ibid.* p. 152.

9. *Ibid.* p. 35.

10. *Ibid.* p. 58.

11. *Ibid.* pp. 85–86.

12. *Ibid.* pp. 97–98.

13. *Ibid.* pp. 98–102. Both Israel and Jordan extract salt from its waters; Israel extracts other minerals as well.

14. Congressional Quarterly Inc., *The Middle East*, fifth edition, p. 172; Peter Gubser, *Jordan: Crossroads of Middle Eastern Events* (Boulder, Colo.: Westview Press, 1983), p. 5.

15. Congressional Quarterly Inc., *The Middle East*, p. 172.

16. Gubser, *Jordan*, p. 7.

17. *Ibid.*

18. W. B. Fisher, "Jordan: a Demographic Shatter-belt" in J. I. Clarke and W. B. Fisher (eds.), *Populations of the Middle East and North Africa: A Geographical Approach* (London: University of London Press Ltd., 1972), p. 205.

19. *Ibid.*; Gubser, *Jordan*, p. 7.

20. The description of the river system derives from the following sources: Moshe Brawer, "The Geographical Background of the Jordan Water Dispute" in Charles A. Fisher (ed.), *Essays in Political Geography* (London: Methuen & Co. Ltd., 1968), pp. 229–31; Kathryn B. Doherty, "Jordan Waters Conflict," *International Conciliation* [Carnegie Endowment for International Peace] no. 553 (May 1965), pp. 3–5; Maurice A. Garbell, "The Jordan Valley Plan," *Scientific American* vol. 212, no. 3 (March 1965), p. 25; Thomas Naff and Ruth C. Matson (eds.), *Water in the Middle East: Conflict or Cooperation?* (Boulder, Colo.: Westview Press, 1984), pp. 17–21; H. A. Smith, "The Waters of the Jordan: A Problem of International Water Control," *International Affairs* vol. 25, no. 4 (October 1949), p. 418.

21. To the west, the Ghor merges with the rolling hills that border Israel's coastal plain, while to the east, it gives way to the vast Jordanian plateau.

22. Charles T. Main, Inc., *The Unified Development of the Water Resources of the Jordan Valley Region* (Boston, Mass., 1953), p. 13; Since the Jordan Valley is a deep rift, the entire Jordan River south of the confluence with the Yarmouk River and most of the Jordan River south of Lake Huleh flows below sea level. As a result, the Jordan cannot provide irrigation water by gravity to agriculture along its banks. Furthermore, the river receives heavy infusions of salt, mostly from subterranean springs. The Yarmouk River, which is above sea level, contributes fresh water to the main stream, thereby acting as a diluting agent that makes possible the use of Jordan River water for certain human purposes. Garbell, "Jordan Valley Plan," p. 26.

23. Brawer, "Geographical Background," p. 229; Naff and Matson, *Water in the Middle East*, pp. 17–19.

24. Naff and Matson, *Water in the Middle East*, p. 17. Throughout this study one million cubic metres (mcm) will be used as the standard measure of water volume. One cubic metre of water equals 1,000 litres or 1,000 kilograms in weight (one metric ton). 1,000 million cubic metres equals one billion cubic metres (bcm).

25. *Ibid.* p. 19. Note that discharge figures are natural averages from the 1950s, prior to the implementation of major development projects using river water. Moreover, discharge figures vary. For example, Main, Inc. (*Unified Development*, p. 7) gauges the discharge of the Hasbani at 157 mcm, Garbell ("Jordan Valley Plan," p. 25) at 150 mcm.

26. Naff and Matson, *Water in the Middle East*, p. 19.

27. *Ibid.* p. 20.

28. *Ibid.* The difference is due to the high degree of direct evaporation from the surface of the lake.

29. Maher Abu Taleb, Jonathan Deason, and Elias Salameh, "The Jordan River Basin," paper delivered at the World Bank International Workshop on Comprehensive Water Management Policy (Washington, D.C., 24–28 June 1991), p. 7.

30. *Ibid.* pp. 20–21.

31. Derived from, Michael Baker Jr., Inc. and Harza Engineering Co., *The*

Hashemite Kingdom of Jordan: Yarmouk–Jordan Valley Project, Master Plan Report, 8 vols. and appendices (Chicago, Ill., 1955), pp. 33–36; Main Inc., *Unified Development*.

32. There is significant variation among authors in discharge figures. C. G. Smith ("The Disputed Waters of the Jordan," *The Institute of British Geographers: Transactions and Papers*, publication no. 40, 1966) writes that average annual runoff of the Jordan and its tributaries to the Dead Sea would, in the absence of any irrigation use of well, spring, or river water, be some 1,850 mcm (p. 112). Main Inc. (*Unified Development*) writes that the Jordan River south of the Yarmouk carries 1,250 mcm; wadis and wells to the east and the west add 382 mcm, giving a total discharge of 1,632 mcm.

33. Brawer, "Geographical Background," p. 233.

34. Aaron Wiener, "The Development of Israel's Water Resources," *American Scientist* vol. 60, no. 4 (July–August 1972), p. 468.

35. M. Jacobs and Y. Litwin, "A Survey of Water Resources Development, Utilization and Management in Israel" in V. T. Chow, S. C. Csallany, R. J. Krizek, and H. C. Preul (eds.), *Water for the Human Environment* vol. 2 (Chicago, Illinois: Proceedings of the First World Congress on Water Resources, 24–28 September 1973), p. 231.

36. *Ibid.* p. 232.

37. Jacobs and Litwin ("Water Resources," p. 232) suggest that Israel requires storage equivalent to about two years' supply of water.

38. J. Schwarz, "Israeli Water Sector Review: Past Achievements, Current Problems, and Future Options" in Le Moigne, Guy, Barghouti, Shawki, Feder, Gershon, Garbus, Lisa, and Xie, Mei (eds.), *Country Experiences with Water Resources Management: Economic, Institutional, Technological and Environmental Issues*, World Bank Technical Paper no. 175 (Washington, D.C.: The World Bank, 1992). Groundwater refers to that part of rainfall that seeps into the ground and upon reaching the water table moves as sub-surface flow. Much of the groundwater appears as the perennial flow in springs and wadis. Where the geological formations are favorable, groundwater may be obtained as a source of supply by pumping from wells. In order to be considered a gain in total water resources, the supply from groundwater thus obtained must be so located that it would not be recoverable from the springs and wadis. Main, Inc., *Unified Development*, p. 19.

39. Jacobs and Litwin, "Water Resources," pp. 226–27; Schwarz, "Israeli Water Sector." According to Associates for Middle East Research, Data Base (Philadelphia, Pa.: University of Pennsylvania), hereafter cited as AMER, Israel drew an annual average of 317 mcm from the coastal basin and 379 mcm from the western basin between 1985/86 and 1989/90.

40. Jacobs and Litwin, "Water Resources," p. 231; Schwarz, "Israeli Water Sector."

41. Indeed, it is only through recycling wastewater that net additions can be achieved. Schwarz, "Israeli Water Sector"; Yaacov Vardi, "National Water Resources Planning and Development in Israel – the Endangered Resource" in

Hillel I. Shuval (ed.), *Water Quality Management under Conditions of Scarcity* (New York: Academic Press, 1980), p. 42.

42. Itzhak Galnoor, "Water Planning: Who Gets the Last Drop?" in R. Bilski *et al.* (eds.), *Can Planning Replace Politics: the Israeli Experience* (The Hague: Martinus Nijhoff Publishers, 1980), pp. 141–42.

43. Interview by author with a spokesman for Mekorot – the country's national water authority, Tel-Aviv, 15 June 1986; Fred Pearce, "Wells of Conflict on the West Bank," *New Scientist* (1 June 1991), p. 37.

44. M. G. Ionides, *Report on the Water Resources of Transjordan and their Development* (published on behalf of the Government of Transjordan by the Crown Agents for the Colonies, London, 1939), pp. 4–5; A. Konikoff, *Transjordan: an Economic Survey* (Jerusalem: Economic Research Institute of the Jewish Agency for Palestine, 1946), p. 13.

45. Michael P. Mazur, "Economic Development of Jordan" in Charles A. Cooper and Sidney S. Alexander (eds.), *Economic Development and Population Growth in the Middle East* (New York: American Elsevier Publishing Co. Inc., 1972), p. 212.

46. Interview by author with a former Jordan Valley Authority official, Amman, 21 November 1985.

47. AMER.

48. The Zarqa River, with a mean annual flow of 92 mcm, is the second most important tributary. Baker and Harza, *Kingdom of Jordan*, p. 8.

49. Elisha Kally, *A Middle East Water Plan Under Peace* (Tel-Aviv University, Interdisciplinary Center for Technological Analysis and Forecasting, March 1986), p. 14. According to one source, the base flow of the Yarmouk is 218 mcm and the floodflow, 182 mcm. Elias Salameh, "Jordan's Water Resources: Development and Future Prospects," *American–Arab Affairs* no. 33 (summer 1990), pp. 70–72.

50. Salameh, "Jordan's Water Resources," p. 76.

51. Selig A. Taubenblatt, "The Jordan River Basin Water Dilemma: A Challenge for the 1990s," in Joyce Starr and Daniel Stoll (eds.), *The Politics of Scarcity: Water in the Middle East* (Boulder, Colo.: Westview Press, 1988). According to Abu-Taleb *et al.* ("Water Resources," p. 25), the total yield from all aquifers in 1990 was about 390 mcm, of which renewable supplies made up 270 mcm and non-renewable, 120 mcm.

52. Abu-Taleb *et al.*, "Water Resources," pp. 32–33; AMER.

53. G. H. Blake, "Israel: Immigration and Dispersal of Population" in Clarke and Fisher (eds.), *Populations*, p. 182.

54. Asher Arian, *Politics in Israel: the Second Generation* (New Jersey: Chatham House Publishers, Inc., 1985), p. 21.

55. See Orni *et al.* (*Geography of Israel*, pp. 262–67) for a discussion of the Jewish groupings in Israel in terms of descent.

56. *Ibid.* p. 261; the number of immigrants in 1949 alone – 240,000 – was equivalent to 26·5 percent of the total number of Jews in the country.

57. Blake, "Israel," p. 185.

58. Orni *et al.*, *Geography of Israel*, p. 259.
59. Kally, "Water Plan under Peace," p. 8; Thomas Naff, "The Jordan Basin: Political, Economic, and Institutional Issues" in Guy Le Moigne *et al.*, *Country Experiences with Water Resources Management*, p. 10. According to the World Bank (*World Development Report 1991*, Oxford University Press, June 1991), the population growth rate of Israel in 1990 was 1·6 percent and Jordan, 3·4 percent; cited in Maher F. Abu-Taleb, "Regional Cooperation in Water Resources Management" in Elise Boulding (ed.), *Peace Building in the Middle East : Challenges for States and for Civil Society* (Boulder, Colo. : Lynne Rienner Publishers, forthcoming).
60. Blake, "Israel," p. 183.
61. Abu-Taleb, "Regional Cooperation," p. 7; Kally, "Water Plan under Peace," p. 8.
62. Arian, *Politics in Israel*, p. 21.
63. *Ibid.*
64. *Ibid.* p. 20.
65. Blake, "Israel," pp. 193–94.
66. *Ibid.* p. 196. For details on the settlement strategy and master plans see, P. Démant, "Les Implantations israéliennes dans les territoires occupés," *Hérodote* (1983); Alain Dieckhoff, *Les Espaces d'Israël* (Paris: Fondation pour les Etudes de Défense Nationale, 1987); Elisha Efrat, *Geography and Politics in Israel since 1967* (London; Totowa, N.J.: Frank Cass, 1988); Baruch Kimmerling, *Zionism and Territory* (Berkeley: Institute of International Studies, University of California, 1983).
67. Quoted in Michael Mandelbaum, *The Fate of Nations : the Search for National Security in the Nineteenth and Twentieth Centuries* (Cambridge: Cambridge University Press, 1988), p. 272, fn. 26.
68. Naseer Aruri, *Jordan : A Study in Political Development (1921–1965)* (The Hague: Martinus Nijhoff, 1972), p. 33; Gubser, *Jordan*, p. 12.
69. Gubser, *Jordan*, p. 12.
70. *Ibid.*
71. *Statistical Abstract of Israel* (Jerusalem, various years), cited in Gubser, *ibid.* p. 12, fn. 4.
72. Congressional Quarterly Inc., *The Middle East*, p. 172; AMER.
73. Gubser, *Jordan*, pp. 15–16.
74. *Ibid.* pp. 13, 25–26.
75. *Ibid.* p. 14.
76. See, in this regard, Richard Hartshorne, "The Functional Approach in Political Geography," *Annals of the Association of American Geographers* vol. 40, no. 2 (June 1950), pp. 95–130.
77. Barry Buzan adds that if the idea of the state is "firmly planted in the minds of other states," then the state probably enjoys a fairly secure external environment as well; *People, States and Fear : the National Security Problem in International Relations* (Chapel Hill: the University of North Carolina Press, 1983), p. 50.
78. For information on Zionism and the Zionist movement see, among others, Ben

Halpern, *The Idea of the Jewish State* (Cambridge: Harvard University Press, 1969); Walter Laqueur, *A History of Zionism* (New York: Schocken Books, 1972).

79. Kimmerling, *Zionism and Territory*, p. 93.
80. Interview by author with a Jordanian scholar, Amman, 4 February 1986.
81. Transjordan was constituted as an independent state – the Hashemite Kingdom of Jordan – by treaty with Britain, on 22 March 1946. On the experience of state-building in Jordan see, Aruri, *Jordan*; Gubser, *Jordan*, pp. 75–95; Benjamin Shwadran, *Jordan, A State of Tension* (New York: Council for Middle Eastern Affairs Press, 1959); P. J. Vatikiotis, *Politics and the Military in Jordan* (London: Frank Cass & Co. Ltd., 1967).
82. In Zionist ideology, *Zion* is an abstract and metaphysical concept; there are no precise definitions of its borders. It did, however, function as the central mobilizing symbol of the Zionist movement.

    With regard to the notions of "return to the land," the glorification of labor and of the laborer, see the ideas of A. D. Gordon. A brief summary is provided in, Laqueur, *Zionism*, pp. 285–86.
83. "The Zionist Organization's Memorandum to the Supreme Council at the Peace Conference" in J. Hurewitz, *Diplomacy in the Near and Middle East* vol. 2 (Princeton: D. Van Nostrand Co., 1956), p. 48.
84. H. F. Frischwasser-Raʿanan, *The Frontiers of a Nation* (Westport, Conn.: Hyperion Press, Inc., 1955), p. 107.
85. Hurewitz, *Diplomacy*, p. 47.
86. For further information on this fascinating story of boundary delineation in the Middle East see, Frischwasser-Raʿanan, *Frontiers of a Nation*; a lighter and less scholarly account can be found in T. E. Lawrence, *Seven Pillars of Wisdom* (Garden City, N.Y.: Doubleday, 1936).
87. Michael Brecher, *Decisions in Israel's Foreign Policy* (New Haven: Yale University Press, 1975), p. 186.
88. In keeping with European Zionists' perception of Palestine as a frontier, Israel Zangwill, one of the movement's most prominent spokesmen, referred to Zionism as "a people without a land, returning to a land without a people."

    For an interesting application of Frederick Jackson Turner's "frontier theory" to discuss the relationship between the character of an immigrant-settler society and its environment, using the example of Jewish settlement in Palestine/Israel in the absence of a frontier, see, Kimmerling, *Zionism and Territory*; Turner's theory is elaborated in Frederick Jackson Turner, *The Frontier in American History* (New York: Henry Holt & Co., 1920).
89. Kimmerling, *Zionism and Territory*, pp. 10–11.
90. American Friends of the Middle East, Inc., *The Jordan Water Problem: an Analysis and Summary of Available Documents* (Washington, D.C., 1964), p. 6; Brecher, *Israel's Foreign Policy*, p. 186.
91. A.-M. Goichon, *L'Eau, Problème Vital de la Région du Jourdain* (Bruxelles: Publication du Centre pour l'Etude des Problèmes du Monde Musulman Contemporain, 1964), pp. 10–11; M. G. Ionides, "The Perspective of Water

231

Development in Palestine and Transjordan," *Journal of the Royal Central Asian Society*, vol. 33, parts 3 and 4 (July–October 1946), pp. 273–74 and "Jordan Valley Irrigation in Transjordan," *Engineering* (13 September 1946), p. 242. These two authors maintain that the Corporation never released water for the use of Transjordan, always claiming that there was no surplus. Until the Arab–Israeli war of 1948–49 and the destruction of the Rutenburg hydro-electric works at the confluence of the Jordan and Yarmouk rivers, the Corporation's monopoly proved to be a major stumbling-block to the economic development of Transjordan.

92. For more information on this period and the land question in particular see, W. Khalidi (ed.), *From Haven to Conquest: the Origins and Development of the Palestine Problem 1897–1948* (Beirut: Institute for Palestine Studies, 1971); Kimmerling, *Zionism and Territory*; Yehoshua Porath, *The Palestinian National Movement: From Riots to Rebellion* (London: Frank Cass, 1977).

93. I. Abu-Lughod (ed.), *The Transformation of Palestine* (Evanston: Northwestern University Press, 1971); Khalidi, *From Haven to Conquest*; Porath, *Palestinian National Movement*. For data on land purchases and the institutions involved see, Kimmerling, *Zionism and Territory*, pp. 38–48, 68–78.

94. Kimmerling, *Zionism and Territory*, pp. 94–95.

95. On the demographic changes as a result of Jewish immigration see, Janet Abu-Lughod, "The Demographic Transformation of Palestine" in Abu-Lughod (ed.), *Transformation of Palestine*, pp. 139–63 and Kimmerling, *Zionism and Territory*, pp. 92–93.

96. Kimmerling, *Zionism and Territory*, p. 94.

97. *Ibid.*; Porath, *Palestinian National Movement*.

98. B. Kalkas, "The Revolt of 1936: A Chronicle of Events" in Abu-Lughod, *Transformation of Palestine*.

99. *Palestine Royal Commission Report* (London: His Majesty's Stationery Office, 1937). Also as a result of the Arab rebellion (1936–39), the British Government, through the publication of the *Land Transfer Ordinances* (1940), drastically limited the rights of Jews to buy additional lands in Palestine. Kimmerling (*Zionism and Territory*, p. 118) maintains, however, that the Ordinances did not limit land purchases.

100. M. G. Ionides (published on behalf of the Government of Transjordan by the Crown Agents for the Colonies, London, 1939).

101. M. G. Ionides, "The Disputed Waters of Jordan," *Middle East Journal* vol. 7, no. 2 (spring 1953), p. 155.

102. Ionides, "Jordan Valley Irrigation," p. 242.

103. *Ibid.*

104. The Jewish Agency was set up in 1922 as part of the World Zionist Organization, to represent the Jewish people in working out a plan with the British Government for a Jewish national home in Palestine. It was one of the dominant governing authorities in the *Yishuv*. After 1948, the spheres of responsibility of the State of Israel were divided between the Agency and the central government. The Agency handles and promotes Jewish immigration to Israel, the absorption

of immigrants, the setting up of settlements, and fund-raising abroad for Israel.

105. For an elaboration of the *Yishuv*'s new territorial conception after 1937, and the land purchasing and settlement policies that supported these views, consult Kimmerling, *Zionism and Territory*, pp. 56, 86–90.

106. Walter C. Lowdermilk, *Palestine Land of Promise* (New York and London: Harper & Brothers Publishers, 1944). See, as well, Sulamith Schwartz, "Blueprint and Vision: The Jordan Valley Authority" in *The Palestine Year Book* vol. 2, 1945–46 (New York: Zionist Organization of America).

107. Lowdermilk's assertion as to the "emptiness" of Palestine harks back to Kimmerling's discussion of the acute contradiction inherent in a situation of "low frontierity" for the aims and ideology of an immigrant-settler society. In order to realize its project, such a society requires an open frontier in its "target land." If there is no frontier, the society must create one. But once created, the frontier must be filled. If not, it will be filled by those who are not part of the immigrant–settler society. See, Kimmerling, *Zionism and Territory*, p. 25.

108. James B. Hays, *TVA on the Jordan: Proposals for Irrigation and Hydro-Electric Development in Palestine* (Washington, D.C.: Public Affairs Press, 1948).

109. Ionides, "Disputed Waters," p. 157.

110. For discussions of these events see, among others, Fred J. Khouri, *The Arab–Israeli Dilemma* (New York: Syracuse University Press, 1968), pp. 43–101; Conor Cruise O'Brien, *The Siege* (New York: Simon and Schuster, 1986), pp. 267–308; Nadav Safran, *From War to War* (New York: Pegasus, 1969), pp. 27–42.

111. Kimmerling, *Zionism and Territory*, p. 122.

112. Gubser, *Jordan*, pp. 10–12.

113. "Refugees and the Jordan," *The Spectator* (19 November 1948), pp. 659–60.

On 11 December 1948, the UN General Assembly passed a resolution to establish a Conciliation Commission, with the task to "take steps to assist the Governments and authorities concerned to achieve a final peace settlement of all questions outstanding between them," and to "facilitate the repatriation, resettlement and economic and social rehabilitation of the refugees and the payment of compensation" to them. But the Commission failed to make important headway in solving the refugee question by political means and so it decided to try an economic approach. In August 1949, it set up an Economic Survey Mission with Gordon Clapp, formerly of the Tennessee Valley Authority, as chairman, with instructions to: "examine the economic situation arising from the recent hostilities in the Near East and…recommend to the Conciliation Commission means of overcoming resultant economic dislocations, of reintegrating the refugees into the economic life of the area, and of creating the economic conditions which will be conducive to the establishment of permanent peace."

Initially, the Mission hoped that it could implement several large-scale projects that would integrate most of the refugees into the economic life of the area. However, it quickly discovered that there were political and emotional obstacles. Moreover, a project such as the comprehensive development of the Jordan River system would require political cooperation between Israel and the Arab states. As that seemed unattainable at the time, Gordon Clapp warned that: "the region is not ready, the projects are not ready, the people and governments are not ready for large-scale development of the region's basic river systems or major undeveloped areas. To press forward on such a course is to pursue folly and frustration and thereby delay sound economic growth." The Mission recommended, instead, small-scale projects that would provide immediate employment for some of the refugees and a first step toward larger projects.

By 1951, the Conciliation Commission had virtually lost hope in making significant inroads in resolving the "Palestine Problem." It suspended all efforts aimed at conciliation. These efforts were never revived, although the Commission did continue to be involved in some of the technical aspects of the refugee problem. Khouri, *Arab–Israeli Dilemma*, pp. 126–33.

114. Kimmerling, *Zionism and Territory*, p. 93 (table 4.1); O'Brien, *The Siege*, pp. 315, 333; Orni and Efrat, *Geography of Israel*, p. 260.
115. Sir M. MacDonald & Partners, *Report on the Proposed Extension of Irrigation in the Jordan Valley* (London, 1951).
116. American Friends, *Jordan Water Problem*, p. 54; quoted from, Pinhas Sapir, "The Development of Israel," *Israel and the Middle East* no. 3–5, vol. 4 (24) (December 1952), p. 62.
117. *Ibid.*
118. American Friends, *Jordan Water Problem*, p. 56, cited from, "Special Reports on Jordan," *Bulletin of Economic Development*, no. 14 (Beirut: UNRWA, July 1956), p. 95.
119. Khalidi, *Haven to Conquest*; Porath, *Palestinian National Movement*.
120. Kimmerling, *Zionism and Territory*, pp. 31–65.
121. *Ibid.*
122. Laqueur, *Zionism*.
123. From, Eliezer Schweid, *The Individual: the World of A. D. Gordon* (Tel-Aviv: Am Oved, 1970), p. 173, quoted in Kimmerling, *Zionism and Territory*, p. 202.
124. Interview by author with an Israeli scholar, Jerusalem, 30 April 1986.
125. Interview by author with an Israeli geomorphologist and author of studies on water development, Haifa, 21 June 1986.
126. For a recent example of the links between access to water and Israel's political and security-related concerns, see chapter 8 (section on the West Bank).
127. See Rosemary Sayigh, *Palestinians: From Peasants to Revolutionaries* (London: Zed Press, 1979).
128. Interviews by author with a Palestinian sociologist, Amman, 4 February 1986; with an Israeli historian of Palestine, Jerusalem, 16 April 1986.
129. Interview by author with a Palestinian sociologist, Amman, 4 February 1986.
130. By the inception of statehood, however, the proportion of the nomadic population relative to the settled was approximately equal. Konikoff, *Transjordan*, p. 19.

131. Interviews by author with a Jordanian journalist, Amman, 27 October 1985; with a Palestinian lawyer, Amman, 6 November 1985. See, Chapter 4, pp. 82, 83, for reference to the Jordan Valley as home to the Palestinians. For information on the British Government's *Palestine Royal Commission* advocacy of resettling Arabs from "Cisjordan" (Palestine) in Transjordan, see, Konikoff, *Transjordan*, pp. 28–29.

3 Riparian disputes compared

1. For an instructive discussion of the comparative case study method of analysis see, Alexander L. George, "Case Studies and Theory Development: The Method of Structured, Focused Comparison" in Paul Gordon Lauren (ed.), *Diplomacy: New Approaches in History, Theory and Policy* (New York: Free Press, 1979), pp. 43–68.
2. Zohurul Bari, "Syrian–Iraqi Dispute over the Euphrates Waters," *International Studies* [Quarterly Journal of the School of International Studies, Jawaharlal Nehru University] vol. 16, no. 2 (April–June 1977), p. 230.
3. Fifteen percent of the basin lies in Saudi Arabia, but it has not been involved in the riparian conflict. Nureddin al-Rifaʿi, "Miyaaʾ Nahr al-Furat bein Turkiya wa-Suriya wal-Iraq" [The Waters of the Euphrates River between Turkey, Syria, and Iraq], *al-Muhandis al-Arabi* [The Arab Engineer] no. 68 (1983), p. 5.
4. Peter Beaumont, "The Euphrates River – an International Problem of Water Resources Development," *Environmental Conservation* vol. 5, no. 1 (spring 1978), p. 36.
5. André Bourgey, "Le Barrage de Tabqa et l'Aménagement du Bassin de l'Euphrate en Syrie," *Revue de Géographie de Lyon* vol. 49 (1974), p. 345. With the construction of the Ataturk dam in Turkey, there will no longer be flooding. The author is grateful to a former United States government official for this information (personal communication, 15 February 1992).
6. *Ibid.*; Beaumont, "The Euphrates River," p. 36.
7. Bourgey, "Barrage de Tabqa"; Nazim Moussly, *Le Problème de l'Eau en Syrie* (Lyon: BOSC Frères, 1951), pp. 15–16. The Euphrates, with its annual average discharge in Syria of approximately 28 bcm, dwarfs all other flows available to the country. The Hasbani River has an average discharge of 130 mcm per annum, while the Orontes, 500 mcm. John Waterbury, "Dynamics of Basin-Wide Cooperation in the Utilization of the Euphrates," paper prepared for the Conference: The Economic Development of Syria: Problems, Progress, and Prospects, Damascus, 6–7 January 1990, p. 7.
8. Julian Rzoska, *Euphrates and Tigris, Mesopotamian Ecology and Destiny* (The Hague: W. Junk bv Publishers, 1980), p. 2; K. Ubell, "Iraq's Water Resources," *Nature and Resources* vol. 7, no. 2 (spring 1978), p. 3. Agriculture in all of northern Iraq is rainfed.
9. Mesopotamia and Iraq have a long history of utilizing Euphrates water for irrigation. A number of "hydraulic civilizations" dependent upon irrigated agriculture waxed and waned in the Mesopotamian plain. Among them, the

Sassanids (AD 226–637) and Abbasids (AD 750–1200) produced the most complex irrigation systems within the region. But from the time of the Abbasids until the late nineteenth century, irrigation development remained largely uncoordinated and of only local importance. River management and extensive use of the river's waters for irrigation were taken up again in earnest in the early part of this century. Barrages to store Euphrates floodwaters were built at al-Hindiya (1913) and at al-Ramadi (1950s). Two other major storage projects were initiated in the late 1970s, but have been delayed as a result of the drastic cutbacks to development projects in the country after the outbreak of the Iran–Iraq war.

10. For information on the various dam projects in Turkey see, John F. Kolars and William A. Mitchell, *The Euphrates River and the Southeast Anatolia Development Project* (Carbondale: Southern Illinois University Press, 1991).

11. Nonetheless, each country, for bargaining purposes, put forth maximum demands: Iraq – 14 bcm, Syria – 13 bcm, Turkey – 18 bcm. These demands exceeded the natural yield of the Euphrates by 15 bcm. Waterbury "Dynamics of Basin-Wide Cooperation," p. 16, based on Bari, "Syrian–Iraqi Dispute," p. 238.

12. Moshe Efrat, "Syria's Dam on the Euphrates," *New Outlook* vol. 10, no. 4 (1967), p. 46. The motivation of the French was to win over Turkey's loyalty and discourage it from joining the war effort on the side of the Axis powers.

13. Waterbury, "Dynamics of Basin-Wide Cooperation," p. 16.

14. Arab Socialist Bʿath Party, *al-Furat... al-ʾazma illathi aftaʿalaha hukaam al-Iraq* (The Euphrates: the Crisis Created by the Rulers of Iraq) (Damascus: Office of Propaganda, Publication, and Information, n.d.), p. 29; Bari, "Syrian–Iraqi Dispute," p. 238; Waterbury, "Dynamics of Basin-Wide Cooperation," p. 17.

15. Col. Roy L. Thompson, "Water as a Source of Conflict," *Strategic Review* vol. 7, no. 2 (spring 1978), p. 67.

16. Whereas until then, 13 bcm of Euphrates water had flowed into Iraq and was used to irrigate 1·2 million hectares, the country had received, by June 1975, only 7 bcm. "Le Partage des Eaux de l'Euphrate," *Maghreb-Machrek* no. 69 (July–August–September 1975), p. 61.

17. Waterbury, "Dynamics of Basin-Wide Cooperation," p. 18.

18. On the relationship between the two Bʿathi regimes in this early period see, Eberhard Kienle, *Baʿth v. Baʿth: the Conflict between Syria and Iraq 1968–1989* (London: I. B. Tauris & Co. Ltd., 1990), pp. 31–86.

19. The Arab League, with the agreement of Syria and Iraq, set up a technical commission to investigate the conflicting claims in the basin. The day it announced its decision that Syria had to release water immediately to meet Iraq's needs, Syria retreated from the commission, charging that Iraq had let loose an "information campaign" against it. Several days later, the Syrian Minister of the Euphrates Dam claimed that at the technical commission talks, Iraq was requesting from Syria more water than what reached the Turkish–Syrian border. The first Saudi Arabian mediation effort met with no greater

success. Although it was announced that a compromise agreement had been reached, the agreement was never made public. Some time later, Iraq announced that negotiations had been sabotaged by the Syrian regime; at the last moment, the Syrian minister had been instructed not to sign the accord. *Maghreb-Machrek* no. 69, pp. 62–63. See, as well, Kienle, *Ba'th v. Ba'th*, p. 100.

20. According to one source, Iraqi officials have said privately that the understanding required Syria to release to Iraq 60 percent of the Euphrates waters reaching its northern border. Thomas Naff and Ruth C. Matson (eds.), "The Euphrates River and the Shatt al-Arab" in *Water in the Middle East : Conflict or Cooperation?* (Boulder, Colo. : Westview Press, 1984), p. 94.

21. For an analysis, along these lines, of the Syrian–Iraqi relationship until 1973 see, note 18 above; Eberhard Kienle, "The Conflict between the Baath Regimes of Syria and Iraq prior to their Consolidation : from Regime Survival to Regional Domination," *Ethnizität und Gesellschaft*, Occasional Papers no. 5 (Freie Universität Berlin, 1985).

22. Bari, "Syrian–Iraqi Dispute," p. 243.

23. Waterbury, "Dynamics of Basin-Wide Cooperation," p. 18. According to the Turks, the Commission's work has been hampered because often, either the Syrian or the Iraqi member does not attend meetings when the other is present. "Turkey Harnesses the Euphrates," *The Middle East* (November 1986), p. 19. According to Naff and Matson (*Water in the Middle East*, p. 99), both Turkey and Iraq claimed in 1984 that Syria had refused to discuss plans to apportion the Euphrates waters since 1972.

24. Kolars and Mitchell, *Euphrates River*, p. 31.

25. For Turkey's Southeast Anatolia Development project (GAP) see, Kolars and Mitchell, *Euphrates River*; "Ataturk Dam – the biggest yet," *The Middle East* (May 1984), pp. 75–76; "Turkey Harnesses the Euphrates," pp. 19–20; "Turkey Taps the Euphrates Resources," *Middle East Economic Digest* (17 July 1981), pp. 50–52.

26. The World Bank and most international funding agencies are not prepared to finance projects in river basins unless there is basin-wide agreement on water utilization. Because of Syrian and Iraqi objections to Turkey's GAP project, Turkey was denied funding for some time. It had to rely on Turkish sources. Since 1985, however, financial institutions and international agencies, including the World Bank, have relaxed their regulations and have been lending assistance. Kolars and Mitchell, *Euphrates River*, p. 32.

27. That is to say, Turkey's motivation is not to engage in strategic games with the downstream states. Besides, it had been involved in projects to develop its portion of the basin long before the issue became geopolitical. (The author wishes to thank a former US government official for this important note; personal communication, 23 February 1992.)

28. The project will put water back into the river system, but that water will be of an inferior quality.

29. Alan George, "Wrangle over the Euphrates," *The Middle East* (October 1987), p. 27.

30. Niranjan Gulhati, *Indus Waters Treaty : An Exercise in International Mediation* (Bombay: Allied Publishers, 1973), p. 18.
31. The tributaries, either two or three at a time, join up to form common channels that meet the Indus and flow through Pakistan. Basheer Khalil Nijim, "The Indus River" in "The Indus, Nile, and Jordan: International Rivers and Factors in Conflict Potential" (doctoral dissertation: Indiana University, June 1969), p. 33.
32. *Ibid.* pp. 40–42.
33. For some idea of the magnitude of the Indus system, consider the following: "The 5 rivers' combined annual discharge of 97 bcm exceeds the Nile's average of 84 bcm, and the Ravi's winter flow of 1·5 bcm exceeds the Jordan's annual flow of 1·2 bcm." *Ibid.* p. 38.
34. *Ibid.* pp. 37–39.
35. Gulhati, *Indus Waters Treaty*, p. 21.
36. Nijim, "The Indus River," pp. 49–50.
37. For details on the population exchange see, Aloys Arthur Michel, *The Indus Rivers – A Study of the Effects of Partition* (New Haven: Yale University Press, 1967), p. 4.
38. The boundary cut across the Bari Doab, almost at right angles to the Ravi and Sutlej Rivers. The Upper Bari Doab Canal system taps the Ravi on the Indian side of the cease-fire line in southeast Kashmir, and irrigates areas on both sides of what has become the international boundary. The Lower Bari Doab Canal also uses Ravi water for areas now in Pakistan. The Sutlej is tapped by the Sirhind Canal in East Punjab and is used entirely in India, but downstream, the Dipalpur and other canals carry Sutlej water to Pakistan. Nijim, "The Indus River," p. 51.
39. Michel, *The Indus Rivers*, p. 8.
40. *Ibid.* p. 197.
41. Nijim, "The Indus River," pp. 54–58.
42. *Ibid.* p. 58.
43. Michel, *The Indus Rivers*, pp. 202–03.
44. Nijim, "The Indus River," pp. 59–60.
45. "Another Korea in the Making?" *Collier's Magazine* (4 April 1951), p. 58.
46. Michel, *The Indus Rivers*, p. 223.
47. Nijim, "The Indus River," pp. 62–65.
48. *Ibid.* p. 65.
49. *Ibid.* p. 67.
50. Gulhati, *Indus Waters Treaty*, p. 139.
51. The same, of course, was true of the Kashmir dispute.
52. It is important to note that there were many Indian statesmen who were opposed to and bitter about the establishment of a separate Muslim state in the sub-continent. They sought to impair Pakistan's viability in order to prove that it could not survive alone. Michel, *The Indus Rivers*, p. 197.
53. For a provocative discussion of "structural political threat," and its application to India and Pakistan see, Barry Buzan, *People, States and Fear : The National*

Security Problem in International Relations (Chapel Hill: The University of North Carolina Press, 1983), pp. 78–79. Buzan argues that such threats arise when "the organizing principles of two states contradict each other in a context where the states cannot simply ignore each other's existence."

54. Pakistan's political development in the early years of statehood was turbulent. Dissension within the ruling Muslim League provoked its eventual factionalization. The country's second prime minister, Liaquat Ali Khan, was assassinated in office (1951). There was much strife between the provincial governments and central power, and between East and West Pakistan. Provincial governments were generally weak, and the central government was constantly changing. From 1951 to 1955, the country had three different prime ministers. And in October 1958, a military *coup d'état* brought the army to power under General Mohamed Ayub Khan.

55. In addition, it is probably fair to say that the World Bank became involved at an opportune moment. India was anxious to enhance its *image* because of historical and security-related circumstances, described above. For a brief discussion on the concern for national image as an incentive toward inter-state cooperation see, David LeMarquand, *International Rivers: the Politics of Cooperation* (Vancouver, B.C.: Westwater Research Centre, University of British Columbia, 1977), p. 12.

56. John Waterbury, *Hydropolitics of the Nile Valley* (New York: Syracuse University Press, 1979), p. 14.

57. Waterbury, *Hydropolitics*, p. 23.

58. Basheer Khalil Nijim, "The Nile River" in "The Indus, Nile, and Jordan: International Rivers and Factors in Conflict Potential" (doctoral thesis, Indiana University, June 1969), pp. 93, 95.

59. John Waterbury, "Legal and Institutional Arrangements for Managing Water Resources in the Nile Basin," *Water Resources Development* vol. 3, no. 2 (1987), p. 92.

60. Waterbury, *Hydropolitics*, pp. 7, 22.

61. *Ibid.* pp. 8–9.

62. *Ibid.* p. 33.

63. The Sudan had just recently begun perennial irrigation.

64. Waterbury, *Hydropolitics*, p. 66.

65. *Ibid.* p. 68.

66. Nijim, "Nile River," p. 124.

67. Waterbury, *Hydropolitics*, p. 70.

68. The 1957 Eisenhower Doctrine provided for direct American military support to Middle Eastern states threatened by "Communist aggression." On Sudanese politics in the 1950s see, P. K. Bechtold, *Politics in the Sudan* (New York: Praeger, 1976).

69. The Aswan High Dam project and its funding became deeply embedded in both superpower politics and the Arab–Israeli conflict. See, Waterbury, *Hydropolitics*, pp. 102–08.

70. Waterbury, "Managing Water Resources," p. 97.

71. Waterbury, *Hydropolitics*, p. 118.
72. Egypt is *the* strongest Arab state in terms of size, population, industrial development, and military capability. It has well-developed institutions and a strong sense of nationhood. It is a unified state, with a strong central government and relatively little, albeit sporadic, domestic political upheaval. It has always exercised a pivotal role in regional affairs, and has been a focus of concern to European states with regard to their Middle East politics. In contrast, the Sudan is a relatively weak state, with an underdeveloped economy. It is a highly rural society that continues to practice subsistence agriculture in much of the country. Central power is weak; it is threatened by primordial tribal allegiances of the population, and has been the target of numerous attempted *coups d'état* (some of which have been successful). And for over three decades, a debilitating civil war has raged in the south. Despite the obvious fact that the power balance is overwhelmingly in Egypt's favor, it is perhaps sobering to note that both states are increasingly being kept afloat by massive injections of foreign aid.
73. Waterbury, *Hydropolitics*, p. 210.
74. See John Waterbury, "Riverains and Lacustrines: Toward International Cooperation in the Nile Basin," Discussion Paper no. 107, *Research Program in Development Studies*, Woodrow Wilson School, Princeton (September 1982), pp. 81–84, for further information on Ethiopia's water resources.
75. *Ibid.* p. 82.
76. Waterbury, *Hydropolitics*, p. 238.
77. Waterbury, "Riverains and Lacustrines," pp. 96–114.
78. Waterbury, "Managing Water Resources," pp. 99–101.
79. The precedent of the 1929 agreement was an active agent, also in a sense stimulated by a third party, the United Kingdom. However, the latter is perhaps best seen as a hegemon. (The author is grateful to John Waterbury for this insight.)

4 The Johnston mission to the Middle East (1953–1956)

1. For discussions of the implementation and violations of the Armistice Agreements see, N. Bar-Yaacov, *The Israel–Syrian Armistice: Problems of Implementation, 1949–1966* (Jerusalem: Magnes Press, 1967); E. L. M. Burns, *Between Arab and Israeli* (Beirut: The Institute for Palestine Studies, 1969); E. H. Hutchison, *Violent Truce* (New York: The Devin-Adair Co., 1956); Fred J. Khouri, *The Arab–Israeli Dilemma* (New York: Syracuse University Press, 1968), pp. 182–203.
2. For details on the Huleh project see, Bar-Yaacov, *Israel–Syrian Armistice*; A.-M. Goichon, *L'Eau, Problème Vital de la Région du Jourdain* (Bruxelles: Publication du Centre pour l'Etude des Problèmes du Monde Musulman Contemporain, 1964), pp. 50–53.
3. Goichon, *L'Eau*, pp. 53–56.
4. On 26 January 1952, the UN General Assembly passed a resolution which authorized UNRWA to carry out a three-year $250,000,000 program to finance

large-scale development projects in the hope that these would resettle most of the refugees. Fred J. Khouri, "The US, the UN, and the Jordan River Issue," *Middle East Forum* (May 1964), p. 22.

5. On why the United States became involved in Jordan Valley water development see, Memorandum from the Legal Advisor of the State Department on Development of Water Resources of the Jordan River Valley, 6 October 1953, United States National Archives (USNA) 684a.85322/10-653; Eric Johnston, "Jordan River Valley Development," *Department of State Bulletin* (28 December 1953), pp. 891–93 and "Arab–Israel Tension and the Jordan Valley," *World Affairs* (summer 1954), pp. 38–41; Dana Adams Schmidt, "Prospects for a Solution of the Jordan River Valley Dispute," *Middle Eastern Affairs* vol. 6, no. 1 (January 1955), pp. 1–12.

6. Memorandum by the Acting Regional Planning Adviser Bureau of Near Eastern, South Asian, and African Affairs, to the Assistant Secretary of State Byroade, Washington, 25 July 1952, *Foreign Relations of the United States, 1952–1954 (FRUS)* vol. 9, part 1 (Washington: United States Government Printing Office, 1986), no. 81, pp. 256–62.

7. *FRUS*, 4 May 1953, no. 604, pp. 1,185–88.

8. The project was outlined in two reports by Bunger, "Prospectus: Yarmouk–Jordan Valley Project, Kingdom of Jordan" and "Information on the Yarmouk River Watershed (Proposed Dam at Maqarin)," n.d., cited in Charles T. Main, Inc., *The Unified Development of the Water Resources of the Jordan Valley Region* (Boston, Mass., 1953), p. 2.

9. Goichon, *L'Eau* pp. 56–59; Yoram Nimrod, "The Unquiet Waters," *New Outlook* vol. 8, no. 4 (June 1965), p. 39. For the Syria–Jordan agreement see, Hashemite Kingdom of Jordan, *al-jarida al-rasmiyya* [Official Gazette], no. 1150 (dated 4 June 1953), pp. 380–84.

10. As we recall, the Yarmouk joins the Jordan River in territory in the hands of Israel – the Adasiye Triangle, formed by the two rivers and Lake Tiberias.

11. Nimrod, "Unquiet Waters," p. 39; Memo of Conversation between Abba Eban and State Department, 19 October 1953, USNA 684a.85/10-1953.

12. See, Bar-Yaacov, *Israel–Syrian Armistice*; Michael Brecher, *Decisions in Israel's Foreign Policy* (New Haven: Yale University Press, 1975), pp. 190–91; Goichon, *L'Eau*, pp. 59–62, 67–73.

13. Memorandum of Agreement between US Department of State and TVA, 18 September 1952, USNA 684.85322/9-1852.

14. Introductory Note by Leslie J. Carver, Acting Director UNRWA, in Charles T. Main, Inc., *Unified Development*, August 1953. It is possible that UNRWA, in requesting such a study, was trying to cover itself; it might have expected a hostile reaction from Israel toward international support for the Bunger project. It is also possible that the United States had encouraged UNRWA to avert antagonizing relations in the Middle East yet further and investigate the potential for water development on a regional cooperative basis.

In May 1953, four months before submission of the Unified Plan, word leaked out to Jordan that the State Department had proposed to delay action on the

Yarmouk project until an agreement on riparian rights could be reached with Israel; Memorandum of Conversation Prepared in US Embassy (Amman), J. F. Dulles and Prime Minister of Jordan, Amman, 15 May 1953, *FRUS*, no. 15, pp. 41–43.

15. Charles T. Main, Inc., *Unified Development*, pp. 10, 12.
16. Secretary of State J. F. Dulles to Eric Johnston, *FRUS*, 13 October 1953, no. 686, pp. 1,348–52.
17. *FRUS*, 11 October 1953, no. 684, pp. 1,345–46 and 13 October 1953, no. 686, pp. 1,348–52.
18. For Israel's explanation for the Qibya attack, see the statement of Prime Minister David Ben-Gurion, broadcast over the Voice of Israel on 19 October 1953, National Archives of the State of Israel (INA), Foreign Ministry documents (Record Group 93), box 360, file 3 (360/3), 20 October 1953. See, as well, E. Hutchison (*Violent Truce*, pp. 43–44) for a discussion of this incident.
19. *FRUS*, 27 October 1953, no. 710, p. 1,389 and 20 October 1953, no. 698, pp. 1,369–71. Israel stopped the work at the site on 28 October in response to the US Government announcement that aid was being withheld.
20. Jordan criticized the US for failing to halt Israeli "acts of aggression." *FRUS*, 18 October 1953, no. 696, pp. 1,367–68. Syria was concerned about developments in the DMZ; it was annoyed by the US' delayed and lame reaction to the Bnot Ya'acov project. USNA, 10 September 1953, 683.84a/9-1053; *FRUS*, 17 October 1953, no. 693, pp. 1,362–63. Furthermore, while the US Government was withholding economic aid to Israel, it made no grants to the Arab states either. *FRUS*, 27 October 1953 no. 709, pp. 1,388–89. Hence, it was difficult for the Arabs to perceive the American gesture as a condemnation of Israel's behavior.
21. *FRUS*, 17 October 1953, no. 693, pp. 1,362–63 and 25 October 1953, no. 706, pp. 1,383–84.
22. *FRUS*, 13 October 1953, no. 687, pp. 1,353–55; USNA, 18 October 1953, 120.280/10-30-53.
23. *FRUS*, 13 October 1953, no. 687, pp. 1,353–55.
24. *FRUS*, 28 October 1953, no. 712, pp. 1,391–92.
25. Brecher, *Israel's Foreign Policy*, p. 194.
26. *FRUS*, 28 October 1953, no. 712, pp. 1,391–92.
27. Quoted in Brecher, *Israel's Foreign Policy*, pp. 195 n. and Nimrod, "Unquiet Waters," p. 41. It is important to note that there was some anti-American sentiment in Israel as well, as a result of the withholding of economic aid and the censure of Israel in the aftermath of the Qibya raid. However, this hostility was dispelled somewhat once aid was reinstated a few days later.
28. Egypt was included among the states that Johnston was to visit. Although not riparian to the Jordan River, it was, by far, the most influential and most powerful Arab state. Washington believed that winning Egypt over to the notion of integrated regional planning of water resources was more than half the battle to securing a basin-wide agreement.
29. *FRUS*, 22 October 1953, no. 703, pp. 1,380–81.

30. *FRUS*, 25 October 1953, no. 706, pp. 1,383–84; USNA, 10 September 1953, 684a.85/9-1053 and 28 October 1953, 120.280/10-2853; *FRUS*, 1 November 1953, no. 720, pp. 1,400–01 and 20 November 1953, no. 736, p. 1,432. In partial explanation of the Arabs' negative response, it became known that the Arab League Political Committee had met in Amman on 23 October and passed the following resolution: "The Political Committee recommends that the three sister Arab States who have common interests in the waters of the Jordan basin ... should refuse to discuss any plan for the joint exploitation of the waters of this river with the enemy Israel and that this resolution should be made quite clear to the western states concerned." (Quoted in a telegram from the US embassy [Amman] to J. F. Dulles, 26 October 1953, USNA 120.280/10-2653.)

31. Israel accepted a temporary stoppage of the Bnot Ya‘acov project on 28 October in response to UN Security Council Resolution 100; Dulles dropped economic sanctions the following day. For Israel's Seven-Year Plan, see, Brecher, *Israel's Foreign Policy*, p. 194; see, chapter 2.

32. Nimrod, "The Unquiet Waters," p. 45.

33. *FRUS*, 28 October 1953, no. 712, pp. 1,391–92 and 29 October 1953, no. 715, pp. 1,394–95; INA, 29 October 1953, "masa u-matan im johnston" [Negotiations with Johnston], box 3688, file 9 (3688/9).

34. *FRUS*, 17 November 1953, no. 732, pp. 1,418–23.

35. *FRUS*, 20 November 1953, no. 734, p. 1,426.

36. From the statement by Ambassador Abba Eban before the Security Council, 30 October 1953, INA 360/6.

37. *FRUS*, 20 November 1953, no. 734, pp. 1,427–28.

38. *FRUS*, 18 November 1953, no. 733, p. 1,425. In US Government circles just prior to Johnston's first visit to the region, it had been hoped that the dispute over the Bnot Ya‘acov project could be effectively dealt with by simply eliminating the DMZ. This however, was not feasible, at least not by way of negotiation; the Syrians wanted the international border to be on the east water line of the Jordan, while Israel did not want Syria to have direct access to the river at all.

39. Report of Conversation with Mahmoud Riad, 15 January 1954, USNA 683.84a322/1-1554.

40. Remarks of the "Arabian Technical Committee" on the Project of "Unified Development of the Water Resources of the Jordan Valley Region," February 1954, USNA 684a.85322/2-1054.

41. At a later session of the Arab Committee (19–21 May), the Plan was amended to allow for the storage of a small amount of Yarmouk water (60–100 mcm, equivalent to an estimate of the river's winter floodwaters) in Lake Tiberias, provided that the Arabs were assured that Israel would not have the power to cut off this supply. Furthermore, the Committee recommended that in order to obviate the passage of water for the West Ghor (in Jordanian territory) through a canal that would take off from Lake Tiberias (in Israeli territory), the East Ghor Canal could be enlarged and have a siphon to the West Ghor; 28 May 1954, USNA, 684a.85322/5-2854.

42. The Cotton Plan for the Development and Utilization of the Water Resources of the Jordan and Litani River Basins, INA, 3688/2, pp. 1–2.
43. Simha Blass, *Mei Meriva u-Maʿas* [Water in Strife and Action] (Israel: Masada Ltd., 1973), pp. 195–96.
44. Observations of a Technical Nature prepared by experts of the Government of Israel on the Main Plan... 29 April 1954, INA, movil ha-mayim ha-artsi [National Water Carrier], box 7, file 61.
45. Israel's attitude toward Unified Plan, 9 February 1954, USNA 684a.85322/2-954.
46. Observations of a Technical Nature prepared by experts of the Government of Israel on the Main Plan, "The Unified Development of the Water Resources of the Jordan Valley Region," 29 April 1954, INA, 7/61. This 35-page report includes a 7-page addendum on the inclusion of the Litani River in Jordan basin development.
47. Brecher, *Israel's Foreign Policy*, p. 197.
48. Goichon, *L'Eau*, p. 80.
49. Brecher, *Israel's Foreign Policy*, p. 196.
50. *FRUS*, 22 June 1954, no. 837, pp. 1,584–85 and 1 July 1954, no. 839, p. 1,586.
51. Yoram Nimrod, "The Jordan's Angry Waters," *New Outlook* vol. 8, no. 5 (July–August 1965), p. 24.
52. However, Johnston did have private indications that they might give ground on this point if the Israelis would accept other elements of the proposals. See, *FRUS*, 17 June 1954, no. 834, pp. 1,578–79.
53. *FRUS*, 17 June 1954, no. 838, pp. 1,585–86; Summary Report of Negotiations held in June 1954 between Ambassador Johnston's Group and Technical Committee of Arab League, February 1955, INA 3688/9.
54. Meetings with Eric Johnston, June 1954; first session, 20 June, INA 3688/9.
55. Most of the secondary literature on the Johnston mission suggests that the demand for inclusion of the Litani was dropped only during the third round of negotiations. This, however, does not concur with the primary sources, most notably, documents reviewed from the State of Israel Archives, the United States National Archives, and in the volume of the *Foreign Relations of the United States*. From the three archival collections, it appears that the demand was withdrawn by the end of the second round in June 1954.
56. "Suggestions for the Formulation of our Position prior to the Coming Negotiations with Ambassador E. Johnston" [heʿarot li-givoosh emdatenu likrat ha-masa u-matan ha-karov im ha-shagrir E. Johnston], INA 3688/10. Simha Blass, in his personal account of the negotiations, writes that the Israeli team announced to Johnston that "without the Litani, Israel will not give its lake for the use of others" [bli ha-litani, lo titen yisrael at ha-yam shela li-shimoosh acherim]. Blass, *Mei Meriva u-Maʿas*, p. 200.
57. Blass, *Mei Meriva u-Maʿas*, p. 199.
58. *Ibid.*
59. Memorandum prepared in the Department of State, Current Status of Jordan Valley Negotiations, *FRUS*, 20 December 1954, no. 938, pp. 1,727–30.

60. As a follow-up to the Bunger Plan of 1952, Michael Baker Jr., Inc. and Harza Engineering Co. had been commissioned to draw up a project for Jordan, for the utilization of the resources of the Yarmouk and Jordan Rivers to irrigate the Jordan Valley and produce hydro-electric power. They had been asked to consider, in the formulation of a scheme, the principles of the "Arab Plan," published by the Technical Committee in March 1954. The new plan, *The Hashemite Kingdom of Jordan: Yarmouk–Jordan Valley Project*, Master Plan report (Chicago, Ill.) was published in eight volumes in 1955.

61. Minutes of the Opening Session: talks between Ambassador Johnston and his party and the members of the Israel government, Thursday a.m. session, 27 January 1955; INA 3688/10.

62. Thursday p.m. session, 27 January 1955, *ibid.*

63. Simha Blass (in *ibid.*), an engineer and member of the Israeli team, based Israel's claim to water from the Yarmouk on present/historic use and riparian rights. It was already using some Yarmouk water for existing settlements in the "Triangle." Israel had a vested interest in the Yarmouk waters.

64. Thursday p.m. session, *ibid.*

65. The matter of international supervision was put aside early on in the talks, after Sharett had announced that if Israel could not have direct cooperation with the Arabs, it would accept only a very restricted role for a water administrator, again, out of concern for its own sovereignty.

66. Minutes from the p.m. session, 29 January 1955; INA 3688/10.

67. Minutes from the a.m. session, 30 January 1955, *ibid.*

68. *Ibid.* 31 January 1955.

69. Although inclusion of the Litani River in the regional scheme had been dropped from the agenda by the end of the second round of talks in June 1954, Israel was now becoming concerned because of rumors of negotiations between the Lebanese and American governments for the development of that national river system. In the opening session of Eric Johnston's third round of talks in Israel, Prime Minister Sharett stated that while Israel had accepted the temporary exclusion of the Litani, it did not want anything done to the river in the meantime that would preclude the eventual joining of its waters with the other rivers of the Jordan system; *ibid.*, 27 January 1955, a.m.; see as well, the entry on the "Jordan River," in *al-mawsuᶜa al-falistiniya* [Palestinian Encyclopaedia] vol. 1 (Damascus, 1984), p. 157.

70. 31 January 1955, INA 3688/10. Blass writes that in an effort to get an agreement, Johnston promised Israel more financial aid and assistance in setting up an atomic power plant for the desalinization of water. He did not promise more water from the Jordan system. Israel, however, "was not going to deliver water [from Lake Tiberias to the Arab states] in exchange for dollars." Blass, *Mei Meriva u-Maᶜas*, p. 205.

71. Telegram from Eric Johnston (US Embassy, Cairo) to the Secretary of State, 10 February 1955; US Department of State documents released to author under the Freedom of Information Act (FOI), Foreign Policy Records, 684a.85322/2-1055.

72. *Ibid.*

73. Nimrod, "Jordan's Angry Waters," p. 28.

74. From Verbatim Text of Tentative Agreement of 19 February telegram from US Embassy (Beirut) to Secretary of State, 20 February 1955, FOI 684a/85322/2-2055.

75. Blass, *Mei Meriva u-Ma^cas*, p. 206.

76. Department of State, Memorandum of Conversation on Jordan Valley Negotiations, 16 March 1955, FOI 684a.85322/3-1655.

77. Blass, *Mei Meriva u-Ma^cas*, pp. 206–07. Blass writes that in a private conversation with Moshe Sharett on the last day of negotiations, Johnston threatened to resign from his mission and blame Israel for refusing to cooperate. The issue, apparently, was Israeli dissatisfaction over the exchange of 100 mcm from the Jordan River to the Kingdom of Jordan for 25 mcm from the Yarmouk. Sharett walked out of the meeting in a huff, and Levi Eshkol, in an effort to appease Eisenhower's special envoy, unilaterally reduced the quantity of water that Israel would release to Jordan "with strings attached."

78. Memorandum to the Files: Ambassador Johnston's Meeting with Mr. Hammarskjold and General Burns, 21 March 1955, FOI 684a.85322/3-2155.

79. For a discussion of the positions taken on the issue by Israel's political parties see, Brecher, *Israel's Foreign Policy*, pp. 178–81.

80. Memorandum to the Files, Ambassador Johnston's Meeting with Mr. Hammarskjold and General Burns, 21 March 1955, FOI 684a.85322/3-2155.

81. Memorandum of Conversation at Foreign Office, London (between officials of the American and British governments) on Progress Made in the Jordan Waters Negotiations, 18 May 1955; Foreign Service Despatch, US Embassy (London) to Department of State, 23 May 1955, FOI 684a.85322/5-2355.

82. Minutes of Meeting, Ambassador Eban and two other Israeli officials, Eric Johnston and two members of his party, 15 June 1955, FOI 684a.85322/6-1555, and Memorandum of Conversation on Jordan Valley Plan, Ambassador Eban and State Department Assistant Secretary George Allen, 23 June 1955, FOI 684a.85322/6-2355.

83. Brecher, *Israel's Foreign Policy*, pp. 202–3. The memorandum states the following: (1) Storage facilities were to be constructed on the Yarmouk at Maqarin. As for Lake Tiberias, final decision on the use of the lake was deferred until 1960, and would be made by the Neutral Engineering Board, (2) Supervision would be exercised by a three-man Neutral Engineering Board, the chairman to be selected by the two members whom Israel and the Arab riparian states would designate, (3) Israeli sovereignty over all Israeli territory was assured, (4) Water allocations were set forth as per the "Gardiner Formula." (p. 203.)

Curiously, in the archival sources consulted, the National Archives of Israel and of the United States, as well as the Freedom of Information Services of the US Department of State, there is no mention of this "Draft Memorandum of Understanding." Brecher does point out that the agreement was never published, but that a copy of it was made available to him (p. 202).

84. Telegram (no. 99) US Embassy (Beirut) to Secretary of State, 27 July 1955, FOI 684a.85322/7-2755. To substantiate the argument that the Plan favored Israel, the Parliament pointed out that the US had committed $40 million in grant aid to Israel for fiscal year 1955, while Lebanon had been having great difficulty obtaining a loan from Washington. Eventually, a loan of $5 million was offered, conditional upon Lebanon's support for the Unified Plan. See, State Department telegram (no. 908) to US Embassy (Beirut), 28 March 1955, FOI 684a.85322/3-855.

85. US Embassy (Amman) to Department of State, 9 August 1955, FOI 684a.-85322/8-955.

86. Telegram (no. 99) US Embassy (Beirut) to Secretary of State, 27 July 1955, FOI 684a.85322/7-2755.

87. Burns, *Between Arab and Israeli*, pp. 123–25; Goichon, *L'Eau*, pp. 84–85; Khouri, *Arab–Israeli Dilemma*, p. 143; Mohamed Ali al-Saadi, "The Jordan River Dispute: a Case Study in International Conflicts" (unpublished Ph.D. dissertation, University of Massachusetts, 1969), p. 172.

88. He did not explain why he was increasing Israel's share, but we do know that Israel wanted 40 mcm from the Yarmouk River. It already had access to 25 mcm by virtue of "historic use" in the Jordan–Yarmouk Triangle.

89. Second Meeting with the Ministerial Committee of Jordan, Amman, 27 August 1955, FOI 684a.85322/8-3055.

90. See, p. 93.

91. Third Meeting with the Ministerial Committee of Jordan, Amman, 28 August 1955, FOI 684a.85322/9-655.

92. Luncheon Meeting with the King and Cabinet, King's Palace, Amman, 28 August 1955, FOI 684a.85322/8-3055.

93. Account of an informal meeting between the Prime Minister of Jordan and Eric Johnston; Telegram (no. 99) US Embassy (Amman) to Secretary of State, 30 August 1955, FOI 684a.85322/8-3055.

94. Telegram (no. 350) US Embassy (Cairo) to Secretary of State, 31 August 1955, FOI 684a.85322/8-3155.

95. Summary Minutes of the Meeting with the Arab Technical Committee at the Office of Mr. Ibrahim ʿAbd-el-Al, Beirut, 8 September 1955, FOI 7.u.684a. 85322/9-1955. According to the Baker–Harza provisions, this represented a reduction in the Kingdom's share of the Jordan and Yarmouk River waters from 537 mcm to 477 mcm, or, of 60 mcm.

96. Memorandum, Results of the Meeting of the Arab Technical Committee for the Exploitation of the Jordan River and its Tributaries, 8–9 September 1955, FOI 684a.85322/9-1955.

97. Memorandum of Conversations, Developments on the Johnston Plan, UN Secretary-General Dag Hammarskjold and other UN officials, 5 April 1956, FOI 684a.85322/4-556.

98. Quoted in Brecher, *Israel's Foreign Policy*, p. 205.

99. Interview by author with a former official of the Israel Foreign Ministry, Jerusalem, 16 June 1986.

100. Telegram, Department of State to US Embassy (Cairo), 23 February 1956, FOI 684a.85322/2-2356; telegram (no. 817), American Embassy (Tel-Aviv) to Secretary of State, 17 February 1956, FOI 684a.85322/2-1656.
101. Telegram (no. 817), 17 February 1956, FOI 684a.85322/2-1656.
102. On the so-called Czech arms deal see, Burns, *Between Arab and Israeli*, pp. 99–102; Khouri, *Arab–Israeli Dilemma*, pp. 202–03.
103. On the two lines in Israel's military and foreign policy, and the replacement of Sharett by Ben-Gurion see, Burns, *Between Arab and Israeli*, pp. 39–48 and Brecher, *Israel's Foreign Policy*.
104. Telegram, Secretary of State to US Embassy (Tel-Aviv), 26 January 1956, FOI 684a.85322/1-2656.
105. Telegram (no. 932), US Embassy (Beirut) to Secretary of State, 14 February 1956, FOI 684a.85322/2-1456.
106. Nimrod, "Jordan's Angry Waters," p. 32. The new government, under the leadership of Saʿid al-Ghazi, feared that the opposition would force it out of office if it accepted the water project.
107. Report of a conversation between the US Ambassador (Egypt) Byroade and President Nasser, 13 March 1956, telegram (no. 1841) from US Embassy (Cairo) to Secretary of State, 14 March 1956, FOI 684a.85322/3-1456.
108. *Ibid.*; Report of conversation between US Embassy (Beirut) officials and Lebanese Foreign Minister, telegram (no. 1029) US Embassy (Beirut) to Secretary of State, 3 March 1956, FOI 684a.85322/3-356.
109. Memorandum of Conversations, Developments on the Johnston Plan, UN Secretary-General Dag Hammarskjold and other UN (and US) officials, 5 April 1956, FOI 684a.85322/4-556.
110. Nimrod, "Jordan's Angry Waters," p. 33.
111. Burns, *Between Arab and Israeli*, p. 174.
112. On the 1956 war see, among others, Donald Neff, *Warriors at Suez* (New York: Linden Press, 1981); Nadav Safran, *From War to War* (New York: Pegasus, 1969), pp. 47–56.
113. Interview by author with a former Government of Israel, Foreign Ministry official, Jerusalem, 29 June 1986.
114. See for example, Constantine Zurayk, *Maʿna al-Naqba* (Beirut: Dar al-ʿIlm l-al-Milayin, 1948), also published as *The Meaning of Disaster*, translated by Bayley Winder (Beirut: Khayat, 1956); on the 1967 defeat, Sadiq al-Azm, *al-Naqd al-Dhati baʿd al-Hazima* [Self-Criticism after the Defeat] (Beirut: Dar al-Taliʿah, 1968).

   In the domain of inter-Arab politics, there was much pressure on Arab governments to demonstrate a "correct" and non-compromising attitude toward the Palestine Question; deviation from that course was threatened with ostracism, as was the experience of Egypt from 1979 to 1987. Moreover, Arab states tended to struggle amongst themselves for rank as the most steadfast *vis-à-vis* Israel. See, for example, the case of Iraq and Syria, chapter 3.
115. Minutes of Meeting with Eric Johnston, June 1954, first session, Jerusalem, 20 June, INA 3688/9.

116. In an interview by this author, a former Jordanian member of the Arab Technical Committee said that Yarmouk water is the only source of food security for Jordan. He went even further and insisted that Yarmouk water is "the basis" – the "top priority" – of the country's national security; it is "more basic than arms, more basic than peace." Amman, 18 November 1985.

117. Quoted in Brecher, *Israel's Foreign Policy*, p. 183 from D. Ben-Gurion, "Israel's Security and her International Position Before and After the Sinai Campaign," in *Government Year-Book 5720, 1959/60* (Jerusalem, 1960), pp. 22–24.

118. Quoted in Brecher, *Israel's Foreign Policy*, p. 184, from *Divrei ha-Knesset*, xv, pp. 270–71, 30 November 1953.

119. Interview by author with former Israel Foreign Ministry official, Jerusalem, 29 June 1986.

120. Report of a conversation between the US Ambassador Byroade and President Nasser, 13 March 1956, telegram (no. 1841) from US Embassy (Cairo) to Secretary of State, 14 March 1956, FOI 684a.85322/3-1456.

121. General Dayan to Assistant Secretary of State Byroade, *FRUS* vol. 9, 18 November 1953, no. 733, p. 1,425.

122. From the Minutes of meetings with Eric Johnston, Jerusalem, June 1954, first session, 20 June, INA 3688/9.

123. See, American Embassy (Damascus) to State Department, 10 September 1953, USNA 683.84a/9-1053; *FRUS*, 1 November 1953, no. 720, pp. 1,400–01; *FRUS* vol. 9, 15 January 1954, no. 767, p. 1,478.

124. Khouri, *Arab–Israeli Dilemma*, p. 203.

125. Report of conversation between King Hussein and the *chargé d'affaires* of the US embassy (Amman), *FRUS*, 11 November 1953, no. 727, pp. 1,410–11.

126. Translation of the memorandum submitted by the Jordan National Socialist Party to the Prime Minister expressing its rejection of the Johnston Project, FOI, 26 September 1955, 684a.85322/9-2655.

127. On the domestic structure of Jordan in the period under review see, Naseer Aruri, *Jordan: A Study in Political Development (1921–1965)* (The Hague: Martinus Nijhoff, 1972); Peter Gubser, *Jordan: Crossroads of Middle Eastern Events* (Boulder, Colo.: Westview Press, 1983); Benjamin Shwadran, *Jordan, A State of Tension* (New York: Council for Middle Eastern Affairs Press, 1959); P. J. Vatikiotis, *Politics and the Military in Jordan* (London: Frank Cass & Co. Ltd., 1967).

128. Telegram, US embassy (Amman) to Secretary of State, 22 September 1955, FOI, 684a.85322/9-2255.

129. Interview by author with a former member of the Arab Technical Committee, Amman, 18 November 1985.

130. Memorandum to the President from J. F. Dulles, 29 April 1954, USNA 120.280/5-154.

131. Nonetheless, the combination of political recognition and the positive involvement of a third party was not enough to insure that the river system would be shared in the optimal fashion suggested in chapter 1.

132. Report of conversation between General Moshe Dayan and Assistant Secretary of State Byroade, *FRUS*, 18 November 1953, no. 733, p. 1,425.

5 Perception and misperception: the Jordan waters crisis (1964) and the onset of war

1. In 1956, Israel's National Water Planning Board adopted a Ten-Year Plan, based upon, but with some modifications of, the earlier Seven-Year Plan.
2. For details on the East Ghor Canal project see, Joseph L. Dees, "Jordan's East Ghor Canal Project," *Middle East Journal* vol. 13, no. 4 (autumn 1959), pp. 357–81; Eliezer Ben-Moshe, "Jordan's Yarmuk Plan," *New Outlook* vol. 5, no. 2 (February 1962), pp. 22–24; Maurice A. Garbell, "The Jordan Valley Plan," *Scientific American* vol. 212, no. 3 (March 1965), pp. 23–31; George E. Gruen, "Jordan's East Ghor Irrigation Project," *New Outlook* vol. 7, no. 5 (1964), pp. 34–37; John S. Haupert, "Recent Progress of Jordan's East Ghor Canal Project," *The Professional Geographer* vol. 18, no. 1 (January 1966), pp. 9–13; C. G. Smith, "Diversion of the Jordan Waters," *The World Today* vol. 22, no. 11 (November 1966), pp. 491–98.
3. Gruen, "East Ghor Irrigation," p. 35.
4. In the late 1950s, the economic situation of the Kingdom was such that maximum utilization of the waters of the Jordan system was deemed imperative. While severely limited in natural resources, technical capacity, and transport facilities, this country, with an estimated population in 1958 of 1,600,000 in an area of just over 60,320 square kilometres, was burdened with refugees, unemployment, and a heavy military budget. And from its inception, the state had been dependent on foreign aid for more than half its annual budget requirements and over 60 percent of its total revenues. At the time, the balance of payments deficit was the highest of any Middle Eastern country except for Israel, while its per capita income of $100 was among the lowest. Lacking mineral resources necessary for an industrial base, the Kingdom had to rely on agriculture for economic growth. However, cultivable land was limited to the Jordan Valley, which represented only 0·6 percent of the country's land area. And agriculture was distinguished by low yields and highly unpredictable harvests, which were barely able to meet the consumption needs of the population in a normal year. Dees, "East Ghor Canal Project," pp. 363–64; Peter Gubser, *Jordan: Crossroads of Middle Eastern Events* (Boulder, Colo.: Westview Press, 1983), pp. 55–68; Haupert, "Jordan's East Ghor Canal," p. 9.
5. Yitzhak Oron (ed.), *Middle East Record* vol. 2, 1961 (Reuven Shiloah Research Center, Tel-Aviv University), p. 220.
6. On the National Water Carrier system see, American Friends of the Middle East, Inc., *The Jordan Water Problem* (Washington, D.C., 1964), pp. 52–63, 84; Moshe Brawer, "The Geographical Background of the Jordan Water Dispute" in Charles A. Fisher (ed.), *Essays in Political Geography* (London: Methuen & Co. Ltd., 1968), pp. 239–42; Garbell, "Jordan Valley Plan," pp. 30–31; Shimon Golani, "Ha-ma'avak al mei ha-yarden" [The Conflict over the Jordan Waters]

in Kliot, Shmueli and Sofer (eds.), *Artsot Ha-Galil* [The Lands of the Galilee] part 2 (1983), pp. 855–56; George E. Gruen, "Water and Politics in the Middle East," *American Jewish Committee : Reports on the Foreign Scene* no. 5 (December 1964), pp. 1–2; Moshe Inbar and Jacob O. Maos, "Water Resource Planning and Development in the Northern Jordan Valley," *Water International* vol. 9 (1984), pp. 20–21.

7. When it became known that the United States was helping Jordan fund the East Ghor Canal project, Israel insisted on parallel treatment in water development. The US eventually agreed to finance the construction of a pipeline from Lake Tiberias to the Beyt She'an Valley, to mitigate the loss from the Yarmouk River incurred by Israel as a result of Jordan's diversion scheme. Interview by author with former Israel Foreign Ministry official, Jerusalem, 16 June 1986.

8. Yoram Nimrod, "Conflict over the Jordan – last stage," *New Outlook* vol. 8, no. 6 (September 1965), p. 5.

9. *Ibid.* p. 7.

10. Yitzhak Oron (ed.), *Middle East Record* vol. 1, 1960 (Reuven Shiloah Research Center: Tel-Aviv University), p. 207.

11. Nimrod, "Conflict over the Jordan," pp. 7–9.

12. Oron, *Middle East Record*, vol. 1, pp. 208–09.

13. British Broadcasting Corporation, *BBC : Summary of World Broadcasts*, part 4: the Middle East (published by the Monitoring Service of the BBC, UK), "Syrian Comment on the Dangers of Israeli Exploitation of the Negev," no. 1470, 4 February 1964 p. A/3; Hassan ʿAbd al-Qader Saleh, "al-asas al-jografi l-il-nizaʿa al-arabi al-israʾili hawl miyaaʾ nahr al-urdun," [The Geographical Bases of the Arab–Israeli Dispute over the Waters of the Jordan River], *majalla kuliya al-ʾadab* [Journal of the Faculty of Letters, University of Jordan] vol. 3, no. 1 (1972), p. 45; Mohamed Ahmed Selim, *Le Problème de l'Exploitation des Eaux du Jourdain* (Paris: Editions Cujas, 1965), pp. 27–28; Interview by author with former Egyptian Foreign Minister, Cairo, 8 May 1986.

14. Note that as of 1949 and the Murdoch MacDonald project to irrigate the Jordan Valley, Arab plans were based on the international legal principle that "the waters in a catchment area should not be diverted outside that area unless the requirements of all those who use or genuinely intend to use the waters within the area have been satisfied." Because of their particular interests in resource development, the Arab states insisted that the waters of the Jordan system must be reserved for intra-basin usage. And Israel, because of its particular interests, asserted that the intra-basin doctrine was outdated and that Jordan waters could be used outside the watershed. Interview by author with former President of Tahal (Water Company for Israel) and technical advisor on the Israeli team during the Johnston mission, Tel-Aviv, 5 May 1986.

15. See note 13 above.

16. As a case in point, consider the aftermath of the dissolution of the Syria–Egypt union (the United Arab Republic) in 1961. Following the break-up, Cairo used the Jordan waters issue in its attacks on the new Kuzbari Government in Syria.

Cairo accused Damascus of first, having given Israel the courage to resume work on its water project by demanding the dissolution of the UAR, and then, standing idly by as Israel diverted the waters of the Dan River within the range of Syrian artillery. Damascus, in turn, accused Cairo of indifference to the Jordan waters question and fear of Israel. Oron, *Middle East Record*, vol. 2, p. 220.

17. Nimrod, "Conflict over the Jordan," pp. 10–11; Note that some of Nimrod's dates appear to be incorrect. According to the BBC, Israel announced a financial push to the National Water Carrier in April 1961, not 1962. And the Arab Chiefs-of-Staff meeting, mentioned below, was in December 1963, and not 1964.

18. ʿAbd al-Nasir reported on this meeting and its recommendations at the first Arab Summit Conference, three years later. See, *BBC*, no. 1453, 15 January 1964, pp. A/1–2.

19. Oron, *Middle East Record*, vol. 2, pp. 218–19.

20. Nimrod, "Conflict over the Jordan," pp. 11–12.

21. *Ibid.*

22. *BBC*, "Statement on the Arab Summit Conference," no. 1456, 18 January 1964, p. A/1; "Arab Press Comment on the Arab Summit Conference," no. 1453, 15 January 1964, p. A/3.

23. *BBC*, "Statement on the Arab Summit Conference," no. 1456.

24. See, in this regard, the monograph written by the former chairman of the Authority: Subhi Kahhaleh, "The Water Problem in Israel and its Repercussions on the Arab–Israeli Conflict," *IPS Papers* no. 9 (Beirut: Institute for Palestine Studies, 1981), pp. 30–32.

25. *BBC*, "Statement on the Arab Summit Conference," no. 1456. "ʿAbd al-Khaliq Hassunah's Press Conference…," no. 1475, 20 January 1964, p. A/2; Muhammad Mehdi, "The Arab Summit," *Middle East Forum* (May 1964), pp. 25–28; Nimrod, "Conflict over the Jordan," p. 12.

26. *BBC*, "Damascus Press Comment on the Cairo Conference," no. 1459, 22 January 1964, p. A/1.

27. *BBC*, "Israeli Press Comment on the Cairo Conference," no. 1457, 20 January 1964, p. A/5.

28. *BBC*, "Israel Comment on the Arab Conference," no. 1456, 18 January 1964, pp. A/3–4; Interview by author with former Israel Government Foreign Ministry official, Jerusalem, 29 June 1986.

29. *BBC*, "Israeli Press Comment on the Arab Summit Conference," no. 1458, 21 January 1964, pp. A/1–2.

30. *BBC*, "Eshkol's Statement on the Cairo Conference," no. 1459, 22 January 1964, pp. A/1–2.

31. *Ibid.*; The last comment was corroborated by the Egyptian *Al-ʾAhram* newspaper, which wrote that: "The battle against the diversion of the Jordan river is one against Israel as a hostile political entity forcibly implanted in the midst of the Arab land." *BBC*, no. 1534, 22 April 1964, p. A/2.

32. Gruen, "East Ghor Irrigation," p. 1.

33. *BBC*, "Comment on Israeli Diversion of Jordan Riverwaters," no. 1548, 8 May 1964, p. A/1.

34. *BBC*, "Damascus Radio Calls for Arab Action Against Israel," no. 1580, 16 June 1964, pp. A/7–9.

35. *BBC*, "Arab Summit Conference Proceedings," no. 1655, 12 September 1964, p. A/2. There were five elements to the diversion scheme proposed by the Authority: (1) divert water from the Hasbani in Lebanon to the Litani basin, and store the water for use in southern Lebanon; (2) carry out the necessary works to exploit the Wazzani springs in Lebanon and the Banias springs in Syria to irrigate agricultural lands in both countries, and transport the surplus water through a canal across the Golan Heights in Syria to Wadi Raqqad (a tributary of the Yarmouk), to be exploited by Jordan; (3) build a dam at the Mukehiba site on the Yarmouk River where it meets Wadi Raqqad, to store the water diverted from Lebanon and Syria in a reservoir with a capacity of 200 mcm, and have it connected by tunnel to the East Ghor Canal in Jordan, to generate electric power and irrigate the Ghor on both banks of the Jordan River; (4) increase the capacity of the East Ghor Canal from 10 to 20 cubic metres per second; (5) build syphons and canals to carry water across the Jordan River to the West Bank for irrigation. Kahhaleh, "Water Problem in Israel," pp. 30–32.

36. Gruen, "Water and Politics," p. 11; Kahhaleh, "Water Problem in Israel," pp. 30–32; Nimrod, "Conflict over the Jordan," p. 15.

37. *BBC*, no. 1655, p. A/2.

38. *Ibid.*

39. *BBC*, "Arab Summit Conference Communique," no. 1656, 14 September 1964, p. A/1.

40. *BBC*, "King Hussein's Press Conference," no. 1656, 14 September 1964, p. A/4.

41. It was Israel's broadcasting services and later, Moroccan radio, that revealed the differences which resulted in near-deadlock. *BBC*, no. 1653, 10 September 1964, pp. A/2, A/4–5.

42. The idea was to move the troops of the unified military command from one Arab country to another, in peace time as well as during war, to meet any anticipated threat. Lebanon, Syria, and Jordan opposed the presence of Egyptian-led troops in countries during peace. And the Lebanese government insisted that no Arab troops could enter its country, under any circumstances, without prior approval from the Lebanese Parliament; Gruen, "Water and Politics," p. 5.

43. *BBC*, no. 1653, 10 September 1964, p. A/4. The Arab riparians saw in Nasir's suggestion a hidden desire to interfere in their domestic politics.

44. *BBC*, "Syrian Comment on the Arab Summit," no. 1658, 18 September 1964, p. A/3.

45. *BBC*, "Syrian Comment on the Conference," no. 1653, 10 September 1964, p. A/3.

46. *BBC*, "Report on the Syrian–Israeli Border Clash," no. 1711, 17 November 1964, p. A/7.

47. *BBC*, "Eshkol's Statement to Foreign Correspondents," no. 1761, 18 January

1965, p. A/1; "Levi Eshkol's Speech at Tiberias," no. 1764, 21 January 1965, p. A/1.

48. See note 47 above, and "Kennedy's Letter to Ben-Gurion Assuring US Support for Israel's Water Project" (13 June 1962) in Mordechai Gazit, *President Kennedy's Policy toward the Arab States and Israel* (Tel-Aviv: The Shiloah Center for Middle Eastern and African Studies, 1983), pp. 95–96.

49. *BBC*, no. 1769, 27 January 1965, pp. A/3–4.

50. *BBC*, "Egyptian Comment on Israeli Reactions," no. 1761, 18 January 1965, p. A/3.

51. Nimrod, "Conflict over the Jordan," p. 17.

52. For information on the Arab Premiers' Conference (9–12 January) and the Foreign Ministers' Meeting (14–15 March) see, *BBC*, no. 1758, 14 January 1965, p. A/1 and no. 1810, 16 March 1965, pp. A/4–5, respectively.

53. The only public expression of doubt and circumspection was Mohamed Hassanein Haykal's. In an article in Egypt's, *Al-ʾAhram* newspaper, this astute observer and judicious critic of regional affairs intimated that the Arab diversion project was doomed. To defend this singular position, he cited three obstacles to the project's realization: (1) Lebanon had made pledges to the scheme, but had not activated any of them thus far, (2) behind Syria's tough exterior and rigid stance was a country in deep turmoil, and (3) the political situation in Jordan, fraught with opposition and threats to the monarchy, was delicate, as well; *BBC*, "Haykal's Review of Situation in Arab World," no. 1815, 22 March 1965, p. A/2.

54. *BBC*, no. 1812, 18 March 1965, p. A/8; no. 1813, 19 March 1965, p. A/7; no. 1859, 15 May 1965, p. A/6; Nimrod, "Conflict over the Jordan," p. 18.

55. *BBC*, "'al-Bʿath' on Need for Arab United Action," no. 1865, 22 May 1965, p. A/6; "Syrian Recommendations to Arab Premiers' Conference," no. 1867, 25 May 1965, pp. A/5–6.

56. *BBC*, "Nasir's Speech to the Palestine National Council," no. 1874, 2 June 1965, p. A/6; "Nasir's Beirut Interview," no. 1879, 9 June 1965, pp. A/5–6.

57. *BBC*, "Nasir's Speech to the Palestine National Council," no. 1874.

58. *BBC*, "Nasir's Speech on the Egyptian Revolution Anniversary," no. 1918, 24 July 1965, p. A/8.

59. *BBC*, "The Representatives' Resolutions on Bourguiba's Statements," no. 1847, 1 May 1965, pp. A/1–2.

60. *BBC*, "PLO Criticism of Jordan," no. 1853, 8 May 1965, pp. A/6–7; "Ahmad ash-Shuqayri's Broadcast," no. 1975, 2 October 1965, p. A/3.

61. There was no respite in the animosity between the Palestinian leadership and the Hashemite king, until after the decimation of the movement in Jordan in 1970–71. See, John Cooley, *Green March, Black September: the Story of the Palestinian Arabs* (London: Cass, 1973).

62. *BBC*, "The Israeli Frontier Raids," no. 1872, 31 May 1965, pp. A/7–8.

63. *BBC*, "Eshkol's Speech on Memorial Day," no. 2145, 26 April 1966, p. A/13.

64. *BBC*, "Israeli–Jordan Frontier Incidents," no. 1953, 7 September 1965, pp. A/2–4; no. 2150, 2 May 1966, p. A/i.

65. *BBC*, no. 1917, 23 July 1965, p. A/4; "Stoppage of Diversion Works," no. 1929, 6 August 1965, p. A/6. In "Les Eaux du Jourdain," *Annuaire Français de Droit International* vol. 11 (1965), Jean-Victor Louis states that, according to *Le Monde* (5 June 1965), very little work had been done on projects in Lebanon before the Government interrupted them. He maintains that the work was stopped because the Government had not been guaranteed air cover (p. 845).
66. *BBC*, no. 327, 13 August 1965, p. A/6.
67. *BBC*, "Comment on the Arab Summit Conference," no. 1965, 21 September 1965, pp. A/2–6; "The Arab Summit Communique," no. 1964, 20 September 1965, pp. A/1–4.
68. *BBC*, "Comment on the Arab Summit Conference," no. 1965.
69. *BBC*, "Haykal on Arab Strategy," no. 1988, 18 October 1965, p. A/2.
70. *BBC*, "Eshkol's Speech on Memorial Day," no. 2145. Despite the interruptions, work on the diversion scheme in Syria eventually picked up again, albeit for a brief period; Louis, "Les Eaux du Jourdain," p. 845.
71. *BBC*, "Ahmed ash-Shuqayri's Broadcast," no. 1975, 2 October 1965, p. A/1; "Haykal on Arab Strategy," no. 1988.
72. *BBC*, "King Hussein's Speech from the Throne," no. 2000, 1 November 1965, p. A/2.
73. *BBC*, no. 1984, 13 October 1965, p. A/9.
74. *BBC*, "Levi Eshkol's Policy Statement," no. 2061, 14 January 1966, p. A/1.
75. *BBC*, "Eshkol on the Arab Summit Conference," no. 1968, 24 September 1965, pp. A/2–3.
76. *BBC*, no. 2149, 30 April 1966, p. A/4.
77. *BBC*, no. 2116, 19 March 1966, p. A/3. It is important to note that, of the immediate neighbors of Israel, Jordan also received arms from the United States.
78. Malcolm H. Kerr, *Regional Arab Politics and the Conflict with Israel* (Research Program on Economic and Political Problems and Prospects of the Middle East – the Rand Corp./Resources for the Future RM-5966-FF, October 1969), p. 23. On the cleavage in the Bᶜath Party between the old guard and the dissenters see, Eberhard Kienle, "The Conflict Between the Baath Regimes of Syria and Iraq prior to their Consolidation," *Ethnizität und Gesellschaft* Occasional Papers no. 5 (Freie Universität Berlin, 1985), pp. 7–11.
79. *BBC*, no. 2159, 12 May 1966, pp. A/7–8; no. 2165, 19 May 1966, p. A/1; "Damascus Radio on Arrests in Jordan," no. 2172, 27 May 1966, p. A/9.
80. *BBC*, no. 2159.
81. Interview by author with former Foreign Minister of Egypt, Cairo, 8 May 1986; Kerr, *Regional Arab Politics*, pp. 27–28.
82. *BBC*, "Cairo Radio on the Next Arab Summit Conference," no. 2180, 7 June 1966, p. A/10; "Nasir's Speech to Celebrate the Anniversary of the Egyptian Revolution," no. 2221, 25 July 1966, pp. A/13–16; Kerr, *Regional Arab Politics*, pp. 27–28.

83. *BBC*, "Nasir's Speech to Celebrate the Anniversary of the Egyptian Revolution," no. 2221, p. A/15.
84. *BBC*, "Saudi Statement on Arab Summit Conference," no. 2228, 2 August 1966, pp. A/4–5; no. 2379, 31 January 1967, p. A/18.
85. Michael Howard and Robert Hunter, "Israel and the Arab World: the Crisis of 1967," *Adelphi Papers* no. 41 (October 1967), p. 13.
86. *BBC*, "Israeli Report of Raid in Syria," no. 2214, 16 July 1966, p. A/2.
87. *BBC*, "Jordan Radio Comment on the Lake Tiberias Engagement," no. 2241, 17 August 1966, pp. A/10–11.
88. *BBC*, "Syrian Foreign Ministry Statement on Israeli Accusations," no. 2291, 15 October 1966, pp. A/1–2.
89. *BBC*, "'Al-Thawrah' Editorial on Israeli Attacks," no. 2214, 16 July 1966, pp. A/5–6.
90. *BBC*, no. 2152, 4 May 1966, p. A/i; "Tunis 'al-ʿAmal' on the Israeli–Syrian Border Engagement," no. 2243, 19 August 1966, p. A/8.
91. *BBC*, "Nasir's Speech to Celebrate the Anniversary of the Egyptian Revolution," no. 2221, p. A/13.
92. Malcolm Kerr (*Regional Arab Politics*, p. 28) has written that, "on paper it was a defense alliance against Israel; in political reality, it was intended as a defense against Saudi Arabia and her supposedly American-supported challenge to Egyptian leadership." This statement helps to clarify why the agreement failed to provide the military defense that was needed in the spring of 1967.
93. *BBC*, "Levi Eshkol's Speech in the Knesset," no. 2294, 19 October 1966, pp. A/3–4.
94. *BBC*, "Israeli Radio Reports on the Border Situation," no. 2296, 21 October 1966, p. A/3.
95. *BBC*, no. 2318, 16 November 1966, pp. A/5–9; no. 2319, 17 November 1966, pp. A/3–6; no. 2323, 22 November 1966, pp. A/5–8.
96. See note 95 above.
97. *BBC*, no. W-399, 13 January 1967, pp. A/1–4.
98. *BBC*, "Meeting of Authority for Exploitation of Jordan Riverwaters," no. 2381, 2 February 1967, pp. A/2–3.
99. *BBC*, no. 2435, 10 April 1967, pp. A/6–8; Yitzhak Rabin, *The Rabin Memoirs* (New York: Little, Brown & Co., 1979), p. 67.
100. *BBC*, "Israeli Broadcasts on the Border Situation," no. 2436, 10 April 1967, pp. A/1–3.
101. *BBC*, no. 2435.
102. "Nasir's May Day Speech," United States, *Foreign Broadcast Information Service (FBIS)*, Daily Report (DR): Middle East, Africa and Western Europe, no. 86, 3 May 1967, p. B-13.
103. *BBC*, no. 2439, 14 April 1967; no. 2, 16 May 1967, p. B-3.
104. *FBIS*, DR no. 93, 12 May 1967, p. H-1.
105. *FBIS*, "State of Emergency Declared for UAR Forces," DR no. 95, 16 May 1967, p. B-1.

106. *BBC*, "Cairo Radio on UAR support for Syria," no. 2468, 18 May 1967, p. A/6.

107. *BBC*, "'al-ᵓAhram' on Prospect of Israeli Attack on Syria,", no. 2466, 16 May 1967, p. A/7; *FBIS*, "Foreign Ministry Spokesman Issues Statement," DR no. 94, 15 May 1967, pp. G-1-2; Interview by author with a former Jordan government official, Amman, 4 December 1985.

108. *BBC*, no. 2376, 27 January 1967, pp. A/1–3.

109. *BBC*, no. 2470, 20 May 1967, p. A/i.

110. *BBC*, "Eshkol's Knesset Statement of 23rd May," no. 2474, 25 May 1967, p. A/18; no. 2475, 26 May 1967, p. A/16.

111. *BBC*, "Israeli Comment on the Crisis," no. 2476, 27 May 1967, pp. A/10–12.

112. For a chronology and analyses of the war, see, among others, Michael Brecher, *Decisions in Israel's Foreign Policy* (New Haven: Yale University Press, 1975), pp. 318–453; Howard and Hunter, "Israel and the Arab World"; Rabin, *Rabin Memoirs*; Eric Rouleau, Jean-Francis Held, Jean & Simonne Lacouture, *Israël et les Arabes : le 3ᵉ combat* (Paris: Éditions du Seuil, 1967); Safran, *From War to War*; Charles W. Yost, "The Arab–Israeli War: How it Began" in J. N. Moore (ed.), *The Arab–Israeli Conflict* vol. 2 (Princeton: Princeton University Press, 1974), pp. 5–21.

113. For a discussion of the concept of encapsulation see, Amitai Etzioni, "On Self-Encapsulating Conflicts," *Journal of Conflict Resolution* vol. 8, no. 3 (September 1964), pp. 242–55.

114. *BBC*, no. 1470, 4 February 1964, p. A/3; no. 1459, 22 January 1964, p. A/1; no. 1456, 17 January 1964, p. A/1.

115. *BBC*, no. 1459, 22 January 1964, p. A/2; Nimrod, "Conflict over the Jordan," p. 17.

116. For a discussion, from a "Great Power" perspective, of the use of hydraulic installations as military targets see, Col. Roy L. Thompson, "Fresh Water Scarcity: Implications for Conflict: an overview" (paper prepared for the Conference on Scarce Resources and International Conflict, International Security Studies Program, The Fletcher School of Law and Diplomacy, Tufts University, 4–6 May 1977), pp. 3–8.

117. The foregoing brief analysis of inter-Arab relations draws heavily upon Kerr, *Regional Arab Politics*, and *The Arab Cold War (1958–1967)* (New York: Oxford University Press, 1967).

118. The coexistence of the pan-Arab ideology and the "Question of Palestine" – both of which functioned as major rallying points – helps to explain the attitude adopted by the Arab states to the Tunisian President when he called for the recognition of the State of Israel. Bourguiba was vilified unsparingly. He was accused of desertion, of treason, of collaboration with Zionism and imperialism. He was isolated, and some Arab leaders even tried to have him ostracized from the Arab League. He had defied two essential binding agents of the "Arab Nation."

119. Kerr, *Regional Arab Politics*, p. 23.

120. *BBC*, no. 1874, 2 June 1965, p. A/17.

121. *BBC*, no. 2214, 16 July 1966, pp. A/5–6.

122. On the brink of war, Nasir's attitude changed markedly, at least in his official discourse. He, too, expressed confidence that if attacked, the Arabs were capable of achieving their basic objective – the destruction of Israel: "If Israel starts any aggressive action against Syria or Egypt, the fight against Israel will be total war. It will not be an engagement restricted to a particular area or the frontiers of Syria or the frontiers of Egypt. It will be total war with the basic object of destroying Israel which we can do." (From Nasir's speech before a delegation of the Arab Workers' Conference, published in *Al-ʾAhram* newspaper, 27 May 1967, quoted in Brecher, *Israel's Foreign Policy*, p. 393.) Nonetheless, Nasir had not wanted the Arabs to initiate war, nor provoke it.

123. *BBC*, "Eshkol's Speech to the Mapai Conference in Tel-Aviv," no. 1789, 19 February 1965, pp. A/1–2.

124. *BBC*, no. 1456, 18 January 1964, pp. A/3–4; Interview by author with former Government of Israel Foreign Ministry official, Jerusalem, 29 June 1986.

125. Brecher, *Israel's Foreign Policy*, p. 333.

126. Quoted in, Gideon Rafael, *Destination Peace – Three Decades of Israeli Foreign Policy* (London: Weidenfeld & Nicolson, 1981), p. 125. For similar statements from other high-policy decision-makers, see, Brecher, *ibid.*

127. *BBC*, "Israeli Comment on the Crisis," no. 2476, 27 May 1967, p. A/12.

128. On this phenomenon – the tendency for actors in an anarchical system to seek maximum power, and the resultant "spiral model" and "security dilemma" – see, John H. Herz, *Political Realism and Political Idealism* (Chicago: University of Chicago Press, 1951), chapters 1 and 2; Robert Jervis, *Perception and Misperception in International Politics* (Princeton: Princeton University Press, 1976), chapter 3, especially pp. 64–68; Arnold Wolfers, "The Pole of Power and the Pole of Indifference" in *Discord and Collaboration: Essays on International Politics* (Baltimore: The Johns Hopkins University Press, 1965), p. 84, and "National Security as an Ambiguous Symbol" in Wolfers, *Discord and Collaboration*, pp. 158–95.

129. *BBC*, "Nasir's May Day Speech," no. 1849, 4 May 1965, p. A/5.

130. *BBC*, no. 1446, 7 January 1964, p. A/3; no. 1459, 22 January 1964, p. A/1; no. 1548, 8 May 1964, p. A/1; no. 1653, 10 September 1964, pp. A/1–5.

131. *BBC*, no. 1456, 18 January 1964, p. A/1; no. 1847, 1 May 1965, pp. A/1–2.

132. *BBC*, no. 1459, 22 January 1964, p. A/1.

133. *BBC*, no. 1769, 27 January 1965, pp. A/3–4.

134. Jervis, *Perception and Misperception*, pp. 153, 203.

135. O. Holsti, "Cognitive Dynamics and Images of the Enemy," *Journal of International Affairs* vol. 21, no. 1 (1967), p. 39.

136. Studies that focus on the role of cognitive processes in political behavior are numerous. Among them see, Robert Axelrod (ed.), *Structure of Decision – the Cognitive Maps of Political Elites* (Princeton: Princeton University Press, 1976); Kenneth Boulding, "National Images and International Systems," *Journal of Conflict Resolution* vol. 3 (1959); Brecher, *Israel's Foreign Policy* and "State Behaviour in International Crisis," *Journal of Conflict Resolution* vol. 23, no. 3

(September 1979), pp. 446–80; David Finlay, Ole Holsti, and Richard Fagen, *Enemies in Politics* (Chicago: Rand McNally & Co., 1967); Holsti, "Cognitive Dynamics"; Jervis, *Perception and Misperception*; H. and M. Sprout, *Man–Mileu Relationship Hypotheses in the Context of International Politics* (Center of International Studies, Princeton University, 1956).

137. Finlay *et al.*, *Enemies in Politics*, pp. 15–22; Jervis, *Perception and Misperception*, chapter 4 and p. 68.

138. On the Manichean character of ideological thought and the "*diabolisation de l'adversaire*," see, Maxime Rodinson, "Sociologie Marxiste et Idéologie Marxiste," *Diogène* no. 64 (octobre–décembre 1968), pp. 85–86.

139. See, Joseph Gabel, "Le Concept de l'Idéologie" in *Idéologies* (Paris: éditions anthropos, 1974), pp. 23–75; Karl Mannheim, *Ideology and Utopia* (London: Routledge & Kegan Paul, 1979 edition), pp. 49–96.

140. For definitions of ideology by a variety of thinkers see, Gabel, "Le Concept de l'Idéologie," pp. 33–35.

141. *BBC*, no. 1847, 1 May 1965, p. A/1.

142. *BBC*, no. 2172, 27 May 1966, pp. A/7–9.

143. *BBC*, no. 2376, 27 January 1967, p. A/2; no. 1459, 22 January 1964, p. A/1.

144. *BBC*, no. 1446, 7 January 1964, p. A/3.

145. *BBC*, no. 1761, 18 January 1965, p. A/3.

146. *BBC*, no. 1548, 8 May 1964, p. A/1; no. 1847, 1 May 1965, pp. A/1–2.

147. *BBC*, no. 1459, p. A/1.

148. *BBC*, no. 1847.

149. *BBC*, no. 1656, 14 September 1964, p. A/1; no. 1653, 10 September 1964, p. A/3.

150. *BBC*, no. 2376, 27 January 1967, p. A/2.

151. *BBC*, no. 2476, p. A/12.

152. *FBIS*, DR no. 93, 12 May 1967, p. H-1.

153. *BBC*, no. 2480, 2 June 1967, p. A/14.

154. *BBC*, no. 2145, 26 April 1966, p. A/13; no. 2484, 7 June 1967, p. A/8.

155. *BBC*, no. 2480, 2 June 1967, p. A/16.

156. *BBC*, no. 2149, 26 April 1966, p. A/13.

157. *FBIS*, "Eshkol Speaks on Defense Against Arabs," DR no. 94, 15 May 1967, p. H-1.

158. *BBC*, no. 2294, 19 October 1966, p. A/4.

159. *BBC*, "Statement by Levi Eshkol," no. 2484, 7 June 1967, p. A/9.

160. Cited in, Brecher, *Israel's Foreign Policy*, p. 334.

161. *BBC*, no. 2483, 6 June 1967, p. i.

162. Finlay *et al.*, *Enemies in Politics*, p. 8.

163. *BBC*, no. 1764, 21 January 1965, p. A/1; no. 2145, 26 April 1966, pp. A/12–13; *FBIS*, DR no. 94, 15 May 1967, p. H-1; Rafael, *Destination Peace*, p. 126; Interview by author with former Israel Foreign Ministry official, Jerusalem, 16 June 1986.

164. *BBC*, "Major-General Rabin's Address to Israeli Armed Forces," no. 2480, 2 June 1967, p. A/12.

165. *BBC*, no. 1649, 5 September 1964, pp. A/1–2; no. 2476, 27 May 1967, p. A/6; Interview by author with former Foreign Minister of Egypt, Cairo, 8 May 1986.
166. *BBC*, no. 1874, 2 June 1965, pp. A/1–14.
167. *BBC*, no. 1653, 10 September 1964, p. A/3.
168. See, for example, *BBC*, no. 2214, 16 July 1966, pp. A/5–6.
169. *BBC*, no. 1711, 17 November 1964, p. A/7.
170. *BBC*, "'Al-Thawrah' editorial on Israeli Attacks," no. 2214, 16 July 1966, pp. A/5–6.
171. *BBC*, no. 1761, 18 January 1965, p. A/3.
172. *BBC*, "'Al-ɔAhram' on Prospect of Israeli Attack on Syria," no. 2466, 16 May 1967, p. A/7.
173. *BBC*, no. 2468, 18 May 1967, p. A/4.
174. Kerr, *Regional Arab Politics*, p. 33.

6 Water and development in Israel and Jordan

1. Gerald H. Blake and Alasdair Drysdale, *The Middle East and North Africa: a Political Geography* (New York: Oxford University Press, 1985), pp. 289–91.
2. *Ibid.* p. 304; Interviews by author with a spokesman for Mekorot, Tel-Aviv, 15 June 1986; with a geomorphologist, Haifa, 25 April 1986; with a hydraulic engineer, Tel-Aviv, 11 June 1986.
3. Rami G. Khouri, *The Jordan Valley: Life and Society below Sea Level* (London: Longman, 1981), p. 103.
4. Peter Gubser, *Jordan: Crossroads of Middle Eastern Events* (Boulder, Colo.: Westview Press, 1983), p. 12.
5. Associates for Middle East Research, Data Base (Philadelphia, Pa.: University of Pennsylvania). The Yarmouk River is 60 km long from the point of confluence with the Jordan River until the point at which both banks are in Syrian territory. Once in Syria, the river separates into several wadis.
6. See, in this regard, Fouad Ajami, *The Arab Predicament: Arab Political Thought and Practice Since 1967* (Cambridge: Cambridge University Press, 1981), pp. 24–75; Sadiq al-Azm, *Al-Naqd al-Dhati Baᶜd al-Hazima* [Self-Criticism after the Defeat] (Beirût: Dar al-Taliᶜah, 1968).
7. I am grateful to a former United States Government official for this clarification. (Personal communication, 21 February 1992.)
8. Itzhak Galnoor, "Water Policymaking in Israel" in Hillel I. Shuval (ed.), *Water Quality Management under Conditions of Scarcity* (New York: Academic Press, 1980), p. 296.
9. Aaron Wiener, "The Development of Israel's Water Resources," *American Scientist* vol. 60, no. 4 (July–August 1972), p. 470; Menachem Cantor, "Ha-Mayim b-Yisrael – Esrim v-Chamesh Shanim la-Medina" [Water in Israel – Twenty-five Years of Statehood] in Israel: Ministry of Agriculture (Office of the Water Commissioner), *Ha-Mayim b-Yisrael* [The Water in Israel] Part 1 (Tel-Aviv, 1973), pp. 1–2. For figures on water consumption, albeit with slight

variations, see, Galnoor, "Water Policymaking in Israel," p. 289; Zvi Grinwald, *Ha-Mayim b-Yisrael* [Water in Israel] (Israel: Hauser Press, 1980), pp. 276–77; Israel: Ministry of Agriculture, *Water in Israel: Consumption and Extraction 1962–1979/80* (Tel-Aviv, 1981), pp. 14, 105.

10. Itzhak Galnoor, "Water Planning: Who Gets the Last Drop?" in R. Bilski *et al.* (eds.), *Can Planning Replace Politics: the Israeli Experience* (The Hague: Martinus Nijhoff Publishers, 1980), pp. 141–42. Note that since the sustainable annual yield is a fixed quantity, excess withdrawals from it by over-pumping or depletion of underground reserves constitute an overdraft that could cause irreversible damage.

11. Galnoor, "Water Planning," p. 175; Wiener, "Development of Israel's Water Resources," pp. 469–70.

12. Yaacov Vardi, "National Water Resources Planning and Development in Israel – the Endangered Resource" in Shuval (ed.), *Water Quality Management*, pp. 42–45; Elisha Kally, "Meshek ha-Mayim ha-Yisraeli u-Baᶜayotav b-Reishit Shnot ha-Shivim" [Israeli Water Management and its Problems at the Beginning of the Seventies] in Israel: Ministry of Agriculture (1973), *Ha-Mayim b-Yisrael*, pp. 84–85; "ha-Kinneret – Makor ha-Mayim shel Mifᶜal ha-Mayim ha-Arzi" [The Kinneret: the Water Source for the National Water Carrier] in Y. Avnimelech *et al.* (eds.), *Kinneret: Ha-Agan v-ha-Kavot* [Kinneret: the Lake and Watershed] (Israel: 1978), pp. 34–36.

13. J. Schwarz, "Israeli Water Sector Review: Past Achievements, Current Problems, and Future Options" in Guy Le Moigne, Shawki Barghouti, Gershon Feder, Lisa Garbus, and Mei Xie (eds.), *Country Experiences with Water Resource Management: Economic, Institutional, Technological and Environmental Issues*, World Bank Technical Paper no. 175 (Washington, D.C.: The World Bank, 1992); Vardi, "National Water Resources," p. 47; Interview by author with a spokesman for Mekorot, the country's National Water Authority, Tel-Aviv, 15 June 1986.

14. Jacobs and Litwin, *Water Resources*, pp. 226–27; Fred Pearce, "Wells of Conflict on the West Bank," *New Scientist*, 1 June 1991; Schwarz, "Israeli Water Sector."

15. Schwarz, "Israeli Water Sector."

16. To wit, agricultural development has remained a national goal, embodying a socially accepted value and dictated by ideology. On the powerful agricultural lobby in Israel and the tensions between it and the government see, Asher Arian, *Politics in Israel: the Second Generation* (New Jersey: Chatham House Publishers, Inc., 1985); Galnoor, "Water Planning" and "Water Policymaking in Israel."

17. "Irrigation: Israel's Water Miracle" in *The Israel Economist* (October 1978), pp. 34–38; Vardi, "National Water Resources," p. 46; Interviews by author with former president of Tahal, Tel-Aviv, 5 May 1986; with a geomorphologist, Haifa, 24 April 1986.

18. This author was doing fieldwork in Israel when this demand was issued by the Water Commissioner. See, *Jerusalem Post*, 24 March 1986, p. 1; 8 April 1986;

11 May 1986, p. 2; 9 June 1986; Galnoor, "Water Planning," p. 184; Vardi, "National Water Resources," p. 46.

19. Pearce, "Wells of Conflict," p. 37.
20. *Ibid.*
21. Schwarz, "Israeli Water Sector." It is estimated that by the year 2000, the consumption of water by agriculture will have fallen to about 62 percent of supply.
22. Interview by author with a geomorphologist, Haifa, 24 April 1986; Meir Ben-Meir, "Water Shortage in the Middle East and the Ensuing Policy in the Region" (paper prepared for conference on US Foreign Policy on Water Resources in the Middle East: Instrument for Peace and Development, Center for Strategic and International Studies, Georgetown University, Washington, D.C., 24–25 November 1986), pp. 1–9.
23. Elisha Kally, *Mayim v-Shalom*, also published as *A Middle East Water Plan Under Peace* (Tel-Aviv University: Interdisciplinary Center for Technological Analysis and Forecasting, February/March 1986).
24. In fact, there have been unconfirmed reports that since the 1982 invasion of Lebanon, Israel has been diverting a portion of the waters of the Litani River into northern Israel. See, among others, the Arab press: *al-Asbuʿa al-ʿArabi* 17 September 1984; *al-Kifah al-ʿArabi* 3 September 1984, 10 September 1984; *al-Qabas* 2 September 1984; *al-Raʾi* 28 August 1984, 14 January 1985; *al-Safir* 10 August 1984, 2 September 1984, 6 January 1985; *al-Thawra* 12 September 1984; John Cooley, "The War over Water," *Foreign Policy* no. 54 (spring 1984); Raghda Jaber, "The Politics of Water in South Lebanon," *Race and Class* vol. 31, no. 2 (1989), pp. 63–67; *Middle East Economic Digest*, 13 May 1983, p. 52.
25. Khouri, *Jordan Valley*, pp. 99, 101; Interview by author with former editor of *Maʿariv* daily, Tel-Aviv, 25 June 1986.
26. Hashemite Kingdom of Jordan, *Agricultural Census* (Amman, 1965), cited in, Khouri, *Jordan Valley*, p. 104; Dar al-Handasah Consulting Engineers and Netherlands Engineering Consultants (NEDECO), *Jordan Valley Project: Agro- and Socio-Economic Study* (Amman: The Hashemite Kingdom of Jordan and the Jordan River and Tributaries Regional Corporation, 1969), p. 64. A different set of figures are provided in Jarir S. Dajani, Jared Hazleton, Richard Rhoda, and David Sharry, *An Interim Evaluation of the Jordan Valley Development Effort: 1973–1980* (prepared for the USAID, Project No. EVALU-ATION 278–0181, August 1980). Abu-Taleb *et al.* gauge irrigable land in Jordan at 55,000 ha, of which 30,000 ha are in the Jordan Valley ("Water Resources Planning and Development in Jordan: Problems, Future Scenarios, and Recommendations" in Guy Le Moigne *et al.* (eds.), *Country Experiences with Water Resources Management*).
27. In 1977, it became the Jordan Valley Authority and its responsibilities were increased considerably; Dajani, *Interim Evaluation*, p. 24; Khouri, *Jordan Valley*, pp. 112–13.
28. Jordan Valley Commission, *Rehabilitation and Development Plan of the Jordan Valley (East Bank): 1973–1975* (Amman, October 1972).

29. In 1979, total exports represented 81 percent of food imports, as opposed to 46 percent in 1972. Dajani, *Interim Evaluation*, p. 27; Khouri, *Jordan Valley*, p. 20.
30. Abu-Taleb *et al.*, "The Jordan River Basin" (paper prepared for the World Bank International Symposium on Comprehensive Water Management Policy, Washington, D.C., 24–28 June 1991), pp. 14, 28.
31. Abu-Taleb *et al.*, "Water Resources."
32. Interview by author with a government official, responsible for Jordan Valley development, Amman, 1 December 1985; United States Government: Foreign Assistance Legislation for Fiscal Year 1981 (Part 3), "Hearings before the Subcommittee on Europe and the Middle East of the Committee on Foreign Affairs" House of Representatives (96th congress, 2nd session), p. 136.
33. Munther Haddadin, "The Water Resources Management Program in Jordan" (paper prepared for conference on US Foreign Policy on Water Resources in the Middle East: Instrument for Peace and Development, Center for Strategic and International Studies, Georgetown University, Washington, D.C., 24–25 November 1986), pp. 7–8; Selig A. Taubenblatt, "The Jordan River Basin Water Dilemma: A Challenge for the 1990s" in Joyce Starr and Daniel Stoll (eds.), *The Politics of Scarcity: Water in the Middle East* (Boulder, Colo.: Westview Press, 1988).
34. Elias Salameh, "Jordan's Water Resources: Development and Future Prospects," *American–Arab Affairs* no. 33 (summer 1990), p. 70.
35. Abu-Taleb *et al.*, "Water Resources."
36. Abu-Taleb *et al.*, "Jordan River Basin," p. 28; Thomas Naff in Testimony before the House Committee on Foreign Affairs: Subcommittee on Europe and the Middle East, *The Middle East in the 1990s: Middle East Water Issues* (Washington, D.C., 26 June 1990), pp. 175–76 (hereafter cited as USG/CFA).
37. Abu-Taleb *et al.*, "Water Resources," p. 120.
38. In 1982, for example, about 30 mcm of water were discovered at Mukheiba on the Yarmouk. Soon after, a conduit was built to link its waters to the East Ghor Canal. Interviews by author with a newspaper editor, Amman, 23 October 1985; with a government official responsible for Jordan Valley development, Amman, 25 October 1985; with a specialist on water resource development, Amman, 27 November 1985. For details on these and other smaller scale projects see, Haddadin, "Water Resources Management Program," pp. 8–9; Khouri, *Jordan Valley*, pp. 214–16.
39. Associates for Middle East Research, Data Base (Philadelphia, Pa.: University of Pennsylvania); Congressional Quarterly Inc., *The Middle East*, fifth edition (Washington, D.C., 1981), p. 172; Salameh, "Jordan's Water Resources."
40. USG/CFA, *Middle East in the 1990s*, p. 188.
41. Interviews by author with a former president of the Jordan Valley Authority, Amman, 3 December 1985; with a government official responsible for Jordan Valley development, Amman, 10 February 1986; Taubenblatt, "Jordan River Basin," p. 10.
42. Cem Duna, "Turkey's Peace Pipeline" in Starr and Stoll (eds.), *Politics of Scarcity*, pp. 119–24; John Kolars, "The Course of Water in the Arab Middle

East," *American–Arab Affairs* no. 33 (summer 1990), p. 61; Joyce Starr, "Water Wars," *Foreign Policy* no. 82 (Spring 1991), pp. 28–29.
43. Naff, "Jordan Basin," p. 115.

7 Riparian relations and the perception of conflict

1. See, chapter 2.
2. Interview by author with a newspaper editor, Amman, 27 October 1985.
3. Gubser, *Jordan: Crossroads of Middle Eastern Events* (Boulder, Colo.: Westview Press, 1983); Paul A. Jureidini and R. D. McLaurin, "Jordan: the Impact of Social Change on the Role of the Tribes," *The Washington Papers* vol. 12, no. 108 (Washington, D.C.: The Center for Strategic and International Studies, Georgetown University, 1984), pp. 3–4.
4. Norman F. Howard, "The Uncertain Kingdom of Jordan," *Current History* vol. 66, no. 390 (February 1974), pp. 64–65; "Jordan: the Price of Moderation," *Current History* vol. 68, no. 402 (February 1975), p. 65; Stephen S. Kaplan, "United States' Aid and Regime Maintenance in Jordan, 1957–73," *Public Policy* vol. 23, no. 2 (spring 1975), pp. 191, 203–04.
5. The Palestinian resistance, considered a profound threat to the monarchy in the late sixties and very early seventies, was quickly and forcefully eliminated after a period of intense social and political turmoil. In the aftermath of the 1967 war, the active Palestinian masses in Jordan attached themselves to the PLO or to its various splinter groups. They were, for the most part, highly critical of King Hussein, his moderate attitude toward Israel, and his attempts to bridle the Palestinian national movement while simultaneously claiming to represent the Palestinians. (Inadvertently, the Palestinians in Jordan were able to exploit a situation characterized by the absence of an agreed idea of "nation" among the Jordanian population and the lack of consensus on an organizing ideology of the state.)

    As the *feda᾽iyin* gained prestige, support, and international attention, the Jordanian army and monarchy felt increasingly humiliated. By 1970, a "protracted contest of authority" emerged between the PLO and the Hashemite regime. During the events that led up to the decimation of the Palestinian resistance in 1970, and then again at Ajloun in 1971, the monarchy feared the overpowering of state institutions and the erosion of its legitimacy. Indeed, threats to the security of state institutions were invoked to justify the full-scale use of force against opponents. For a detailed study of the events leading up to the decimation of the Palestinian resistance see, John Cooley, *Green March, Black September: the Story of the Palestinian Arabs* (London: Cass, 1973). See, as well, Adam M. Garfinkle, "Negotiating by Proxy: Jordanian Foreign Policy and US Options in the Middle East," *Orbis* vol. 24 (winter 1981), p. 853.
6. To the more radical Arab regimes, Jordan's close alliance with the United States (prior to the 1991 Gulf war) has been looked upon with suspicion and contempt. This alliance is frowned upon by some Jordanians, as well, who claim that the

regime is constantly having to suffer humiliation as a result of the conditions that the US places on continued support; interviews by author with a government official, responsible for critical development issues, Amman, 25 October 1985; with an underground political activist, a former government official, Amman, 4 December 1985; with a newspaper editor, Amman, 23 October 1985.

7. Interviews by author with a member of the royal family, Amman, 23 November 1985; with a government official, Amman, 25 October 1985; with a newspaper editor, Amman, 27 October 1985; with a Palestinian lawyer, Amman, 6 November 1985.

8. Interview by author with a newspaper editor, Amman, 27 October 1985.

9. Interview by author with a government official, Amman, 25 October 1985.

10. Oded Yinon, *Kivunim: a Journal for Judaism and Zionism*, no. 14 (February 1982), pp. 52, 57.

11. See the editorial in the *New York Times*, 5 March 1990 (p. A-15) written by Ariel Sharon, Israel's then Minister of Housing.

12. See, chapter 2.

13. See, chapter 5. Consider the following statement by Gideon Rafael: Since the 1967 war, "nothing could happen internally in the area against Israel's will, because of its military preponderance." *Destination Peace – Three Decades of Israeli Foreign Policy* (London: Weidenfeld & Nicolson, 1981), p. 207.

14. Howard, "Jordan: the Price of Moderation," p. 64; Bassam Saket, "The Jordanian Economy" in A. B. Zahlan and Subhi Qasem (eds.), *The Agricultural Sector of Jordan* (London: Ithaca Press, 1985), pp. 9–39; Fahd Salih Natur, "Water Supply for the Agricultural Sector" in Zahlan and Qasem (eds.), pp. 197–273.

15. Alasdair Drysdale and Gerald H. Blake, *The Middle East and North Africa: a Political Geography* (New York: Oxford University Press, 1985), p. 307.

16. Interviews by author in Jordan and Israel, October 1985 to July 1986.

17. Moshe Zak, "Israeli–Jordanian Negotiations," *Washington Quarterly* vol. 8, no. 1 (winter 1985), pp. 167–76. Moreover, Israeli radio announced in 1985 that there had been approximately 500 hours of direct talks between the two countries. This information has not been confirmed by the Hashemite regime.

18. *Ibid.* p. 170.

19. Gubser, *Jordan*, pp. 103–04; Kaplan, "United States' Aid," pp. 196–97.

20. Zak, "Israeli–Jordanian Negotiations," p. 171.

21. Ian Lustick, "Israel and Jordan: the Implications of an Adversarial Partnership," *Policy Papers in International Affairs* no. 6 (Institute of International Studies: University of California, Berkeley, 1978), pp. 9–10.

22. Interview by author with former editor of *Maʿariv* daily, Tel-Aviv, 24 June 1986.

23 See, chapter 6. Israel was reluctant to allow the sandbar to be cleared since it allowed it to pump a larger volume of river water to its side; Interview by author with a government official, Amman, 10 February 1986. (This author was given an unpublished, confidential document that treats this issue.) Thomas Stauffer, "Tightening the

265

Squeeze on Jordan's Water," *Middle East International* no. 223 (20 April 1984), p. 13.

24. Lustick, "Israel and Jordan."
25. Interview by author with newspaper editor, Amman, 23 October 1985.
26. Interviews by author with a minister in the Jordanian government, Amman, 24 November 1985; with a Jordanian scholar, Amman, 11 November 1986; with a former government official, Amman, 4 December 1985.
27. Interview by author with a prominent Jordanian economist, Amman, 17 November 1985.
28. *Ibid.*
29. Interviews by author with a senior official of Tahal, Tel-Aviv, 10 June 1986; with an Israeli professor of International Law, Jerusalem, 24 June 1986; with former editor of *Maʿariv* daily, Tel-Aviv, 24 June 1986; with a water engineer, formerly with Tahal, Tel-Aviv, 11 June 1986.
30. Interviews by author with professor of International Law, Jerusalem, 24 June 1986; with professor of Middle East politics, Tel-Aviv, 25 June 1986. On King Abdullah's dealings with the Israeli political establishment see, among others, Avi Shlaim, *Collusion across the Jordan: King Abdullah, the Zionist Movement, and the Partition of Palestine* (New York: Columbia University Press, 1988).
31. Interview by author with a former Israel Government Foreign Ministry official, Jerusalem, 16 June 1986.
32. Interview by author with a professor of International Law, Jerusalem, 24 June 1986.
33. Lustick, "Israel and Jordan," pp. 22–29.
34. Edward Azar notes that we should not be deluded by the emergence of cooperative arrangements in situations of protracted conflict: "Conflictual and cooperative events flow together even in the most severe of intense conflicts. Cooperative events are sometimes far more numerous than conflictual ones even in the midst of intense social conflict situations... Cooperative events are not sufficient to abate protracted social conflicts." ("Protracted International Conflicts: Ten Propositions," *International Interactions* vol. 12, no. 1 (1985), p. 62.) Indeed, they are indicative of particular national interests and pressures, especially to satisfy domestic needs.
35. Interview by author with a former president of the Jordan Valley Authority, Amman, 21 November 1985.
36. Interview by author with a former government official, Amman, 4 December 1985.
37. Interview by author with an economist at the Royal Scientific Society, Amman, 20 October 1985.
38. Interviews by author with government official responsible for Jordan Valley development, Amman, 25 October 1985; with a press secretary attached to the Palace, Amman, 6 November 1985; with a Jordanian scholar, Amman, 11 November 1986.
39. Interview by author with Jordanian university administrator, Amman, 11 November 1985.

40. Interview by author with a press secretary attached to the Palace, Amman, 6 November 1985.
41. Interview by author with a former president of the Jordan Valley Authority, Amman, 21 November 1985; with a Jordanian university administrator, Amman, 11 November 1985.
42. Interview by author with a Jordanian scholar, Amman, 11 November 1985.
43. *Ibid.* In the late 1960s, for example, and after Israel and Jordan had had several encounters on the Yarmouk River, "Israel made it perfectly clear that Jordanian pumping [from the river] would be dependent on Israeli pumping." Amir Shapira in *al-Hamishmar*, 7 January 1977.
44. Interview by author with newspaper editor, Amman, 23 October 1985.
45. Interviews by author with a senior official at Tahal, Tel-Aviv, 10 June 1986; with a water engineer, formerly with Tahal, Tel-Aviv, 11 June 1986; with a former Water Commissioner, Tel-Aviv, 3 July 1986.
46. Interview by author with a water engineer, formerly with Tahal, Tel-Aviv, 11 June 1986.
47. *Ibid.* In fact, the Johnston Plan is not followed. Israel takes approximately 100 mcm per annum from the Yarmouk River, while the Plan had allocated only 25–40 mcm. As for the waters of the Upper Jordan River, Israel does not release the 100 mcm it was supposed to release for Jordan. Jordan, however, does release 25 mcm from the Yarmouk for Israel during the summer months. Interview by author with a former Israel Government Foreign Ministry official, Jerusalem, 16 June 1986.
48. Interview by author with a senior official at Tahal, Tel-Aviv, 3 July 1986.
49. Interview by author with a professor of Middle East politics, Tel-Aviv, 25 June 1986.
50. Interview by author with a water engineer, formerly with Tahal, Tel-Aviv, 11 June 1986.
51. Interviews by author with former Israel Government Foreign Ministry official, Jerusalem, 29 June 1986; with a professor of Middle East politics, Tel-Aviv, 25 June 1986; with a geographer, Haifa, 22 June 1986.
52. It is important to note that only those in very high-ranking positions in Jordan – either in the political establishment and closely linked to the monarchy, or in state institutions responsible for economic development – were able to comment authoritatively on this matter.
53. Interview by author with a former president of the Jordan Valley Authority, Amman, 3 December 1986.
54. Interview by author with a Jordanian economist, Amman, 17 November 1985.
55. Interview by author with a press secretary, attached to the Royal Palace, Amman, 6 November 1985.
56. Interview by author with an economist at the Royal Scientific Society, Amman, 20 October 1985.
57. Thucydides, *The Peloponnesian War* (New York: Random House, Inc., 1982), Book V, p. 351.

8 Riparian disputes since 1967

1. See, chapter 4.
2. Amir Shapira, "Return to the Struggle over the Water," *Hotam* (*al-Hamishmar*'s weekly supplement), 24 December 1976.
3. Foreign Assistance Legislation for FY 1979 (Part 5) [95th congress, second session, February/March 1978], "Hearings Before the Subcommittee on Europe and the Middle East of the Committee on International Relations," House of Representatives (Washington: US Government Printing Office, 1978), p. 80.
4. Shapira, "Return to the Struggle."
5. *Ibid.*
6. Amir Shapira, "Struggle over the Height of the Dam," *Hotam*, 31 December 1976; "The Controversial Yarmouk," *Hotam*, 11 August 1978. According to Arnon Sofer and Nurit Kliot, the Johnston Plan stated that the West Bank was entitled to receive some 150 mcm of water from the Yarmouk via the West Ghor Canal. "The Water Resource of the Jordan Catchment: Management Options," paper presented at the BRISMES Annual Conference at the School of Oriental and African Studies, University of London, July 1991, p. 4.
7. Shapira, "Return to the Struggle."
8. *Ibid.*
9. Jordan Valley Authority, *Jordan Valley Irrigation Project Stage II – Feasibility Study* (Chicago: Harza Overseas Engineering Company, January 1978).
10. *Ibid.*, Preface, pp. 3–5.
11. Foreign Assistance Legislation for FY 1979 (Part 5), *Subcommittee on Europe and the Middle East*, p. 100.
12. International Development and Food Assistance Act of 1978, House of Representatives [95th congress, second session, report no. 95–1087], "Report of the Committee on International Relations" (Washington: US Government Printing Office, 1978), p. 39.
13. Selig A. Taubenblatt, "The Jordan River Basin Water Dilemma: a Challenge for the 1990's" in Joyce Starr and Daniel Stoll (eds.), *The Politics of Scarcity: Water in the Middle East* (Boulder, Colo.: Westview Press, 1988).
14. They were: the International Bank for Reconstruction and Development (World Bank), the US Agency for International Development, the Arab Fund for Economic and Social Development, the European Common Market, Government of West Germany, Government of France, and the OPEC Special Fund. John Cooley, "Jordan and the Politics of Water," *Middle East International* (30 January 1981), p. 10.
15. More importantly, however, the dam project was of geopolitical interest to Syria; it symbolized a respite in the often tense relations with Jordan. Interview with a former United States Government official, Washington, D.C., 21 February 1992.
16. Economic Support Fund Programs in the Middle East [Committee Print, 96th congress, first session], "Report of a Staff Study Mission to Egypt, Syria,

Jordan, the West Bank, and Gaza," 24 November – 15 December 1978, to the Committee on Foreign Affairs, US House of Representatives, April 1979 (Washington: US Government Printing Office, 1979), p. 60.

17. Foreign Assistance Legislation for Fiscal Years 1980–81 (Part 3) [96th congress, first session, February/March 1979], "Hearings and Markup before the Subcommittee on Europe and the Middle East of the Committee on Foreign Affairs," House of Representatives (Washington: US Government Printing Office, 1979), p. 270.

18. Interview by author with a high-ranking official in Tahal, the Water Company for Israel, Tel-Aviv, 13 April 1986.

19. Shapira, "Struggle over the Height of the Dam."

20. As part of the project, a weir, or diversion dam, was to be constructed downstream of the Maqarin dam, at the point where Jordan would take water for the East Ghor Canal and Israel would take water for the Yarmouk Triangle.

21. "Parting of the Jordan Likely to Cause Waves," *Jerusalem Post* 22 February 1980. It is important to remember that during Round Four of the Johnston negotiations, Eisenhower's Special Emissary announced to Jordan that he was increasing Israel's allocation for the Yarmouk Triangle to 40 mcm. This was presented to the Arabs as a *fait accompli*. Seven months earlier (February 1955), Johnston had promised Israel that while he could guarantee only 25 mcm for the Triangle, he would do his best to secure an additional 15 mcm. In September 1955, the Arab Technical Committee decided to approve the Revised Unified Plan, and hence the 40 mcm allocation, despite its reservations. However, given that both Israeli and Arab sources have told this author that the respective teams had each been given a different document to sign, we will never know whether the Arabs actually agreed in writing to the greater allocation of Yarmouk water for Israel, or whether the document signed by Israel stipulated 25 mcm or 40 mcm for the Triangle. (Interviews by author with the former president of Tahal and technical representative on Israel's team with the Johnston mission, Tel-Aviv, 5 May 1986; with a former Foreign Minister of Egypt, Cairo, 8 May 1986; with a former US government official, Washington, D.C., 15 February 1992.) We do know, though, that in the late 1970s, Israel insisted that it had a document from Eric Johnston recognizing its need for 40 mcm (*Jerusalem Post*, 22 February 1980).

22. Shapira, "Controversial Yarmouk."

23. See, chapter 6.

24. *Jerusalem Post*, 22 February 1980.

25. *Ibid.*

26. John Cooley, "Success of Palestinian Talks May Hinge on a Dam," *Christian Science Monitor*, 10 July 1980.

27. Congress of the United States, Committee on Foreign Affairs, "Memorandum: to Members of the Committee on Foreign Affairs, from Chairman of the Committee," House of Representatives, 6 July 1979.

28. Foreign Assistance Legislation for Fiscal Years 1980–81 (Part 3), p. 250.

29. Cooley, "Success of Palestinian Talks," p. 11.

30. Foreign Assistance Legislation for FY 1980–81 (Part 3), "Subcommittee on Europe and the Middle East," p. 270; Foreign Assistance Legislation for FY 1981 (Part 3) [96th congress, second session, January/February/March 1980], "Hearings before the Subcommittee on Europe and the Middle East of the Committee on Foreign Affairs," House of Representatives (Washington: US Government Printing Office, 1980), p. 136.

31. Ellen Laipson, *Memorandum: Policies of the American, Israeli and Jordanian Governments on Use of the Jordan River Waters* (Library of Congress: Congressional Research Service, 12 October 1979), p. 7.

32. *Ibid.* p. 8.

33. "Israel and Jordan Negotiate Indirectly about a Dam," *New York Times*, 18 May 1980.

34. See in this regard, Patrick Seale, *Asad: the Struggle for the Middle East* (Berkeley: University of California Press, 1989), pp. 320–34.

35. *Ibid.* p. 462; Cooley, "Success of Palestinian Talks," p. 11; interview by author with Syrian specialist of International Law, Damascus, 30 January 1986.

36. Interview by author with an official with the Jordan Valley Authority, Amman, 1 December 1985.

37. Foreign Assistance Legislation for Fiscal Year 1982 (Part 3) [97th congress, 1st session, February/March/April 1981], "Hearings and Markup before the Subcommittee on Europe and the Middle East of the Committee on Foreign Affairs," House of Representatives (Washington: US Government Printing Office, 1981), p. 58.

38. Interviews by author with Jordanian journalist, Amman, 23 October 1985; with a former official with the Jordan Valley Authority, Amman, 11 November 1985.

39. Interview by author with a Syrian official, Damascus, 3 February 1986.

40. *Ibid.*

41. See, chapters 5 and 6.

42. We know from well-informed sources that Syria has placed ground-to-air missiles at the site of the Euphrates Dam. Interview by author, Damascus, 30 January 1986.

43. Interviewees in Israel, Jordan, and the United States have insisted that Syria was the chief obstacle to the realization of the Maqarin scheme.

44. Information on this dam project derives from Testimony before the House Committee on Foreign Affairs: Subcommittee on Europe and the Middle East, *The Middle East in the 1990s: Middle East Water Issues* (Washington, D.C., 26 June 1990) [hereafter cited as USG/CFA], and from personal interviews with US government officials, Washington, April 1991.

45. The two countries agreed to leave aside the question of whether Yarmouk water should go to the West Bank. Neither party wanted the talks to founder on this issue. (Personal communication with a former United States government official, 15 February 1992.)

46. For a perverse twist to the story of water utilization in the basin, consider the following: the waters of Israel's coastal plain aquifer are recharged by water taken from Lake Tiberias via the National Water Carrier System. Hence, as long

as there is no dam on the Yarmouk, the waters of that river help to replenish Israel's over-exploited aquifers. See, chapter 6.

47. Interviews by author with Israeli geomorphologist, Haifa, 24 April 1986; with Jordanian official with the Jordan Valley Authority, Amman, 1 December 1985.
48. Interviews by author with Israeli geomorphologist, Haifa, 24 April 1986; with a senior official at Tahal, Tel-Aviv, 10 June 1986; with a water engineer, formerly with Tahal, Tel-Aviv, 11 June 1986. It is interesting to note that a well-informed former US government official was amazed to learn that those Israelis interviewed expressed this position (personal communication, 15 February 1992).
49. *Ibid.*
50. Interview with a former Israeli Water Commissioner, Tel-Aviv, 3 July 1986. This interviewee added that Israel could eventually release some 80 mcm of Yarmouk water, stored in Lake Tiberias, to Jordan.
51. It is interesting to note that in the late 1980s, the Israeli press disclosed that the country diverts as much as 80 mcm of Yarmouk water to Lake Tiberias.
   According to a senior Jordanian official, Israeli pumpage from the Yarmouk includes: (1) the allocation for the Yarmouk Triangle, (2) a part of the winter floodwaters, stored in Lake Tiberias, (3) an undisclosed quantity for irrigation in the West Jordan Valley, and (4) an undisclosed quantity near Hamma, for use in the Golan Heights. Moreover, in an interview with an Israeli geomorphologist (Haifa, 21 June 1986), this author was told that Israel takes about 15 mcm directly from the Lower Jordan River for use in the Beyt She'an Valley.
52. Associates for Middle East Research, Data Base (Philadelphia, Pa.: University of Pennsylvania), hereafter cited as AMER.
53. Interviews by author with Jordanian water specialist, Amman, 27 November 1985; with Israeli water engineer, Tel-Aviv, 11 June 1986.
54. Interview by author with a Jordanian historian, Amman, 11 November 1985.
55. *Foreign Relations of the United States, 1952–1954* vol. 9, part 1 (Washington: United States Government Printing Office, 1986), no. 604, 4 May 1953, pp. 1,185–88.
56. Interview by author with spokesman for Mekorot, Tel-Aviv, 15 June 1986; J. Schwarz "Israeli Water Sector Review: Past Achievements, Current Problems, and Future Options" in Guy Le Moigne, Shawki Barghouti, Gershon Feder, Lisa Garbus, and Mei Xie (eds.), *Country Experiences with Water Resources Management: Economic, Institutional, Technological and Environmental Issues*, World Bank Technical Paper no. 175 (Washington, D.C.: The World Bank, 1992).
57. Declassified document on West Bank water provided to the author by the Government of the United States, Department of State (n.d.), hereafter cited as USG/DS.
58. J. Schwarz, "Water Resources in Judea, Samaria, and the Gaza Strip" in Daniel Elazar (ed.), *Judea, Samaria, and Gaza: Views on the Present and the Future* (Washington: American Enterprise Institute for Public Policy Research, 1982), pp. 88–91.

59. Naff ("The Jordan Basin," p. 3) gauges total discharge at 650 mcm, Schwarz ("Water Resources," pp. 85, 90) at 685–745 mcm, and Ibrahim Dakkak ("al-Siyaasa al-Maʾiya f-il-Dafa al-Gharbiya al-Muhtala" [Water Policy on the Occupied West Bank] *Shuʾun Filastiniya* vol. 126, May 1982) at 900 mcm. USG/DS gauges groundwater alone at 850 mcm.

60. Dakkak, "al-Siyaasa al Maʾiya," pp. 38–39; David Kahan, *Agriculture and Water in the West Bank and Gaza* (Jerusalem: The West Bank Data Base Project, 1983), p. 25; Shawkat Mahmoud, "al-Ziraʿa w-al-Miyaaʾ f-il-Dafa al-Gharbiya taht al-Ihtilaal al-Israʾili" [Agriculture and Water on the West Bank under the Israeli Occupation], *Samed al-Iqtisadi* vol. 6, no. 52 (November–December 1984), p. 19; Schwarz, "Water Resources," p. 91.

61. Dakkak, "al-Siyaasa al-Maʾiya," pp. 41–42. Irrigated agriculture on the West Bank has remained limited, in part because of the topography of the territory. Nonetheless, if the Palestinians had greater access to the local water supply, they would most likely use it for supplemental irrigation of rainfed agriculture, as well as for personal consumption. They could also use it to extend the irrigated area, to some degree. Interview with former United States Government official, Washington, D.C., 21 February 1992.

62. Thomas Stauffer, "The Price of Peace: the Spoils of War," *American–Arab Affairs* no. 1 (summer 1982), p. 45.

63. Kahan, *Agriculture and Water*, p. 28; Lea Spector, "Waters of Controversy: Implications for the Arab–Israel Peace Process" (New York: Foreign Affairs Department, the American–Jewish Committee, December 1980), p. 4. J. Schwarz ("Water Resources," pp. 92–93) notes that groundwater is over-exploited at a rate of 30–40 mcm per annum in the western basin and 10 mcm per annum in the two northeastern basins. Moreover, "continued over-pumpage is likely to cause saline water intrusion to the main pumpage areas of the aquifers, particularly in the plains adjoining Judea and Samaria."

64. John Kolars, "The Course of Water in the Arab Middle East," *American–Arab Affairs* no. 33 (summer 1990), p. 66.

65. *Ibid.* In contrast, AMER estimates the average annual water deficit during the drought years of 1987–91 at 100–150 mcm.

66. Schwarz, "Water Resources," pp. 92–93. The (south)eastern water table, the smallest of the three West Bank basins, is the principal Palestinian water source and the only one that is not yet overused. USG/DS.

67. USG/DS.

68. Uri Davis, Antonia Maks and John Richardson, "Israel's Water Policies," *Journal of Palestine Studies* vol. 9, no. 2 (winter 1980), p. 13.

69. Dakkak, "al-Siyaasa al-Maʾiya," p. 58.

70. Meron Benvenisti, *The West Bank Data Project: a Survey of Israel's Policies* (Washington: American Enterprise Institute for Public Policy Research and West Bank Data Base Project, 1984), p. 14; Jeffrey D. Dillman, "Water Rights in the Occupied Territories," *Journal of Palestine Studies* vol. 19, no. 1 (autumn 1989), p. 56; USG/CFA, p. 187; USG/DS.

71. David Kahan, *Agriculture and Water*, p. 28.

72. Ned Temko, "Water – Toughest Issue on West Bank," *The Christian Science Monitor*, Tuesday, 18 September 1979.
73. Interview by author with Israeli water engineer, formerly with Tahal, Tel-Aviv, 26 June 1986.
74. Interview by author with former Deputy-Mayor of Jerusalem, Jerusalem, 8 June 1986.
75. USG/CFA, p. 187. In hot, dry climates, the best times of day for irrigating during the six-month long hot season are early in the morning or late in the afternoon and the evening. Irrigating at night is not uncommon. At these times, evaporation is significantly less than it is between 10 a.m. and 4 p.m., the hottest part of the day. Moreover, during these times, there is less risk of destroying plants and their roots. Intense watering turns soil to mud; when hot sun beats down on mud, plants rot.
76. Interview by author with former Deputy-Mayor of Jerusalem, Jerusalem, 8 June 1986; Dakkak, "al-Siyaasa al-Maʾiya," pp. 44, 60; Kahan, *Agriculture and Water*, p. 167; Mahmoud, "al-Ziraʿa w-al-Maiyaaʾ," p. 21.
77. USG/CFA, p. 187.
78. *Ibid.*
79. USG/DS.
80. Kahan, *Agriculture and Water*, p. 167; Mahmoud, "al-Ziraʿa w-al-Miyaaʾ," p. 8; USG/DS.
81. Dakkak, "al-Siyaasa al-Maʾiya," *Agriculture and Water*, pp. 165–67.
82. J.-P. Langellier, "Guerre de l'Eau en Cisjordanie," *Le Monde*, 7 November 1987.
83. USG/DS.
84. Dakkak, "al-Siyaasa al-Maʾiya," p. 44; Paul Quiring, "Israeli Settlements and Palestinian Rights, Part 2," *Middle East International* (October 1978), pp. 14–15; Temko, "Water–Toughest Issue"; Khalil Touma, "Bethlehem Plan Further Threatens Scarce Water Resources," *Al-Fajr* (26 July 1987), pp. 8–9; "Proposed Israeli Well will Deepen West Bank Water Crisis", *Al-Fajr* (5 July 1987), p. 3; "Water Supply under Occupation," *Al Awdah* English Weekly (12 October 1987), pp. 19–23; United Nations, Committee on the Exercise of the Inalienable Rights of the Palestinian People, "Israel's Policy on the West Bank Water Resources" (New York: United Nations, 1980), pp. 13–15.
85. USG/DS.
86. Kahan, *Agriculture and Water*, pp. 20–23, 111. See, note 61 of this chapter for a different view regarding the possibility of extending irrigated agriculture on the West Bank.
87. Interview by author with an Israeli water engineer, formerly with Tahal, Tel-Aviv, 26 June 1986.
88. Elisha Kally, "A Middle East Water Plan under Peace" (Tel-Aviv University, Interdisciplinary Center for Technological Analysis and Forecasting, March 1986), p. 5.
89. Interview by author with a water engineer, Tel-Aviv, 26 June 1986.
90. See in this regard, Ludwik A. Teclaff and Albert E. Utton, *International*

Groundwater Law (London/Rome/New York: Oceana Publications, Inc., 1981), pp. 1–75; Robert Hayton and Albert E. Utton, "Transboundary Groundwaters: The Bellagio Draft Treaty," *Natural Resources Journal* vol. 29 (summer 1989), pp. 663–722.

91. Interview by author with a water engineer, formerly with Tahal, Tel-Aviv, 26 June 1986.

92. To quote one Israeli analyst: "The Arab population in Judea and Samaria may have a claim to the waters that flow underground, and that is one-third of Israel's water supply. The Arabs could say that Israel is using their water." Interview by author with Israeli geographer, Haifa, 22 June 1986.

93. Shaul Ramati, "Water War and the Mideast," *Chicago Tribune*, 2 March 1985. A similar statement, albeit far more blunt and with less hyperbole, was made by the *Likud* Party in its campaign literature before the Israeli election of November 1988:

> Judea and Samaria boast 40 percent of Israel's available fresh water supply... Water is our life. As such, it makes no sense to place it in the hands of those whose intentions towards us may not always be the kindest.

Alan Cowell, "Next Flashpoint in Middle East: Water," *New York Times*, 16 April 1989.

94. Spector, "Waters of Controversy," p. 11.

9 Conclusion: the conduct of riparian dispute and the potential for cooperation in international river basins

1. See, chapter 4.
2. *Ibid.*
3. See, chapter 8.
4. On the variance in concern for relative gains and its effects on prospects for cooperation see, Duncan Snidal, "Relative Gains and the Pattern of International Cooperation," *American Political Science Review* vol. 85, no. 3 (September 1991). See, as well, Robert Powell, "Absolute and Relative Gains in International Relations Theory," *American Political Science Review* vol. 85, no. 4 (December 1991).
5. See, chapters 4 and 8.
6. Joseph Grieco, *Cooperation Among Nations: Europe, America, and the Non-Tariff Barriers to Trade* (Ithaca, N.Y.: Cornell University Press, 1990), pp. 47, 48, chapter 7. While it is true that we do not know exactly what constitutes an equitable distribution of benefits, the fact that in the Jordan basin, for example, there was not the perception of one, is sufficient. See in this regard, Helen Milner, "International Theories of Cooperation among Nations: Strengths and Weaknesses," *World Politics* vol. 44, no. 3, April 1992.
7. Robert O. Keohane, "Neoliberal Institutionalism: A Perspective on World Politics" in *International Institutions and State Power: Essays in International Relations Theory* (Boulder, Colo.: Westview Press, 1989), p. 2.
8. No doubt, the members of the "epistemic community" – to the extent that one

existed – had little or no access to the policy process in their respective states. Thus, they were unable to influence domestic politics in such a way that policy-makers perceived it to be in the national interest to cooperate in this matter. Peter Haas, *Saving the Mediterranean: the Politics of International Environmental Cooperation* (New York: Columbia University Press, 1990), pp. 218–19.

9. Stephan Haggard and Beth Simmons, "Theories of International Regimes," *International Organization* vol. 41, no. 3 (summer 1987), p. 511; Robert Jervis, "Realism, Game Theory, and Cooperation," *World Politics* vol 40, no. 3 (April 1988), pp. 324–25; Ronnie D. Lipschutz, *When Nations Clash: Raw Materials, Ideology and Foreign Policy* (Cambridge, Mass.: Ballinger Publishing Co., 1989); Harold and Margaret Sprout, *Man–Milieu Relationship Hypotheses in the Context of International Politics* (Center of International Studies, Princeton University, 1956).

10. See, note 8 of this chapter. Haas hypothesizes: "The strength of cooperative arrangements will be determined by the domestic power amassed by members of the epistemic community within their respective governments." (*Saving the Mediterranean*, p. 57.) His study shows that where epistemic communities are most active in domestic politics, they can reshape "their states' definition of the national interest in ways that allow[ed] those states to be more cooperative." (Milner, "International Theories," p. 479.) Consider, in this regard, the following: it has come to the attention of this author that a recent water study, researched and written by the Jaffee Center for Strategic Studies at Tel-Aviv University, and using data and documentation provided by Israel's Water Commission Administration, has been denied publication by the Ministry of Agriculture, because its conclusions run counter to the political position of the *Likud* government (1977–92). The study shows that Israel does not need to hold onto the West Bank in order to have access to its water resources. (Reference to this study has been made in *Al-Fajr*, 6 March 1992, p. 1, as well as in a personal communication with a member of the Jaffee Center, March 1992.)

11. See, chapter 4.

12. Keohane, "Neoliberal Institutionalism," p. 18 fn. 20.

13. See in this regard, Robert O. Keohane, *After Hegemony: Cooperation and Discord in the World Political Economy* (Princeton: Princeton University Press, 1984), pp. 85–132. On what constitutes "context," see, Robert Jervis, *Perception and Misperception in International Politics* (Princeton: Princeton University Press, 1976), pp. 153, 203.

14. Lipschutz, *When Nations Clash*.

15. It seems fair to say, however, that what may be sub-optimal relative to an ideal type – as the one posited in the first chapter (p. 1) – may not necessarily be sub-optimal. In some cases, and certainly in the particular case of the Indus conflict, assigning property rights may, in fact, be optimal: the best one can expect under the circumstances.

Helen Milner ("International Theories," p. 486) rightly suggests that studies of international cooperation need to consider the nature of the cooperative solution arrived at. Different arrangements have different implications for aggregate welfare and the distribution of goods. Moreover, they may elucidate something about the concerns and interests of states in their international relations, as well as the potential for future collaboration.

16. See, Oran Young, *International Cooperation: Building Regimes for Natural Resources and the Environment* (Ithaca and London: Cornell University Press, 1989), pp. 84–86.

17. See, chapter 5.

18. See, chapter 8.

19. See, chapter 5.

20. Failing that, the two downstream states would benefit from bilateral cooperation to counterbalance Turkey, whose relative power is growing. (This, however, would require a favorable political climate.) See, in this regard, Milner's critique ("International Theories," p. 484) of Grieco's argument (*Cooperation Among Nations*, p. 47) about the need for states to depend on their own capabilities in a world of anarchy. Milner maintains that his argument is valid only in the case of two-person games. In three-person games, as in the Euphrates basin, bilateral cooperation – what Duncan Snidal calls "defensive cooperation" through the formation of a "cooperative cluster" – would certainly be more favorable than each state "going it alone." In that way, Syria and Iraq would achieve relative gains collectively. See, "International Cooperation among Relative Gains Maximizers," *International Studies Quarterly* vol. 35 (1991).

21. David Mitrany, *A Working Peace System* (Chicago: Quadrangle Books, 1986) [first published in 1943]; Robert Axelrod, *The Evolution of Cooperation* (New York: Basic Books, 1984); Haas, *Saving the Mediterranean*, p. 184.

22. Grieco, *Cooperation Among Nations*, p. 231; Haas, *Saving the Mediterranean*, p. 184.

23. Axelrod, *Evolution of Cooperation*; Kenneth Oye (ed.), *Cooperation under Anarchy* (Princeton: Princeton University Press, 1986).

24. E. Haas, *Beyond the Nation-State* (Stanford: Stanford University Press, 1964), p. 48.

25. See, chapter 7.

26. *Ibid.*

27. See, note 20 of this chapter.

28. See, note 4 of this chapter.

29. In this regard, it is important to remember that during the Jordan waters crisis, the Arabs retreated from the diversion scheme soon after Israel began flexing its muscles; see chapter 5.

Select bibliography

Newspapers

Chicago Tribune (United States)
Christian Science Monitor (United States)
al-Fajr (West Bank)
ha-Aretz (Israel)
Hotam [*al-Hamishmar* weekly supplement] (Israel)
Jerusalem Post (Israel)
Le Monde (France)
New York Times (United States)

Books and articles

Abu-Lughod, I. (ed.), *The Transformation of Palestine* (Evanston: Northwestern University Press, 1971)

Abu-Taleb, Maher, "Regional Cooperation in Water Resources Management" in Elise Boulding (ed.), *Building Peace in the Middle East: Challenges for States and for Civil Society* (Boulder, Colo.: Lynne Rienner Publishers, 1994)

Abu-Taleb, Maher F., Deason, Jonathan P., and Salemeh, Elias, "The Jordan River Basin," paper presented at the World Bank International Workshop on Comprehensive Water Management Policy, Washington, D.C., 24–28 June 1991

Abu-Taleb, Maher F., Deason, Jonathan P., Salameh, Elias, and Kefaya, Boulos, "Water Resources Planning and Development in Jordan: Problems, Future Scenarios, and Recommendations" in Guy Le Moigne, Shawki Barghouti, Gershon Feder, Lisa Garbus, and Mie Xie (eds.), *Country Experiences with Water Resources Management: Economic, Institutional, Technological and Environmental Issues*, World Bank Technical Paper no. 175 (Washington, D.C.: The World Bank, 1992)

Ajami Fouad, *The Arab Predicament: Arab Political Thought and Practice since 1967* (Cambridge: Cambridge University Press, 1981)

Ali, Ali Muhamad, *Nahr al-Urdan wal-Mu'amara al-Sahyuniya* [The Jordan River and the Zionist Conspiracy] (Cairo: al-Dar al-Qawmiya, n.d.) [in Arabic]

American Friends of the Middle East, Inc., *The Jordan Water Problem: an Analysis and Summary of Available Documents* (Washington, D.C., 1964)

American Society of International Law, *Legal Questions Arising out of the Construction of a Dam at Maqarin on the Yarmuk River* [report for the US Agency for International Development, Contract AID/NE-C-1256] (Washington, D.C., 31 July 1977)

"Arab Plan for Development of Water Resources in the Jordan Valley" in *The Egyptian Economic and Political Review* vol. 2, no. 2 (October 1955), pp. 42–46

Arab Socialist B'ath Party: *al-Furat . . . al-'azma illati afta'alaha hukaam al-Iraq* [The Euphrates: the Crisis Created by the Rulers of Iraq] (Damascus: Office of Propaganda, Publication and Information, n.d.) [in Arabic]

Arad, Ruth W., Arad, Uzi B., McCulloch, Rachel, Piñera, Jose, and Hollick, Ann L., *Sharing Global Resources* (Council on Foreign Relations, McGraw-Hill Book Co., 1979)

Arian, Asher, *Politics in Israel: the Second Generation* (New Jersey: Chatham House Publishers Inc., 1985)

Aron, Raymond, trans. Richard Howard and Annette Baker Fox, *Peace and War: A Theory of International Relations* (Garden City, New York: Doubleday & Co., Inc., 1966)

Aruri Naseer, *Jordan: A Study in Political Development (1921–1965)* (The Hague: Martinus Nijhoff, 1972)

Associates for Middle East Research, Data Base (Philadelphia, Pa.: University of Pennsylvania)

"Ataturk Dam – the biggest yet," *The Middle East* (May 1984), pp. 75–76

Axelrod, Robert, *The Evolution of Cooperation* (New York: Basic Books, 1984)

Axelrod, Robert (ed.), *Structure of Decision – the Cognitive Maps of Political Elites* (Princeton: Princeton University Press, 1976)

Azar, Edward, "Protracted International Conflicts: Ten Propositions," *International Interactions* vol. 12, no. 1 (1985), pp. 59–70

Azar, Edward, Jureidini, Paul and McLaurin, Ronald, "Protracted Social Conflict: Theory and Practice in the Middle East," *Journal of Palestine Studies* vol. 8, no. 1 (1978), pp, 41–60

al-Azm, Sadiq, *al-Naqd al-Dhati ba'd al-Hazima* [Self-Criticism after the Defeat] (Beirut: Dar al-Tali'ah 1968) [in Arabic]

Baker, Jr. Inc., Michael and Harza Engineering Co., *The Hashemite Kingdom of Jordan: Yarmouk–Jordan Valley Project*, Master Plan Report, 8 vols. and appendices (Chicago, Ill., 1955)

Bar-Yaacov, Nissim, *The Israel–Syrian Armistice: Problems of Implementation, 1949–1966* (Jerusalem: Magnes Press, 1967)

Bari, Zohurul, "Syrian–Iraqi Dispute over the Euphrates Waters," *International Studies* (Quarterly Journal of the School of International Studies, Jawaharlal Nehru University) vol. 16, no. 2 (April–June 1977)

Beaumont, Peter, "The Euphrates River – an International Problem of Water Resources Development," *Environmental Conservation* vol. 5, no. 1 (spring 1978)

Ben-Moshe, Eliezer, "Jordan's Yarmuk Plan," *New Outlook* vol. 5, no. 2 (February 1962), pp. 22–24

Biswas, Asit K. (ed.), *International Waters of the Middle East: From Euphrates–Tigris to Nile* (Delhi: Oxford University Press, 1994)

Blake, G. H., "Israel: Immigration and Dispersal of Population" in J. I. Clarke and W. B. Fisher (eds.), *Populations of the Middle East and North Africa: A Geographical Approach* (London: University of London Press Ltd., 1972)

Blass, Simha, *Mei Meriva u-Ma'as* [Water in Strife and Action] (Israel: Masada Press, Ltd., 1973) [in Hebrew]

Boneh, Y. and Baida, U., "Mekorot ha-Mayim v-Nitsulam b-Yehuda v-Shomron" [Water Resources and their Exploitation in Judea and Samaria] in Shmueli, A. *et al.* (eds.), *Yehuda v-Shomron: Prakim bi-Geografia Yishuvit* [Judea and Samaria: Essays in Settlement Geography] Part 1 [in Hebrew] (Jerusalem: Canaan Publishing House, 1977)

Boulding, Kenneth, "National Images and International Systems," *Journal of Conflict Resolution* vol. 3 (1959)

Bourgey, André, "Le Barrage de Tabqa et l'Aménagement du Bassin de l'Euphrate en Syrie," *Revue de Géographie de Lyon* vol. 49 (1974)

Bourne, C. B., "The Development of International Water Resources: the Drainage Basin Approach," *The Canadian Bar Review* vol. 47, no. 1 (March 1969), pp. 62–82

Brawer, Moshe, "The Geographical Background of the Jordan Water Dispute" in Charles A. Fisher (ed.), *Essays in Political Geography* (London: Methuen & Co. Ltd., 1968)

Brecher, Michael, *Decisions in Israel's Foreign Policy* (New Haven: Yale University Press, 1975)

"State Behaviour in International Crisis," *Journal of Conflict Resolution* vol. 23, no. 3 (September 1979), pp. 446–80

"International Crises and Protracted Conflicts," *International Interactions* vol. 11, nos. 3–4 (1984), pp. 237–97

Brecher, Michael and Wilkenfeld, Jonathan, "Protracted Conflicts and Crises" in Brecher and Wilkenfeld, *Crisis, Conflict and Instability* (New York: Pergamon Press, 1989), pp. 127–40

British Broadcasting Corporation, *Summary of World Broadcasts*, part 4: Middle East, 1964–67 (United Kingdom: Monitoring Service of the BBC)

Burns, E. L. M., *Between Arab and Israeli* (Beirut: Institute for Palestine Studies, 1968)

Buzan, Barry, *People, States and Fear: the National Security Problem in International Relations* (Chapel Hill: University of North Carolina Press, 1983)

Cantor, Menachem, "Ha-Mayim b-Yisrael – Esrim v-Chamesh shanim la-medina" [Water in Israel – Twenty-five Years of Statehood] in Israel: Ministry of Agriculture (Office of the Water Commissioner), *Ha-Mayim b-Yisrael* [The Water in Israel] Part 1 (Tel-Aviv, 1973)

Choucri, N. and North, R., *Nations in Conflict* (San Francisco: W. H. Freeman, 1975)

Congressional Quarterly Inc., *The Middle East*, fifth edition (Washington, D.C., 1981)

Colley, John, *Green March, Black September: the Story of the Palestinian Arabs* (London: Cass, 1973)

"Jordan and the Politics of Water," Middle East International (30 January 1981)

"The War over Water," *Foreign Policy* no. 54 (spring 1984)

Dakkak, Ibrahim, "al-Siyaasa al- Ma'iya f-il-Dafa al-Gharbiya al-Muhtala" [Water Policy on the Occupied West Bank], *Sh'un Filastiniyah* vol. 126 (May 1982)

Davis, Uri, Maks, Antonia, and Richardson, John, "Israel's Water Policies," *Journal of Palestine Studies* vol. 9, no. 2 (winter 1980)

Dees, Joseph L., "Jordan's East Ghor Canal Project," *Middle East Journal* vol. 13, no. 4 (autumn 1959), pp. 357–81

Demant, P., "Les implantations israëliennes dans les territoires occupés," *Hérodote* (1983)

Devlin, John F., *Syria: Modern State in an Ancient Land* (Boulder, Colo.: Westview Press, 1983)

Dieckhoff, Alain, *Les espaces d'Israël* (Paris: Fondation pour les Etudes de Défense Nationale, 1987)

Dillman, Jeffrey D., "Water Rights in the Occupied Territories," *Journal of Palestine Studies* vol. 19, no. 1 (autumn 1989)

Doherty, Kathryn B., "Jordan Waters Conflict," *International Conciliation* [Carnegie Endowment for International Peace] no. 553 (May 1965)

Drysdale, Alasdair and Blake, Gerald H. *The Middle East and North Africa: A Political Geography* (New York: Oxford University Press, 1985)

Duna, Cem, "Turkey's Peace Pipeline" in Joyce Starr and Daniel Stoll (eds.), *The Politics of Scarcity: Water in the Middle East* (Boulder, Colo.: Westview Press, 1988)

Efrat, Moshe, "Syria's Dam on the Euphrates," *New Outlook* vol. 10, no. 4 (1967)

Farid, Abdel Majid and Sirriyeh, Hussein (eds.), *Israel and Arab Water* (London: Ithaca Press, 1985)

Fisher, W. B., "Jordan: a Demographic Shatter-belt" in J. I. Clarke and W. B. Fisher (eds.), *Populations of the Middle East and North Africa: A Geographical Approach* (London: University of London Press Ltd., 1972)

The Middle East: A Physical, Social, and Regional Geography (London: Methuen & Co., 1978)

Foreign Relations of the United States, 1952–1954, vol. 9, part 1 (Washington: United States Government Printing Office, 1986)

Frantz, H. R., "The Water Master Plan of Jordan" (paper delivered at Jordan's National Water Symposium, Amman, 19–22 March 1978)

Frischwasser-Ra'anan, H. F., *The Frontiers of a Nation* (Westport, Conn.: Hyperion Press, Inc., 1955)

Gabel, Joseph, "Le Concept de l'Idéologie" in *Idéologies* (Paris: éditions anthropos, 1974), pp. 23–75

Galnoor, Itzhak, "Water Planning: Who Gets the Last Drop?" in Raphaella Bilski, Itzhak Galnoor, Dan Inbar, Yohanan Manor, and Gabriel Sheffer (eds.), *Can Planning Replace Politics: the Israeli Experience* (The Hague: Martinus Nijhoff Publishers, 1980)

"Water Policymaking in Israel" in Hillel Shuval (ed.), *Water Quality Management under Conditions of Scarcity* (New York: Academic Press, 1980

Garbell, Maurice A., "The Jordan Valley Plan," *Scientific American* vol. 212, no. 3 (March 1965), pp. 23–31

Garfinkle, Adam M., "Negotiating by Proxy: Jordanian Foreign Policy and US Options in the Middle East," *Orbis* vol. 24 (winter 1981)

Garretson, A. H., Hayton, R. D., Olmstead, C. J., and Baxter, Richard R. (eds.), *The Law of International Drainage Basins* (Dobbs Ferry: Oceana Publications, 1967)

Gazit, Mordechai, *President Kennedy's Policy toward the Arab States and Israel* (Tel-Aviv; Shiloah Center for Middle Eastern and African Studies, 1983)

George, Alan, "Wrangle over the Euphrates," *The Middle East* (October 1987)

George, Alexander L., "Case Studies and Theory Development: the Method of Structures, Focused Comparison" in Paul Gordon Lauren (ed.), *Diplomacy: New Approaches in History, Theory and Policy* (New York: Free Press, 1979), pp. 43–68

Gilpin, Robert, *US Power and the Multinational Corporation: The Political Economy of Foreign Direct Investment* (New York: Basic Books, 1975)

War and Change in World Politics (Cambridge: Cambridge University Press, 1981)

"The Richness of the Tradition of Political Realism" in Robert O. Keohane (ed.), *Neorealism and its Critics* (New York: Columbia University Press, 1986)

The Political Economy of International Relations (Princeton: Princeton University Press, 1987)

Gleick, Peter H., "Water and Conflict: Fresh Water Resources and International Security," *International Security* vol. 18, no. 1 (summer 1993), pp. 79–112

Goichon, A.-M., *L'Eau, Problème Vital de la Région du Jourdain* (Brussels: Centre pour l'Etude des Problèmes du Monde Musulman Contemporain, 1964)

Golani, Shimon, "Ha-Ma'avak al Mei ha-Yarden" [The Conflict over the Jordan Waters] in Kliot, Shmueli and Sofer (eds.), *Artsot Ha-Galil* [The Lands of the Galilee] part 2 (1983) [in Hebrew]

Grieco, Joseph M., "Anarchy and the Limits of Cooperation: a Realist Critique of the Newest Liberal Institutionalism," *International Organization* vol. 42, no. 3 (summer 1988), pp. 486–507

Cooperation among Nations: Europe, America, and Non-Tariff Barriers to Trade (Ithaca, N.Y.: Cornell University Press, 1990)

Grinwald, Zvi, *ha-Mayim b-Yisrael* [Water in Israel] (Hauser Press, 1980) [in Hebrew]

Groom, A. J. R. and Taylor, Paul (eds.), *Functionalism: Theory and Practice in International Relations* (London: University of London Press, 1975)

Gruen, George E., "Jordan's East Ghor Irrigation Project," *New Outlook* vol. 7, no. 5 (1964), pp. 34–37

"Water and Politics in the Middle East," *American Jewish Committee: Reports on the Foreign Scene* no. 5 (December 1964)

Gubser, Peter, *Jordan: Crossroads of Middle Eastern Events* (Boulder, Colo.: Westview Press, 1983)

Gulhati, Niranjan, *Indus Waters Treaty: an Exercise in International Mediation* (Bombay: Allied Publishers, 1973)

Haas, Ernst, *The Uniting of Europe: Political, Social, and Economic Forces, 1950–1957* (Stanford: Stanford University Press, 1958)
Beyond the Nation-State: Functionalism and International Organization (Stanford: Stanford University Press, 1964)
"International Integration: the European and the Universal Process," *International Organization* no. 15 (1961)
"The 'Uniting of Europe' and the Uniting of Latin America," *Journal of Common Market Studies* vol. 5 (June 1967)
Haas, Peter, *Saving the Mediterranean: the Politics of International Environmental Cooperation* (New York: Columbia University Press, 1990)
Haggard, Stephan and Simmons, Beth A., "Theories of International Regimes," *International Organization* vol. 41, no. 3 (summer 1987), pp. 491–517
Hardin, Garrett, "The Tragedy of the Commons," *Science* 162 (1968), pp. 1,243–48
Hartshorne, Richard, "The Functional Approach in Political Geography," *Annals of the Association of American Geographers* vol. 40, no. 2 (June 1950), pp. 95–130
Hashemite Kingdom of Jordan, *al-Jarida al-Rasmiyya* (Official Gazette), no. 1150 (4 June 1953), pp. 380–84 [in Arabic]
Haupert, John S., "Recent Progress on Jordan's East Ghor Canal Project," *The Professional Geographer* vol. 18, no. 1 (January 1966), pp. 9–13
Hays, James B., *TVA on the Jordan: Proposals for Irrigation and Hydro-Electric Development in Palestine* (Washington, D.C.: Public Affairs Press, 1948)
Hayton, Robert and Utton, Albert E., "Transboundary Groundwaters: The Bellagio Draft Treaty," *Natural Resources Journal* vol. 29 (summer 1989), pp. 663–722
Heradstveit, D., *The Arab–Israeli Conflict: Psychological Obstacles to Peace* (Oslo: Universitetsforlaget, 1979)
Herz, John H., *Political Realism and Political Idealism* (Chicago: University of Chicago Press, 1951)
Hillel, Daniel, *Rivers of Eden: The Struggle for Water and the Quest for Peace in the Middle East* (New York: Oxford University Press, 1994)
Hoffman, Stanley, "The Fate of the Nation-State," *Daedalus* vol. 95, no. 3 (summer 1966)
Holsti, O., "Cognitive dynamics and Images of the Enemy," *Journal of International Affairs* vol. 21, no. 1 (1967)
Holsti, O., Finlay, David, and Fagen, Richard, *Enemies in Politics* (Chicago: Rand McNally & Co., 1967)
Howard, Michael and Hunter, Robert, "Israel and the Arab World: the Crisis of 1967," *Adelphi Papers* no. 41 (October 1967)
Howard, Norman F., "The Uncertain Kingdom of Jordan," *Current History* vol. 66, no. 390 (February 1974)
"Jordan: the Price of Moderation," *Current History* vol. 68, no. 402 (February 1975)
Hutchison, Elmoe H., *Violent Truce* (New York: the Devin-Adair Co., 1956)
Inbar, Moshe and Maos, Jacob O., "Water Resource Planning and Development in the Northern Jordan Valley," *Water International* vol. 9, no. 1 (1984), pp. 18-25
Ionides, M. G., *Report on the Water Resources of Transjordan and their Development*

(published on behalf of the Government of Transjordan by the Crown Agents for the Colonies, London, 1939)

"The Perspective of Water Development in Palestine and Transjordan," *Journal of the Royal Central Asian Society* vol. 33, parts 3 and 4 (July–October 1946)

"Jordan Valley Irrigation in Transjordan," *Engineering* (13 September 1946)

"Refugees and the Jordan," *The Spectator* (19 November 1948), pp. 659–60

"The Disputed Waters of Jordan," *Middle East Journal* vol. 7, no. 2 (spring 1953)

Israel: Ministry of Agriculture (Office of the Water Commissioner), *ha-Mayim b-Yisrael* [The Water in Israel] part 1 (Tel-Aviv, 1973)

Israel: Ministry of Agriculture, *Water in Israel: Consumption and Extraction 1962–1970/80* (Tel-Aviv, 1981)

Jacobs, M. and Litwin, Y., "A Survey of Water Resources Development, Utilization and Management in Israel" in V. T. Chow, S. C. Csallany, R. J. Krizek, and H. C. Preul (eds.), *Water for the Human Environment* vol. 2 (Chicago, Illinois: Proceedings of the First World Congress on Water Resources, 24–28 September 1973)

Jamous, Haroun, *Israël et ses Juifs* (Paris: François Maspéro, 1982)

Jervis, Robert, *Perception and Misperception in International Politics* (Princeton: Princeton University Press, 1976)

"Realism, Game Theory, and Cooperation," *World Politics* vol. 40, no. 3 (1988), pp. 317–49

Johnston, Eric, "Jordan River Valley Development," *Department of State Bulletin* (28 December 1953), pp. 891–93

"Arab–Israel Tension and the Jordan Valley," *World Affairs* (summer 1954), pp. 38–41

"Jordan River," *al-Mawsu'a al-Falistiniya* [Palestinian Encyclopaedia] vol. 1 (Damascus, 1984) [in Arabic]

Jordan Valley Authority, *Jordan Valley Irrigation Project Stage II – Feasibility Study* (Chicago: Harza Overseas Engineering Company, January 1978)

Jureidini, Paul A. and McLaurin, R. D., "Jordan: the Impact of Social Change on the Role of the Tribes," *The Washington Papers* vol. 12, no. 108 (The Center for Strategic and International Studies, Georgetown University, 1984)

Kahan, David, *Agriculture and Water in the West Bank and Gaza* (Jerusalem: The West Bank Data Base Project, 1983)

Kahhaleh, Subhi, "The Water Problem in Israel and its Repercussions on the Arab–Israeli Conflict," *IPS Papers* no. 9 (Beirut: Institute for Palestine Studies, 1981)

Kally, Elisha, *Mayim v-Shalom*, also published as *A Middle East Water Plan Under Peace* (Tel-Aviv University, Interdisciplinary Center for Technological Analysis and Forecasting, March 1986)

Kaplan, Stephen S., "United States' Aid and Regime Maintenance in Jordan, 1957–73," *Public Policy* vol. 23, no. 2 (spring 1975)

Kemp, Geoffrey, "Scarcity and Strategy," *Foreign Affairs*, vol. 56, no. 2 (January 1978)

Keohane, Robert, "The Theory of Hegemonic Stability and Changes in International Economic Regimes, 1967–77" in Ole Holsti, Randolph M. Siverson, and

Alexander L. George (eds.), *Change in the International System* (Boulder, Colo.: Westview Press, 1980), pp. 131–62

After Hegemony: Cooperation and Discord in the World Political Economy (Princeton: Princeton University Press, 1984)

"Neoliberal Institutionalism: A Perspective on World Politics" in *International Institutions and State Power: Essays in International Relations Theory* (Boulder, Colo.: Westview Press, 1989)

"Institutionalist Theory and the Realist Challenge after the Cold War" in David Baldwin (ed.), *Neorealism and Neoliberalism: The Contemporary Debate* (New York: Columbia University Press, 1993)

"Multilateralism: an Agenda for Research," *International Journal* vol. 45, no. 4 (autumn 1990)

Kerr, Malcolm, *The Arab Cold War (1957–1967)* (New York: Oxford University Press, 1967)

Regional Arab Politics and the Conflict with Israel (Research Program on Economic and Political Problems and Prospects of the Middle East – Rand Corp./ Resources for the Future RM-5966-FF, October 1969)

Khouri, Fred J., "The US, the UN and the Jordan River Issue," *Middle East Forum* (May 1964)

The Arab–Israeli Dilemma (New York: Syracuse University Press, 1968)

Khouri, Rami G., *The Jordan Valley: Life and Society below Sea Level* (London: Longman, 1981)

Kienle, Eberhard, "The Conflict between the Baath Regimes of Syria and Iraq prior to their Consolidation," *Ethnizität und Gesellschaft* Occasional Papers no. 5 (Freie Universität Berlin, 1985)

Ba'th v. Ba'th: the Conflict between Syria and Iraq 1968–1989 (London: I. B. Tauris & Co. Ltd., 1990)

Kimmerling, Baruch, *Zionism and Territory* (Berkeley: Institute of International Studies, University of California, 1983)

Kolars, John, "The Course of Water in the Arab Middle East," *American–Arab Affairs* no. 33 (summer 1990)

Kolars, John and Mitchell, William A., *The Euphrates River and the Southeast Anatolia Development Project* (Carbondale: Southern Illinois University Press, 1991)

Konikoff, A., *Transjordan: An Economic Survey* (Jerusalem: Economic Research Institute of the Jewish Agency for Palestine, 1946)

Krasner, Stephen D., "Global Communications and National Power: Life on the Pareto Frontier," *World Politics* 43 (April 1991)

Krasner, Stephen (ed.), *International Regimes* (Ithaca, N.Y.: Cornell University Press, 1983)

Laipson, Ellen, "Memorandum: Policies of the American, Israeli and Jordanian Governments on Use of the Jordan River Waters," Library of Congress: Congressional Research Service (12 October 1979)

LeMarquand, David, *International Rivers: the Politics of Cooperation* (Vancouver, B.C.: Westwater Research Centre, University of British Columbia, 1977)

"Le Partage des Eaux de l'Euphrate," *Maghreb-Machrek* no. 69 (July–August–September 1975)

Lepawsky, Albert, "International Development of River Resources," *International Affairs* vol. 39 (1963), pp. 533–50

Lipschutz, Ronnie D., *When Nations Clash: Raw Materials, Ideology and Foreign Policy* (Cambridge, Mass.: Ballinger Publishing Co., 1989)

Lipson, Charles, "Why are some International Agreements Informal?" *International Organization* vol. 45, no. 4 (autumn 1991)

Lonergan, Stephen and Brooks, David B., *Watershed: The Role of Fresh Water in the Israeli–Palestinian Conflict* (Ottawa, Canada: International Development Research Centre, 1994)

Louis, Jean-Victor, "Les Eaux du Jourdain," *Annuaire Français de Droit International* vol. 11 (1965)

Lowdermilk, Walter C., *Palestine, Land of Promise* (New York and London: Harper & Brothers Publishers, 1944)

Lowi, Miriam R., "The Politics of Water under Conditions of Scarcity and Conflict: the Jordan River and Riparian States" (Ph.D. dissertation, Princeton University, 1990)

"West Bank Water Resources and the Resolution of Conflict in the Middle East," *Environmental Change and Acute Conflict* (American Academy of Arts and Sciences), Occasional Paper no. 1 (September 1992), pp. 29–60

"Bridging the Divide: Transboundary Resource Disputes and the Case of West Bank Water," *International Security* vol. 18, no. 1 (summer 1993)

"Conflict and Cooperation in Resource Development," in Elise Boulding (ed.), *Building Peace in the Middle East: Challenges for States and for Civil Society* (Boulder, Colo.: Lynne Rienner Pubishers, 1994)

"Rivers of Conflict, Rivers of Peace," *Journal of International Affairs* vol. 49, no. 1 (summer 1995)

"Resource Scarcity and Protracted Conflict" in Daniel Deudney and Richard Matthew (eds.), *Contested Ground: Security and Conflict in the New Environmental Politics* (Albany, N.Y.: State University of New York Press, 1995)

Lowi, Miriam R. and Rothman, Jay, "Arabs and Israelis: the Jordan River" in Guy Olivier Faure and Jeffrey Z. Rubin (eds.), *Culture and Negotiation: the Resolution of Water Disputes* (California: Sage Publications, 1993)

Mahmoud, Shawkat, "al-Zira'a w-al-Miyaa' f-il-Dafa al-Gharbiya taht al-Ihtilaal al-Isra'ili" [Agriculture and Water on the West Bank under the Israeli Occupation], *Samed al-Iqtisadi* vol. 6, no. 52 (November–December 1984) [in Arabic]

Main, Charles T. Inc., *The Unified Development of the Water Resources of the Jordan Valley Region* (Boston, Mass., 1953)

Mannheim, Karl, *Ideology and Utopia* (London: Routledge & Kegan Paul, 1979)

Matar, Ibrahim, "Israeli Settlements in the West Bank and Gaza Strip," *Journal of Palestine Studies* vol. 11, no. 1 (autumn 1981)

Mazur, Michael P., "Economic Development of Jordan" in Charles A. Cooper and Sidney S. Alexander (eds.), *Economic Development and Population Growth in the Middle East* (New York: American Elsevier Publishing Co. Inc., 1972)

Mehdi, Muhammad, "The Arab Summit," *Middle East Forum* (May 1964)

Michel, Aloys Arthur, *The Indus River – a Study of the Effects of Partition* (New Haven: Yale University Press, 1967)

Milner, Helen, "The Assumption of Anarchy in International Relations Theory: a critique," *Review of International Studies* no. 17 (1991), pp. 67–85

"International Theories of Cooperation among Nations: Strengths and Weaknesses,' *World Politics* vol. 44, no. 3 (April 1992)

Mitrany, David, *A Working Peace System* (Chicago: Quadrangle Books, 1966) [first published 1943]

The Functional Theory of Politics (New York: St. Martin's Press, 1975)

Moravcsik, Andrew, "Liberalism and International Relations Theory," Working Paper no. 92–6, Center for International Affairs, Harvard University (October 1992)

Morgenthau, Hans, *Politics among Nations*, 4th edition (New York: Knopf, 1966) [first published in 1948]

Moussly, Nazim, *Le Problème de l'Eau en Syrie* (Lyon: BOSC Frères, 1951)

Muhamad, 'Abd al-Hafiz, *Al-Nahr illadi Wahada al-Arab Nahr al-Urdun al-Xalid, w-Mashari' al-Tahwil* (The River which United the Arabs, the Jordan River, and Development Projects) (Cairo, 1964) [in Arabic]

Naff, Thomas, 'The Jordan Basin: Political, Economic, and Institutional Issues" in Guy Le Moigne, Shawki Barghouti, Gerson Feder, Lisa Garbus, and Mei Xie (eds.), *Country Experiences with Water Resources Management: Economic, Institutional, Technological and Environmental Issues*, World Bank Technical Paper no. 175 (Washington, D.C.: The World Bank, 1992)

Naff, Thomas and Matson, Ruth C. (eds.), *Water in the Middle East: Conflict or Cooperation?* (Boulder, Colo.: Westview Press, 1984)

"Nahr al-Urdun," [Jordan River] *al-Mawsu'a al-Falistiniya* [Palestinian Encyclopaedia] vol. 1 (Damascus, 1984) [in Arabic]

National Archives of the State of Israel, Foreign Ministry Documents (Record Group 93), 1953–55

National Archives of the United States, Foreign Policy Records, 1952–54

Nijim, Basheer Khalil, "The Indus, Nile, and Jordan: International Rivers and Factors in Conflict Potential" (unpublished Ph.D. thesis: Indiana University, June 1969)

Nimrod, Yoram, "The Unquiet Waters," *New Outlook* vol. 8, no. 4 (June 1965)

"The Jordan's Angry Waters," *New Outlook* vol. 8, no. 5 (July–August 1965)

"Conflict over the Jordan . . . last stage," *New Outlook* vol. 8, no. 6 (September 1965)

North, R., 'Toward a Framework for the Analysis of Scarcity and Conflict," *International Studies Quarterly* vol. 21, no. 4 (December 1977)

Nye, Joseph, *Peace in Parts: Integration and Conflict in Regional Organization* (Boston: Little, Brown & Co., 1971)

O'Brien, Conor Cruise, *The Siege* (New York: Simon and Schuster, 1986)

Orni, Efraim and Efrat, Elisha, *Geography of Israel* (Jerusalem: Israel Universities Press, 1971)

Oron, Yitzhak (ed.), *Middle East Record* vols. 1 and 2, 1960 and 1961 (Reuven Shiloah Center, Tel-Aviv University)

Orr, David, "Modernization and Conflict: Second Image Implications of Scarcity," *International Studies Quarterly* vol. 21, no. 4 (December 1977)

Oye, Kenneth (ed.), *Cooperation under Anarchy* (Princeton: Princeton University Press, 1986)

Palestine Royal Commission Report (London: His Majesty's Stationery Office, 1937)

Pearce, Fred, "Wells of Conflict on the West Bank," *New Scientist* no. 1 (June 1991)

Powell, Robert, "Absolute and Relative Gains in International Relations Theory," *American Political Science Review* vol. 85, no. 4 (December 1991)

Quiring, Paul, "Israeli settlements and Palestinian Rights, Part 2," *Middle East International* (October 1978)

Rabin, Yitzhak, *The Rabin Memoirs* (New York: Little, Brown & Co., 1979)

Rafael, Gideon, *Destination Peace – Three Decades of Israeli Foreign Policy* (London: Weidenfeld & Nicolson, 1981)

al-Rafa'i, Nureddin, "Miyaa' Nahr al-Furat bein Turkiya wa-Suriya wal-Iraq" [The Waters of the Euphrates River between Turkey, Syria, and Iraq] *al-Muhandis al-'Arabi* [The Arab Engineer] no. 68 (1983) [in Arabic]

Rogers, Peter and Lydon, Peter (eds.), *Water in the Arab World: Perspectives and Prognoses* (Cambridge, Mass.: Harvard University Press, 1994)

Rothman, Jay and Lowi, Miriam, "Culture, Conflict and Cooperation: the Jordan River Basin" in Gershon Baskin (ed.), *Water: Conflict or Cooperation*, Israel/Palestine Center for Research and Information vol. 1, no. 2 (May 1992)

al-Rumeihy, Mohamed, "al-Miyaa'al-'Arabiya wa-Hadith 'an al-Xatar al-Mustatir" [Arab Water and the Hidden Danger] *al-'Arabi* (Kuwait) no. 311 (October 1984), pp. 10–22 [in Arabic]

al-Saadi, Mohamad Ali, "The Jordan River Dispute: a Case Study in International Conflicts" (unpublished Ph.D. dissertation, University of Massachusetts, 1969)

Safran, Nadav, *From War to War* (New York: Pegasus, 1969)

Saket, B., Smadi, M. and Amerah, M., "The Significance of Some West Bank Resources to Israel (Revised Edition)" Amman: Royal Scientific Society – Economics Department, April 1979)

Saket, B., Assaf, G. and Siraj, M., "Continued Exploitation in Spite of the World: Israeli Colonization of the West Bank" (Amman: Royal Scientific Society – Economics Department, November 1980)

Salameh, Elias, "Jordan's Water Resources: Development and Future Prospects," *American–Arab Affairs* no. 33 (summer 1990)

Saleh, Hassan 'Abd al-Qader, "al-Asas al-Jografi l-il-Niza'a al 'Arabi al-Isra'ili hawl Miyaa' Nahr al-Urdun" [The Geographical Bases of the Arab–Israeli Dispute over the Waters of the Jordan River] *Majalla kuliyat al-'Adab* [*Journal of the Faculty of Letters*] University of Jordan, vol. 3, no. 1 (1972) [in Arabic]

Sayigh, Rosemary, *Palestinians: From Peasants to Revolutionaries* (London: Zed Press, 1979)

Schmidt, Dana Adams, "Prospects for a Solution of the Jordan River Valley Dispute," *Middle Eastern Affairs* vol. 6, no. 1 (January 1955), pp. 1–12

Select bibliography

Schwartz, Sulamith, "Blueprint and Vision: the Jordan Valley Authority" in *The Palestine Year Book* vol. 2, 1945–46 (New York: Zionist Organization of America)

Schwarz, J., "Water Resources in Judea, Samaria, and the Gaza Strip" in Daniel Elazar (ed.), *Judea, Samaria, and Gaza: Views on the Present and the Future* (Washington: American Enterprise Institute for Public Policy Research, 1982)

"Israeli Water Sector Review: Past Achievements, Current Problems, and Future Options" in Guy Le Moigne, Shawki Barghouti, Gershon Feder, Lisa Garbus, and Mei Xie (eds.), *Country Experiences with Water Resources Management: Economic, Institutional, Technological and Environmental Issues*, World Bank Technical Paper no. 175 (Washington, D.C.: The World Bank, 1992)

Seale, Patrick, *Asad: the Struggle for the Middle East* (Berkeley: University of California Press, 1989)

Selim, Mohamed Ahmed, *Le Problème de l'Exploitation des Eaux du Jourdain* (Paris: Editions Cujas, 1965)

Shwadran, Benjamin, *Jordan, A State of Tension* (New York: Council for Middle Eastern Affairs Press, 1959)

Smith, C. G., "The Disputed Waters of the Jordan," *The Institute of British Geographers: Transactions and Papers*, publication no. 40 (1966)

"Diversion of the Jordan Waters," *The World Today* vol. 22, no. 11 (November 1966), pp. 491–98

"Water Resources and Irrigation Development in the Middle East," *Geography* vol. 55, part 4 (November 1970)

Smith, H. A., "The Waters of the Jordan: A Problem of International Water Control," *International Affairs* vol. 24, no. 4 (October 1949)

Snidal, Duncan, "Relative Gains and the Pattern of International Cooperation," *American Political Science Review* vol. 85, no. 3 (September 1991)

"International Cooperation among Relative Gains Maximizers," *International Studies Quarterly* vol. 35 (1991)

Soffer, Arnon, *Naharot shel Esh* [Rivers of Fire] (Tel Aviv: Am Oved Publisher, 1992) [in Hebrew]

Soffer, Arnon and Kliot, Nurit, "The Water Resources of the Jordan Catchment: Management Options," paper presented at the *BRISMES* Annual Conference at the School for Oriental and African Studies, University of London, July 1991

Spector, Lea, "Waters of Controversy: Implications for the Arab–Israel Peace Process," (New York: Foreign Affairs Department, the American–Jewish Committee, December 1980)

Sprout, Harold and Sprout, Margaret, *Man–Milieu Relationship Hypotheses in the Context of International Politics* (Center of International Studies, Princeton University, 1956)

"Environmental Factors in the Study of International Politics," *Journal of Conflict Resolution* vol. 1, no. 4 (1957), pp. 309–28

"Geography and Politics in an Era of Revolutionary Change," *Journal of Conflict Resolution* vol. 4, no. 1 (1960)

Starr, Joyce R., "Water Wars," *Foreign Policy* no. 82 (spring 1991), pp. 17–36

Stauffer, Thomas, "The Price of Peace: the Spoils of War," *American–Arab Affairs* no. 1 (summer 1982)

Taubenblatt, Selig, "The Jordan River Basin Water Dilemma: a Challenge for the 1990s" in Joyce Starr and Daniel Stoll (eds.), *The Politics of Scarcity: Water in the Middle East* (Boulder, Colo.: Westview Press, 1988)

Teclaff, Ludwick A., *The River Basin in History and Law* (The Hague: Martinus Nijhoff, 1967)

Teclaff, Ludwick and Utton, Albert E., *International Groundwater Law* (London/ Rome/New York: Oceana Publications, Inc., 1981)

Thompson, Col. Roy L., "Fresh Water Scarcity: Implications for Conflict – an overview" (paper prepared for the conference on Scarce Resources and International Conflict, International Security Studies Program, The Fletcher School of Law and Diplomacy, Tufts University, 4–6 May 1977)

"Water as a Source of Conflict," *Strategic Review* vol. 6, no. 2 (spring 1978)

Touval, Saadia *The Peace Brokers: Mediators in the Arab–Israeli Conflict, 1948–1979* (Princeton: Princeton University Press, 1982)

"Turkey Harnesses the Euphrates," *The Middle East* (November 1986), pp. 19–20

"Turkey Taps the Euphrates Resources," *Middle East Economic Digest* (17 July 1981), pp. 50–52

Ubell, K., "Iraq's Water Resources," *Nature and Resources* vol. 7, no. 2 (spring 1978)

United Nations, "Economic Activity and Access to National Resources: Legal "Restrictions on Access to Land and Water in Israel" (paper prepared for the International Conference on the Question of Palestine, A/CONF.114/6, 20 June 1983)

United Nations, "Israel's Policy on the West Bank Water Resources" (prepared for the Committee on the Exercise of the Inalienable Rights of the Palestinian People, New York, 1980)

United States, Congress of the United States, Committed on Foreign Affairs, "Memorandum: to Members of the Committee on Foreign Affairs, from Chairman of the Committee," House of Representatives, 6 July 1979 (Washington: US Government Printing Office, 1979)

United States, Economic Support Fund Programs in the Middle East [Committee Print, 96th congress, first session], "Report of a Staff Study Mission to Egypt, Syria, Jordan, the West Bank, and Gaza," 24 November–15 December 1978, to the Committee on Foreign Affairs, US House of Representatives, April 1979 (Washington: US Government Printing Office, 1979)

United States, Foreign Assistance Legislation for Fiscal Year 1979 (Part 5) [95th congress, second session, February/March 1978], "Hearings Before the Sub-committee on Europe and the Middle East of the Committee on International Relations," House of Representatives (Washington: US Government Printing Office, 1978)

United States, Foreign Assistance Legislation for Fiscal Years 1980–81 (Part 3) [96th congress, first session, February/March 1979], "Hearings and Markup before the Subcommittee on Europe and the Middle East of the Committee on Foreign

Affairs," House of Representatives (Washington: US Government Printing Office, 1979)

United States, Foreign Assistance Legislation for Fiscal Year 1981 (Part 3) [96th congress, second session, January/February/March 1980], "Hearings before the Subcommittee on Europe and the Middle East of the Committee on Foreign Affairs," House of Representatives (Washington: US Government Printing Office, 1980)

United States, Foreign Assistance Legislation for Fiscal Year 1982 (Part 3) [97th congress, first session, February/March/April 1981], "Hearings and Markup before the Subcommittee on Europe and the Middle East of the Committee on Foreign Affairs," House of Representatives (Washington: US Government Printing Office, 1981)

United States, House Committee on Foreign Affairs: Subcommittee on Europe and the Middle East, *The Middle East in the 1990s: Middle East Water Issues* (Washington: US Government Printing Office, 26 June 1990)

United States, International Development and Food Assistance Act of 1978 [95th congress, second session, report no. 95–1087], "Report of the Committee on International Relations," House of Representatives (Washington: US Government Printing Office, 1978)

United States, Department of State, *Foreign Policy Records, 1955–56*, Freedom of Information Act

United States, *Foreign Broadcast Information Service*, Daily Report: Middle East, Africa, and Western Europe, 1967

Vardi, Yaacov, "National Water Resources Planning and Development in Israel – the Endangered Resource" in Hillel I. Shuval (ed.), *Water Quality Management under Conditions of Scarcity* (New York: Academic Press, 1980)

Vatikiotis, P. J., *Politics and the Military in Jordan* (London: Frank Cass & Co. Ltd., 1967)

Wagner, R. Harrison, "The Theory of Games and the Problem of International Cooperation," *American Political Science Review* vol. 77, no. 2 (June 1983)

Waltz, Kenneth, *Man, The State and War* (New York: Columbia University Press, 1959)
  Theory of International Politics (Reading, Mass.: Addison-Wesley, 1979)

Waterbury, John, *Hydropolitics of the Nile Valley* (New York: Syracuse University Press, 1979)
  "Legal and Institutional Arrangements for Managing Water Resources in the Nile Basin," *Water Resources Development* vol. 3, no. 2 (1987)
  "Riverains and Lacustrines: Toward International Cooperation in the Nile Basin," Discussion Paper no. 107, *Research Program in Development Studies* (Princeton University: Woodrow Wilson School, September 1982)
  "Dynamics of Basin-Wide Cooperation in the Utilization of the Euphrates" (paper prepared for the conference, The Economic Development of Syria: Problems, Progress and Prospects, Damascus, 6–7 January 1990)
  "Transboundary Water and the Challenge of International Cooperation in the Middle East" in Peter Rogers and Peter Lydon (eds.), *Water in the Arab World: Perspectives and Prognoses* (Cambridge, Mass.: Harvard University Press, 1994)

West Bank Studies, *Towards a Data Base Study of Palestinian Needs: a Synopsis* (Amman, Jordan, May 1985)

Westing, Arthur H. (ed.), *Global Resources and International Conflict: Environmental Factors in Strategic Policy and Action* (Oxford: Oxford University Press, 1986)

Wiener, Aaron, "The Development of Israel's Water Resources," *American Scientist* vol. 60, no. 4 (July–August 1972)

Wishart, David Merkle, "The Political Economy of Conflict over Water Rights in the Jordan Valley from 1890 to the Present" (unpublished Ph.D. thesis: University of Illinois, Urbana-Champaign, 1985)

Wolfers, Arnold, "The Pole of Power and the Pole of Indifference" in *Discord and Collaboration: Essays in International Politics* (Baltimore: Johns Hopkins University Press, 1965)

"National Security as an Ambiguous Symbol" in *Discord and Collaboration: Essays in International Politics* (Baltimore: Johns Hopkins University Press, 1965)

Young, Oran, "International Regimes: Problems of Concept Formation," *World Politics* no. 32 (April 1980)

Resource Regimes: Natural Resources and Social Institutions (Berkeley: University of California Press, 1982)

International Cooperation: Building Regimes for Natural Resources and the Environment (Ithaca and London: Cornell University Press, 1989)

Zacher, Mark W. and Matthew, Richard A., "Liberal International Theory: Common Threads, Divergent Strands" in Charles Kegley (ed.), *Controversies in International Relations Theory: Realism and the Neoliberal Challenge* (New York: St. Martin's Press, 1995)

Zahlan, A. B. and Qasem, Subhi (eds.), *The Agricultural Sector of Jordan* (London: Ithaca Press, 1985)

Zak, Moshe, "Israeli–Jordanian Negotiations," *Washington Quarterly* vol. 8, no. 1 (winter 1985)

"The Zionist Organization's Memorandum to the Supreme Council at the Peace Conference" in Hurewitz, J. (ed.), *Diplomacy in the Near and Middle East* vol. 2 (Princeton: D. Van Nostrand Co., 1956), p. 48

Index

'Abd al-Nasir, Gamal
  and inter-Arab relations, 124, 126, 129,
    130, 131, 134–35, 143–44
  and Johnston mission, 103, 104, 109,
    112
  and National Water Carrier project, 121
  and nationalization of Suez Canal,
    104–05
  and 1967 war, 131–32, 143–44, 258 n.
  strategy *vis-à-vis* Israel, 121, 135, 142
agriculture
  importance to Zionists/Israelis, 51; to
    Palestinians, 52; to East Bankers,
    52–53
  in Israel, 150, 151, 153
  in Jordan, 158, 171–72
  in West Bank, 185, 272 n.
Alexandretta, 57, 60, 236 n.
Arab diversion scheme, 119, *120*, 121,
    122, 123, 124, 125, 126, 128, 131,
    133, 135, 176, 199, 253 n.
Arab–Israeli conflict, 2, 104, 132–33, 196
  and development of Jordan Valley, 105,
    106, 112, 177–80, 195
  US involvement in, 81–82, 100, 205–06
Arab–Israeli wars
  of 1948–49, 46–47
  of 1967, 115, 132, 143, 147, *148*, 163
Arab-Jewish relations pre-1948, 41,
    42–43, 46, 49–50
Arab League
  and Johnston mission, 89, 96–97, 100,
    102, 104, 195, 243 n.
  and National Water Carrier project,
    118–19, 121, 122, 123
Arab Plan (1954), 89, *90*, 92, 209–10,
    243–44 n.
Armistice Demarcation Lines, 80, 86, 91,
    104, 108, 131, 185
  "Green Line," 147, 183, 185, 187, 190

Aswan High Dam, 71, 104–05, 240 n.

Baghdad Pact, 81, 96, 98, 129
Baker and Harza Co., 93, 96, 101, 245 n.
  Harza Engineering, 173
B'athism, 58–59, 60
  Syrian B'ath Party, 119, 126, 129, 132,
    134–35, 140, 142–43, 144
Ben-Gurion, David, 103, 107, 136
border clashes, 98, 103
  Israel–Jordan, 87, 92, 104, 127, 130–31
  Israel–Syria, 92, 124–25, 126, 127, 130,
    131
Bourguiba, Habib, 126, 137, 257–58 n.
Bunger Plan, 82–83, 172, 245 n.

conflict resolution
  efforts at, 11, 74
  role of third party, 74, 75–76, 112, 113,
    196
  core values/organizing principles, 11, 74,
    75, 132, 133–34, 202
  of Arabs, 105, 106, 108–09, 133, 137,
    257–58 n.
  in Indus basin, 113
  of Israel, 105, 106, 137
  and outcome of Johnston mission, 113,
    195, 197–98
Cotton Plan, 90–91, *92*, 211

Dayan, Moshe, 109, 118, 141
demilitarized zones (DMZ), 80, 88, 131,
    237 n.
Dulles, John Foster, 87, 100, 104–05

East Ghor Canal (project), 82, 116, 150,
    154–55, 164, 165, 177
Egypt, 134, 149, 240 n., 243 n.
  reaction to Revised Unified Plan, 103
  see also Nile River basin

292

Cambridge Middle East Library